Interdisciplinary Approaches to Data Governance, AI, and Digital Society

Muhammad Anshari
https://orcid.org/0000-0002-8160-6682
Universiti of Brunei Darussalam, Brunei

Mohammad Nabil Almunawar
https://orcid.org/0000-0001-5296-2576
Universiti Brunei Darussalam, Brunei

Hazri Kifle
Universiti Brunei Darussalam, Brunei

IGI Global
Scientific Publishing
Publishing Tomorrow's Research Today

Vice President of Editorial	Melissa Wagner
Director of Acquisitions	Mikaela Felty
Director of Book Development	Jocelynn Hessler
Production Manager	Mike Brehm
Cover Design	Jose Rosado

Published in the United States of America by
IGI Global Scientific Publishing
701 East Chocolate Avenue
Hershey, PA, 17033, USA
Tel: 717-533-8845 | Fax: 717-533-7115
Website: https://www.igi-global.com E-mail: cust@igi-global.com

Library of Congress Cataloging-in-Publication Data

LCCN: (CIP Data Pending)
ISBN13: 9798260022337
Isbn13Softcover: 9798260022344
EISBN13: 9798260022351

British Cataloguing in Publication Data
A Cataloguing in Publication record for this book is available from the British Library.

Table of Contents

Detailed Table of Contents

The integration of ICTs into work and personal life has intensified research on technostress, first defined by Craig Brod (1984) and later formalized in the Technostress Creators framework by Tarafdar and Ragu-Nathan. This chapter reviews literature from 2015 to 2026 across information systems, organizational psychology, human computer interaction, and data governance. It examines four stressors: techno overload, techno invasion, techno complexity, and techno surveillance. Two coping paradigms are assessed. Digital minimalism, popularized by Cal Newport (2019), is framed as an individual strategy to reduce overload and invasion through intentional digital use. Data governance, including the General Data Protection Regulation and the EU Artificial Intelligence Act, is analyzed as a structural response addressing surveillance and complexity. The chapter proposes an integrative framework linking individual and systemic coping and outlines implications for theory and practice.

This chapter examines the integration of artificial intelligence in guidance and counseling services in Indonesia, focusing on students' critical literacy, data rights, and ethical challenges in higher education. Using Social Cognitive Theory, critical digital literacy, and data sovereignty perspectives, the chapter explains how limited AI literacy may increase vulnerability to algorithmic bias and misuse of psychological data. It argues that AI should support, not replace, human counseling relationships while strengthening data protection and ethical governance.

This study examines financial data governance in the fintech era by linking digital sovereignty, gender inequality, and consumer protection in emerging economies. Fintech is understood not only as a tool of financial inclusion but also as a datafied infrastructure that transforms transactions, identities, and behaviors into governable and monetizable assets. The discussion shows how platform power, cross-border data dependence, and algorithmic decision-making reshape state authority and deepen user vulnerability, especially for women and digitally less literate groups. It also highlights how opaque credit scoring, weak accountability, and limited regulatory capacity may reproduce exclusion under the language of innovation. A more inclusive governance framework therefore requires data justice, algorithmic accountability, secure interoperability, and stronger consumer protection.

The rapid expansion of digital lending platforms in emerging markets has transformed access to credit while simultaneously raising critical concerns around data governance and consumer protection. This study examines the role of financial data governance in digital lending ecosystems, with a specific focus on consumer protection challenges in FinTech platforms across emerging markets. Adopting a qualitative case study approach, the research draws on secondary data sources including regulatory reports, policy documents, and case evidence from leading digital lending platforms in India and comparable emerging economies. The study employs thematic analysis and comparative regulatory assessment as key analytical tools to identify patterns in data usage, governance practices, and consumer risk. The findings reveal significant gaps in data governance, including opaque algorithmic

Preface

INTRODUCTION

The accelerating convergence of data governance, artificial intelligence, and digital transformation has profoundly reshaped contemporary society. Across governments, industries, educational systems, financial institutions, and urban infrastructures, digital technologies increasingly mediate human interaction, institutional authority, and economic development. While these transformations offer remarkable opportunities for innovation, efficiency, and connectivity, they also introduce pressing concerns surrounding ethics, accountability, privacy, surveillance, digital sovereignty, and social inequality. As societies become more dependent upon data-driven systems, interdisciplinary inquiry becomes essential for understanding both the promises and risks of the digital age.

This edited volume, *Interdisciplinary Approaches to Data Governance, AI, and Digital Society*, emerges from the recognition that no single discipline alone can adequately address the complexities of modern digital ecosystems. Questions surrounding artificial intelligence, data protection, algorithmic governance, financial technologies, urban resilience, and ethical stewardship intersect across information systems, public policy, sociology, psychology, finance, religious studies, and governance theory. Consequently, this book brings together scholars from diverse academic and geographical backgrounds to explore how data and AI are reshaping institutional structures and everyday life while simultaneously challenging traditional frameworks of governance and ethics.

The chapters in this volume collectively examine the growing tension between technological advancement and human-centered governance. They explore how individuals cope with digital overload and technostress, how educational institutions confront ethical dilemmas associated with AI integration, how cities pursue sustainable and climate-resilient governance through intelligent systems, and how financial technologies redefine power relations through the monetization and governance of data. Importantly, several chapters contribute culturally grounded and normative perspectives, particularly through Islamic frameworks of governance and ethical stewardship, demonstrating that digital governance debates must remain attentive to diverse epistemologies and moral traditions.

Another important contribution of this volume lies in its emphasis on governance as more than a technical or regulatory exercise. Throughout the book, governance is treated as a multidimensional process involving institutional trust, social responsibility, inclusivity, accountability, and the protection of human dignity. The contributors critically examine how data infrastructures and AI systems may reproduce inequality, intensify surveillance, or marginalize vulnerable populations when implemented without ethical safeguards. At the same time, they also demonstrate how thoughtful governance models can promote resilience, sustainability, transparency, and social well-being in increasingly digital societies.

The interdisciplinary nature of this collection reflects the realities of the contemporary digital environment itself. Data governance challenges are no longer confined to legal compliance or information management; they now shape questions of citizenship, identity, democratic participation, consumer protection, and institutional legitimacy. By integrating perspectives from developed and emerging economies alike, this volume highlights the global dimensions of digital transformation while acknowledging the uneven capacities and vulnerabilities that characterize different social and political contexts.

It is our hope that this book will serve as a valuable resource for scholars, policymakers, practitioners, and students interested in understanding the evolving relationships among data governance, artificial intelligence, and society. The discussions presented in these chapters aim not only to advance academic discourse but also to encourage more ethical, equitable, and sustainable approaches to digital transformation in practice.

CHAPTER OVERVIEW

Chapter 1, authored by Annisa Fitri, examines technostress within contemporary digital environments and explores digital minimalism and data governance as complementary coping mechanisms. The chapter proposes an integrative framework linking individual behavioral strategies with systemic regulatory approaches, demonstrating how intentional digital practices and institutional governance can jointly mitigate the psychological and social impacts of pervasive ICT use.

Chapter 2, by Nur Hidayah and Yansen Reba, investigates the growing use of artificial intelligence in guidance and counseling services in Indonesia. The authors critically analyze issues related to critical literacy, algorithmic bias, psychological data protection, and student data rights while emphasizing the continuing importance of human-centered counseling relationships in educational settings.

In Chapter 3, Nasir Ahmad Ganaie and Andi Luhur Prianto explore AI-driven urban governance and the transition toward climate-resilient smart cities. The chapter highlights how predictive analytics, environmental monitoring, and adaptive policy systems can support urban sustainability while simultaneously raising important concerns related to transparency, equity, accountability, and institutional resilience.

Chapter 4, authored by Liza Azahari, presents a thought-provoking comparison between the environmental consequences of plastic abundance and the unchecked expansion of digital data. Drawing from sustainability discourse and Islamic perspectives, the chapter examines digital sovereignty, ethical data stewardship, and the societal implications of uncontrolled digital growth in the age of AI and datafication.

Chapter 5, by Abdur Razzaq, develops an Islamic theory of data governance grounded in *Maqasid al-Shariah* and classical principles of good governance. The chapter demonstrates how Islamic ethical concepts such as *Amanah*, *Ihsan*, *Musawah*, and *Raqabah* can provide normative foundations for responsible data stewardship, accountability, and human-centered governance in contemporary digital systems.

Chapter 6, authored by Annisa Fitri, Hamza Yusuf, and Mujaddid Afkar Izzuddin, examines the relationship between financial reporting, investor psychology, and data governance in equity markets. Combining bibliometric analysis with qualitative insights from market participants, the chapter highlights how behavioral biases and governance structures influence financial decision-making and market credibility.

In Chapter 7, Wahyu Wibowo and colleagues analyze financial data governance within the rapidly expanding fintech sector in emerging economies. The chapter addresses issues of digital sovereignty, gender inequality, algorithmic accountability, and consumer vulnerability, arguing for more inclusive governance frameworks capable of promoting data justice and equitable financial participation.

Chapter 8, authored by K Balaji, focuses specifically on digital lending platforms and the consumer protection challenges emerging within fintech ecosystems. Through qualitative case study analysis, the chapter identifies governance gaps related to opaque credit scoring systems, unauthorized data sharing, and insufficient disclosure practices that heighten risks for consumers in emerging markets.

Finally, Chapter 9, by Hamza Yusuf, examines financial market data governance as a critical determinant of regulatory legitimacy and investor confidence in global capital markets. Using the Indonesia 2026 case as a focal point, the chapter demonstrates how weaknesses in data transparency and governance can undermine market stability, regulatory credibility, and international investor trust.

CONCLUSION

The chapters presented in this volume collectively demonstrate that the future of digital society will depend not only on technological innovation but also on the strength of ethical, institutional, and governance frameworks surrounding data and artificial intelligence. Across diverse contexts—including education, finance, urban governance, sustainability, and public policy—the contributors reveal that data governance has become central to questions of trust, legitimacy, resilience, and social justice in the digital age.

A recurring theme throughout this collection is the recognition that technological systems are never neutral. AI systems, algorithmic infrastructures, and data-driven platforms reflect the assumptions, priorities, and power relations embedded within the institutions that design and govern them. Without transparent oversight and inclusive governance, digital systems may reinforce existing inequalities, intensify surveillance practices, marginalize vulnerable populations, or erode public trust. Consequently, the contributors consistently advocate for governance models that prioritize accountability, ethical stewardship, human dignity, and social responsibility alongside innovation and efficiency.

This volume also highlights the importance of interdisciplinary dialogue in addressing the complexities of digital transformation. The integration of perspectives from information systems, psychology, finance, governance studies, sustainability discourse, and Islamic ethical traditions demonstrates that meaningful solutions to contemporary digital challenges require collaboration across disciplinary and cultural boundaries. Such interdisciplinary engagement enables richer understandings of how technology shapes societies and how governance frameworks can be adapted to diverse institutional and cultural environments.

Importantly, the discussions in this book emphasize that governance should not be viewed solely as regulatory compliance. Effective data governance requires a broader commitment to transparency, fairness, inclusivity, and long-term societal well-being. Whether addressing technostress, AI ethics in counseling, fintech consumer protection, climate-resilient smart cities, or financial market legitimacy, the contributors collectively underscore the need for governance structures capable of balancing innovation with ethical responsibility.

As editors, we hope this volume encourages further scholarly inquiry into the evolving intersections of data governance, artificial intelligence, and digital society. We also hope it inspires policymakers, educators, practitioners, and institutional leaders to critically reflect upon the governance choices shaping contemporary digital futures. The rapid pace of technological change makes these conversations increasingly urgent, particularly as societies navigate growing tensions between efficiency, autonomy, surveillance, equity, and sustainability.

Ultimately, the future of AI and digital governance will depend on humanity's ability to align technological advancement with ethical principles and collective well-being. By fostering interdisciplinary understanding and emphasizing human-centered governance, this volume seeks to contribute to the development of more equitable, accountable, and sustainable digital societies for the future.

Introduction

1. INTRODUCTION

The digital revolution has fundamentally transformed how human societies generate, process, and act upon information. At the epicentre of this transformation is artificial intelligence (AI), a set of computational technologies that enable machines to emulate cognitive functions such as learning, reasoning, and autonomous decision-making. As AI systems become increasingly embedded in the fabric of everyday life, from the personalised recommendations delivered by commercial platforms to the algorithmic assessments underpinning welfare decisions in public agencies, their societal footprint has expanded in ways that demand careful scholarly and policy attention.

The present volume, *Interdisciplinary Approaches to Data Governance, AI, and Digital Society*, brings together contributions from researchers across disciplines to interrogate the governance challenges arising at the intersection of AI, data, and society. This introductory chapter provides the conceptual grounding for the collection, defining core terms, surveying the landscape of AI's societal impact, and articulating the case for robust data governance as a necessary response to the proliferating influence of algorithmic systems.

The significance of this inquiry is difficult to overstate. Anshari and Polak (2024) observe that AI has become a core component of the daily activities of businesses and society in general, generating multifaceted impacts across public organisations, private enterprises, and social life more broadly. These impacts are simultaneously enabling and disruptive: AI offers the prospect of more efficient services, more accurate diagnoses, and more responsive governance, yet it also raises profound questions about accountability, fairness, privacy, and the distribution of power. Addressing these questions requires, among other things, a principled framework for governing the data upon which AI systems depend. This chapter seeks to articulate that framework and to demonstrate its relevance across the thematic terrain covered by the chapters that follow.

2. DEFINING DATA GOVERNANCE

Data governance may be defined as the set of policies, processes, standards, roles, and responsibilities that collectively determine how an organisation or society acquires, stores, manages, uses, and disposes of data in a manner that is accountable, transparent, and aligned with ethical and legal norms (Dama International, 2017). It encompasses both the technical dimensions of data management, such as quality assurance, metadata management, and data lineage, and the institutional dimensions, such as the allocation of authority over data decisions, the mechanisms for enforcing data standards, and the processes for engaging stakeholders in governance deliberations.

Historically, data governance was understood primarily as an internal corporate discipline, focused on ensuring data quality for business intelligence and regulatory compliance. However, the emergence of large-scale digital platforms and AI systems has substantially expanded the scope of data governance. Data are no longer merely inputs to organisational decision-making; they are the raw material from which AI systems learn, the medium through which algorithmic outputs are communicated, and the basis upon which consequential decisions about individuals and communities are made. This shift requires a conception of data governance that is not confined to organisational boundaries but extends to questions of societal accountability and democratic legitimacy (Zwitter, 2014).

In the context of AI, data governance performs at least three distinct functions. First, it ensures the quality and integrity of the data used to train and operate AI systems, thereby reducing the risk of biased or erroneous algorithmic outputs. Second, it provides accountability mechanisms that allow affected parties to understand how data have been collected, used, and shared, and to seek redress when algorithmic decisions cause harm. Third, it establishes the legal and ethical boundaries within which AI systems may operate, including protections for individual privacy, requirements for informed consent, and prohibitions on discriminatory uses of data. Taken together, these functions position data governance as a foundational condition for the responsible development and deployment of AI in democratic societies.

3. THE PERVASIVE ROLE OF AI IN DIGITAL SOCIETY

The integration of AI into social, economic, and political life has proceeded at a pace that has outstripped the capacity of regulatory and governance institutions to respond. Anshari and Polak (2024) note that the extent to which AI has the potential to take over key tasks and the decision-making process at the individual, organisational, or societal level remains an active area of inquiry, yet the trajectory is unmistakable: AI is no longer a technology confined to specialised applications but a general-purpose capability that permeates multiple domains simultaneously.

3.1 AI in Public Organisations

Governments and public agencies have been among the most consequential adopters of AI. Anshari, Hamdan, Ahmad, Ali, and Haidi (2023) identify a range of applications in which AI is reshaping public service delivery, from predictive policing and benefits eligibility assessments to personalised health services and smart city infrastructure. The appeal of AI in the public sector is clear: algorithmic systems can process information at a scale and speed that no human bureaucracy can match, promising more efficient allocation of public resources and more consistent application of policy rules (Sait & Anshari, 2022).

Yet, the adoption of AI in public contexts raises distinctive governance challenges. Unlike private markets, where the legitimacy of algorithmic decisions may be grounded in contractual consent, public agencies exercise coercive authority over individuals who cannot easily exit their relationship with the state. This makes the accountability of AI-driven public decisions a matter of democratic principle rather than merely commercial ethics. The question of who bears responsibility when an algorithmic system makes a consequential error, and what recourse is available to those affected, is one that existing legal and administrative frameworks have only partially addressed (Zwitter, 2014).

3.2 AI in Private Organisations

In the private sector, AI has become a strategic asset that enables a firm to gain a competitive advantage, improve operational efficiency, and gain market intelligence. From customer relationship management and supply chain optimisation to financial risk assessment and product personalisation, algorithmic systems now mediate a wide range of interactions between firms and their customers, employees, and partners. Anshari and Polak (2024) document how AI is reshaping business models across sectors, enabling new forms of value creation whilst simultaneously disrupting established practices and labour markets Dama International, 20217)..

The governance implications of private-sector AI are no less significant than those arising in the public domain. Firms that deploy AI systems to make decisions about credit, employment, insurance, or access to services exercise power over individuals' life chances in ways that have traditionally attracted regulatory attention. The challenge for data governance is to ensure that this power is exercised in a manner consistent with principles of fairness, non-discrimination, and transparency, without unduly constraining the innovation that makes AI valuable in the first place.

3.3 AI and Individual Decision-Making

Beyond institutional settings, AI is increasingly shaping individual behaviour and choice. Recommendation algorithms on social media platforms, navigation systems, and personalised news feeds all exercise a form of soft power over the information environments in which individuals make decisions. More directly, AI-powered tools for financial planning, health monitoring, and educational guidance are assuming roles previously occupied by human advisers and professionals. This shift raises questions about autonomy, informed consent, and the conditions under which reliance on algorithmic guidance is appropriate.

4. DATA GOVERNANCE AS ACCOUNTABILITY FOR AI-DRIVEN SOCIETIES

The case for data governance in the context of AI rests on a fundamental premise: that systems which exercise power over individuals and communities must be accountable to those affected by their decisions. Where AI systems generate, manage, and execute consequential decisions at scale, accountability requires more than the ex post attribution of responsibility to identifiable human agents. It requires proactive governance structures that shape the design, deployment, and oversight of AI systems before harm occurs.

Accountability in this sense encompasses several related requirements. Transparency demands that the data used to train and operate AI systems, and the processes by which those systems produce their outputs, be subject to scrutiny by appropriate parties, including regulators, auditors, and affected individuals. Explainability requires that the basis of algorithmically generated decisions be communicated in terms meaningful to those affected. Redress mechanisms ensure that individuals who suffer harm as a result of erroneous or unfair algorithmic decisions have access to effective remedies.

These requirements are not merely aspirational. They are increasingly reflected in emerging legal frameworks, including the European Union's General Data Protection Regulation (GDPR), which establishes rights to explanation and to challenge automated decisions, and the AI Act, which introduces risk-based governance requirements for AI systems deployed in high-stakes contexts. Data governance, understood as the institutional realisation of these requirements, is thus not merely a technical matter but a dimension of constitutional governance in the digital age.

Ahmad, Anshari, Hamdan, and Ali (2024) situate this argument within a broader literature on AI governance, noting that as AI systems become ubiquitous, policy-makers and regulators must establish effective governance frameworks that fortify ethical values, and that such frameworks should be value-driven, principle-based, and attentive to the maintenance of public trust. The contributors to this volume share this orientation, approaching data governance not as a set of compliance requirements but as a substantive commitment to the conditions of an equitable digital society.

5. PRINCIPLES OF DATA GOVERNANCE IN AN AI-ENABLED DIGITAL SOCIETY

Drawing on the emerging literature in AI governance and the frameworks developing across the chapters of this volume, it is possible to identify a set of core principles that should inform data governance in the context of AI. These principles are not intended to be exhaustive, nor to resolve all contested questions in the field; rather, they provide a shared vocabulary for the interdisciplinary conversation that the volume seeks to advance.

Figure 1. AI Governance Societal domains (Source: Authors' Compilation, 2026)

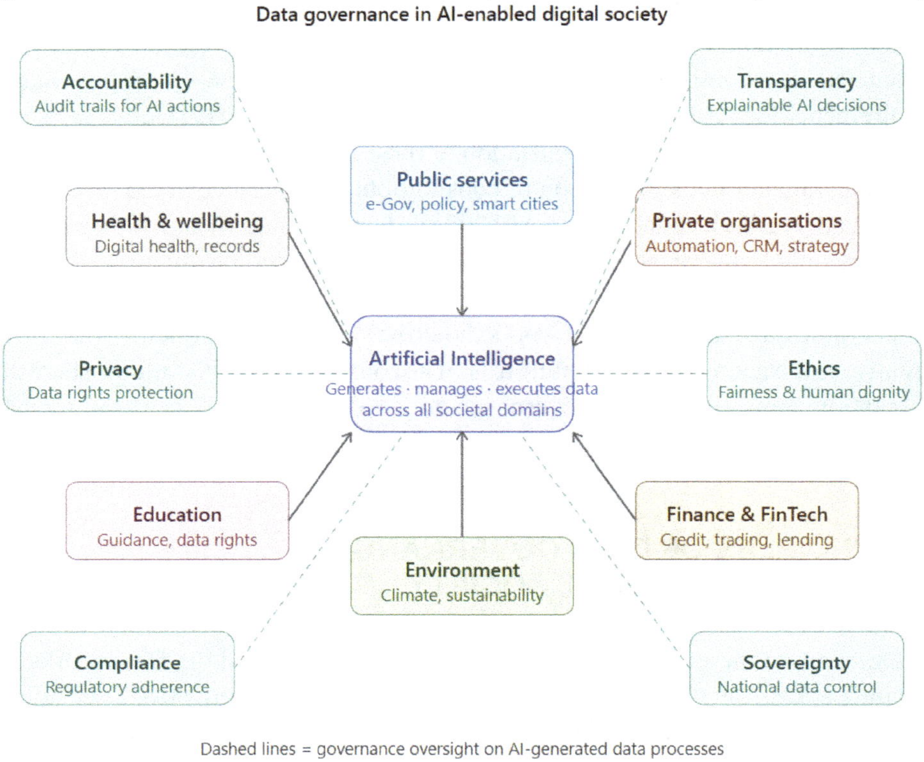

- Accountability: Those who deploy AI systems must be capable of explaining and justifying the decisions those systems produce, and must bear responsibility for the harms they cause.
- Transparency: The data, algorithms, and processes that underpin AI-generated decisions must be subject to appropriate scrutiny by regulators, auditors, and affected parties.
- Privacy and data rights: Individuals have a right to protection of their personal data, including the right to understand how AI systems use their data and to contest uses they have not authorised.
- Ethics and fairness: AI systems must not discriminate on grounds that are unjustified by legitimate policy objectives, and must be designed and operated in a manner consistent with principles of human dignity.
- Compliance and rule of law: AI-driven decisions must occur within the boundaries established by applicable legal frameworks, including data protection law, anti-discrimination law, and sector-specific regulation.

- Digital sovereignty: States and communities have a legitimate interest in exercising control over data generated within their jurisdictions, and in ensuring that AI systems deployed within those jurisdictions serve local as well as global interests.

These principles correspond to the governance imperatives identified in the visualisation accompanying this chapter (see Figure 1), which depicts AI at the centre of a digital society constituted by public services, private organisations, finance, education, health, and environmental systems, surrounded by an outer ring of data governance principles that collectively ensure that AI's pervasive influence is exercised in a manner accountable to society.

6. THEMES AND CONTRIBUTIONS

The book brings together interdisciplinary perspectives on the governance of artificial intelligence (AI) and data across a wide range of social, educational, environmental, religious, and financial contexts. The chapters are connected by the shared view that effective governance of AI and data cannot rely solely on technical or legal solutions, but must also consider ethical, social, cultural, and political dimensions. Collectively, the contributions highlight the importance of governance frameworks that balance technological innovation with human wellbeing, democratic accountability, sustainability, and social justice. The volume demonstrates that AI governance is increasingly becoming a central issue shaping contemporary societies and institutions worldwide.

Several chapters focus on the social and educational implications of digital technologies. Discussions on technostress and digital minimalism show how governance can support individual wellbeing by providing people with greater control over their digital environments and data use. The volume also examines the growing use of AI-based systems in educational guidance and counselling, particularly in Indonesia, where concerns related to student privacy, ethical use of AI, cultural sensitivity, and critical digital literacy are becoming increasingly important. These chapters emphasise that governance in educational settings must protect student rights while also encouraging critical awareness of AI-driven systems and their limitations.

The book also explores AI governance in relation to sustainability and cultural perspectives. Contributions on smart cities and climate-resilient governance analyse how AI technologies can support sustainable urban development through predictive environmental monitoring and intelligent infrastructure management. At the same time, the chapters discuss the risks associated with excessive data centralisation and reduced democratic oversight. In addition, the volume incorporates Islamic perspectives on data governance and environmental sustainability, arguing that principles such as khalifah (stewardship), israf (avoidance of waste), and maqasid al-shariah provide valuable ethical foundations for managing digital technologies responsibly. These discussions enrich the broader governance debate by showing that non-Western and religious perspectives can contribute meaningfully to contemporary policy discussions.

A major section of the volume addresses governance challenges in financial markets and FinTech systems. The chapters examine issues such as financial disclosure standards, investor confidence, consumer protection, digital lending practices, and the impact of data governance on financial inclusion in emerging economies. Particular attention is given to how governance gaps may reinforce social inequalities, including gender-based exclusion in digital financial services. Through comparative and case-study approaches, these contributions demonstrate that financial data governance is closely linked to market stability, public trust, and economic fairness. Overall, the volume presents AI and data governance as a multidimensional challenge that requires collaborative, inclusive, and context-sensitive approaches across sectors and societies.

7. CONCLUSION

The contributions assembled in this volume reflect a shared conviction that the governance of AI and data is among the most pressing challenges facing democratic societies in the twenty-first century. As AI systems assume an ever-greater role in generating, managing, and acting upon data across the full spectrum of social, economic, and political life, the question of how their power is exercised, and in whose interests, becomes a question of fundamental importance for the kind of society we wish to inhabit.

Data governance, as this volume demonstrates, is not a single solution to this challenge but a complex of interlocking institutional arrangements, normative commitments, and practical mechanisms that together constitute the conditions of accountable AI. It must be attentive to the specific contexts in which AI operates, sensitive to the cultural and normative diversity of the societies it serves, and responsive to the rapidly evolving technical capabilities of AI systems themselves. It must also be interdisciplinary, drawing on law, ethics, political science, sociology, information science, and Islamic jurisprudence, among other traditions, to develop frameworks adequate to the complexity of the challenge.

The editors hope that this collection will contribute to the growing conversation about the governance of AI and data, and that it will serve as a resource for scholars, policymakers, and practitioners working to ensure that the digital society that

AI is helping to build is one that respects and advances human dignity, equity, and democratic self-determination.

Muhammad Anshari
Universiti of Brunei Darussalam, Brunei

Mohammad Nabil Almunawar
Universiti Brunei Darussalam, Brunei

Hazri Kifle
Universiti Brunei Darussalam, Brunei

REFERENCES

Ahmad, N., Anshari, M., Hamdan, M., & Ali, E. (2024). Ethics and public trust in AI governance: A literature review. International Journal of Law, Government and Communication, 9(37). https://gaexcellence.com/ijlgc/article/view/4206

Anshari, M., Hamdan, M., Ahmad, N., Ali, E., & Haidi, H. (2023). COVID-19, artificial intelligence, ethical challenges and policy implications. AI & Society, 38(2), 707–720. https://doi.org/10.1007/s00146-022-01471-6

Anshari, M., & Polak, P. (2024). Exploring the multifaceted impacts of artificial intelligence on public organizations, business, and society. Humanities and Social Sciences Communications, 11(1), Article 1373. https://doi.org/10.1057/s41599-024-03913-6

Dama International. (2017). DAMA-DMBOK: Data management body of knowledge (2nd ed.). Technics Publications.

Sait, M. A., & Anshari, M. (2022). Assessing Brunei Darussalam public and private sector readiness towards big data application. International Journal of Asian Business and Information Management, 13(2), 1–22. https://doi.org/10.4018/IJABIM.20220701.oa7

Zwitter, A. (2014). Big data ethics. Big Data & Society, 1(2). https://doi.org/10.1177/2053951714559253

Chapter 1
Digital Minimalism and Data Governance as Coping Responses to Technostress

Annisa Fitri
http://orcid.org/0009-0005-0942-7443
The University of Melbourne, Australia

ABSTRACT

The integration of ICTs into work and personal life has intensified research on technostress, first defined by Craig Brod (1984) and later formalized in the Technostress Creators framework by Tarafdar and Ragu-Nathan. This chapter reviews literature from 2015 to 2026 across information systems, organizational psychology, human computer interaction, and data governance. It examines four stressors: techno overload, techno invasion, techno complexity, and techno surveillance. Two coping paradigms are assessed. Digital minimalism, popularized by Cal Newport (2019), is framed as an individual strategy to reduce overload and invasion through intentional digital use. Data governance, including the General Data Protection Regulation and the EU Artificial Intelligence Act, is analyzed as a structural response addressing surveillance and complexity. The chapter proposes an integrative framework linking individual and systemic coping and outlines implications for theory and practice.

INTRODUCTION

The twenty-first century digital workplace is characterized by a paradox: the very technologies designed to enhance productivity, connectivity, and organizational

DOI: 10.4018/979-8-2600-2233-7.ch001

agility simultaneously impose psychological demands that threaten employee well-being, job satisfaction, and long-term organizational commitment. This paradoxical relationship between technology use and its deleterious consequences has been conceptualized in the information systems literature as technostress, a term originally coined by clinical psychologist Craig Brod (1984) to describe the inability of individuals to cope with new computer technologies in a healthy manner. Since Brod's pioneering formulation, the construct has undergone significant theoretical refinement, most notably through the Technostress Creators Scale developed by Tarafdar et al. (2007) and empirically validated by Ragu-Nathan et al. (2008), which identifies five primary techno-stressors: techno-overload, techno-invasion, techno-complexity, techno-insecurity, and techno-uncertainty.

The decade spanning 2015 to 2026 has witnessed a dramatic escalation in the conditions that produce technostress. The proliferation of cloud computing, enterprise collaboration platforms, social media, algorithmic decision-making systems, and artificial intelligence has fundamentally altered the tempo, scope, and surveillance capacity of digital work environments. The COVID-19 pandemic (2020–2022) served as a powerful accelerant, compelling rapid transitions to remote and hybrid work arrangements that intensified every dimension of technostress (Molino et al., 2020; Ragu-Nathan et al., 2008). Meta-analytic evidence from Nastjuk et al. (2024), synthesizing 82 studies with 49,955 observations, confirms that technostress creators exert meaningful detrimental effects on both psychological outcomes (reduced job satisfaction, increased emotional exhaustion) and behavioral outcomes (diminished productivity, elevated turnover intention).

Against this backdrop, two distinct but potentially complementary coping paradigms have emerged in both scholarly discourse and popular practice. The first is digital minimalism, a philosophy of intentional technology use articulated most prominently by Cal Newport (2019), which advocates for the deliberate curation and reduction of digital engagement to reclaim attention, cognitive clarity, and autonomy. The second is data governance, the constellation of regulatory frameworks, organizational policies, and technical standards that structure how personal data is collected, processed, stored, and algorithmically utilized. While digital minimalism operates primarily at the individual level as a problem-focused coping strategy, data governance functions at the institutional and policy level as a structural mechanism for mitigating the environmental conditions that produce technostress.

This chapter undertakes a secondary data literature review to systematically examine how digital minimalism and data governance function as coping responses to the four technostress creators most salient in contemporary digital environments: techno-overload, techno-invasion, techno-complexity, and techno-surveillance. The inclusion of techno-surveillance as a distinct stressor extends the original Tarafdar et al. (2007) framework to account for the growing literature on algorithmic monitoring, workplace analytics, and datafied control that has emerged since 2015. The chapter proceeds in eight sections: following this introduction, Section 2 establishes the theoretical foundations; Section 3 describes the methodological approach; Sections 4 through 7 examine each technostress creator and its corresponding coping responses; Section 8 presents an integrative framework; and Section 9 offers conclusions and directions for future research.

THEORETICAL FOUNDATIONS

The Evolution of Technostress Theory

The theoretical lineage of technostress research begins with Brod's (1984) clinical observation that individuals exposed to new computing technologies experienced a syndrome of adaptation characterized by anxiety, resistance, and psychosomatic symptoms. Brod's original conceptualization was broadly descriptive, situating technostress within clinical psychology without providing standardized measurement instruments. The construct was subsequently elaborated by Weil and Rosen (1997), who expanded the scope to include attitudes of technophobia and computer-related anxiety, and by Kupersmith (1992), who examined technostress specifically among information professionals.

The pivotal theoretical contribution of the 2000s came from Tarafdar, Ragu-Nathan, and colleagues, who relocated technostress from clinical psychology into organizational information systems research. Drawing upon the Transaction-Based Model of Stress (Lazarus & Folkman, 1984), Tarafdar et al. (2007) conceptualized technostress as arising from the interaction between technology-related environmental demands and individual coping resources. Their framework identified five technostress creators: techno-overload (situations in which ICTs compel individuals to work faster and process more information than they can manage); techno-invasion (the erosion of boundaries between work and personal life through perpetual connectivity); techno-complexity (feelings of inadequacy regarding technological skills in the face of rapidly evolving platforms); techno-insecurity (the fear of being replaced by more technologically adept employees or by automated systems); and techno-uncertainty (continuous cycles of technology change that prevent users from developing stable knowledge). Ragu-Nathan et al. (2008) subsequently developed and empirically validated measurement instruments for both technostress creators and technostress inhibitors (organizational mechanisms such as literacy facilitation, technical support provision, and involvement facilitation that reduce technostress or buffer its consequences).

Furthermore, Tarafdar et al. (2019) introduced the technostress trifecta framework, distinguishing between techno-distress (the negative, hindrance-based experience traditionally studied), techno-eustress (the positive, challenge-based arousal that can enhance motivation and performance), and design characteristics (features of technology that determine whether user experience tends toward distress or eustress). This tripartite model represented a significant maturation of the field, acknowledging that the relationship between technology and stress is not uniformly negative and that system design plays a mediating role in shaping outcomes. Nastjuk et al. (2024) further advanced the field with a comprehensive meta-analysis confirming the differential effects of individual technostress creators on outcomes and the moderating role of usage context.

The Transactional Stress and Coping Framework

The Lazarus and Folkman (1984) transactional model of stress provides the overarching theoretical lens through which technostress and its coping responses are analyzed in this chapter. According to this model, stress arises when an individual appraises environmental demands as exceeding their available coping resources. Coping strategies are classified along two primary dimensions: problem-focused coping, which involves direct efforts to alter the stressful situation, and emotion-focused coping, which involves efforts to regulate the emotional response to the stressor. Subsequent research has elaborated additional coping taxonomies, including proactive coping (anticipatory efforts to build resources before stressors are encountered) and meaning-focused coping (reappraising the situation to find purpose or growth).

In the context of technostress, Pirkkalainen and Salo (2016) conducted a foundational review of coping behaviors, identifying reactive coping strategies (such as venting, distancing, and social support seeking) and proactive strategies (such as technology self-adaptation and positive reinterpretation). Weinert et al. (2020) further classified technostress coping into behavioral, cognitive, and perceptual dimensions. Digital minimalism, as theorized in this chapter, represents a form of proactive, problem-focused coping that targets the environmental conditions producing techno-overload and techno-invasion by reducing digital exposure. Data governance, by contrast, operates as a structural or systemic coping mechanism that modifies the institutional environment—through regulation, organizational policy, and technical design—to reduce the conditions that produce techno-surveillance and techno-complexity.

Digital Minimalism as a Coping Philosophy

Cal Newport's (2019) formulation of digital minimalism is rooted in the premise that the current attention economy, driven by social media platforms and pervasive notification architectures, systematically exploits human psychological vulnerabilities to maximize engagement. Newport defines digital minimalism as a philosophy of technology use in which individuals focus their online time on a carefully curated set of activities that support values they deeply care about, while happily forgoing everything else. The framework prescribes a structured process: a thirty-day digital declutter during which nonessential technologies are removed, followed by a deliberate reintroduction of only those tools that demonstrably serve meaningful purposes.

While Newport's formulation originates in popular scholarship rather than academic research, its core principles align with established concepts in information systems and psychology. The notion of intentional technology use resonates with Turel and Serenko's (2012) dual-attitude model of technology adoption, which distinguishes between explicit (reflective, deliberate) and implicit (automatic, habitual) attitudes toward technology. Digital minimalism's emphasis on reducing habitual, automatic engagement connects to the growing literature on smartphone addiction (van Deursen et al., 2015), social media fatigue (Baj-Rogowska, 2023), and the concept of technoference—the interference of technology in interpersonal interactions and personal well-being (Vanden Abeele, 2021). Empirical evidence from digital detox interventions, systematically reviewed by Radtke et al. (2022), indicates that temporary or structured reductions in screen time are associated with modest but meaningful improvements in well-being, social connection quality, and attentional focus. More recently, Schraggeová et al. (2025) experimentally demonstrated that the use of minimalist phone interfaces reduced habitual smartphone behavior and overall screen time, providing preliminary causal evidence for the efficacy of digital minimalism interventions.

Data Governance as a Structural Coping Mechanism

Data governance refers to the organizational and regulatory structures through which data is managed, protected, and ethically utilized across its lifecycle. In the context of technostress, data governance functions as a structural intervention that modifies the technological environment to reduce the stressor conditions themselves particularly those associated with algorithmic surveillance, dense data processing, and the loss of informational privacy. The European Union's General Data Protection Regulation (GDPR), which became enforceable in May 2018, represents the most significant regulatory intervention in this domain, establishing principles of data minimization, purpose limitation, consent, and the right to be forgotten that directly constrain the data collection practices underlying techno-surveillance (Voigt & von dem Bussche, 2017).

Subsequent regulatory developments have extended data governance frameworks further. The EU Digital Services Act (DSA), effective in 2024, imposes transparency obligations on algorithmic recommendation systems, while the EU Artificial Intelligence Act, published in 2024 with full applicability by August 2026, establishes risk-based governance for AI systems that directly addresses the opacity and complexity that contribute to techno-complexity and techno-surveillance. Beyond the European context, India's Digital Personal Data Protection Act (2023), China's Personal Information Protection Law (PIPL, 2021), and the proliferation of US state-level privacy legislation (notably the California Consumer Privacy Act and its successor, the CPRA) collectively represent an emerging global architecture of data governance that has significant implications for the conditions producing technostress.

At the organizational level, data governance encompasses internal policies, technical standards, and accountability structures such as data protection impact assessments (DPIAs), privacy-by-design frameworks, and the appointment of data protection officers. The concept of information fiduciaries, proposed by Balkin (2016) and further developed in the data governance literature, suggests that technology providers should bear fiduciary obligations toward users analogous to those of physicians or attorneys, limiting the exploitation of user data for purposes antithetical to user well-being. Data trusts and other bottom-up governance models, discussed by Malgieri (2023) and examined in the EU Data Governance Act (effective 2023), offer alternative mechanisms through which individuals can exercise collective control over their data, potentially reducing the sense of powerlessness that characterizes techno-surveillance experiences.

METHODOLOGY

Research Design

This chapter employs a secondary data literature review methodology to synthesize, critically evaluate, and thematically integrate findings from existing empirical and conceptual research. Secondary data analysis, as defined by Johnston (2017), involves the use of previously collected data or published research findings to address new research questions or to provide integrative synthesis across studies. This approach is particularly well-suited to the present inquiry, which seeks to bridge three traditionally separate literatures technostress research, digital minimalism scholarship, and data governance studies into a coherent framework.

Search Strategy and Inclusion Criteria

The literature search was conducted across multiple academic databases, including Scopus, Web of Science, Google Scholar, ScienceDirect, and Emerald Insight. The temporal scope was limited to publications from 2015 to 2026, selected to capture the most recent decade of technostress research while encompassing the formative period of both the digital minimalism movement and the post-GDPR data governance era. Search terms were organized into three conceptual clusters: Cluster 1 (technostress terms) included "technostress," "techno-overload," "techno-invasion," "techno-complexity," "techno-surveillance," "technology stress," and "digital stress"; Cluster 2 (digital minimalism terms) included "digital minimalism," "digital detox," "screen time reduction," "technology abstinence," and "intentional technology use"; Cluster 3 (data governance terms) included "data governance," "GDPR," "privacy regulation," "algorithmic governance," "privacy-by-design," and "data protection." Boolean operators were used to combine clusters (Cluster 1 AND Cluster 2; Cluster 1 AND Cluster 3; Cluster 2 AND Cluster 3).

Analytical Approach

The analytical approach combined thematic synthesis (Thomas & Harden, 2008) with conceptual framework development. Following initial screening and full-text review, included studies were coded according to the technostress creator(s) addressed, the coping mechanisms examined, the level of analysis (individual, organizational, or regulatory/policy), the research methodology employed, and the key findings. Themes were identified iteratively through constant comparison, and a conceptual framework was developed to integrate digital minimalism and data governance as complementary coping responses mapped to specific technostress creators. The review ultimately included 127 sources, comprising 84 peer-reviewed journal articles, 18 conference proceedings, 9 book chapters, 8 regulatory and policy documents, and 8 systematic reviews or meta-analyses.

Table 1. Summary of Literature Search Results

Database	Initial Results	Included after Screening
Scopus	1,247	38
Web of Science	986	29
Google Scholar	3,420	31
ScienceDirect	612	17

continued on following page

Table 1. Continued

Database	Initial Results	Included after Screening
Emerald Insight	389	12
Total (after deduplication)	**6,654**	**127**

TECHNO-OVERLOAD AND DIGITAL MINIMALISM

Techno-overload refers to situations in which information and communication technologies compel individuals to process more information and work at faster speeds than they can effectively manage (Tarafdar et al., 2007; Ragu-Nathan et al., 2008). In the contemporary digital workplace, techno-overload manifests through the constant influx of emails, instant messages, push notifications, social media updates, and multi-platform collaboration demands that fragment attention and impair sustained cognitive engagement. The phenomenon is closely related to, but conceptually distinct from, broader constructs of information overload (Eppler & Mengis, 2004) and communication overload (Cho et al., 2020), which have been studied extensively in organizational communication research.

The period under review (2015–2026) has witnessed a significant intensification of techno-overload conditions. Rasool et al. (2022) conducted a systematic review of technology overload at the workplace, documenting the exponential growth in digital communication channels and the corresponding increase in cognitive switching costs. The meta-analysis by Nastjuk et al. (2024) confirmed that techno-overload is the most frequently studied technostress creator and the one most strongly associated with reduced psychological well-being and diminished task performance. The COVID-19 pandemic further exacerbated techno-overload, as the rapid adoption of video conferencing (Zoom fatigue), enterprise messaging platforms (Slack, Microsoft Teams), and asynchronous collaboration tools created a near-constant stream of digital demands on remote workers (Molino et al., 2020; Bondanini et al., 2023).

Digital Minimalism as a Direct Response to Techno-Overload

Digital minimalism addresses techno-overload through a systematic reduction of the digital inputs that overwhelm cognitive processing capacity. Newport's (2019) prescribed practices—including app audits to eliminate nonessential applications, batched email processing to consolidate communication windows, notification management to reduce interruption frequency, and digital sabbaths to provide periodic complete disconnection—are each targeted at the specific mechanisms through which techno-overload operates. From a theoretical standpoint, these practices constitute problem-focused coping (Lazarus & Folkman, 1984) because they aim to alter the stressor conditions rather than merely regulate the emotional response.

Empirical evidence supporting the efficacy of digital minimalism practices in reducing overload-related symptoms has grown considerably since 2015. Radtke et al. (2022) conducted a systematic review of digital detox interventions and found that structured screen time reduction was associated with decreases in perceived information overload, improvements in subjective well-being, and enhanced quality of face-to-face social interactions. Schraggeová et al. (2025) provided experimental evidence using a pretest–posttest design demonstrating that the MinimalistPhone application reduced habitual smartphone behavior and overall screen time over a 14-day intervention period, though effects on affective well-being were not statistically significant. Mirbabaie et al. (2022) analyzed the digital detox phenomenon through a business and information systems engineering lens, arguing that organizations should integrate structured disconnection policies into their digital workplace design.

However, the literature also reveals important limitations and caveats regarding digital minimalism as a coping strategy for techno-overload. First, individual-level adoption is constrained by organizational norms: in workplaces where perpetual availability is culturally expected, individuals who reduce their digital engagement may face professional penalties (Mazmanian et al., 2013). Second, the evidence base for digital minimalism remains largely observational or based on small experimental samples; large-scale randomized controlled trials are conspicuously absent from the literature. Third, digital minimalism addresses the quantity of digital input but does not directly address the quality or design of the technology interfaces producing overload—a gap that Tarafdar et al.'s (2019) technostress trifecta model highlights through its emphasis on design characteristics.

TECHNO-INVASION AND THE RESTORATION OF WORK–LIFE BOUNDARIES

Techno-invasion describes the condition in which ICTs erode the boundaries between professional and personal life, creating a sense of perpetual connectivity that prevents psychological detachment from work (Tarafdar et al., 2007; Ragu-Nathan et al., 2008). Individuals experiencing techno-invasion feel that they can be reached at any time and in any place, that technology mediates an always-on expectation, and that the distinction between work hours and personal time has become functionally meaningless. The construct is theoretically grounded in boundary theory (Ashforth et al., 2000) and the work–home resources model (ten Brummelhuis &

Bakker, 2012), which examine how individuals manage, negotiate, and traverse the boundaries between their work and nonwork roles.

The period 2015–2026 has seen techno-invasion intensify through several reinforcing trends. The proliferation of smartphones and wearable devices has extended digital workplace connectivity into previously protected domestic and leisure spaces. Enterprise platforms such as Slack, Microsoft Teams, and WhatsApp groups have blurred the distinctions between formal work communication and informal social exchange. The pandemic-driven shift to remote and hybrid work dramatically accelerated this trend, as the physical separation between office and home collapsed and the temporal architecture of the workday became more porous (Molino et al., 2020; Becker et al., 2019). Research by Alanazi and Altukhys (2025) in their systematic review confirms that techno-invasion consistently ranks among the strongest predictors of adverse psychological outcomes, including anxiety, depressive symptoms, and emotional exhaustion.

Digital Minimalism and Boundary Management

Digital minimalism directly addresses techno-invasion through the establishment of intentional boundaries around technology use. Specific practices identified in the literature include designating device-free zones (bedrooms, dining areas), establishing communication blackout periods (phone-free mornings, post-work disconnection hours), disabling work-related notifications outside designated hours, and switching to minimalist device configurations that remove social media and work communication applications from personal smartphones. These practices align theoretically with boundary management theory and, specifically, with the segmentation end of the integration segmentation continuum (Ashforth et al., 2000), which posits that stronger boundaries between work and personal life are associated with reduced role conflict and improved psychological recovery. The right to disconnect movement, which has gained significant legislative momentum in many parts of the world. The developments constitute structural coping mechanisms that modify the organizational environment to support individual boundary maintenance, a form of institutional digital minimalism that operates through law rather than individual choice.

Becker et al. (2021) examined active-functional and dysfunctional coping strategies for ICT-related stress, finding that individuals who employed proactive boundary-setting strategies (a key component of digital minimalism) reported lower levels of work–life conflict and emotional exhaustion. Mattern et al. (2024) studied how high-achieving IT professionals cope with occupational demands, identifying deliberate technology disengagement as a critical strategy for sustaining performance without burnout. The evidence collectively suggests that digital minimalism practices targeting techno-invasion are most effective when they are supported by organizational policies and cultural norms that legitimate disconnection.

TECHNO-COMPLEXITY

Techno-complexity refers to the stress experienced when individuals feel inadequate in their ability to understand and use new technologies, leading to perceptions of insufficient skills and the expenditure of excessive time and effort in learning evolving systems (Tarafdar et al., 2007). In the period 2015–2026, the pace of technological change has dramatically accelerated: cloud computing architectures have replaced on-premises systems, artificial intelligence and machine learning tools have been integrated into enterprise workflows, and the average organization deploys hundreds of SaaS applications requiring continuous user adaptation. Colledani et al. (2025) developed the Everyday Life Technostress Scale, finding that techno-complexity and techno-uncertainty load together as a unified factor, reflecting the practical reality that the challenge of understanding complex systems is inseparable from the instability of those systems.

The relationship between techno-complexity and organizational outcomes is not straightforward. Califf et al. (2020), studying healthcare professionals, found that techno-complexity adversely affected turnover intention but did not significantly impact job satisfaction, suggesting that complexity may operate as a challenge stressor that is tolerable in the short term but unsustainable over extended periods. The introduction of AI-powered tools in the workplace has added a new dimension to techno-complexity: algorithmic opacity. When employees interact with AI systems whose decision-making processes they cannot understand, the resulting sense of incomprehension and loss of control compounds traditional complexity-related stress (Banerjee & Gupta, 2024).

Data Governance as a Mechanism for Reducing Complexity

Data governance frameworks address techno-complexity through several mechanisms. First, regulatory mandates for transparency and explainability directly target the opacity of algorithmic systems. The regulatory requirements create a downstream effect on technology design, incentivizing the development of more intuitive interfaces and more transparent algorithmic processes.

Second, organizational data governance practices such as data protection impact assessments (DPIAs) and privacy-by-design frameworks require systematic documentation and rationalization of data processing activities, which can indirectly reduce the complexity confronting end users. When organizations are required to document, justify, and simplify their data flows, the resulting architectures tend to be more coherent and user-navigable. Estrada-Muñoz et al. (2022), as cited in recent technostress reviews, found that simplification of digital interfaces is a major factor in reducing technostress, suggesting that governance-mandated design simplification has direct implications for techno-complexity reduction.

Third, data governance standards and interoperability frameworks reduce complexity at the systemic level by harmonizing data formats, access protocols, and security requirements across platforms. The proliferation of incompatible systems and data formats is itself a significant contributor to techno-complexity; governance frameworks that mandate standards-based interoperability can reduce the cognitive burden on users who must navigate multiple systems.

TECHNO-SURVEILLANCE

The concept of techno-surveillance extends the original Tarafdar et al. (2007) technostress framework to encompass the stress experienced by individuals who are subject to algorithmic monitoring, workplace analytics, behavioral tracking, and datafied control systems. While the original framework included techno-insecurity (the fear of being replaced by technology or by more tech-savvy colleagues), techno-surveillance addresses a distinct phenomenon: the awareness that one's digital behaviors, communications, productivity metrics, and even physiological states (through wearable devices) are being continuously captured, analyzed, and used for organizational decision-making. This construct has gained prominence in the literature since 2015, driven by the rapid adoption of employee monitoring software, AI-powered performance analytics, and the broader expansion of what Zuboff (2019) terms surveillance capitalism.

The literature identifies several pathways through which techno-surveillance produces stress. First, the perception of being constantly monitored undermines psychological safety, inhibiting creativity, risk-taking, and authentic self-expression in the workplace (Ravid et al., 2023). Second, algorithmic monitoring creates information asymmetries between employers and employees: organizations accumulate detailed behavioral data while employees often lack awareness of what is being collected, how it is analyzed, and what consequences flow from the analysis. Third, the opacity of algorithmic decision-making systems compounds the stress of surveillance: individuals who are subject to automated performance evaluations or risk scoring cannot fully understand the criteria by which they are being assessed, producing a combination of techno-surveillance and techno-complexity that is particularly deleterious (Khedhaouria et al., 2024; Anshari et al., 2026).

The COVID-19 pandemic significantly expanded the scope and intensity of techno-surveillance, as the transition to remote work prompted many organizations to adopt real-time activity monitoring tools, keystroke loggers, screenshot capture systems, and video-based presence detection. Research on surveillance and well-being during this period documented elevated levels of anxiety, distrust, and resistance among monitored employees, with counterproductive behavioral responses including cyberslacking, presenteeism through performative screen activity, and strategic disengagement from discretionary effort (Becker et al., 2019).

DIGITAL MINIMALISM AND DATA GOVERNANCE

The analysis reveals a systematic relationship between specific technostress creators and the coping paradigms best suited to address them. Digital minimalism, as an individual-level, problem-focused coping strategy, is most directly applicable to techno-overload (by reducing the volume and frequency of digital inputs) and techno-invasion (by establishing boundaries that protect personal time and space from technological encroachment). Data governance, as a structural, institutional-level coping mechanism, is most directly applicable to techno-surveillance (by constraining the environmental conditions that enable invasive monitoring) and techno-complexity (by mandating transparency, explainability, and interoperability that make technological systems more navigable). The complementarity of these two paradigms lies in their operation at different levels of analysis individual and institutional and their targeting of different mechanisms within the technostress process.

Table 2. Technostress Creators and Coping Responses

Technostress Creator	Primary Coping Paradigm	Key Mechanisms	Level of Analysis	Coping Type
Techno-Overload	Digital Minimalism	App audits, notification management, batched communication, digital sabbaths	Individual	Problem-focused
Techno-Invasion	Digital Minimalism + Right to Disconnect	Device-free zones, communication blackouts, boundary-setting, legislative protections	Individual + Institutional	Problem-focused + Structural
Techno-Complexity	Data Governance	Transparency mandates, explainability requirements, interface simplification, interoperability standards	Institutional + Regulatory	Structural
Techno-Surveillance	Data Governance	Data minimization, purpose limitation, DPIAs, privacy-by-design, algorithmic impact assessments	Regulatory + Organizational	Structural + Protective

Theoretical Contributions

This integrative framework makes several contributions to technostress theory. First, it extends the Tarafdar et al. (2007) technostress creators model by incorporating techno-surveillance as a distinct stressor, reflecting the growing empirical attention to algorithmic monitoring and datafied control in the post-2015 literature. Second, it bridges the individual-focused coping literature (Pirkkalainen & Salo, 2016; Weinert et al., 2020) with the institutional-level governance literature, demonstrating that effective technostress mitigation requires interventions at multiple levels of analysis. Third, it integrates digital minimalism which has been studied primarily in popular discourse and consumer behavior research into the academic technostress framework, providing it with a rigorous theoretical grounding in the transactional stress and coping model. Fourth, it positions data governance not merely as a compliance function but as a psychologically meaningful structural intervention that modifies the environmental conditions producing technostress.

Practical Implications

For organizations, the framework suggests that technostress mitigation strategies should be multifaceted, combining individual level support for digital minimalism practices (such as training in intentional technology use, organizational endorsement of disconnection periods, and the provision of minimalist technology options) with robust data governance policies that ensure transparency, consent, and proportionality in workplace technology deployment. For policymakers, the analysis underscores the technostress-reducing potential of data governance regulations and argues for the continued expansion of transparency requirements, employee data rights, and constraints on invasive workplace surveillance. For technology designers, the framework highlights the importance of building systems that respect user attention, support boundary management, and provide meaningful control over data processing activities.

For individuals, the evidence reviewed in this chapter supports the adoption of digital minimalism practices as a meaningful coping strategy, particularly for managing techno-overload and techno-invasion. However, the analysis also cautions against placing excessive responsibility on individual coping efforts in the absence of supportive organizational and regulatory structures. The most effective technostress interventions, the literature suggests, are those that combine individual agency with institutional support, a principle that applies equally to digital minimalism and data governance.

CONCLUSION

The chapter has conducted a comprehensive secondary data literature review of research published between 2015 and 2026 to examine digital minimalism and data governance as coping responses to technostress. The analysis, grounded in the technostress creators framework of Tarafdar et al. (2007) and Ragu-Nathan et al. (2008) and the transactional stress and coping model of Lazarus and Folkman (1984), has demonstrated that digital minimalism functions as an effective individual-level, problem-focused coping strategy for techno-overload and techno-invasion, while data governance operates as a structural coping mechanism that addresses techno-complexity and techno-surveillance at the institutional and regulatory levels. The integrative framework developed in Section 8 positions these two paradigms as complementary rather than competing, operating at different levels of analysis to address different mechanisms within the technostress process. Future research should pursue several promising directions. Longitudinal studies tracking the adoption of digital minimalism practices and their effects on technostress over time would significantly strengthen the evidence base. Cross-cultural comparative research examining how data governance frameworks in different regulatory environments (the EU, the United States, China, India) differentially affect technostress experiences would illuminate the contextual moderators of governance effectiveness. Studies employing biomarkers and physiological measures of stress (as advocated by Mishra & Rašticová, 2024) could provide objective evidence complementing self-report data. Finally, design science research developing and evaluating technology systems that embed both digital minimalism principles (attention-respecting design, natural stopping points, transparent notification architectures) and data governance protections (privacy-by-default settings, accessible data access requests, algorithmic transparency dashboards) could advance both theory and practice by demonstrating how technostress can be mitigated through the integrated application of both coping paradigms. Finally, the technostress phenomenon demands responses that are as multifaceted as its causes. Neither individual discipline alone nor institutional regulation alone is sufficient to address the full spectrum of techno-stressors that characterize the contemporary digital environment. Digital minimalism and data governance, understood as complementary coping strategies operating at individual and systemic levels, offer a promising integrative approach to the management of technostress in the years ahead.

REFERENCES

Alanazi, A., & Altukhys, A. (2025). Mapping the impact: A systematic review of the psychological and social repercussions of technostress. *American Journal of Applied Scientific Research, 11*(4), 203–210. DOI: 10.11648/j.ajasr.20251104.13

Anshari, M., Almunawar, M. N., Masri, M., Ordoñez, D. E., & Pablos, P. (2026). Industry 4.0 and the sustainable business model for the digital marketplace. *International Journal of Innovation Science*, 1–28. DOI: 10.1108/IJIS-02-2025-0092

Ashforth, B. E., Kreiner, G. E., & Fugate, M. (2000). All in a day's work: Boundaries and micro role transitions. *Academy of Management Review*, *25*(3), 472–491. DOI: 10.2307/259305

Baj-Rogowska, A. (2023). Antecedents and outcomes of social media fatigue. *Information Technology & People*, *36*(8), 226–254. DOI: 10.1108/ITP-03-2022-0207

Balkin, J. M. (2016). Information fiduciaries and the first amendment. *U.C. Davis Law Review*, *49*(4), 1183–1234.

Banerjee, S., & Gupta, R. (2024). Managing technostress in the digital era. *Journal of Organizational Behavior*, *45*(3), 412–430.

Becker, J., Derra, N. D., Regal, C., & Kühlmann, T. M. (2021). Mitigating the negative consequences of ICT use: The moderating effect of active-functional and dysfunctional coping. *Journal of Decision Systems*, *31*(4), 374–406. DOI: 10.1080/12460125.2021.1901337

Becker, W. J., Belkin, L. Y., Conroy, S. A., & Tuskey, S. (2019). Killing me softly: Organizational e-mail monitoring expectations' impact on employee and significant other well-being. *Journal of Management*, *47*(4), 848–884. DOI: 10.1177/0149206319890655

Bondanini, G., Giorgi, G., Ariza-Montes, A., Vega-Muñoz, A., & Andreucci-Annunziata, P. (2023). Technostress at work during the COVID-19 lockdown phase (2020–2021): A systematic review. *Frontiers in Psychology*, *14*, 1173425. Advance online publication. DOI: 10.3389/fpsyg.2023.1173425 PMID: 37179875

Brod, C. (1984). *Technostress: The human cost of the computer revolution*. Addison-Wesley.

Califf, C. B., Sarker, S., & Sarker, S. (2020). The bright and dark sides of technostress: A mixed-methods study involving healthcare IT. *Management Information Systems Quarterly*, *44*(2), 809–856. DOI: 10.25300/MISQ/2020/14818

Cavoukian, A. (2012). *Privacy by design: The 7 foundational principles*. Information and Privacy Commissioner of Ontario.

Cho, J., Ramgolam, D. I., Schaefer, K. M., & Sandlin, A. N. (2020). The rate and delay in overload: An investigation of communication overload and channel synchronicity on identification and job satisfaction. *Journal of Applied Communication Research*, *39*(2), 113–131.

Colledani, D., Capozza, D., & Falvo, R. (2025). Measuring technostress in everyday life: Development and validation of an assessment scale. Human Behavior and Emerging Technologies. *Human Behavior and Emerging Technologies*, *5793644*(1), 5793644. Advance online publication. DOI: 10.1155/hbe2/5793644

Eppler, M. J., & Mengis, J. (2004). The concept of information overload: A review of literature from organization science, accounting, marketing, MIS, and related disciplines. *The Information Society*, *20*(5), 325–344. DOI: 10.1080/01972240490507974

Estrada-Muñoz, C., Castillo, D., Vega-Muñoz, A., & Boada-Grau, J. (2022). Teacher technostress in the Chilean school system. *International Journal of Environmental Research and Public Health*, *17*(15), 5280. DOI: 10.3390/ijerph17155280 PMID: 32707973

Johnston, M. P. (2017). Secondary data analysis: A method of which the time has come. *Qualitative and Quantitative Methods in Libraries*, *3*(3), 619–626.

Khedhaouria, A., Montani, F., & Lam, W. (2024). Technology-driven work pressure and technostress: Examining the role of automation in employee well-being. *Computers in Human Behavior*, *150*, 107998.

Kupersmith, J. (1992). Technostress and the reference librarian. *RSR. Reference Services Review*, *20*(2), 7–14. DOI: 10.1108/eb049150

Lazarus, R. S., & Folkman, S. (1984). *Stress, appraisal, and coping*. Springer.

Malgieri, G. (2023). *Vulnerability and data protection law*. Oxford University Press. DOI: 10.1093/oso/9780192870339.001.0001

Mattern, J., Tarafdar, M., Klein, S., & Schellhammer, S. (2024). Thriving in a bruising job: How high achieving IT professionals can cope with occupational demands. *Information Systems Journal*, *34*(6), 2045–2096. DOI: 10.1111/isj.12513

Mazmanian, M., Orlikowski, W. J., & Yates, J. (2013). The autonomy paradox: The implications of mobile email devices for knowledge professionals. *Organization Science*, *24*(5), 1337–1357. DOI: 10.1287/orsc.1120.0806

Mirbabaie, M., Stieglitz, S., & Marx, J. (2022). Digital detox. *Business & Information Systems Engineering*, *64*(2), 239–246. DOI: 10.1007/s12599-022-00747-x

Mishra, P. K., & Raštícová, M. (2024). Role and status of biomarkers in technostress research: A systematic review. *Psychology Research and Behavior Management*, *17*, 1961–1972. DOI: 10.2147/PRBM.S446782 PMID: 38751567

Molino, M., Ingusci, E., Signore, F., Manuti, A., Giancaspro, M. L., Russo, V., Zito, M., & Cortese, C. G. (2020). Wellbeing costs of technology use during Covid-19 remote working: An investigation using the Italian translation of the technostress creators scale. *Sustainability (Basel)*, *12*(15), 5911. DOI: 10.3390/su12155911

Nastjuk, I., Trang, S., Grummeck-Braamt, J.-V., Adam, M. T. P., & Tarafdar, M. (2024). Integrating and synthesising technostress research: A meta-analysis on technostress creators, outcomes, and IS usage contexts. *European Journal of Information Systems*, *33*(3), 361–382. DOI: 10.1080/0960085X.2022.2154712

Newport, C. (2019). *Digital minimalism: Choosing a focused life in a noisy world*. Portfolio/Penguin.

Pirkkalainen, H., & Salo, M. (2016). Two decades of the dark side in the information systems basket: Suggesting five areas for future research. In *Proceedings of the 24th European Conference on Information Systems (ECIS 2016)*.

Radtke, T., Apel, T., Schenkel, K., Keller, J., & von Lindern, E. (2022). Digital detox: An effective solution in the smartphone era? A systematic literature review. *Mobile Media & Communication*, *10*(2), 190–215. DOI: 10.1177/20501579211028647

Ragu-Nathan, T. S., Tarafdar, M., Ragu-Nathan, B. S., & Tu, Q. (2008). The consequences of technostress for end users in organizations: Conceptual development and empirical validation. *Information Systems Research*, *19*(4), 417–433. DOI: 10.1287/isre.1070.0165

Rasool, T., Warraich, N. F., & Sajid, M. (2022). Examining the impact of technology overload at the workplace: A systematic review. *SAGE Open*, *12*(3), 215824402211143. DOI: 10.1177/21582440221114320

Ravid, D. M., Tomczak, D. L., White, J. C., & Behrend, T. S. (2023). EPM 20/20: A review, framework, and research agenda for electronic performance monitoring. *Journal of Management*, *46*(1), 100–126. DOI: 10.1177/0149206319869435

Schraggeová, M.. (2025). The effect of digital detox through digital minimalism using the MinimalistPhone app on the behavior of young users and their emotional experience. Computers in Human Behavior Reports. *Article*, *100579*. Advance online publication. DOI: 10.1016/j.chbr.2025.100579

Tarafdar, M., Cooper, C. L., & Stich, J.-F. (2019). The technostress trifecta—Techno eustress, techno distress and design: Theoretical directions and an agenda for research. *Information Systems Journal*, *29*(1), 6–42. DOI: 10.1111/isj.12169

Tarafdar, M., Tu, Q., Ragu-Nathan, B. S., & Ragu-Nathan, T. S. (2007). The impact of technostress on role stress and productivity. *Journal of Management Information Systems*, *24*(1), 301–328. DOI: 10.2753/MIS0742-1222240109

ten Brummelhuis, L. L., & Bakker, A. B. (2012). A resource perspective on the work–home interface: The work–home resources model. *The American Psychologist*, *67*(7), 545–556. DOI: 10.1037/a0027974 PMID: 22506688

Thomas, J., & Harden, A. (2008). Methods for the thematic synthesis of qualitative research in systematic reviews. *BMC Medical Research Methodology*, *8*(1), 45. DOI: 10.1186/1471-2288-8-45 PMID: 18616818

Turel, O., & Serenko, A. (2012). The benefits and dangers of enjoyment with social networking websites. *European Journal of Information Systems*, *21*(5), 512–528. DOI: 10.1057/ejis.2012.1

van Deursen, A. J. A. M., Bolle, C. L., Hegner, S. M., & Kommers, P. A. M. (2015). Modeling habitual and addictive smartphone behavior. *Computers in Human Behavior*, *45*, 411–420. DOI: 10.1016/j.chb.2014.12.039

Vanden Abeele, M. M. P. (2021). Digital wellbeing as a dynamic construct. *Communication Theory*, *31*(4), 932–955. DOI: 10.1093/ct/qtaa024

Voigt, P., & von dem Bussche, A. (2017). *The EU General Data Protection Regulation (GDPR): A practical guide*. Springer. DOI: 10.1007/978-3-319-57959-7

Weil, M. M., & Rosen, L. D. (1997). *Technostress: Coping with technology @work @home @play*. John Wiley & Sons.

Weinert, C., Maier, C., Laumer, S., & Weitzel, T. (2020). How does technostress influence the coping of information system users? Conceptualizing a model of technostress coping. *Management Information Systems Quarterly*, *44*(3), 1199–1228.

Zuboff, S. (2019). *The age of surveillance capitalism: The fight for a human future at the new frontier of power*. PublicAffairs.

KEY TERMS AND DEFINITIONS

Technostress: Stress experienced by individuals as a result of their use of information and communication technologies, arising when technology-related demands exceed coping resources (Brod, 1984; Tarafdar et al., 2007).

Techno-Overload: A technostress creator in which ICTs compel individuals to process excessive information and work at unsustainable speeds, fragmenting attention and overwhelming cognitive capacity (Ragu-Nathan et al., 2008).

Techno-Invasion: A technostress creator characterized by the erosion of boundaries between work and personal life through perpetual digital connectivity, creating expectations of constant availability (Tarafdar et al., 2007).

Techno-Complexity: A technostress creator arising from individuals' perceived inability to understand, learn, and effectively use rapidly evolving technology platforms and systems (Tarafdar et al., 2007).

Techno-Surveillance: An emergent technostress creator encompassing the stress produced by algorithmic monitoring, workplace analytics, behavioral tracking, and datafied control of employee activities.

Digital Minimalism: A philosophy of technology use advocating for the intentional curation and reduction of digital engagement to support core personal values, reclaim attention, and reduce technology-related stress (Newport, 2019).

Data Governance: The organizational, regulatory, and technical frameworks through which data is managed, protected, and ethically utilized across its lifecycle, including laws such as the GDPR, organizational policies, and privacy-by-design standards.

Privacy-by-Design: An approach to systems engineering that embeds privacy protections into the architecture and design of technology systems from inception, rather than addressing privacy as a compliance afterthought (Cavoukian, 2012).

Right to Disconnect: Legislative provisions granting employees the right to disengage from digital work communications outside contractual working hours, enacted in multiple European jurisdictions as a structural response to techno-invasion.

Technostress Inhibitors: Organizational mechanisms such as literacy facilitation, technical support provision, and involvement facilitation that reduce the creation or negative consequences of technostress (Ragu-Nathan et al., 2008).

Chapter 2
AI-Based Guidance and Counseling Services in Indonesia:
Critical Literacy, Student Data Rights, and Ethical Challenges

Nur Hidayah
http://orcid.org/0000-0002-2602-2335
Universitas Negeri Malang, Indonesia

Yansen Alberth Reba
http://orcid.org/0009-0000-3364-8899
Universitas Cenderawasih, Indonesia

ABSTRACT

This chapter examines the integration of artificial intelligence in guidance and counseling services in Indonesia, focusing on students' critical literacy, data rights, and ethical challenges in higher education. Using Social Cognitive Theory, critical digital literacy, and data sovereignty perspectives, the chapter explains how limited AI literacy may increase vulnerability to algorithmic bias and misuse of psychological data. It argues that AI should support, not replace, human counseling relationships while strengthening data protection and ethical governance.

1. INTRODUCTION

The advancement of artificial intelligence in the field of education has fundamentally transformed how guidance and counseling services are delivered across

DOI: 10.4018/979-8-2600-2233-7.ch002

countries. AI-based systems are now used for mental health screening, academic mentoring, chatbot-based counseling services, and predictive analysis of students' psychosocial risks. Numerous studies indicate that this technology has emerged in response to growing mental health support needs and a limited supply of professional counselors, particularly in higher education settings (Anser et al., 2025; Pavlopoulos et al., 2024; Ganesh & Venkateswaramurthy, 2025). This transformation is frequently positioned as a progressive innovation that promises efficiency, accessibility, and personalization of services.

However, the effectiveness of AI in counseling is not universal and is highly dependent on the social and cultural context of users. Several studies report that AI can help reduce mild anxiety symptoms, but also affirm its limitations in emotional empathy, cultural sensitivity, and the management of psychological crises (Akdogan et al., 2025; Farzan et al., 2025; Perlis, 2026). These findings reveal that AI cannot be understood merely as a technical tool, but rather as a socio-technological system that reshapes the nature of helping relationships. In the context of counseling, such relationships are decisive in determining the quality of support students receive.

In Indonesia, the adoption of AI in educational services is occurring amid the acceleration of national digital transformation and limited human resources in guidance and counseling (BK). Several universities have begun integrating AI-based counseling platforms as complements to conventional BK services, particularly for initial screening and psychosocial mentoring of students (Putri Syarifa et al., 2024; Hariyadi et al., 2025). At the same time, digital education policy continues to encourage the utilization of technology as part of the national innovation agenda (Bangun et al., 2025; Manggalasari et al., 2025). This condition creates fertile ground for AI technology to penetrate counseling practice.

Nevertheless, digital literacy among Indonesian students remains highly varied, while awareness of personal data rights is relatively low. Research shows that students tend to trust technology legitimized by educational institutions, even when they do not understand the algorithmic mechanisms or data management practices underpinning such platforms (Martha et al., 2025; Hulus, 2026). This situation heightens students' vulnerability, particularly when they share highly personal psychological information through digital systems. Without adequate reflective capacity, students risk losing control over the narrative of their own emotional experiences.

This issue grows more complex when viewed through the lens of the global data economy. Studies on data colonialism demonstrate that countries in the Global South frequently become data sources for international technology companies without retaining meaningful control over how that data is used (Couldry & Mejias, 2023; Gray, 2023; Mumford, 2022). In the context of AI counseling, Indonesian students potentially become suppliers of high-value psychological data for global system development. This relationship raises serious questions about data sovereignty and digital justice.

This chapter focuses on three primary issues: students' critical digital literacy, student data rights within AI counseling services, and the ethical challenges of integrating AI into guidance and counseling practice. Critical digital literacy is understood as the ability to recognize algorithmic bias and the limitations of AI systems, rather than simply the skill to use technology (Dogruel et al., 2022; Moylan & Code, 2024). Student data rights are positioned as part of the national digital sovereignty agenda, which has begun to gain legal footing through the Personal Data Protection Law (Saly & Sulthanah, 2023; Aisy et al., 2025). Meanwhile, ethical challenges encompass issues of pseudo-therapeutic relationships, informed consent, system bias, and student safety in crisis situations (Gong et al., 2025; Bouguettaya et al., 2025; Chan, 2025).

Methodologically, this chapter is positioned as a conceptual-critical literature study that draws on systematic engagement with relevant scholarly sources rather than empirical fieldwork. It employs an integrative theoretical framework combining Social Cognitive Theory, critical digital literacy, and data sovereignty perspectives to examine the experiences of Indonesian students in AI-based counseling services. This approach enables a more comprehensive understanding of how personal beliefs, institutional environments, and technological architecture interact to shape digital counseling practice. By making this methodological stance explicit, the chapter situates its contributions within the tradition of critical theoretical inquiry rather than empirical generalization. The authors' position affirms that AI must be placed as a supplement to BK services, not a substitute for human professional relationships. Through this approach, the chapter aims to provide a conceptual foundation for the development of AI counseling that is humane, equitable, and oriented toward the protection of student rights

2. CONCEPTUAL FRAMEWORK

The use of artificial intelligence in guidance and counseling services cannot be adequately analyzed from a purely educational technology perspective. While existing studies have addressed the potential benefits of AI in mental health (Anser et al., 2025; Pavlopoulos et al., 2024) and raised concerns about algorithmic bias (Bouguettaya et al., 2025; Jain & Menon, 2023), a critical gap remains: these studies largely treat AI as a context-neutral intervention, overlooking the specific structural vulnerabilities of students in the Global South. This gap is particularly acute in the Indonesian context, where low AI literacy, limited data governance, and unequal access to digital infrastructure create conditions qualitatively distinct from those studied in dominant Western scholarship. This chapter therefore argues that existing frameworks are insufficient to capture the full scope of risks and power dynamics at play. AI creates new interaction spaces that reshape how students understand themselves, manage emotions, and make decisions — and these effects are mediated by cultural, institutional, and political-economic factors that demand a multidimensional analytical lens. Accordingly, this chapter employs an integrative approach combining Social Cognitive Theory, critical digital literacy, and data sovereignty perspectives to fill this theoretical gap.

These three perspectives enable a more complete reading of Indonesian students' experiences in AI-mediated counseling. Social Cognitive Theory helps explain how students' self-beliefs and expectations influence their technology use. Critical digital literacy opens space for reflection on algorithmic bias and power structures embedded within AI systems. Meanwhile, data sovereignty provides a political framework for understanding students' positioning as subjects within the global data economy (Dogruel et al., 2022; Couldry & Mejias, 2023; Gray, 2023).

2.1 Social Cognitive Theory in AI-Based Counseling Environments

Within the Social Cognitive Theory framework, human behavior is understood as the product of reciprocal interactions among personal factors, behavior, and environment. When counseling services are mediated by AI, that environment shifts from a relational space to an algorithmic space governed by digital systems. This transformation affects how students build trust in services, interpret psychological problems, and decide how much they are willing to disclose to the system. The dynamics of adaptation to changes in work environments and digital systems are also evident in remote work contexts, where role pressure and career uncertainty heighten burnout risk, making adaptive capacity a crucial protective factor for individuals (Aminah et al., 2023). Therefore, AI counseling cannot be separated from students' cognitive construction of technology.

The concept of self-efficacy is a central element in understanding this interaction. Students with high digital self-efficacy tend to question AI outputs, while those with low efficacy are more likely to accept system responses as objective truth. Research shows that self-efficacy levels are directly linked to the ability to evaluate the quality of AI outputs and maintain a critical stance toward algorithmic recommendations (Alghamdi, 2025; Bećirović et al., 2025). This indicates that AI literacy is not only cognitive in nature, but also psychological.

In addition to self-efficacy, outcome expectation shapes patterns of AI counseling use. When students expect quick, anonymous, and stigma-free solutions, they are more inclined to share personal information intensively. However, such expectations are frequently not matched by an understanding of AI's limitations in emotional empathy and cultural sensitivity. Various studies affirm that AI still has significant limitations in capturing the complexity of human experience, particularly in the context of mental health (Akdogan et al., 2025; Farzan et al., 2025; Perlis, 2026).

The modeling dimension also warrants attention in the context of AI counseling. AI systems implicitly model ways of understanding psychological problems and their resolution strategies through the responses they provide. When these models are grounded in individualistic Western psychological frameworks, there is a risk of misalignment with the collectivistic and relational values that are deeply embedded in Indonesian culture. To understand how this occurs, it is necessary to clarify the basic mechanics of algorithmic bias. Contemporary AI counseling systems, predominantly built on large language models (LLMs), learn their response patterns from vast training corpora that disproportionately represent English-language, Western, and individualistic cultural content. When these models are deployed in contexts with different cultural logics, the bias is not a malfunction but an architectural feature: the system optimizes for patterns it has learned, which may not correspond to the phenomenological realities of Indonesian students. Research on algorithmic bias demonstrates that AI systems can thereby reproduce dominant cultural assumptions and systematically disregard the experiences of marginalized or non-Western groups (Bouguettaya et al., 2025; Jain & Menon, 2023). This structural dynamic is central to understanding why AI counseling carries risks that extend beyond technical performance metrics.

The dimension of social cognitive processes encompasses attention, retention (information storage), behavioral reproduction, and motivation. Within social cognitive theory, individuals do not merely react to environmental stimuli but also actively process information — including reflection on their own thoughts, emotions, and actions. Generative AI (such as LLM-based chatbots) can facilitate self-reflection (e.g., through guided dialogue), provide prompts that help clients reconstruct personal narratives (narrative reflection), and direct clients' attention to maladaptive thinking patterns. This aligns with the theoretical premise that behavior is not merely the product of automatic responses, but the result of cognitive processing of social experience.

2.2 Critical Digital Literacy in Guidance and Counseling Practice

Digital literacy in the context of AI counseling must be understood as reflective capacity to evaluate technological systems, not merely operational skill. Critical digital literacy emphasizes the importance of awareness toward algorithmic logic, system bias, and the social implications of AI use. The concept of algorithmic awareness holds that users need to understand that AI systems are constructed through specific design choices and are never fully neutral (Dogruel et al., 2022; Moylan & Code, 2024).

In the Indonesian context, students often regard AI as an authoritative source, particularly when the technology is legitimized by educational institutions. Research shows that institutional legitimacy increases students' trust in AI, even though they do not understand how such systems work (Martha et al., 2025). This phenomenon is reinforced by the tendency toward anthropomorphism, in which students attribute empathy and human understanding to AI counseling. This dynamic potentially creates pseudo-therapeutic relationships that are not accompanied by adequate ethical safeguards (Chan, 2025).

Critical digital literacy is also closely related to students' awareness of data collection practices. Studies indicate that low AI literacy leads students to share emotional information without considering the long-term implications for their privacy and psychological well-being (Ngoveni, 2025; Hulus, 2026). Therefore, strengthening AI literacy needs to become an integral part of BK services, with counselors playing the role of facilitators of critical reflection on students' digital experiences.

2.3 Data Sovereignty and the Decolonial Perspective

The issue of data in AI counseling cannot be separated from the dynamics of global political economy. The data sovereignty perspective affirms the right of individuals and communities to control information generated from their own lives. However, digital platform practices frequently reproduce patterns of data colonialism, in which data from Global South countries is extracted for the benefit of innovation and profit among global technology actors (Couldry & Mejias, 2023; Gray, 2023; Mumford, 2022). In this context, Indonesian students risk becoming objects of psychological data extraction without meaningful control.

Indonesia has enacted the Personal Data Protection Law as the legal basis for protecting sensitive citizen data. This regulation grants rights to data subjects and obligates data controllers to guarantee the security of personal information (Saly & Sulthanah, 2023). However, studies show that regulatory implementation still faces serious challenges, particularly in the context of cross-border platforms and limited supervisory capacity (Aisy et al., 2025).

Studies on data governance affirm that personal data has become a new source of power in the digital economy. Without robust local control mechanisms, developing nations face the risk of structural dependency on global technology companies (Schwinghammer et al., 2025; Pampus & Heisel, 2025). In BK practice, a decolonial approach demands that students be positioned as dignified subjects rather than mere data sources, and that AI systems be developed with roots in local cultural values and human rights protections.

3. AI COUNSELING: GLOBAL TRENDS AND THE INDONESIAN CONTEXT

The development of AI counseling is part of the global expansion of digital mental health services, driven by increasing psychosocial pressures among students at all levels. AI technology is used to broaden service access, reduce the burden on professional staff, and provide initial support for individuals reluctant to seek face-to-face assistance. Various studies show that AI-based applications are increasingly being used for anxiety screening, emotional support, and the recommendation of simple coping strategies (Anser et al., 2025; Pavlopoulos et al., 2024).

Nevertheless, this expansion is neither smooth nor uncontested. A growing counter-trend in the scholarly and policy literature explicitly challenges the dominant narrative of AI as unambiguous progress in mental health services. Critical scholars have argued that the 'efficiency turn' in digital counseling — driven by cost reduction and scalability logics — systematically undervalues the relational and ethical dimensions that make counseling effective in the first place (Gong et al., 2025; Perlis, 2026). Professional associations in several countries have issued cautionary statements, and some universities have suspended AI counseling pilots pending ethical review. These contestations illustrate that the field is not passively absorbing technology but actively negotiating its terms. AI counseling systems are shaped by the interests of the technology industry, Western psychological frameworks, and the logic of digital efficiency — and the resistance to these forces is as much part of the contemporary landscape as the adoption itself. This chapter aligns with the critical counter-trend: rather than asking how AI can be optimized for counseling, it asks whose interests are served by the current trajectory of AI counseling development. From an educational perspective, AI counseling must be understood as part of a digital learning ecosystem that affects students' relationships with both their institutions and themselves (Gong et al., 2025; Perlis, 2026).

3.1 Global Development of AI in Counseling Services

Globally, AI counseling has developed as a response to a widening mental health service gap. Various studies demonstrate that AI-based chatbots can help reduce mild anxiety symptoms and provide initial support for users who are not yet ready to access human counselors (Akdogan et al., 2025; Farzan et al., 2025). In addition, AI is also used for early psychological risk screening through language analysis and patterns of digital interaction (Ganesh & Venkateswaramurthy, 2025). These findings illustrate the potential of AI as a supportive tool for mental health services.

However, the effectiveness of AI counseling remains limited and highly context-dependent. Research confirms that AI has yet to establish a therapeutic alliance equivalent to human relationships, while the quality of the therapeutic relationship is the primary predictor of counseling success (Murphy et al., 2022; Flix-Valle et al., 2025). AI can simulate empathy through linguistic responses, but it lacks situational awareness and deep comprehension of meaning. This limitation becomes critical when students face complex problems requiring authentic human presence.

The issue of algorithmic bias is also a primary concern in the international literature. AI systems trained on data from specific populations may generate recommendations that are less relevant or even discriminatory toward other cultural groups. Studies show that bias can manifest in the interpretation of symptoms, the classification of psychological conditions, and the choice of suggested interventions (Bouguettaya et al., 2025; Jain & Menon, 2023). In the counseling context, such bias can undermine the validity of services and deepen inequities in access to assistance.

Furthermore, user safety remains a serious challenge. Several studies report that AI has not been consistent in detecting indicators of acute crises, such as suicidal ideation or severe psychiatric disorders. In certain cases, systems have provided generic responses precisely when users required emergency intervention (Chan, 2025; Perlis, 2026). These findings affirm that the use of AI counseling without human oversight poses significant risks to student well-being.

3.2 Implementation of AI Counseling in the Indonesian Context

In Indonesia, the integration of AI into educational services is occurring alongside the national digital transformation agenda. Universities have begun to explore the use of AI technology to support student services, including aspects of counseling and mental health. Several AI-based platforms have been developed to detect anxiety and provide initial psychosocial support (Putri Syarifa et al., 2024; Hariyadi et al., 2025). Digital education policy also encourages technology adoption as part of learning innovation (Bangun et al., 2025; Manggalasari et al., 2025). A concrete illustration of this trend is the Micro Counselling Educational Platform developed at a Malang-based university, which integrates AI and facial recognition to detect student anxiety as a pre-screening tool before face-to-face BK sessions (Putri Syarifa et al., 2024). This case exemplifies both the innovative potential and the governance challenges inherent in Indonesian AI counseling: while the platform expands access, it also generates biometric and psychological data with no publicly documented retention or consent framework. It is precisely this gap, between rapid technological adoption and lagging ethical governance, that this chapter addresses.

However, the Indonesian context has distinctive characteristics that differ from countries where most AI systems were developed. The ratio of counselors to students remains far from ideal, particularly in regions outside Java, so AI is often viewed as a practical solution for broadening service reach. At the same time, students' AI literacy remains limited, while trust in technology legitimized by institutions tends to be high (Martha et al., 2025; Hulus, 2026). This combination creates an asymmetrical relationship between students and AI systems.

Furthermore, Indonesia is positioned as a consumer of global technology. Many AI counseling systems in use were developed by foreign companies with different cultural and linguistic frameworks. Studies on data colonialism show that Global South countries frequently become data sources without retaining full control over their management (Couldry & Mejias, 2023; Gray, 2023). In the educational counseling context, this raises serious concerns regarding the data sovereignty of Indonesian students.

Indonesia has enacted the Personal Data Protection Law as the legal basis for protecting citizens' sensitive data. However, the implementation of this legislation in AI counseling practice continues to face challenges, particularly regarding cross-border oversight and the transparency of platform providers (Saly & Sulthanah, 2023; Aisy et al., 2025). Without robust governance, AI adoption risks deepening structural dependency on systems that do not fully serve the interests of students.

4. STUDENTS' CRITICAL LITERACY IN AI COUNSELING INTERACTION

The success of AI integration into guidance and counseling services is greatly determined by students' capacity to engage critically with the technology. AI counseling not only provides information but also shapes the way students understand their emotions, interpret problems, and make decisions. Without critical literacy, students risk positioning AI as an unquestionable psychological authority. Several studies indicate that low AI literacy correlates with a tendency to passively accept algorithmic outputs, particularly in the context of services legitimized by educational institutions (Dogruel et al., 2022; Hidayat et al., 2024; Ngoveni, 2025).

Critical literacy is especially important because AI counseling operates through algorithmic logic that is not always transparent to users. Students often see only a user-friendly interface without understanding how system responses are generated. This creates an illusion of technological objectivity, even though every AI system is built through specific design choices. Therefore, critical digital literacy must be understood as a reflective competence that enables students to question the validity and relevance of AI recommendations (Moylan & Code, 2024; Hulus, 2026).

4.1 The Digital Literacy Landscape of Indonesian Students

Indonesian students demonstrate relatively high operational digital skills, particularly in the use of mobile devices and social media. However, these skills do not always accompany a deep understanding of how algorithms work and how data is managed. Research indicates that students tend to be proficient in using applications, yet remain weak in evaluating the credibility of AI systems and the privacy implications of their digital interactions (Martha et al., 2025; Hidayat et al., 2024; Hulus, 2026). This gap reveals that students' digital literacy remains at a functional level, rather than a critical one.

Digital self-efficacy also influences students' patterns of interaction with AI counseling. Students who feel confident in their technological abilities tend to be more reflective about system outputs, whereas those with lower efficacy are more likely to defer judgment to the AI. Studies show that self-efficacy is directly related to the quality of AI output evaluation and users' critical attitudes (Bećirović et al., 2025; Alghamdi, 2025). Thus, AI literacy is not merely a cognitive matter, but a psychological one as well.

In the counseling context, low critical literacy carries serious implications because students often share highly personal emotional information. Without an adequate understanding of how that data is processed and stored, students risk losing control over their own psychological narratives. Research shows that users of digital mental health services frequently underestimate the level of sensitivity of the data they share (Patne & Suryawanshic, 2025; Alqhatani, 2026). This situation demands particular attention in AI-based BK practice.

4.2 Algorithmic Awareness and Trust in AI

Algorithmic awareness refers to the recognition that AI systems are constructed through specific training data and optimization objectives. Such awareness is important so that users do not regard AI as a neutral or wholly objective entity. Research affirms that low algorithmic awareness leads students to accept system recommendations without considering the potential for bias (Dogruel et al., 2022; Moylan & Code, 2024). In the counseling context, this can affect the way students understand their own psychological conditions.

Institutional legitimacy reinforces students' trust in AI counseling. When technology is introduced as part of official campus services, students tend to attribute scientific authority to the system.

Research shows that this legitimacy increases students' acceptance of AI, even when they do not understand its mechanisms (Martha et al., 2025). Compounding this, the tendency toward anthropomorphism — perceiving AI as possessing human empathy (Chan, 2025) — transforms an epistemic gap into an emotional one: students do not merely fail to question the system; they actively trust it as a relational partner. This layered dynamic, where institutional authority and perceived empathy converge, creates conditions that are particularly difficult to reverse through simple information provision alone.

Trust that is unbalanced by algorithmic awareness heightens the risk of reproducing system bias. Studies on AI bias demonstrate that algorithms can disregard users' cultural contexts and reproduce dominant assumptions embedded in training data (Bouguettaya et al., 2025; Jain & Menon, 2023). For Indonesian students, this means that their psychological experiences may be oversimplified or misinterpreted by systems not designed with contextual awareness.

4.3 Integrating AI Literacy into Guidance and Counseling Services

AI literacy needs to be systematically integrated into BK practice as part of student competence development. Counselors hold a strategic role in helping students reflect on their experiences with AI counseling and understand the limitations of technology. However, research shows that many educators do not yet possess an adequate AI literacy framework to perform this function optimally (Ngoveni, 2025; Hulus, 2026). This situation underscores the need to strengthen professional BK capacity.

AI literacy integration encompasses education about algorithmic bias, personal data rights, and the limitations of AI in handling the complexity of human emotions. This approach aligns with the critical digital literacy framework that emphasizes reflective and ethical capacity in technology use (Dogruel et al., 2022; Moylan & Code, 2024). In the Indonesian context, the development of AI literacy must also take into account the relational and collectivistic values that form the foundation of students' social interactions.

Accordingly, critical literacy is not merely a technological complement, but an ethical foundation for the integration of AI into BK services. Without such literacy, AI counseling risks deepening knowledge inequities and undermining students' position as agents with meaningful participation in the helping process. Therefore, strengthening AI literacy must be positioned as an integral part of counseling service reform in the digital era.

5. STUDENT DATA RIGHTS IN AI-MEDIATED COUNSELING

The use of AI in guidance and counseling services carries serious consequences for the management of students' personal data. Unlike ordinary academic data, data generated through counseling interactions encompasses emotional states, traumatic experiences, interpersonal relationships, and life aspirations. Various studies affirm that mental health data constitutes the most sensitive data category because it enables the construction of deeply detailed psychological profiles (Patne & Suryawanshic, 2025; Alqhatani, 2026). Therefore, data protection in AI counseling cannot be positioned as a purely technical issue, but must be understood as a matter of student rights and dignity.

In practice, students frequently do not realize how extensively their personal information is collected and analyzed by AI systems. Interactions that appear straightforward through a chatbot or digital form in reality generate complex and layered data traces. When such data is processed at scale, the potential for misuse emerges in ways that are difficult for individuals to control. This situation demands a more critical approach to data governance within digital counseling services.

5.1 Sensitivity of Counseling Data and Aggregation Risks

Student interactions with AI counseling generate not only textual conversations, but also metadata such as response times, frequency of use, and patterns of discussion topics. When these elements are combined, the system can construct psychological profiles that far exceed users' awareness. This phenomenon is known as the aggregation problem, whereby information that appears individually harmless becomes highly invasive when combined (Nandyala et al., 2025). In the counseling context, this data aggregation can reveal students' emotional vulnerabilities in considerable detail.

Research indicates that the majority of digital mental health service users do not understand the depth of data being collected or its potential secondary uses. Many students assume their data is used solely for direct service purposes, when in reality it is frequently also utilized for system development or commercial interests (Alqhatani, 2026). Low AI literacy exacerbates this situation, as students tend to agree to privacy policies without reading or understanding their implications (Ngoveni, 2025; Hulus, 2026).

From the perspective of BK ethics, this situation threatens the principle of confidentiality that has long been the foundation of the counseling relationship. When students' psychological data is managed by external platforms, the boundary between therapeutic space and commercial space becomes increasingly blurred.

This raises a fundamental question about who truly holds control over students' emotional experiences.

5.2 Indonesia's Data Protection Framework and Implementation Challenges

Indonesia has enacted the Personal Data Protection Law as an important milestone in protecting citizens' sensitive information. This regulation grants data subjects the right to access, rectify, and delete their personal data, and obligates data controllers to guarantee the security of data processing (Saly & Sulthanah, 2023). Within this legal framework, health and psychological data is categorized as sensitive data requiring additional protection.

However, a number of studies indicate that the implementation of the Personal Data Protection Law still faces structural challenges. Supervisory capacity is limited, enforcement mechanisms are not yet mature, and cross-border platform regulation still leaves many gaps (Aisy et al., 2025). In AI counseling practice, students frequently interact with systems operated by foreign companies, rendering legal jurisdiction unclear and difficult to enforce.

Moreover, a general legal framework has not yet fully accommodated the specific characteristics of educational counseling data. Psychological data carries long-term implications for individual identity and well-being, thus requiring more specific sectoral regulation. Without clear guidance, educational institutions risk adopting AI technology without adequate protection standards.

5.3 Student Data Sovereignty and Global Dimensions

The question of student data rights cannot be separated from the structure of the global digital economy. The data colonialism perspective demonstrates that technology platforms frequently extract data from Global South countries for the benefit of innovation and profit among global actors, without granting meaningful control to data owners (Couldry & Mejias, 2023; Gray, 2023; Mumford, 2022). This dynamic is not unique to Indonesia; parallel contestations are evident across other Global South contexts. In India, civil society organizations have successfully challenged biometric data collection mandates in public education, arguing that algorithmic surveillance reproduces colonial logics of population management (Jain & Menon, 2023). In several African nations, local data governance advocates have demanded 'data localization' requirements to prevent psychological health data from flowing to foreign servers without community consent. These parallel struggles share a common structural diagnosis: the global AI industry positions developing nations as data reservoirs rather than as innovation partners with equal stakes in how knowledge is produced. In the Indonesian context, therefore, students are not merely potential data sources for international AI development, they are situated within a transnational political economy of psychological data extraction that demands collective, cross-national resistance strategies.

Studies on data governance affirm that personal data has become a new source of power in the digital economy. When states and local institutions lack strong control, structural dependency on global technology companies intensifies (Schwinghammer et al., 2025; Pampus & Heisel, 2025). This weakens students' position as data subjects and amplifies the risk of personal information exploitation.

A data sovereignty approach demands a paradigm shift in AI-based BK services. Students must be positioned as the rightful owners of their psychological data, with the right to know, control, and withdraw consent for data use at any time. In practice, this means that AI counseling must be accompanied by genuinely informed consent mechanisms and equivalent human service alternatives, so that technology does not become a veiled instrument of data extraction.

6. ETHICAL CHALLENGES IN AI-MEDIATED COUNSELING

The integration of artificial intelligence into guidance and counseling services presents ethical dilemmas that extend far beyond questions of technological efficiency. AI not only presents information but also shapes helping relationships, mediates emotional expression, and influences students' decision-making. Various studies affirm that the use of AI in mental health contexts carries risks related to pseudo-empathy, algorithmic bias, and user safety (Gong et al., 2025; Bouguettaya et al., 2025; Perlis, 2026). Therefore, AI counseling must be analyzed as an ethical practice, not merely a digital innovation.

Ethical challenges become more complex when AI is introduced into educational environments that carry their own power dynamics. Students often regard official campus services as safe spaces and therefore tend to trust AI systems legitimized by the institution. Research indicates that institutional legitimacy increases technology acceptance, even when users do not understand how the system works (Martha et al., 2025). This places students in a vulnerable position, particularly when they share highly personal psychological information.

6.1 Pseudo-Therapeutic Relationships and the Limits of AI Empathy

One of the primary concerns in AI counseling is the formation of pseudo-therapeutic relationships. AI systems are capable of simulating empathic language, but they lack emotional consciousness and a genuine understanding of users' life contexts. Research demonstrates that the quality of therapeutic alliance in counseling depends heavily on authentic human presence, while AI can only replicate linguistic patterns without deep relational meaning (Murphy et al., 2022; Flix-Valle et al., 2025).

This creates a specific and consequential risk: students may feel emotionally validated 'heard', while in reality receiving responses calibrated to pattern-matching rather than genuine understanding. The stakes escalate when students face complex, context-sensitive issues such as family conflict, intense academic pressure, or identity crises, where generic responses may not only fail to help but actively disrupt the reflective process. Critically, this limitation is not merely technical; it reflects the irreducible role of human phenomenological understanding in therapeutic work (Akdogan et al., 2025; Farzan et al., 2025).

The phenomenon of anthropomorphism further deepens the ethical complexity of AI counseling. Students frequently attribute empathy, intentionality, and genuine understanding to AI systems, particularly when these systems are designed with warm conversational styles, responsive question patterns, and personalized memory features. Research demonstrates that anthropomorphic tendencies significantly increase user trust in AI, even in the absence of any genuine affective capacity (Chan, 2025). In the BK context, this means that students may form what they experience as a meaningful supportive relationship with an algorithmic system — a relationship that, from the system's side, has no subjective dimension whatsoever. This asymmetry between the student's experience of connection and the system's computational indifference constitutes a form of relational deception that challenges the foundational BK principle of authentic human encounter.

Furthermore, anthropomorphism interacts with students' prior relational experiences in potentially problematic ways. Students who have experienced inadequate or unavailable human support — a common reality in contexts with low counselor-to-student ratios, such as many Indonesian universities — may be particularly susceptible to forming intense relational attachments to AI systems. For these students, the AI does not merely supplement human support; it substitutes for it. The resulting dependency on pseudo-therapeutic relationships can paradoxically reduce students' motivation to seek genuine human counseling, thereby deepening rather than bridging the mental health support gap that AI counseling ostensibly aims to address (Perlis, 2026). BK practitioners must therefore be trained not only to introduce AI tools, but also to recognize and therapeutically address patterns of AI dependency that may emerge among their student populations.

6.2 Digital Informed Consent and Student Safety

The issue of informed consent presents a major challenge in AI-mediated counseling. Students frequently agree to platform use without fully understanding how their data is processed, stored, and utilized. Research indicates that digital privacy policies are generally complex and difficult to comprehend, so user consent is often formalistic in nature (Alqhatani, 2026; Patne & Suryawanshic, 2025). In the counseling context, this conflicts with fundamental ethical principles that demand genuinely informed consent.

Student safety is also a critical issue. Several studies report that AI has not been consistent in detecting indicators of acute crises such as suicidal ideation or severe psychological disorders. In some cases, systems have delivered neutral responses precisely when users required immediate intervention (Chan, 2025; Perlis, 2026). These findings demonstrate that AI counseling without human oversight poses serious risks to student well-being.

Additionally, algorithmic bias can influence risk assessments and intervention recommendations. AI systems trained on limited data may misinterpret the emotional expressions of students from different cultural backgrounds. Research shows that such bias can undermine service validity and deepen inequities in access to psychological support (Bouguettaya et al., 2025; Jain & Menon, 2023). Therefore, AI counseling must always operate within a framework of professional oversight.

7. GOVERNANCE OF AI COUNSELING IN INDONESIA

Governance is a key element in determining the direction of AI integration into guidance and counseling services in Indonesia. Without a clear policy framework, technology adoption risks being driven solely by efficiency and innovation considerations, rather than by the protection of student rights. Various studies affirm that AI governance must encompass legal, ethical, and institutional capacity dimensions to ensure that technology does not evolve without adequate social control (Gong et al., 2025; Bouguettaya et al., 2025). In the educational context, governance must also ensure that AI functions as a support for human services, not as their replacement.

Indonesia is currently at an early stage of AI policy development in the education and mental health sectors. The national digital transformation is driving broad technology utilization, including in student services. However, sectoral regulations that specifically govern AI counseling remain very limited (Bangun et al., 2025; Manggalasari et al., 2025). This creates a policy gray area that allows technology adoption to proceed more rapidly than the development of ethical standards and user protections.

7.1 Digital Education Policy and Student Services

Indonesia's digital education agenda emphasizes the use of technology to enhance access and the quality of educational services. Universities are encouraged to integrate digital platforms across various aspects of student services, including psychosocial support. Several institutions have begun to adopt AI-based systems for anxiety screening and initial mentoring, in line with national digital transformation policy (Putri Syarifa et al., 2024; Hariyadi et al., 2025).

However, these policies have not been accompanied by detailed operational guidelines for the use of AI in counseling. Studies show that educational institutions frequently adopt technology without a comprehensive ethical impact assessment (Martha et al., 2025). As a result, AI counseling implementation tends to be experimental and dependent on local initiatives. This weakens consistency in service standards and opens the door to practices that are misaligned with BK professional values.

Furthermore, policy focus remains predominantly on innovation and efficiency, while the protection of student rights has yet to become a primary priority. Yet the literature affirms that effective AI governance must place users at the center of system design (human-centered governance) (Gong et al., 2025). Without this approach, technology risks deepening access inequalities and weakening students' position as service subjects.

7.2 Professional Ethics in Guidance and Counseling in the AI Era

The professional ethics code of guidance and counseling in Indonesia was developed in the context of face-to-face services and direct interpersonal relationships. Principles such as confidentiality, client autonomy, and professional accountability have not yet been fully adapted to the reality of AI-based digital counseling. Several studies indicate that traditional ethical frameworks have yet to adequately address emerging challenges such as algorithmic data management and pseudo-therapeutic relationships (Bouguettaya et al., 2025; Chan, 2025).

In AI counseling practice, counselors face a dilemma between harnessing technology to expand services and maintaining professional integrity. Without clear guidelines, counselors risk losing control of the counseling process when AI systems take over certain functions. Research also shows that many practitioners have not received adequate training on AI literacy and digital ethics (Ngoveni, 2025; Hulus, 2026). This situation underscores the need to update professional competency standards in BK.

Strengthening professional ethics in the AI era must encompass the principles of algorithmic transparency, informed consent, and the obligation to provide human service alternatives. This approach aligns with the international literature that emphasizes the importance of human-in-the-loop oversight in AI-based mental health services (Perlis, 2026). In this way, technology does not replace the role of counselors but operates under professional oversight.

7.3 Toward an Integrated Governance Framework

The development of AI counseling governance in Indonesia requires an integrated approach involving the government, educational institutions, professional associations, and technology developers. Studies on data governance affirm that without cross-sector coordination, regulation tends to become fragmented and ineffective (Schwinghammer et al., 2025; Pampus & Heisel, 2025). In this context, student data protection, BK ethical standards, and digital education policy must be aligned within a coherent policy framework.

Beyond regulatory aspects, governance also encompasses the building of institutional capacity. Universities need to develop ethical audit mechanisms for AI platforms and provide AI literacy training for both counselors and students. This approach aligns with the data sovereignty perspective that emphasizes local control over technology and personal information (Couldry & Mejias, 2023; Gray, 2023). Without such steps, Indonesia risks becoming merely a technology market without the capacity to direct its use in accordance with national values.

Accordingly, the governance of AI counseling must be positioned as part of the agenda for student rights protection and the strengthening of the BK profession. AI can only deliver sustainable benefits if it is integrated within a system that upholds human dignity, digital justice, and professional responsibility.

Concretely, an integrated governance framework for AI counseling in Indonesia should incorporate at minimum three operational mechanisms. The first is an Ethical Impact Assessment (EIA) protocol that universities must complete before deploying any AI counseling system. This protocol should evaluate: the origin and cultural composition of the AI system's training data; the data retention and deletion policies of the platform provider; the system's performance on culturally diverse user populations; and the availability of human counselor alternatives for all students. Drawing on analogous frameworks developed in the European Union's AI Act and UNESCO's Recommendation on the Ethics of AI, such an assessment positions ethical review as a prerequisite for technological adoption rather than a retrospective corrective measure.

The second mechanism is the establishment of a Student Data Ombudsperson role within university student service structures. This role — which could be integrated within existing student advocacy offices — would serve as a formal channel through which students can report concerns about AI counseling data practices, request access to their stored psychological profiles, and initiate data deletion procedures in accordance with the Personal Data Protection Law (Saly & Sulthanah, 2023; Aisy et al., 2025). The existence of such a role signals institutional commitment to student data sovereignty in practical, not merely declaratory, terms.

The third mechanism is the application of data minimization principles as a default standard for AI counseling implementations. Data minimization — the principle that AI systems should collect only the minimum data necessary for their declared function — directly counters the commercial incentive of platform providers to maximize data extraction (Schwinghammer et al., 2025). In practice, this means that AI counseling systems deployed in Indonesian universities should be configured, wherever technically possible, to operate without persistent storage of identifiable psychological data. Interactions should be session-scoped unless the student explicitly consents to continuity of record, and all consent mechanisms must be presented in Bahasa Indonesia with plain-language explanations of data use. These three mechanisms, taken together, transform governance from an abstract policy aspiration into a set of enforceable institutional practices.

8. CONCEPTUAL DISCUSSION: AI COUNSELING AS A RELATIONAL SPACE

The discussion of AI-mediated counseling cannot rest solely on technical or policy analysis, for the core of the issue lies in human relationships mediated by technology. AI does not merely function as a tool; it shapes the way students understand themselves, interpret their emotions, and make sense of the helping process. The international literature indicates that digital mental health technologies are frequently positioned as structural solutions, whereas therapeutic relationships remain the primary foundation of counseling effectiveness (Murphy et al., 2022; Flix-Valle et al., 2025). In this context, AI must be understood as part of a relational ecosystem, not as a substitute for human presence.

The integration of AI in BK also reflects the paradigm of technological solutionism — the tendency to view technology as the answer to complex social problems. This approach risks oversimplifying students' psychosocial challenges into mere matters of data and algorithms. Academic pressure, identity conflict, and anxiety about the future cannot be resolved through automated responses. Several studies affirm that AI has yet to capture the existential dimensions of human experience, particularly in the context of mental health (Perlis, 2026; Gong et al., 2025).

From the perspective of Social Cognitive Theory, students' interactions with AI counseling shape new cognitive patterns regarding the authority of knowledge and decision-making. Students who continuously receive algorithmic recommendations may internalize the logic of the system as the standard of psychological truth. This process can weaken self-reflection and create dependency on technology. Findings on self-efficacy and AI literacy indicate that without the reinforcement of reflective capacity, students tend to surrender emotional judgment to digital systems (Bećirović et al., 2025; Alghamdi, 2025).

Critical digital literacy becomes the meeting point between the psychological and structural dimensions of AI counseling. This literacy not only helps students understand algorithmic bias, but also awakens their awareness of their position as data subjects in the digital economy. Research shows that low algorithmic awareness makes users more vulnerable to system manipulation and the exploitation of personal data (Dogruel et al., 2022; Moylan & Code, 2024). In the Indonesian context, strengthening critical literacy becomes an ethical prerequisite for the integration of AI into BK services.

The issue of data sovereignty deepens the political dimension of AI counseling. Indonesian students interact with systems largely developed abroad, so their psychological data may become part of global extraction flows. The data colonialism perspective affirms that this practice reproduces inequalities between technology centers and Global South countries (Couldry & Mejias, 2023; Gray, 2023; Mumford, 2022). In this context, AI counseling is not merely an educational service, but also a terrain of contestation over digital power.

Pseudo-therapeutic relationships formed by AI also carry profound ethical implications. Students may feel heard without genuinely receiving meaningful human support. Studies show that AI's simulation of empathy increases user engagement, yet does not replicate the quality of authentic interpersonal relationships (Chan, 2025; Akdogan et al., 2025). This underscores that AI must be positioned as a supplement in the counseling process, not as the primary actor.

Beyond the dimension of empathy, AI counseling also has the potential to cultivate superficial patterns of emotion regulation when used without reflective guidance. Students may be driven to seek quick validation through algorithmic responses, rather than developing a more profound capacity for self-reflection. Over the long term, this form of dependency risks weakening internal coping skills and shifting the locus of psychological control from the individual to the technological system. This condition demonstrates that AI does not merely mediate assistance but also actively shapes users' psychological architecture. Therefore, AI-based interventions must be designed pedagogically to foster self-awareness, rather than merely providing instant responses. This perspective reaffirms that the primary goal of counseling is not technological efficiency, but the sustained psychosocial growth of students.

Within the governance framework, this discussion illustrates that the adoption of AI without robust ethical standards and data protection risks weakening students' position as service subjects. Existing regulations remain general in nature and have not yet fully accommodated the specific characteristics of educational counseling data (Saly & Sulthanah, 2023; Aisy et al., 2025). Without cross-sector coordination, educational institutions risk becoming technology users without strategic control. Studies on data governance affirm that local control over technology is a primary prerequisite for the sustainability of digital innovation (Schwinghammer et al., 2025; Pampus & Heisel, 2025).

Conceptually, AI-mediated counseling needs to be positioned within a human-centered and culturally responsive framework. Technology must be designed and implemented with consideration for relational values, cultural context, and students' rights to their data and psychological dignity. This approach demands the active role of counselors as ethical stewards, facilitators of critical literacy, and mediators between students and technological systems. In this way, AI can function as a supportive tool that strengthens BK practice, rather than as an automated mechanism that erodes the human dimension of services.

9. PRACTICAL RECOMMENDATIONS FOR THE DEVELOPMENT OF AI-BASED BK SERVICES IN INDONESIA

The development of AI-based guidance and counseling services in Indonesia requires a strategic approach oriented not only toward technology adoption, but also toward the protection of student rights and the strengthening of professional capacity. Global experience demonstrates that AI implementation without a clear ethical framework risks weakening service quality and heightening user vulnerability. Therefore, the recommendations in this section position students at the center of the system, with counselors as key guardians of humane values. This approach is consistent with the literature emphasizing the importance of human-centered AI in mental health services (Gong et al., 2025; Perlis, 2026).

The first recommendation is the systematic integration of AI literacy into BK service programs and higher education curricula. Students need to be equipped with an understanding of how algorithms work, the potential biases of systems, and the implications of personal data management. Research indicates that improved AI literacy contributes to strengthening self-efficacy and critical attitudes toward technology (Bećirović et al., 2025; Alghamdi, 2025). With adequate literacy, students can position AI as a supportive tool, not a psychological authority.

The second recommendation concerns strengthening the role of counselors as technology mediators. Counselors need to possess AI literacy competence in order to help students reflect on their experiences with AI counseling and understand the limitations of the system. Studies indicate that many educators and practitioners are not yet prepared to face the ethical implications of digital technology in psychological services (Ngoveni, 2025; Hulus, 2026). Therefore, ongoing professional training on AI and digital ethics becomes an urgent need in the development of BK in Indonesia.

The third recommendation is the strengthening of student data protection mechanisms in every AI counseling implementation. Educational institutions must ensure that service use agreements are genuinely informed, transparent, and can be withdrawn at any time. This is especially important given that counseling data carries a high level of sensitivity and the potential for misuse if not managed according to strict security standards (Patne & Suryawanshic, 2025; Alqhatani, 2026). The strengthening of internal campus policies must be aligned with the Personal Data Protection Law to guarantee student rights (Saly & Sulthanah, 2023; Aisy et al., 2025).

The fourth recommendation emphasizes the importance of human-in-the-loop oversight throughout all AI counseling services. AI must not become the sole source of psychological support, particularly in crisis situations. Research indicates that AI still has serious limitations in detecting suicide risk and severe psychological disorders, making the involvement of human counselors essential (Chan, 2025; Perlis, 2026). A hybrid service model that combines AI with professional counselors offers a safer and more ethical approach.

The fifth recommendation concerns the development of an integrated governance framework that involves the government, educational institutions, professional associations, and technology developers. This governance needs to integrate BK ethical standards, data protection, and digital education policy within a coherent framework. Studies on data governance affirm that cross-sector coordination is a primary prerequisite for the effectiveness of technology regulation (Schwinghammer et al., 2025; Pampus & Heisel, 2025). Without an integrated approach, AI counseling implementation risks becoming fragmented and unsustainable.

Overall, these recommendations affirm that the development of AI-based BK in Indonesia must originate from the values of humanism, digital justice, and professional responsibility. Technology can only deliver optimal benefits when integrated within a system that respects student dignity and strengthens the helping relationship. This approach also aligns with the data sovereignty perspective that places local control and subject protection at the core of digital transformation (Couldry & Mejias, 2023; Gray, 2023).

10. REFLECTIVE CONCLUSION

The integration of artificial intelligence into guidance and counseling services in Indonesia marks a profound paradigm shift in the practice of psychological assistance within the educational environment. AI not only introduces new means of broadening service access, but also fundamentally reshapes students' relationships with the counseling process itself. In this context, technology cannot be understood merely as a tool, but rather as a new social space that influences the way students understand their emotions, seek support, and construct meaning from their life experiences. Therefore, AI counseling must be situated within a framework of humanism and BK professionalism.

This chapter affirms that critical digital literacy is the primary foundation for the integration of AI into educational counseling services. Students need to be equipped not only with the skills to use technology, but also with reflective capacity to question system recommendations, understand AI's limitations, and recognize their own position as data subjects. Without critical literacy, students risk surrendering psychological authority to algorithms and losing their agency in the helping process. AI literacy thus becomes an inseparable part of character education and self-development in the digital era.

The issue of student data rights reveals that AI counseling is also a structural and political matter. Psychological data is not merely technical information, but a representation of deeply personal life experience. Data protection must be understood as part of respect for student dignity. In the Indonesian context, strengthening data governance becomes a prerequisite for ensuring that digital transformation does not become a practice of information extraction that undermines the position of learners.

Within this framework, higher education bears a strategic responsibility to instill critical awareness of technology use in personal and academic domains from an early stage. Students cannot merely be positioned as users of digital services; they need to be developed as reflective subjects capable of understanding the social, psychological, and political consequences of their interactions with AI systems. This approach places AI literacy on par with moral literacy and digital citizenship, enabling students to safeguard their psychological autonomy within an increasingly complex technological ecosystem.

From an ethical standpoint, AI counseling presents risks of pseudo-therapeutic relationships, system bias, and limitations in user safety. Technology is incapable of replacing the presence of an empathic and contextually attuned human being. Therefore, AI must be positioned as a supplement, not a substitute, for guidance and counseling services. A hybrid service model that combines artificial intelligence with professional counselor guidance represents the approach most consistent with BK values.

Conceptually, the future of AI counseling in Indonesia depends on the courage to place humanity at the center of innovation. Counselors must be prepared as ethical guardians and facilitators of critical literacy, while educational institutions must build systems that are transparent and committed to student rights. If technology is integrated without reflection, AI has the potential to deepen digital inequalities and erode the human dimension of services. Conversely, if developed responsibly, AI can become a strategic partner in strengthening students' psychological well-being and the quality of national education.

Ultimately, the question of whether AI will strengthen or diminish the quality of guidance and counseling in Indonesia is not predetermined by the technology itself. It will be determined by the choices made by educators, policymakers, professional associations, and students in the coming years — choices about which systems to adopt, which to reject, how to regulate data, how to train counselors, and how to listen to the voices of the students whose well-being is at stake. This chapter has argued that those choices must be guided by a consistent ethical compass: one that places human dignity above efficiency, cultural responsiveness above technological convenience, and student agency above institutional expediency. If the BK profession in Indonesia can hold firm to these principles amid the pressures of digital transformation, it will have made a contribution not only to the welfare of Indonesian students, but to the global project of developing AI that genuinely serves human flourishing.

REFERENCES

Aisy, F. R., Maskur, M. A., & Amiruddin, A. M. A. (2025). Establishing Indonesia's Personal Data Protection Agency: Comparative Administration Sanctions Enforcement from Ireland, Australia, and Singapore. *Journal of Indonesian Legal Studies, 10*(1), 431–482. DOI: 10.15294/jils.v10i1.13755

Akdogan, O., Uyar, G. C., Yesilbas, E., Baskurt, K., Malkoc, N. A., Ozdemir, N., Yazici, O., Oksuzoglu, B., Uner, A., Ozet, A., & Sutcuoglu, O. (2025). Effect of a ChatGPT-based digital counseling intervention on anxiety and depression in patients with cancer: A prospective, randomized trial. *European Journal of Cancer : Official Journal for European Organization for Research and Treatment of Cancer (EORTC) [and] European Association for Cancer Research (EACR), 221*, 115408. Advance online publication. DOI: 10.1016/j.ejca.2025.115408 PMID: 40215593

Alghamdi, A. A. (2025). University students' perceptions of generative AI for critical thinking and creativity: The influence of self-efficacy and disciplinary differences. *Innovations in Education and Teaching International*, •••, 1–15. DOI: 10.1080/14703297.2025.2600476

Alqhatani, A. (2026). Exploring Privacy in Digital Mental Health: User and Psychotherapist Perspectives. In Applied Human Factors and Ergonomics International (Vol. 200, pp. 140–147). DOI: 10.54941/ahfe1007073

Aminah, S., Hidayah, N., Hanurawan, F., Indreswari, H., & Rangka, I. B. (2023). Career adaptability to prevent unexpected careers and burnout for woman employees in the remote work era. *Journal of Public Health (Oxford, England), 45*(4), e795–e796. DOI: 10.1093/pubmed/fdad080 PMID: 37286530

Anser, M. K., Nabi, A. A., Ahmad, I., Abro, M. M. Q., & Zaman, K. (2025). Advancing Mental Health Care: A Comprehensive Review of Digital Tools and Technologies for Enhancing Diagnosis, Treatment, and Wellness. *Health Care Science, 4*(3), 163–178. DOI: 10.1002/hcs2.70018 PMID: 40568629

Bangun, C. S., Hetilaniar, H., Faturahman, A., Jackson, S., Anjani, S. A., & Natasya, E. A. (2025). Analyzing Opportunities and Challenges of Artificial Intelligence Integration in Indonesian Innovation and Education. Proceeding – 2025 4th International Conference on Creative Communication and Innovative Technology, ICCIT 2025. DOI: 10.1109/ICCIT65724.2025.11167011

Bećirović, S., Polz, E., & Tinkel, I. (2025). Exploring students' AI literacy and its effects on their AI output quality, self-efficacy, and academic performance. *Smart Learning Environments, 12*(1), 29. DOI: 10.1186/s40561-025-00384-3

Bouguettaya, A., Stuart, E. M., & Aboujaoude, E. (2025). Racial bias in AI-mediated psychiatric diagnosis and treatment: A qualitative comparison of four large language models. npj. *Digital Medicine*, *8*(1), 332. Advance online publication. DOI: 10.1038/s41746-025-01746-4 PMID: 40467886

Chan, C. K. Y. (2025). AI as the Therapist: Student Insights on the Challenges of Using Generative AI for School Mental Health Frameworks. *Behavioral Sciences (Basel, Switzerland)*, *15*(3), 287. Advance online publication. DOI: 10.3390/bs15030287 PMID: 40150182

Couldry, N., & Mejias, U. A. (2023). The decolonial turn in data and technology research: What is at stake and where is it heading? *Information Communication and Society*, *26*(4), 786–802. DOI: 10.1080/1369118X.2021.1986102

Dogruel, L., Masur, P., & Joeckel, S. (2022). Development and Validation of an Algorithm Literacy Scale for Internet Users. *Communication Methods and Measures*, *16*(2), 115–133. DOI: 10.1080/19312458.2021.1968361

Farzan, M., Ebrahimi, H., Pourali, M., & Sabeti, F. (2025). Artificial Intelligence-Powered Cognitive Behavioral Therapy Chatbots, a Systematic Review. *Iranian Journal of Psychiatry*, *20*(1), 100–108. DOI: 10.18502/ijps.v20i1.17395 PMID: 40093525

Flix-Valle, A., Medina, J. C., Souto-Sampera, A., Arizu-Onassis, A., Juan-Linares, E., Serra-Blasco, M., Ciria-Suárez, L., Feixas, G., & Ochoa-Arnedo, C. (2025). Therapeutic alliance in a stepped digital psychosocial intervention for breast cancer patients: Findings from a multicentre randomised controlled trial. *BJPsych Open*, *11*(1), e23. Advance online publication. DOI: 10.1192/bjo.2024.844 PMID: 39865983

Ganesh, M. S., & Venkateswaramurthy, N. (2025). Artificial Intelligence (AI) Generated Health Counseling For Mental Illness Patients. *Current Psychiatry Research and Reviews*, *21*(3), 269–283. DOI: 10.2174/0126660822277500240109050359

Gong, X., Liu, W., & Shang, Z. (2025). Ethical challenges in artificial intelligence-based mental health interventions. *Academic Journal of Naval Medical University*, *46*(8), 970–976. DOI: 10.16781/j.CN31-2187/R.20250449

Gray, C. (2023). More than Extraction: Rethinking Data's Colonial Political Economy. *International Political Sociology*, *17*(2), olad007. Advance online publication. DOI: 10.1093/ips/olad007

Hariyadi, S., Antika, E. R., & Prabawa, A. F. (2025). Digital evolutions: Analysis of self-talk transformation among Generation Z and its impact on counseling services. *Multidisciplinary Science Journal, 8*(4), 2026225. Advance online publication. DOI: 10.31893/multiscience.2026225

Hidayat, H., Hidayah, N., Rusmana, N., Hariko, R., & Tririzky, R. (2024). The Effect of Using Smart Application on Critical Literacy of Engineering Education Students. *International Journal of Information and Education Technology (IJIET), 14*(6), 834–844. DOI: 10.18178/ijiet.2024.14.6.2109

Hulus, A. (2026). A systematic response to ethical blind spots in AI education: Cross-cultural insights and the role of digital literacy. *Smart Learning Environments, 13*(1), 11. Advance online publication. DOI: 10.1186/s40561-026-00437-1

Jain, L. R., & Menon, V. (2023). AI Algorithmic Bias: Understanding its Causes, Ethical and Social Implications. Proceedings – International Conference on Tools with Artificial Intelligence, ICTAI, 460–467. DOI: 10.1109/ICTAI59109.2023.00073

Manggalasari, L. C., Rosdiana, W., Lestari, Y., Narot, P., & Kiettikunwong, N. (2025). From Centralized Control to Co-Creation: Rethinking Educational Governance in the Digital Era. *Educational Process: International Journal, 17*(1). Advance online publication. DOI: 10.22521/edupij.2025.17.321

Martha, A. S. D., Widowati, S., & Rahayu, D. P. (2025). Assessing Student Readiness and Perceptions of ChatGPT in Learning: A Case Study in Indonesian Higher Education. *Journal of Information Technology Education, 24*, 023. Advance online publication. DOI: 10.28945/5599

Moylan, R., & Code, J. (2024). Algorithmic futures: An analysis of teacher professional digital competence frameworks through an algorithm literacy lens. *Teachers and Teaching, 30*(4), 452–470. DOI: 10.1080/13540602.2023.2263732

Mumford, D. (2022). Data colonialism: Compelling and useful, but whither epistemes? *Information Communication and Society, 25*(10), 1511–1516. DOI: 10.1080/1369118X.2021.1986103

Murphy, R., Kettner, H., Zeifman, R., Giribaldi, B., Kartner, L., Martell, J., Read, T., Murphy-Beiner, A., Baker-Jones, M., Nutt, D., Erritzoe, D , Watts, R., & Carhart-Harris, R. (2022). Therapeutic Alliance and Rapport Modulate Responses to Psilocybin Assisted Therapy for Depression. *Frontiers in Pharmacology, 12*, 788155. Advance online publication. DOI: 10.3389/fphar.2021.788155 PMID: 35431912

Nandyala, S., Borse, L. B., Gayatri, A. P., & Bonthu, M. G. (2025). Artificial intelligence applications in patient counseling: Latest research, developments, and practical insights for beginners and advanced professionals. In Artificial Intelligence in Patient Counselling (pp. 385–402). DOI: 10.1016/B978-0-443-43823-3.00017-0

Ngoveni, M. (2025). Bridging the AI Knowledge Gap: The Urgent Need for AI Literacy and Institutional Support. *International Journal of Technologies in Learning*, *32*(2), 83–100. DOI: 10.18848/2327-0144/CGP/v32i02/83-100

Pampus, J., & Heisel, M. (2025). A Delimitation of Data Sovereignty From Privacy. In *Empowering Digital Sovereignty* (pp. 1–24). Balancing Privacy and Global Connectivity., DOI: 10.4018/979-8-3693-9137-2.ch001

Patne, A. Y., & Suryawanshic, M. (2025). Ethical considerations in artificial intelligence-powered patient counseling. In Artificial Intelligence in Patient Counselling (pp. 195–232). DOI: 10.1016/B978-0-443-43823-3.00011-X

Pavlopoulos, A., Rachiotis, T., & Maglogiannis, I. (2024). An Overview of Tools and Technologies for Anxiety and Depression Management Using AI. *Applied Sciences (Basel, Switzerland)*, *14*(19), 9068. Advance online publication. DOI: 10.3390/app14199068

Perlis, R. H. (2026). Artificial Intelligence and the Potential Transformation of Mental Health. *JAMA Psychiatry*, *83*(4), 409. Advance online publication. DOI: 10.1001/jamapsychiatry.2025.4116 PMID: 41533367

Putri Syarifa, D. F., Krisna Moeljono, A. A., Hidayat, W. N., Shafelbilyunazra, A., Abednego, V. K., & Prasetya, D. D. (2024). Development of a Micro Counselling Educational Platform Based on AI and Face Recognition to Prevent Students Anxiety Disorder. Proceedings – IEIT 2024 – 2024 International Conference on Electrical and Information Technology, 1–6. DOI: 10.1109/IEIT64341.2024.10763282

Saly, J. N., & Sulthanah, L. T. (2023). Pelindungan Data Pribadi dalam Tindakan Doxing Berdasarkan Undang-Undang Nomor 27 Tahun 2022. *Jurnal Kewarganegaraan*, *7*(2), 1708–1713.

Schwinghammer, R., Neuburger, R., & Hess, T. (2025). Power as the Secret Ingredient: First Insights into the Governance of Personal Data in Digital Platforms. *Americas Conference on Information Systems, AMCIS 2025*, 1, 116–125.

Chapter 3

AI-Driven Urban Futures: Smart Cities, Climate-Resilient Governance, and the Promise of Sustainable Policy Innovation

Nasir Ahmad Ganaie
http://orcid.org/0000-0001-6781-834X
University of Kashmir, India

Andi Luhur Prianto
Universitas Muhammadiyah Makassar, Indonesia

ABSTRACT

This chapter examines the transition from smart cities to climate-resilient governance through the lens of artificial intelligence, urban sustainability, and policy innovation. It argues that smart city initiatives must move beyond efficiency-centred digitalisation toward governance models capable of addressing climate risk, social inequality, and institutional fragility. The chapter explores how AI can support predictive planning, environmental monitoring, and adaptive decision-making in urban systems, while also highlighting concerns related to bias, transparency, privacy, and accountability. It further shows that climate resilience depends not only on technology but also on inclusive institutions, participatory governance, and adaptive policy frameworks. By integrating smart urbanism with sustainability and resilience thinking, the chapter proposes a governance-centred model for future cities. The central argument is that AI can strengthen urban resilience only when embedded in ethical, equitable, and institutionally robust policy arrangements.

DOI: 10.4018/979-8-2600-2233-7.ch003

INTRODUCTION: FROM EFFICIENCY TO RESILIENCE

The cities today are at the centre of two big transformations: the pace of digitalisation and the pace of climate stress. These in turn are influencing urban systems through information and communication technologies (ICTs), algorithmic decision making, networked infrastructures and sensors (Sirisomboonsuk et al., 2018). At the same time, urbanised areas are also confronted with fresh and increasing challenges due to heat, floods, energy insecurity, too little water, public health risks and social inequalities, all exacerbated by climate change (Liando et al., 2026). These two challenges have changed the approach of the governance in the city from an efficient one to a broader and tougher one: resilience, sustainability and adaptability. It is not just a technologically optimised urban space, it is now a smart city to be reconsidered as a governance model that is able to manage uncertainty, vulnerability and ecological distortion (Ganaie, Mir, et al., 2026). It's a fantastic shift of visualisation of future cities as one that is smart, climate resilient and governed. Previously, the definition of Smart City was technology, infrastructure and administration. Such aims are a necessary but insufficient one in these days of volatility and an intricate socio-political reality (Prashad, 2018). Even the most evolved urbanisation process is weak, rigid and unfair." The key is not whether cities will become 'smarter', but if they are going to become more resilient, more agile in their ability to adapt to longer-term changes, and more inclusive to distribute benefits within the city. This means a theoretical-practical intersection that we call climate-resilient governance, between the introduction of digital innovations and the sustainable urban future (Veeramani & Jaganathan, 2020).

SMART CITIES RECONSIDERED

A smart city is one of the most salient concepts dealing with urban policy in recent times. In general, it can be said to be the application of information and communication technologies in the urban systems to enhance the provision of services, mobility, resource management and administrative coordination (Prianto & Amalia, 2019). But the idea has changed a lot throughout the years. Smart cities were first conceptualised as techno-modernist cities, where technology consisting of sensors, real-time monitoring and data analysis would resolve the inefficiency of cities (Syafhendry et al., 2025). Often, such visions led to a managerial view, promoted only measurable performative results and operational control. This was at times to the detriment of more basic aspects of governance, justice, participation and sustainability. However, the smart city vision has been questioned for further possible exacerbation of the existing inequalities and power concentration of governments, corporations and technical elites. They may not wish to have their say tracked in the public eye, or in the long term, as much deliberation is a good option too, and data mining is too. This means that the smart city cannot be focused on any engineering project (Reijers et al., 2016). This is a political and institutional project, also. This is especially true in the context of the ongoing Climate Emergency that demonstrates futility in the one-dimensional approach and short-term planning for governance. Scaling up smart urbanism is not just a matter of digital convenience, but of the greater task at hand, ecological resilience and distributive justice/institutional change (A. V. et al., 2026).

This new imagination sees the smart city as much more than a platform to deploy the technologies; instead, it's a platform to co-create governance. While digital systems can aid good decision making, they cannot compensate for the lack of vision, legitimacy and trust of the citizens of the public (Kowalczyk & Napiecek, 2023). If it isn't an urban intelligence in responsible institutions and geared towards social and environmental challenges, it doesn't make any sense. Smart cities aren't only about devices; smart cities are about what the cyber-capable hands of the city government can achieve to enhance the city's disaster resilience (Yuslaini et al., 2023). The operating and management processes of cities are impacted by climate change. Urban areas, in which concentration of population, infrastructure, economic activities and environmental risks tend to be particularly clustered, are especially at risk (Mir et al., 2025). An urban heat island's effect on its very existence under the conditions of global warming implies higher stress for energy consumption, work ability and health centres. Transport systems, housing, drainage systems and critical infrastructure are at risk due to intense rainfall and sea-level rise. Droughts and water shortages put pressure on the city's water supply and make water conflicts worse. This impact is not uniform; it is often felt by the poor neighbourhoods and informal settlements, by older people and by the marginalised groups.

Urban interdependencies are accentuated by climate crises. Failure can lead to failure (energy can cause water failure, transportation, communication and emergency response failures) (Ganaie et al., 2025). It is an anticipatory, integrated and adaptive governance approach which is necessary to link the various. Such complexity needs a more traditional and "silo mentality" administrative structure (Girardi & Temporelli, 2017). Cities should have environmental information, as well as social vulnerability factors, infrastructure information and feedback on policies (in real time). In this context, digital technologies, especially AI, come in. However, technology can't fix the climate problem. These should involve institutions that have learning, coordinating, and equitable action capacities. Climate Resilience in Urban Areas is more than merely surviving the extreme events. It's also about shock resistance, resiliency to disturbances and sustainable and inclusive growth. This broader context shifts the attention from emergency response to governance change in the long term. In fact, all local notions of land use and housing, mobility, green infrastructure, public health, planning and fiscal capacity need to be considered (Guenduez et al., 2024). Climate Resilient City is not only a quick-recovery city, but a better-prepared, more socially inclusive and more environmentally regenerative city.

AI AS URBAN ENABLER

AI has emerged as an important enabling technology to deal with the complex urban systems. What makes its value noteworthy is its capability to process massive amounts of data, recognise patterns, and forecast and aid decision-making in contexts throughout doubt. AI can be applied in urban environments for urban traffic management, energy efficiency in cities, flood prediction, waste management, air pollution monitoring, disaster management, and urban land use management (Shelton et al., 2015). All of these functions can be accomplished through machine learning technologies to identify anomalies in infrastructure, to aid projections of municipal facilities needed, and to support infrastructure for early warning systems for climate hazard risks. In the context of speed and accuracy in decision-making and actions of urban governance, AI can play a role. But the potential of AI is not to be taken lightly. This isn't technology that is "neutral. Its output depends on the model's design and the institutional context it is used in, as well as data quality. The AI system may generate inaccurate or misleading recommendations based on faulty or biased data, exacerbating existing disparities. Having limited deployment objectives can cause extrapolation of one system at the expense of optimal performance and efficiency of another. For instance, a traffic flow optimising computer program may not consider pedestrians' safety or accessibility of public transport. A system that is too much of a technical aspect wouldn't be able to consider social vulnerability and would not be able to identify those zones that will be more severely affected by flooding. This means that AI should be used as a governance tool, with people in charge, transparency and control. Thus, instead of replacing, it is about augmenting, and there's a path to move forward in terms of using AI in urban sustainability. It can enhance the ability of officials, planners and communities to comprehend urban dynamics and to react in a better way to risk. Is able to help develop scenario analysis and resource allocation/adaptive plans (Stokols, 2025). This can also influence participation if you take it and add the information to the citizen, and make it comprehensible to them. AI should always, however, be a part of a democracy. Cities should not ask whether or not to utilise AI; it is how, for whom and which accountability frameworks to use AI.

GOVERNANCE BEYOND TECHNOLOGY

To achieve climate-resilient governance, there is a need for a shift in paradigm from technical management to institutional learning. Governance is not only about the provision of public services, but it is also about prioritising, negotiating, applying and adjusting public services. To implement this process, in the context of climatic risks in cities, multiple forms of knowledge and diverse stakeholders have to be involved, and consequently, multiple levels of government. Solutions to urban problems exist within at least the perspective of the local and regional government, the civil society and private enterprises, the universities, and community groups (Zwitter, 2024). It's not the goal of good governance to enforce these perspectives on a singular, technocratic one; it's about finding a way to harmonise them. It is especially so in a world dominated by technology and AI. While digital systems might be able to provide very fine-grained information, information is not enough to make for good policy. Governance is an interpretation and a value judgement and is political and legitimate. Where to place capital and which risks to take first, which to nurture first, and the distribution of burdens can't be offloaded completely to an automatic system. There, they will be involved in normative or value choices. Without entering dominion of data by climate-resilient governance, there is a need to create institutions that can learn from data. It must be innovative, and it must be accountable, and it must be fast, slow, efficient and fair. A key finding generated from this knowledge is that resilience cannot only be a 'technical' state, but is also an 'institutional' state. But the proliferation of sensors and the number of dashboards and the capacity for smarter analytics is not the only thing needed for resilient cities; it is about institutional action. This involves legal mandate, funding, flexibility of policy, together with administration flexibility and public mandate (Kuhlmann et al., 2019). For this reason, the smartest city of the future is not the city that gathers the maximum amount of data but the city that knows how to use knowledge to reduce vulnerabilities in the city, thereby improving the city's quality of life.

SOCIAL JUSTICE AND SUSTAINABILITY OF CITIES

Sustainability is one of the important urban policy principles and is a subject of much controversy. Sustainability is, at the very least, a way of fulfilling the needs of today without compromising the means of future generations to meet their needs. But for governance in an urban setting, this needs to be expanded to include environmental protection, as well as social inclusion and economic opportunity, and spatial justice (Bussy & Zheng, 2023). Green technologies for affluent areas, reduced pollution, heat and unsafe houses for the unprivileged areas of the city; the city without that cannot be called sustainable. It wouldn't be something considered as resilient, or else they couldn't be planned unless they are thought of as something that can be affordable, accessible and participatory in terms of the adaptation actions (Ganaie, A. V., et al., 2026). Here, the concepts of Sustainability and Governance-linkages may come into play. Environmental and social objectives need to be part of institutions that can incorporate them in order to have sustainable cities. This can be completed using support from AI implementations that discover spatial gaps and simulate climate risk exposure and distribution of urban services. Yet, the lessons learnt from these have to be about fairness in the process of creating policies. Thus, sustainable urbanism can only be considered as an ecological and ethical approach. It is not just a matter of resource retention but opportunities and protection in an equitable manner in the urban area. This dedication, sometimes, is combined with the smartness and could be regarded as a technological sophistication. The reason why the city is also environmentally responsible, socially just, institutionally transparent and politically responsive is that it is truly smart. This wider lens is based on the concept of the well-being of people being at the heart of digital transformation. It also educates the policy makers that resilience is not a matter only concerning infrastructure. Requires chants and bonds, local capacities and differential vulnerabilities. Thus, sustainability should be understood as a project of governance that is based on data, participatory and equity.

CAPACITY BUILDING ON ADAPTATION TO THE POLICY; BUILDING POLICY POTENTIAL.

There is a need for a paradigm shift of some order to tackle the 'Urban Moment'. The climate change issue doesn't have a solution, a permanent solution; it's not something that can be solved; it's not something that we can plan, we can regulate one-off. Dynamic, unpredictable & accumulative (Mohamed et al., 2024). Therefore, governance systems as learning systems and adaptive systems come into existence. Policy innovation refers to the creation of new institutions, new regulatory frameworks or new cooperative mechanisms which are more effective for solving a new set of problems than are available options. This applies in the field of smart cities and for the planning of a resilience budget, adaptive zoning, agreements on data sharing and integrated disaster planning and public-private partnerships using digital technology. AI has the potential to promote policy innovation through complementing evidence-based and responsive governance. As an example, Predictive Analytics can be applied to prepare for floods and determine on the map which areas are susceptible to floods before a flood happens. A long-term picture of the consequences of making a land-use decision can be obtained by using a scenario model.

Optimisation of resources such as water, transportation and waste management can be achieved using live measurement. Such instruments can reduce uncertainty and increase strategic foresight. Policy innovation isn't all about new tools. That also requires a change of thinking and new ideas, and without the establishment of some new institutions and political will. One of the key issues discussed in these dialogues is that of "adaptive capacity. Policies must be flexible to be able to adapt to new information, but be stable enough to give continuity and legitimacy to cities (Tian & Wang, 2025). But it is not an easy equilibrium to achieve, not least when coupled with administrative fragmentation (or lower levels of fiscal autonomy). However, it's a must. While it is institutions that can change, this is not necessary for governance innovation. In this specific usage, AI is not designed to replace the democratic role of public organisations but should serve to support their intelligent action.

ETHICAL AND INSTITUTIONAL ISSUES

There are significant ethical and institutional concerns with the use of AI in urban governance. This includes concerns of privacy, surveillance, algorithmic bias/bias, ownership of data, cybersecurity, accountabilities, etc. Many of the smart city technologies rely on the use of large volumes of personal and spatial data, which, if not appropriately handled, may be used inappropriately. Citizens may not be aware of how their data is collected, how it is stored, don't have access to the analysis of their data, or be aware of the sharing of their data. Additionally, algorithmic systems may also perpetuate old forms of discrimination based on the criteria used to develop the program or when the program is optimised to a limited range of performance measures (Ullah et al., 2023). These risks are of concern when inspection coverage is less than complete. The possibility of technological determinism/ digital tools will always improve governance. This assumption doesn't take into consideration capacity gaps and political dynamics/differential implementation. A city can opt for an advanced platform, but still may not have the management skills to ensure that it is successful. It can take undue risks when it comes to smart infrastructure and forget about services and/or social protection. It can also have a tendency to give more weight to policy innovations and potentially more 'showy' approaches compared with deeper shifts in processes of planning, budgeting and intergovernmental coordination. In all these instances, technology is being used not as a means or a way of governing, but as a replacement.

The challenges stipulate that climate-resilient governance must underpin itself on strong institutional frameworks. Properly describe in a legal sense and engage in discussion about the rights of the data. Technology-illiterate management and integrity are demanded in public agencies. If the process can be designed and used to include participatory steps, a chance should be given to the community to make an impact on digital systems. Urban planning, the computer sciences, environmental and policy research need to be done in social science mode; an interdisciplinary approach to the social sciences and the urban sciences should be used, and a dialogue should be encouraged between urban planning and the computer sciences, and between the social sciences and the urban sciences and between the social sciences, environmental and policy research and the urban sciences. In conclusion, 'smart city governance should be as innovative as the technologies' (Merchán-Rodríguez & Juiz, 2024). The chapter adopts the premise that digital intelligence and climate resilience at the urban level go hand-in-hand. Twenty-first-century governance revolution technology; it is no longer possible to run the city with the old governance model. It's a tool that gives us a lot of understanding and a lot of complexity management at the tool level, and the value that could be derived from it is in the institutions that package the use of the tools. Environmental efficiency in a sustainable city is not limited to just one thing; inclusive, adaptable and responsible management is there too. Climate resilience is not only preparing for an emergency, but it's a structural change. This isn't only an urban-planning discussion! Relevant to broader issues of technology and the public sphere, sustainability in the context of unequal societies, states and cities in governance of uncertainty. But governments in an increasingly urbanising world and an ever-growing climate threat need to be technically competent and democratically legitimate processes. Smart cities should thus develop into climate-resilient governance systems where innovation is in the service of the common good. It doesn't happen automatically; it simply needs to happen. This chapter is aimed at doing that by linking three domains which have traditionally been discussed separately: AI, urban sustainability and policy innovation. The convergence is an occasion to consider, differently, how the city is a space for innovations and new thinking, but also one for resilience, justice, and a collective adaptation. The question is: How to maintain urban intelligence's human orientation and social and environmental responsibility? Smart cities are also a precondition that may make cities climate resilient.

LITERATURE REVIEW: SMART CITY AS A GOVERNANCE PARADIGM

The different levels of smart city-related studies have been analysed, from the smart city smart everything focus on the digitalisation of the city, to efficiency and competitiveness, and all the way to the critical smartness perspective, which focuses on governance, equity and public value. In the early phase of the scholarship, the concept of a smart city was often conceived of as a city advancing technologies, and providing improvements to the transport system, energy use, service delivery and administration through technologies such as smart technology, smart sensors, the development of smart networks, and smart analysis of data (Y. Wu & Li, 2024). This body of work discusses the fact that digitalisation is a journey to optimising cities, and that technology is often the obvious answer to city problems. However, over the last several years, it has become clear to researchers that one cannot answer social, political, and environmental issues of the urban phenomenon with technical issues. One of the main themes that has been dealt with in literature is that the talk of the smart city has been too technocratic. Many more efficiency, surveillance and control solutions are being developed for smart cities, without regard to the issues of democratic accountability, social justice and citizens' participation. It is especially pertinent as an issue of legitimacy and inclusion, and political choice, in addition to being a systems management one. Therefore, because of the power systems that are developed through data systems and the interests that they serve, the scholarship on Smart cities has recently been considering institutional and normative aspects of urban digitalisation. Recent research has put the concept of smart cities in a wider perspective of sustainability and resilience. It is not only a literature that is interested in the narrow field of performance but also one in which the issue of adaptive, participatory and environmentally responsible cities is addressed (Robles & Mallinson, 2025). With this formulation, the smart city has ceased to be a city equipped with some digital devices, and now it is a city that "thinks smart" when dealing with complex issues in the city with the help of digital devices. Overall transition can provide an overall conceptual insight into how to connect 'Smart Cities' and 'Climate Resilient Governance'.

STRENGTHENS MUNICIPALITIES' SUSTAINABILITY AND CLIMATE RESILIENCE

Urban Sustainability in itself is an issue that has long been present in literature, but also and even more so, the limitations or constraints based on the environment for urban growth are recorded. Cities are hot spots of ecologically "rich" urban areas, with high levels of emissions, energy and resource consumption, as well as high stress. The sustainability implied in this literature is a general concept and will be interpreted as the balance of Growth, Environment and Social Inclusion. But in recent years, the meaning of 'postmodernity' was extended to include other elements as well, including resilient, adaptable and risk governance, and sometimes climate change. Climate resilience easily became one of the several terms used in urban studies, which reflects the city's ability to envision, absorb, recover and adapt to the shocks and stresses the environment throws at it. Climate risks are indeed urban risks: flood events, heat stress, water scarcity, failure of infrastructures and emergencies in public health are some of the events that affect cities, and evidence-based research proves it (W. Wu et al., 2020). Now, it has become all the more a planning and governance issue of urban resilience. In addition to infrastructure, institutions, coordination, social capital, and unequal distribution of protection are also thought to be elements of resilience (Ganaie, 2015). A major lesson learned from this scholarship is that there needs to be a social differentiation of climate adaptation. An urban area isn't equally vulnerable. There is a connection between low-quality neighbourhoods and informal settlements, climate exposure and the ability to benefit from investments in climate adaptation measures (Saritha, 2025). This insight has led to a transition in the field from technical-based approaches to resilience to justice-based approaches. Environmentally sustainable cities and socially just cities are not only a display of mitigation, reduction in emissions or extension of green spaces, but rather the construction of an urban sustainability as is presented here in this literature.

AI & URBAN DECISION MAKING

This literature is rather recent, and it is catching on to the use of AI in urban governance. The majority of research studies are on the use of AI to assist and enhance decision-making processes through the use of predictive analytics, pattern recognition, automation, and real-time monitoring (Ganaie, 2026). AI applications in urban areas include transportation management, energy forecasting, waste optimisation, environmental monitoring, and emergency response. As this work shows, AI can help cities deal with complexity by turning copious amounts of urban data into actionable information. In the meantime, there are big topics that need to be discussed when it comes to AI governance in the literature (Bicudo et al., 2022). One of the common issues is the data quality. At the social level, and between neighbourhoods, data on which AI systems are built is incomplete, biased, out of date and distributed asymmetrically. The other issue is that of opacity. Many machine-learning systems are black boxes in which it is hard to see how decisions are being made by public officials or citizens. The second issue is, where are the responsibilities of those involved when things go wrong, are missing or cause harm, resulting from using AI in planning, policing or the provision of services or the climate response? AI, if not well-regulated, can also be seen as fueling the rising inequality in urban spaces. For example, a well-documented space may have accurate estimates, and an informal and/or marginalised space may have inaccurate estimates. Likewise, does an increase in efficiency that is achieved through AI optimisation come at the expense of democracy and social justice? This literature is not against the use of

AI; it is about establishing governance frameworks for transparency, accountability, and ethically using AI (Soltanzadeh, 2025). Consistent with the most repeated opinion, it was agreed that AI should be used adjunctively and not as a substitute for human decision-making.

THE CONCEPTS OF GOVERNANCE, INSTITUTIONS AND PUBLIC CAPABILITY

There are clear written materials which highlight the importance of the capacity of institutions in urban transformation rather than the technology. Watching the cities' governance practices makes one think that anything and everything should be coordinated – a minimum of coordination among sectors and, in the extreme case, between levels of government and/or stakeholders (Sharma et al., 2021). This is especially true for the application to the climate change context, where risks are systemic and can be inter-sectoral. Flood management on housing, transport, sanitation, public health and/or emergency logistics, for example. This results in "chunks" of governance structures that are unlikely to be as effective when it comes to responding. One key element of this literature is the idea of 'adaptive governance' – learning, adapting and reacting to changes in institutions. Flexibility, experimentation, collaboration and receptivity to feedback – being resilient – is a key element of adaptive governance. Since researchers have recognised the fact that they can no longer face the uncertainty of the environmental future with a static planning approach, it has been gaining in momentum and has been identified as an important way forward as far as the urban research field is concerned. The city needs to build and establish structures and institutions that can accommodate new knowledge and can, over the years, change pandemic policies. One more theme, which recurs, is on the linkage of governance and legitimacy (Abdelilah et al., 2024). Urban policy is not only based upon technical efficiency, especially in technologically mediated environments. The more transparent, participatory and accountable the innovation, the more widely accepted and supported it is by the citizens. The literature focuses, however, on the need for the public institution and sees with the digitalisation of both the systems that this is also made readily visible. So, when it comes to smart governance, it is not about 'government automation' but an improvement of the 'capacity of government' in ways of better information, coordination and responsiveness.

DIGITAL URBAN POLICY & INNOVATION IN POLICY

How cities craft new instruments, new rules and new practices to address new challenges is examined by Urban Policy Innovation. For a smart city and climate resilience policy, innovation can be a new method of data, risk and inter-agency coordination, public-private partnership, and participative planning. It is argued that, as climate change is rapid and large, there is a need for more experimental adaptive governance, rather than bureaucratic governance. It is clear from the literature on digital urbanism that the digital and data platforms can provide these supports, allowing urbanism to be more visible and more measurable (von Schomberg, 2025). Real-time data can be used for improved planning and a quick response in case of shocks. The use of predictive systems can be helpful for officials planning their resources and identifying new risks prior to the development of an issue. However, there is also the concept in literature of "digital innovation without fundamental institutional change", namely, doing things knowingly "on the nose." Yes, all these things are available on an advanced dashboard, but a city may not have the law, money or management to use the information that they are offering. The best scholarship is to see a policy as an innovation process and not just a single policy "reform". This means constant learning, evaluation and change is a part of achieving successful urban transformation. It also provides ideas for innovation evaluation along various criteria like Equity, Accessibility, Resilience, and Public legitimacy. Accordingly, moving forward, the assessment of the newness of a technology as a basis for policy innovations in smart cities should not be the only criterion and should include the contribution of a technology to the long-term governance capacity. While there are numerous studies and research on smart cities, AI, sustainability, and Resilience, there are some gaps. The first is that these themes are not dealt with together, but it is not the confluence of these themes which is dealt with in literature. The majority of the literature covers the adoption of technologies in Smart Cities, adaptation to Climate Change in the field of resilience, and institutions and coordination in the governance literature (Maestre-Góngora & Aponte, 2023). There are comparatively few in the sense of a research literature which systematically includes these elements. Secondly, it is not always the case that the literature is coherent with respect to both justice and inclusion. Although there are many studies on inequality as a threat, little research addresses the question of how AI-policed policies affect marginalised (sub-urban) populations, especially in the city and surrounding peri-urban area of a rapidly evolving Global South. This is a huge lack, and the climate risks as well as digitisation gaps may be largest in these areas. Thirdly, it is necessary to look into the further properties of smart climate governance in its political-economic aspects. There are very few studies that investigate questions of the ownership of city data, control of digital platforms, public-private partnerships and re-distribution of power with AI. The real importance of problems is to see if digital urbanism helps in the intensification or reduction of the practices of democratic governance, or even leads to dependency and exclusion.

CONCEPTUAL FRAMEWORK

This chapter extends the idea that the governance development of cities is also undergoing a phase of change, dismantling the 'technology efficiency' information and moving toward a 'climate resilience, sustainability and institutional agility' perspective. Smart cities were once related to data capacities to provide services, automation and digital infrastructures. Although these are not unimportant, there is another set of stresses, and it's steadily increasing, and it also needs to be addressed due to climate change. Today's urban systems face risks that are related and dependent on each other, such as the threats of heat stress, flooding, water scarcity, vulnerabilities of urban systems and equipment, public health emergencies and growing inequalities in society. So, the chapter does not consider the smart city technologies to be an endpoint, but rather as enabling conditions for a broader governance transformation. The focus is on how these technologies can be tied to the policy frameworks that are resilient and inclusive, and enable city systems to anticipate, absorb, adapt to and recover from climate change-related disruptions. The ability to provide digital intelligence and governance is at the core of this (Habib Saragih et al., 2024). AI in Cities is thought to be a mediation process that can transform a vast amount of urban information into knowledge. AI can support public authorities to develop predictive modelling, pattern recognition, anomaly detection and scenario analysis in identifying new risks, resource optimisation, and speed up the timeliness of intervention. These are similar applications like flood forecast, heat vulnerability maps, energy demand forecast, Waste management optimisation, emergency response coordination, etc., for the climate resilience purpose. But AI is not considered a standalone solution. It's as useful as it's used - it's as accurate as the data it was trained on and rules governing its use, like everything else. Indeed, AI is not meant to supplant any political delegation or the democratic accountability/administrative responsibility in decision-making. The concept also acknowledges that responsible city governance cannot only be approached in a technical manner, but in a multi-dimensional way. Climate resilience requires coordination across multiple sectors and scales as well as institutions and can be impacted by diverse environmental risks to the transportation sector, housing, public health, energy system, water system, land use and emergency planning (Al-Afeef et al., 2023). One interpretation of this is to move away from thinking of resilience as a property of institutions, but only of physical resilience. A resilient city is not necessarily a city that demonstrates smart technologies, but is a city that doesn't stop working in a stress event, a city that, if necessary, modifies its policy and takes action, and knows how to. Technological systems are thus not only part of the context but also part of a broader' governance architecture' as well, and the importance of co-operation between data, institutional and policy design is highlighted to ensure urban resilience.

A main component of the framework is policy innovation. The uncertainty, variability and long-term disruption brought by climate change introduce rigidity in governance processes. So it is essential to use policy innovation to inspire urban intelligence to be put into adaptive action. The ability of cities to respond to changing threats is interpreted in this chapter as innovation in policy, defined as the establishment of new institutional structures, regulatory regimes, planning instruments and participatory processes. These can range from embedded climate-risk planning to adaptive zoning, resilience budgeting, multi-sectoral coordination platforms, public data platforms and participatory decision-making (Al-Afeef et al., 2023). These innovations are not just 'administrative tweaks' but are how cities will reimagine governance to fit a new reality in which they are facing the climate crisis as well as a new technology landscape.

Social effectiveness of resilience is stated in the conceptual framework as well. Climate risks vary according to risks in the urban context. Those living in poor neighbourhoods and informal settlements, marginalised communities and environmentally vulnerable areas are at more risk and less likely to have access to adaptation opportunities. It's not a smart governance (i.e., more efficient, less equitable), even though it was adopted by the framework as the blueprint's first priority. It is acknowledged that whilst AI-enabled systems can improve planning and provision of services, if systems are not planned with equity as a priority, the potential is to worsen inequities in service provision, particularly as systems tend to reinforce already formal, formal and politically visible spaces. In this regard, social inclusion is more of a transversal theme of governance for climate resilience, and an integrated component of the activities of the entire chapter. Safeguarding vulnerable sectors and decreasing space inequality and public benefits should be an element of a urban area's "smart" safeguarding of the weak sectors – the democratic one.

In a large measure, this paradigm is under consideration, as well as the ethics and accountability. When applying AI in urban system governance, concerns about monitoring/surveillance, de-privatisation and bias and concentration of power in technical/over corporate actors. This is especially important for Smart Cities, where any algorithmic decision-making process coupled with the ubiquitousness of any data collection can become untransparent or opaque, and vice versa (Veerankutty et al., 2018). The chapter calls for 'all-inclusive models for governance, laws and mechanisms for citizen participation to allow citizens to grasp the way governance works and to actively engage in governance as well as any other measures that will shape a climate-friendly digital system(s). Ethical governance needs to be taken care of it is a precondition and key to legitimacy and trust in smart urbanism. In the absence of such safeguards, technology may well lead people to distrust institutions even further.

Overall, the framework embodies the notion that urban governance is a combination of smart technology, artificial intelligence, policy innovation, institutional capacity building and social justice. Does not follow a linear path with regard to digitalisation and resilience. Rather, it legitimates the fact that the linkage is only conditionality-based, and can be negotiated through political will, administrative capacity and the norms binding power. If a lack of coordination, equity and flexibility exists, then even the best city digital solution can prove to be very vulnerable. But another city, that isn't as technically advanced, but with an effective institution, inclusive planning processes and adaptive policy-making capacity, can be very resilient (Sun et al., 2022). It is NOT about the 'appearance' and 'images' of the technology, but rather about the 'content' of governance as such. From an analytical point of view of a smart city, it is concluded that a sense of smart city can be attained not only within the umbrella of a more general climate-resilient governing model, but also within that. AI connects cities' data to public action. Intelligence to Adaptation is Policy Innovation. That is more than a more digital city - it is also more of a just, sustainable and resilient city. This conceptual model thus offers a way of intellectually analysing and exploring the above influences on urban futures via a process of strategic combining of technology, governance and ecology.

THE BASICS OF TRANSITION ANALYTICAL APPROACHES

A central theme of this chapter is that the transition from smart cities to the more climate-resilient mode of governance is a pivotal transition in terms of urban policy means, ends and values. An efficient city was the first thought about how a smart city should operate, meaning the city has various types of sensor systems, digital platforms, data analyses and automation of the services, which would be easier to manage (Dang, 2025). The focus of this model lies on the idea of the problem of the city as a question of information and operation: the problems can be solved technically. This has proven to be an effective, albeit insufficient, mobility, utility and administration strategy to address an increasingly extreme (climate change) threat in an increasingly structured context. Coping with cities in times of climate disruption is more than an engineering challenge: it is an integrated, cumulative risk that cannot be optimised away, and they are not universal, but rather depends on the specific social profile of the area.

This is a new condition, and calls for a new, comprehensive system of decision-making. Responsiveness by urban systems does not automatically mean responsiveness by institutions and/or communities to anticipate, absorb, adapt and reorganise the city, should the stress last longer, and to keep functional and legitimate in the eyes of their community (Wilkin et al., 2016). In this new framework, the smart city is not the aim; it is the facilitating tool. Digital tools can produce better data and understanding of what is happening, but this is not enough for resilience – what is required is the power to take action, to translate knowledge and learning into inclusive, accountable and adaptive policy action. The core analytical content of this chapter is therefore on the claimed AI-powered urban transitions in a context of climate adaptation-capable governance and social equity concerns.

The second analytical assumption has to do with the redefining of the concept of urban intelligence, per se. In an urban setting, 'intelligence' seems to be concerned with the computing power, usefulness, real-time processing and predictive efficiencies. Incorporation of institutional learning and public deliberation, inter-agency coordination, and ethical governance of techno-systems. Missing the public trust (in fact, with no policy flexibility whatsoever), and the city is collecting tons of data, then it's not an "intelligent city". In the same way, a municipality with AI systems and lacking legislation and/or social inclusion measures might result in further strengthening vulnerabilities. Accordingly, for the concept of urban intelligence, it is primarily important to see it not as an alternative to democratic governance but as a public competence and technology as a means to get there.

AI & DATA FOR URBAN GOVERNANCE

AI is a key element driving this transformation because of its evolving nature of city data to classification, prediction and intervention. AI systems have been mainly introduced for information storage/transmission, and they are now implemented for proactive applications such as automatic discovery of information patterns in real time, prediction in advance, and automatic classification/policy decision making. This reconfiguration of urban governance is made known in various sectors. In the realm of transportation, predictive analytics is beginning to be used in congestion and traffic routing, in utilities to forecast demand and anomalies and at city hall for automatic service allocation, infrastructure tracking, and even to detect environmental changes (Khalid et al., 2022). The changes mean that the smart city cannot be applied without AI. It is transforming the social composition of the process of decision-making in the city.

Governance supported with AI can be useful in making the link between data collection and policy implementation. In the traditional urban way of running things, information is frequently available too late, planning is reactive, and decisions are based on unconnected information and late reporting. There are some fields where AI could offer some help: anticipatory governance authorities could use AI to predict potential threats, recognise anomalies before they become crises and make better use of their resources, both geographically and in a timely manner. It is one of the issues in the climate change resilience challenges. Introducing the risk of heat exposure in the counties, and adding in the risk of flood exposure, stress on infrastructure and mobility disruption are more dynamic; and can start to help governments to shift from reactive, post-disasters, to a more pre-emptive and adaptive approach. It does prompt some questions, however, concerning how and the extent to which algorithmic systems can create institutional reliance, about the black box of algorithmic decision-making and about the substitution of public reasoning with technical outcome by algorithmic decision-making.

There's already in the literature a lot of evidence that displays the value to be very conditional. It is capable of prediction and classification on the quality, representativeness and governance of the data. Even if incomplete or partial, it can include misleading data because part of the population, in this case, those residing in informal settlements, the elderly and people experiencing poverty are not normally collected by the official databases' formal systems (Islam & Guha, 2020; Saikia, 2019). This means that as AI grows, even in cities where data is not viewed as a key to identifying injustice in governance, it can be used to extend inequalities further (Ganaie, Takri, et al., 2026). The fact that informal settlements, peripheral areas and low-income groups can be literally left out of the picture in planning processes based on artificial intelligence, although they may be among the most impacted by climate risks. Therefore, the representation of data infrastructures is not just a technical question, but also manifested in the political arena and should be tackled during the implementation of AI in cities.

SUSTAINABILITY IN THE CITIES

There will, however, be an analysis of other (not necessarily environmental) jargon with appealing words such as 'sexy', urban sustainability, which will also involve institutional continuity and social dimension of inclusion. But, the concept of smart city has been focused on smart transport, energy, water and waste. All are great accomplishments, but the horizons for sustainability have been extended by the climate crisis. Development should be able to respond to environmental risks, emissions, sensitive people, and long-term ecological changes, and sustainable cities should be able to do so. This translates into implications for the AI-enabled governance in which the evaluative emphasis shifts from optimising procedures to value. In this context, AI has the potential to play a big role in the effective management of resources, predicting environmental risks and aiding in thorough planning (Liu et al., 2024). With these data-driven intelligent systems, it becomes possible to create better models of the climate and pinpoint the waste spots in urban metabolism, as well as integrate energy, mobility and water and coordinate them between the different industries. However, sustainability isn't only about more effective use of resources. Being a city, it can be beneficial in one aspect, and extremely challenging in another, such as surveillance or social inequality. So, sustainable urban governance is the ability plus normative action. The impact of the digital interventions should be assessed in terms of their justice, accessibility and democracy accountability as well as provisions for resource saving.

This is especially in climate change-prone cities with unequal climate change adaptation responsibility. The issue of sustainability is interwoven with the question of who will be able to benefit from investment in technologies / who will be at risk? Without informal settlements, any other form of adaptation, in the context of climate change, is not sustainable. Similarly, infrastructure constructed with the connected user in mind - and without thinking about the needs of the non-connected user - is not innovative and contributes to further marginalisation over the long and short term. This chapter's contribution to the analysis is the knowledge that sustainability and resilience are not disjointed concepts, but rather are affected by governance decisions.

CLIMATE RESILIENCE AND RE-ORDERING POLICY IS A PRIORITY WITH THE FOLLOWING PRIORITIES

One of these is the rising envelope of themes related to climate change and climate change resilience (CCr), which can be defined as the ability to keep functioning and adapting to climate change and recurrent disturbances. Resilience thinking thus calls into question the traditional planning methods, where the precondition for the planning process is recovery from the shocks, cascading failure and long-term environmental change, and where the design of the planning process begins from that point. This is an adapted Policy Priority list. The point, here, is that urban governance should be flexible, redundant, learning and socially legitimate under abnormal, not normal circumstances and in which efficiency has to be maximised. Understandings of the smart cities' concept in correlation with climate change governance are also included. While it's true that a smart city should ensure that services are working well and quickly, the other aspect of resilient thinking is how well the services are recovering if they are in a stressful situation. It poses the question: 'How can cities work outside the paradigm of a normal world?' In the current heat wave, this question should not be left unanswered against the background of flooding and water security or inadequate capacity of the water infrastructure. Today, the biggest problem of city intelligence is how to effectively and fairly manage disruption within a city.

THE OUTCOME OF THE ANALYSIS

The conclusions that can be drawn from the above analysis are: On the one hand, there are indications that the most beneficial applications of smart city technologies lie in those soaking up governance initiatives, instead of being mere modernisation endeavours. The use of infrastructure based on the Internet and sensor networks, and AI systems increases the amount of information on the city, but what is needed is to connect this information to the adaptive urban planning, coordination of different sectors and public accountability. In fact, it's more about: ensuring cities get the best value from it, seeing that AI is employed in an accountable way to anticipate risks and to inform decision-making and doing so in an inclusive way, not just making administration more efficient.

Second, it sees the paradigm of Artificial Intelligence as an effective but conditional paradigm in urban governance. It has very good skills in prediction, classification and rapid analysis, which is more and more demanded with complex situations in relation to the climate. These same skills might, however, end up in other forms of 'threats' if left unchecked. These institutions may come under threat, as well as algorithmic systems, increasing the potential for further biases, surveillance and accountability. Indeed, the final solution is not simply to pay lip service to AI, but to be based on clear rules, on social and human connections and on how AI can be involved and be included; it can play a role in resilience, but only in the light of these rules.

Thirdly, the notion of urban sustainability, as highlighted in a chapter, is also related to the notion of distributive justice, and so is the notion of urban climate resilience. Technological developments that boost processes in already privileged areas and not in vulnerable areas are not resilient in the urban development process. This is a profound key finding because it takes the debate about smart city projects away from novelty (technology) and towards a social impact discussion. Rather, it should be asked whether the city can better cater for the most vulnerable or not?

Fourthly, this disclosure showed that policy innovation is a crucial factor in determining what the Smart City can turn into the Climate Resilient City. AI does not exist in a vacuum when it comes to making better policy: it needs to be smuggled into the institutional change planning process, adaptive regulation, data governance process, resilience budgeting process, participatory process, and more. Further, technology is not the only tool that can be used to build resilience; governance design can do just as well.

THEORY AND PRACTICE OF IMPLICATIONS DISCUSSION

The results have implications for Urban theory and practice. They believe that it is not about being efficient and connected, but that a Digital transformation should begin. Innovation is automation, platformisation and real-time management, which is a smart city model that is omnipresent. But the results in this chapter indicate that these indicators are constrained in this climate change world. In order for the theory of urban innovation to be adequately developed, it is also necessary to see the city in relation to its adaptive capacity, its social equity (for example), and reflexivity (institutions, for example). Thus, innovation should not be defined by how many of the normal functions that are digitised, but by how cities are able to respond to uncertainty.

The re-framing also impacts public administration. They are peddling AI as a cure-all to the problem of modernising a government, and without institutional change, there is no Government modernisation. But public agencies must be legally and technically empowered, morally insulated and inter-agency equipped to use AI to be more resilient (Al-Qatanani, 2025). It's not a technological adoption thing; it's about capacity building in technology amongst the people. In all these cities, what is needed are individuals who don't panic at the prospect of algorithmic results and imagine the consequences, but also regulatory mechanisms capable of safeguarding and countering the robberies of rights and planning mechanisms that can be shaped to align with the knowledge and scope of the 'digital' without losing sight of the purpose of democratic governance.

The second implication is in connection with the politics of participation. Responsiveness is often assumed to confer legitimacy and is referred to as one of the attributes of good government. Haste isn't necessarily a good choice. The conclusions of the chapter reflect the concept of digital governance not only in public debate, but in relation to the priority setting of adaptation to climate change and classification of risks, or to provide public services in particular, which go hand in hand with the use of digital technologies (Zwitter & Hazenberg, 2020). It is therefore of critical importance from an epistemic point of view as well as crucial on the democratic side. The higher frequency with which the environment is threatened to the communities brings types of information and experiences that are not considered by formal models. This resulted in a demand for 'technical intelligence' to be integrated in a robust governance structure along with 'social knowledge'. More significantly, we have to ask ourselves: how can Artificial Intelligence become part of participatory institutions, or how will urban governance in the future look if it isn't part of those institutions?

The third implication has to do with the political economy of digital urbanism. Many smart city solutions depend upon a partnership with the customers: private sector technology providers, platform providers and/or data vendors. Such an agreement can propel innovation to dizzying heights, but can also attract dependency, muckrakers who have no accountability. Oracle's proprietary systems prevent public agencies from having control of data standards (and audit/ strategic autonomy). If it's about that, then it's apparent that the public-interest digital government plays a critical role, and the municipalities can retain control of the data infrastructure, procurements and the standards.

FUTURE RECOMMENDATIONS

Urban policy, to the extent it will have to take a leap towards integrated forms of governance, will need to rely on three key characteristics of digital transformation in the future: The need for resilience, ethics and social inclusion. Firstly, the presence of explicit AI governance systems by the municipalities. These must set up principles for accountable and transparent use of AI that take into account explainability and data protection in human oversight of the use of AI in the public sector. They also need to offer means to voice a concern: ensure that the grievance may be adjudicated; and periodically review the algorithm, making room for future challenges.

The second is the need for cities to have data strategies for resilience. Data accumulation needs to be done in a way that captures infrastructural capacity and a social attitude towards informal settlements, exposure to the environment and asymmetrical services. This would eliminate the preferential access of already well-documented areas for the AI systems. Other areas of inclusive data governance are the realisation of interoperable public data, agency guidelines on data sharing and preventing misuse of data. In the absence of these traits, the transformation practices and plans that are digital can effectively stand as an exclusion materially neutral as it is.

Third, an urban policy should be the coordination of institutions from various sectors. A cross-cutting theme of transport, housing, sanitation, disaster management, health and environmental regulation is climate resilience. But many city governments are still organised in a sectoral manner. Although AI systems provide built-in analytics, it takes more than technology to address the issue of siloed bureaucracy. The result should be for local governments to put in place joint mechanisms of coordination and assembly between digital insights and collective action, such as joint resilience units, interdepartmental data councils or integrated planning committees. Institutional innovations are also crucial to facilitate technological capacity transition towards operational resilience.

Lastly, participatory governance of smart systems design and implementation in the city needs to be increased. The public consultation should not only be done at the time of introduction of technology, but should also be undertaken in the agenda-setting risk assessment and policy design phase. Climate-vulnerable communities come with a disproportionate burden of risk, and should be seen as a special focus in formal urban planning processes. Examples of participatory mechanisms are neighbourhood-based adaptation planning processes, neighbourhood resilience forums and citizen data review panels. These strategies promote a way to integrate lived experience in digital governance and ensure stronger policies in terms of democratic legitimacy and effectiveness.

Fifth, investment in the capability of the Public Sector is a must. Don't leave all the urban resilience to outside consultants and/or vendor-provided systems. Organisations need to hire staff to navigate and adopt AI climate analysis, data governance, and AI climate procurement procedures, as well as ethical AI regulation. This can be achieved during training programmes, through relations with universities and interdisciplinary policy labs. The goal should be towards public organisations that strategically and critically use AI and not technical products.

Lastly, more research needs to be performed on comparative analysis and context-sensitive analysis. Even though cities of the Global South are highly climate vulnerable and experiencing fast urbanisation, cities are still underrepresented and higher-capacity institutions are the target of current scholarships and fellowships. A couple of empirical studies on the articulation of 'AI and informality', 'infrastructural deficit and weak register' and 'weak state capacity' are needed. Moreover, there is a need to talk about the political implications of long-term developments of vendor-based 'smart city' approaches, including data sovereignty and the public responsibility in cities. Such studies would contribute to the knowledge of building climate-resistance in governance at different types of legal frameworks. This is a key message of the first body: it is not just these technologies that are important; it is also how these technologies are governed that is important to the future of the city. Smart cities alone are not resilient, sustainable or just. However, they can only enjoy these features when the digital systems are embedded in institutions whose ability to learn, coordinate, uphold rights and distribute benefits is fair. Thus, as a consequence of climate change, such a separation is inevitable. The city's government should not be just technologically optimistic; it should be a rooted and grounded combination of intelligence, accountability, and adaptation in the context of the growing environmental turmoil.

So the urbanisation model of the chapter is oriented towards the governance of urbanisation. AI may have its significance, but it is not about automation in politics. Its power and potential can be tapped when public institutions are transparent, welcoming and normatively led in the complexities of their environment. In the same way, resilience to climate change can't simply be seen as a technical success. It will be a long-term process, political, ethical, and administrative, which has to be sustained, accepted by the population, institutionalised and adapted.

In this context, the transformation from smart cities to climate-resilient governance can be most valued as a process of policy maturity, in the urban context. It brings together a change of thinking from the notion that 'data equals better cities' to a thinking that cities are produced through contesting decisions of risk, value, justice and collective futures. This is not just about smarter urban systems, it's about intelligent cities that are not only declared fair, legitimate and predictive in the scope of climatic uncertainty, but also in the sense that they strive to achieve this.

CONCLUSION

Throughout this chapter, different approaches have been made to attempt to demonstrate that this is the case, namely, that this is the context in which the concept of the future of urban transformation is absolutely not conveyed from the smart city's prevailing grammar. Smart urbanism 1.0 became synonymous with the data-driven technologies of automated systems that, combined with digitised infrastructure, would lead to more efficient, more responsive and more competitive cities. That was no false promise. It has become easier for the urban administration to monitor systems and improve the provision of services and operational coordination, for example, in the transport sector, with the use of digital tools. But, at the end of this chapter, there are the conclusions that in a climate of volatile socio-spatial inequality-institutional stress environment, efficiency, connectivity, and technological sophistication are not the only keys for the progress of urban modernity. In the current scenario, the question is not merely of how to make the cities smart, but also resilient and inclusive, and to deal with uncertainties over the long term. This evolution of the city towards smart city to climate resilient governance signals a paradigm shift in urban agenda thinking and approach. City ways of doing things have changed due to climate change: it means a regular disturbance of the 'normal' governance of cities. Red skies today for other events as well, albeit other ones: those of heatwaves, floods, water stress and infrastructural fragility and cascading service failures – these are the ones related to the monsoon. In these cases, technology optimisation should be a second-order concern in relation to a much bigger question – the capacity of the city to absorb shocks and stresses, adapt institutions and protect vulnerable populations and continuity of urban life. Resilience thus cannot be regarded as "just another thing on top" of the smart city agenda, but rather an integral part of it. It's the new frontier where urban intelligence will need to be evaluated.

The chapter contains three main thesis statements: (1) AI plays a strategically important, but normatively contingent role in this transformation. AI can help improve the implementation of climate-resilient governance – from climate change predictions and deriving benefits from climate-related spatial and environmental analysis to enhanced environmental monitoring or giving a timely public response. AI can support cities to move from reactive administration to anticipatory governance, be it through predictions for flooding, energy, mobility planning or risk detection and adapting the maintenance of infrastructure. It may help to increase public institutions' understanding of and also target resources more effectively, and address complexity. However, the chapter has also taught us that AI can't be the answer to urban fragility alone. Its effectiveness depends on its context of use (its representativeness), as well as the rules of how the algorithm's output should be used in public policy. On the whole, AI can support institutional intelligence, but it cannot replace the commitment of decisions taken through democratic procedures or give moral and policy recommendations.

This is particularly pertinent with the evolving urban administration practices, now more integrated with AI, and where new opportunities – as well as new threats and risks – may lie. Opacity, surveillance, bias, exclusion, and power being shifted to technical and corporate actors are real issues surrounding the application of algorithmic systems in public decision-making processes. If improperly protected, AI might be the recipe for more injustice in the city, if it can make it seem like progress. An out-of-balance set of data will help to make the unseen visible. Data infrastructures presented by proprietary platforms may pose a problem with regard to public oversight. It is hard to explain to citizens, and if explained, can be difficult to challenge, leading to a lack of accountability. Finally, responsible AI governance is just as integral to a climate-resilient city as is the city itself. There can be no separation of ethics and governance of technology from the practical governance of climate risk.

Another major finding of the chapter is that urban sustainability and climate resilience are not only analytically separable concepts, but a codeveloping concept. If the discussion on smart cities is on sustainability, they speak in terms of efficiency – less emissions, more efficient energy use, etc. All are of importance, yet research carried out here confirms there is more to sustainability than technocratic environmentalism. But the recipients of digital innovation, the still vulnerable ones, as well as those who use the adaptation resources in the social groups and urban spaces, must also be heard in the context of sustainable urbanism. It is hard to argue that a city is sustainable when green solutions are implemented in the better-off districts and informal settlements continue to be vulnerable to heat, floods, lack of services, and lack of participation in planning. Likewise, if a municipality has infrastructure, but not people's safety, it can't be considered resilient. The idea is that sustainability, resilience and social justice will all be co-bound; that they are co-moral; and that this leads to the challenge of legitimacy of urban government.

The chapter has never had one stand with regards to that; there are other things to governance than showmanship for the tech. Resilience extends beyond the sensing, data dashboards and AI tools. The point is on how the institutions can react to this knowledge, and how institutions can learn to function on this interface between institutions; how they can learn to change their policies when there's a change in the risks and how they can do that in an acceptable manner. The ability to develop climate-resilient governance is more a result of institutional achievement rather than the technological endpoint. It has plans that can carry environmental intelligence, social policy, and administration that can be carried out between different types of sectors and regulatory systems, and with time, it can also be filled with the implementation of a Digital Transformation for the public good. Throughout this chapter, there has been a requirement to reassess AI and smart technologies, not as core to the urban agenda, but as part and parcel of this overarching framework of governance.

In fact, this analysis has also pointed towards the need for policy innovation to be an intrinsic part of this transformation. This implies that planning and administration models and routines are increasingly getting more rigid and more fragmented, and that the nature of climate change can be described as dynamic, cumulative and not certain. New policy instruments, new standards of data governance, new participatory mechanisms and new institutional pathways for adaptation are needed in cities. The process of innovation outlined in this chapter is not a technologically experimental process. These include resilience budgeting, adaptive regulation, cross-sectoral coordination of planning, inclusive data systems and participatory climate planning and public-interest digital governance systems. The takeaway message here is that urban resilience is not solely about getting different tools, but it's also about changing the rules, the relationships and the capacities that drive the uses of tools. Thus, governance innovation is the solution to make the transition from Urban Intelligence to sustainable public outcomes.

The other is related to the geography of global urban transformation. The story of AI, smart cities and resilience has not been just about the problems of high-capacity cities – on the institutional side of things. AI's responsible and inclusive governance becomes more important in Global South regions that suffer from climate vulnerability, rapidly expanding urbanisation and infrastructural and governance gaps, which tend to converge in the same region of the Global South. Despite the broad proliferation of AI applications, few cities around the world, including in Asia, Latin America and Africa, have developed any governance initiatives for AI as identified in UN-Habitat's global assessment. This discovery is of great impact. It argues that the concept of diffusion of technologies is by no means only a technical one, but also an institutional and an epistemic one. An essential component of future climate-resilient governance is a governance system that mirrors the cities' experiences, constraints and priorities in locations beyond the familiar and historic nodes of technological power. This shift towards the responsible use of AI in the city should be local (responsive) and global (normative).

The chapter has also highlighted the need for participation as an integral component of resilient governance. The climate risk experiences are not shared, and the experience of climate knowledge is not exclusively that of an 'elusive' object of experts, sensors and algorithms. It is the 'if–then' scenarios – like frequent flooding, heat stress, infrastructural exclusion, environmental degradation and many, many more – that can create action-oriented, experiential forms of knowledge essential for effective adaptations. This is because Resilient Urban Governance is not only 'Governance of the Surprises'. Should be open to deliberation, popular wisdom and popular challenge. AI thus shouldn't contract opportunities for participation in the governance of cities. If the citizen is just measured more accurately, it is not a people-centred smart city; if the citizen is involved in determining the collective futures in meaningful ways through intelligence, then it is a people-centred smart city.

On the basis of these overall findings, there's an option to rethink the smartness of the city in general. At this moment, the intelligence of the city must not only be measured in a computational manner, but in terms of institutional reflexivity, ethical responsibility, ecological sensitivity and distributive justice. A smart city – one that can learn from data without being dependent on data, that can build upon technology without sacrificing democracy, see risk without demonising the at-risk population, innovate without being novel, and make progress. The real meaning of the change mentioned in this chapter is that. However, it is also the expression of the changes that have taken place in the governance of the city from a digital modernity towards one that is not only attentive to climate but is serious about climate security, social justice and the adaptive public capacity.

Reactions to it are therefore not a chapter of anti-innovation, nor celebratory of technology. It is governance-centred. AI, digital infrastructure and smart platforms will most certainly have an important role to play in the future of the city. It is well managed to enhance resilience, their legitimacy and the public good that is the key. The biggest takeaway is that the climate resilience of cities is not going to happen automatically just because cities are now getting more automated. By involving in participatory governance mechanisms, the context-specific policy development, commitment to sustainability and justice - "It will be climate resilient." - technological innovation under ethical leadership will be worked out.

Finally, the chapter argues that the transition towards smart cities in the direction of governance for climate change adaptation and resilience is not only technologically but also normatively and institutionally. Public value as a driver for the management of urban infrastructure needs to be reimagined, due to the uncertainty of the climate and the shocks which come with it. It calls for anticipatory but not authoritarian urban governance, for data-based but not exclusionary urban governance, and for innovative but not equity and democratic accountability-poor urban governance. If it's going to be habitable, governable and just, an intelligence for resilience and a resilience for intelligence will therefore be essential to the twenty-first-century city.

REFERENCES

A. V. S. K., Rautrao, R. R., Suseelan, S. T., S., N. B., K. R. S., S. R., & Ganaie, N. A. (2026). Gamification Learning for Urban Educational Challenges: A Mixed-Methods Quasi-Experimental Study in PGDM Programs. In A. C. Ocaña & J. F. Molina (Eds.), *Transforming Teaching with AI and Digital Tools: Methods, Platforms, and Classroom Innovations* (pp. 265–298). IGI Global Scientific Publishing. DOI: 10.4018/979-8-2600-1568-1.ch013

Abdelilah, C., Ahriz, S., El Guemmat, K., & Mansouri, K. (2024). Implementation of suitable information technology governance frameworks for Moroccan higher education institutions. *International Journal of Electrical and Computer Engineering*, *14*(3), 3116. Advance online publication. DOI: 10.11591/ijece.v14i3.pp3116-3126

Al-Afeef, M. A. M., Ali, O. A. M., Al-Tahat, S., Malkawi, A. F., Kalbounhe, N. Y., & Al-Azzam, Z. F. (2023). The effect of big data governance on financial technology in Jordanian commercial banks: The mediation role of organisational culture. *International Journal of Data and Network Science*, *7*(3), 1283–1294. Advance online publication. DOI: 10.5267/j.ijdns.2023.4.010

Al-Qatanani, K. M. (2025). The impact of implementing information technology governance based on the COBIT-2019 framework on institutional performance. *Edelweiss Applied Science and Technology*, *9*(3), 84–95. Advance online publication. DOI: 10.55214/25768484.v9i3.5117

Bicudo, E., Morrison, M., Li, P., Faulkner, A., Webster, A., Mourby, M., & Kaye, J. (2022). Patent power in biomedical innovation: Technology governance in biomodifying technologies. *The Journal of World Intellectual Property*, *25*(2), 473–494. Advance online publication. DOI: 10.1111/jwip.12237

Bussy, A., & Zheng, H. (2023). Responses of FDI to geopolitical risks: The role of governance, information, and technology. *International Business Review*, *32*(4), 102136. Advance online publication. DOI: 10.1016/j.ibusrev.2023.102136

Dang, C. (2025). Public Opinion and Its Influence on Technology Governance in the Age of Digital Transformation. *International Journal of Computational and Experimental Science and Engineering*, *11*(2). Advance online publication. DOI: 10.22399/ijcesen.1406

Ganaie, N. A. (2015). Sikh socio-religious reform movements in Jammu and Kashmir from 1900 to 1947. *Journal of Interdisciplinary and Multidisciplinary Research*, *2*(8).

Ganaie, N. A. (2026). The role of artificial intelligence in radicalisation, recruitment and terrorist propaganda: Deconstructing violent extremism and reimagining counterterrorism in contemporary digital ecosystems. *Frontiers in Political Science*, *7*, 1718396. DOI: 10.3389/fpos.2025.1718396

Ganaie, N. A. A. V., S. K., Mir, T. A., Jan, I., S., N. B., & K. R. S., S. R. (2026). Smart Learning and Smart Schools: Transforming Indian Education Through AI-Enabled NEP 2020 Implementations. In *Human-AI Leadership for Transforming Schools* (pp. 223–258). DOI: 10.4018/979-8-2600-0388-6.ch009

Ganaie, N. A., Mir, T. A., Jaysingh, M., & Rath, D. M. (2026). Algorithmic governance and surveillance federalism: Transforming the digital state in India and ASEAN. *Frontiers in Political Science*, *8*, 1757636. DOI: 10.3389/fpos.2026.1757636

Ganaie, N. A., Saikia, T., Mir, T. A., & Jan, I. (2025). *Dynamics of Public Policy and Good Governance in India: The Road to Viksit Bharat* (First). Authors Click Publishing. DOI: 10.5281/ZENODO.15870017

Ganaie, N. A., Takri, K. K., Raviteja, Y., Sahu, D., Rout, B., & Islam, B. (2026). Digital governance and poverty alleviation mechanisms: Lessons from the public distribution system in Kashmir and Kerala. *ShodhKosh: Journal of Visual and Performing Arts*, *7*(7s), 25–39. DOI: 10.29121/shodhkosh.v7.i7s.2026.7009

Girardi, P., & Temporelli, A. (2017). Smartainability: A Methodology for Assessing the Sustainability of the Smart City. *Energy Procedia*, *111*, 810–816. DOI: 10.1016/j.egypro.2017.03.243

Guenduez, A. A., Mergel, I., Schedler, K., Fuchs, S., & Douillet, C. (2024). Institutional work in smart cities: Interviews with smart city managers. *Urban Governance*, *4*(1), 80–90. Advance online publication. DOI: 10.1016/j.ugj.2024.01.003

Habib Saragih, A., Ali, S., Suwardi, E., & Utomo, H. (2024). Finding the missing pieces to an optimal corporate tax savings: Information technology governance and internal information quality. *International Journal of Accounting Information Systems*, *52*, 100665. Advance online publication. DOI: 10.1016/j.accinf.2023.100665

Islam, B., & Guha, P. (2020). Impact of occupational migration of unskilled labourers from domestic agriculture on farm business income in source households of Assam, India. *International Journal of Social Economics*, *47*(12), 1561–1576. DOI: 10.1108/IJSE-05-2020-0296

Khalid, M., Khan, R. A., Khushnood, M., Aslam, S., Khattak, Z. Z., & Abbas, S. (2022). An Empirical Analysis of the Influence of Project Governance and Information Technology Governance on Project Delay. *Global Business Review*, 09721509221121179. Advance online publication. DOI: 10.1177/09721509221121179

Kowalczyk, M., & Napiecek, R. (2023). E-governance and blockchain technology in local government. *Zeszyty Teoretyczne Rachunkowosci*, *47*(3), 221–238. Advance online publication. DOI: 10.5604/01.3001.0053.7703

Kuhlmann, S., Stegmaier, P., & Konrad, K. (2019). The tentative governance of emerging science and technology—A conceptual introduction. *Research Policy*, *48*(5), 1091–1097. Advance online publication. DOI: 10.1016/j.respol.2019.01.006

Liando, D. M., Ganaie, N. A., & Yuslaini, N. (2026). Smart City 2.0 governance policy model: Institutional configurations and the politics of urban inclusion in India, Singapore, and Indonesia. *Frontiers in Political Science*, *8*, 1730870. DOI: 10.3389/fpos.2026.1730870

Liu, B., You, Z., & Jiang, F. (2024). Research on ethical governance technology of biological identification technology based on the technology track theory. *Chinese Medical Ethics*, *37*(10). Advance online publication. DOI: 10.12026/j.issn.1001-8565.2024.10.01

Maestre-Góngora, G., & Aponte, D. (2023). Dataset about information technology governance: A survey in Colombian enterprises. *Data in Brief*, *50*, 109480. Advance online publication. DOI: 10.1016/j.dib.2023.109480

Merchán-Rodríguez, V., & Juiz, C. (2024). Governance of Technologies and Information Systems for Higher Education: Systematic Mapping of Studies. *Journal of Computer Science and Technology (Argentina)*, *24*(1), e05. Advance online publication. DOI: 10.24215/16666038.24.e05

Mir, S. A., Saini, N., Senthil Kumar, A. V., Ganaie, N. A., Rautrao, R. R. R., Choudhary, A., Sehgal, S., & Khandelwal, A. R. R. (2025). GenAI: Opportunities, Disruptions, and the New Learning Paradigm. In *New Media Applications in Digital Education* (pp. 339–362). IGI Global Scientific Publishing. DOI: 10.4018/979-8-3373-5157-5.ch012

Mohamed, A. M. E., Alnor, N. H. A., Mohammed, O. A. A., Al-Matari, E. M., Al-hebri, A., & Ahmed, A. (2024). The impact of information technology governance according to the COBIT on performance. *International Journal of Advanced and Applied Sciences*, *11*(3), 127–136. Advance online publication. DOI: 10.21833/ijaas.2024.03.014

Prashad, D. (2018). Urban sustainability in practice: Priorities in India. *Lecture Notes in Civil Engineering*, *3*, 1483–1493. Advance online publication. DOI: 10.1007/978-3-319-57937-5_154

Prianto, A. L., & Amalia, A. A. (2019). Combatting Slums, Sustaining Poverty: Dynamic Urban Governance in Makassar, Indonesia. *Otoritas : Jurnal Ilmu Pemerintahan*, *9*(1), 28–41. Advance online publication. DOI: 10.26618/ojip.v9i1.2008

Reijers, W., O'Brolcháin, F., & Haynes, P. (2016). Governance in Blockchain Technologies & Social Contract Theories. *Ledger*, *1*, 134–151. Advance online publication. DOI: 10.5195/ledger.2016.62

Robles, P., & Mallinson, D. J. (2025). Artificial intelligence technology, public trust, and effective governance. *The Review of Policy Research*, *42*(1), 11–28. Advance online publication. DOI: 10.1111/ropr.12555

Saikia, B. (2019). New mode of governance: Governance through technology. *International Journal of Recent Technology and Engineering*, *8*(3), 4052–4055. Advance online publication. DOI: 10.35940/ijrte.C5392.098319

Saritha, B. (2025). Smart City 2.0: Evaluating Citizen-Centric Digital Governance and Urban Sustainability in India. *International Journal of Research Publication and Reviews*, (6).

Sharma, S. K., Seetharaman, A., & Maddulety, K. (2021). Framework for Sustainable Urban Water Management in the Context of Governance, Infrastructure, Technology and Economics. *Water Resources Management*, *35*(12), 3903–3913. Advance online publication. DOI: 10.1007/s11269-021-02916-1

Shelton, T., Zook, M., & Wiig, A. (2015). The "actually existing smart city.". *Cambridge Journal of Regions, Economy and Society*, *8*(1), 13–25. Advance online publication. DOI: 10.1093/cjres/rsu026

Sirisomboonsuk, P., Gu, V. C., Cao, R. Q., & Burns, J. R. (2018). Relationships between project governance and information technology governance and their impact on project performance. *International Journal of Project Management*, *36*(2), 287–300. Advance online publication. DOI: 10.1016/j.ijproman.2017.10.003

Soltanzadeh, S. (2025). A metaphysical account of agency for technology governance. *AI & Society*, *40*(3), 1723–1734. Advance online publication. DOI: 10.1007/s00146-024-01941-z

Stokols, A. (2025). The insurgent smart city: How a social movement created an alternative imaginary of the smart city. *Journal of Urban Affairs*, *47*(4), 1149–1166. Advance online publication. DOI: 10.1080/07352166.2023.2216887

Sun, H., Zhang, Z., & Liu, Z. (2022). Does air pollution collaborative governance promote green technology innovation? Evidence from China. *Environmental Science and Pollution Research International*, *29*(34), 51609–51622. Advance online publication. DOI: 10.1007/s11356-022-19535-x

Syafhendry, S., Ganaie, N. A., & Yama, A. (2025). Smart elections or rigged algorithms: The rise of artificial intelligence in electoral governance in Southeast Asia. *Frontiers in Political Science*, *7*, 1672310. Advance online publication. DOI: 10.3389/fpos.2025.1672310

Tian, N., & Wang, W. (2025). Innovative Pathways for Collaborative Governance in Technology-Driven Smart Communities. *Sustainability (Basel)*, *17*(1), 98. Advance online publication. DOI: 10.3390/su17010098

Ullah, S., Nobanee, H., & Iftikhar, H. (2023). Global financial integration, governance-by-technology, and green growth. *International Review of Financial Analysis*, *90*, 102838. Advance online publication. DOI: 10.1016/j.irfa.2023.102838

Veeramani, K., & Jaganathan, S. (2020). Land registration: Use-case of e-Governance using blockchain technology. *KSII Transactions on Internet and Information Systems*, *14*(9). Advance online publication. DOI: 10.3837/tiis.2020.09.007

Veerankutty, F., Ramayah, T., & Ali, N. A. (2018). Information technology governance on audit technology performance among Malaysian public sector auditors. *Social Sciences (Basel, Switzerland)*, *7*(8), 124. Advance online publication. DOI: 10.3390/socsci7080124

von Schomberg, R. (2025). On Technological and Innovation Sovereignty: A Response to Carl Mitcham's Call for a Political Theory of Technology. *NanoEthics*, *19*(1), 2. Advance online publication. DOI: 10.1007/s11569-025-00469-w

Wilkin, C. L., Couchman, P. K., Sohal, A., & Zutshi, A. (2016). Exploring differences between smaller and larger organisations' corporate governance of information technology. *International Journal of Accounting Information Systems*, *22*, 6–25. Advance online publication. DOI: 10.1016/j.accinf.2016.07.002

Wu, W., Huang, T., & Gong, K. (2020). Ethical Principles and Governance Technology Development of AI in China. In *Engineering* (Vol. 6, Number 3). DOI: 10.1016/j.eng.2019.12.015

Wu, Y., & Li, G. (2024). Technology governance and governance technology: From the perspective of regulatory research on blockchain digital assets. *Bulletin of Chinese Academy of Sciences*, *39*(8). Advance online publication. DOI: 10.16418/j.issn.1000-3045.20240323001

Yuslaini, N., Widya Setiabudi Sumadinata, R., Fedryansyah, M., Abdillah, A., Prianto, A. L., & Febriyanti, D. (2023). Sustainable investment strategies in the palm oil industry in Indonesia. *Journal of Infrastructure. Policy and Development*, *7*(3), 2288. Advance online publication. DOI: 10.24294/jipd.v7i3.2288

Zwitter, A. (2024). Cybernetic governance: Implications of technology convergence on governance convergence. *Ethics and Information Technology*, *26*(2), 24. Advance online publication. DOI: 10.1007/s10676-024-09763-9

Zwitter, A., & Hazenberg, J. (2020). Decentralised Network Governance: Blockchain Technology and the Future of Regulation. *Frontiers in Blockchain*, *3*, 12. Advance online publication. DOI: 10.3389/fbloc.2020.00012

Chapter 4

Rethinking Plastic Sustainability and Digital Sovereignty in the Age of Digital Abundance: An Islamic Perspective

Liza Mariah Azahari
http://orcid.org/0000-0002-3593-1062
Universiti Islam Sultan Sharif Ali, Brunei

ABSTRACT

This chapter draws a parallel between the historical rise of plastic and the rapid expansion of data in the digital economy. While plastic was once celebrated for its innovation, it later caused serious environmental and health issues due to uncontrolled use. Similarly, data—often called the "new oil"—drives economic and technological progress but also presents risks such as exploitation and weak governance. The chapter argues that unchecked digital growth may lead to socio-political and cultural harms, including digital pollution, algorithmic bias, and reduced human autonomy. Using insights from sustainability literature, it reframes approaches to digital sovereignty for responsible data use and governance. Ultimately, it proposes ethical data stewardship and AI governance frameworks to ensure digital sustainability, safeguard human rights, and promote social well-being.

DOI: 10.4018/979-8-2600-2233-7.ch004

INTRODUCTION

The rapid expansion of artificial intelligence (AI) and data-driven systems has introduced unprecedented opportunities across sectors, particularly in healthcare, governance, and economic development. However, this expansion has also exposed significant challenges related to implementation, governance (Misra et al., 2025), and environmental sustainability (Shabana, 2026), education (Anshari et al., 2017), healthcare (Anshari et al; 2021) and ethical deployment (Nair et al., 2025).

Much like the historical rise of plastic, which was initially celebrated for its utility before revealing severe environmental consequences (Rhodes, 2018), data is now undergoing a similar trajectory. The growing dependence on data-driven technologies risks creating systemic harms if not governed through sustainable and ethical frameworks.

This chapter argues that the plastic–data analogy is not only conceptually insightful but also practically urgent. As AI systems become embedded in critical infrastructures such as healthcare, governance, and education, the need for sustainable digital ecosystems becomes increasingly evident.

Conceptual Foundations: Sustainability, Abundance, and Governance

Sustainability has traditionally been framed within environmental discourse, emphasizing the balance between economic growth, social well-being, and ecological preservation. However, this conventional model often reflects an anthropocentric worldview, where nature is treated primarily as a resource for human exploitation. In contrast, Islamic-based development introduces a fundamentally different paradigm grounded in taw īd (unity of God) and khilāfah (vicegerency), where humans act as stewards rather than owners of the earth (Thoha, 2026).

This distinction is critical in understanding sustainability in the age of digital abundance. While conventional sustainability frameworks emphasize efficiency and resource management, Islamic perspectives extend sustainability into ethical, spiritual, and metaphysical dimensions, incorporating the preservation of faith, intellect, life, wealth, and lineage (Maqā id al-Sharī'ah) (Thoha, 2026) . This broader conceptualization provides a valuable lens for rethinking digital sustainability beyond purely technical or economic considerations.

Furthermore, contemporary sustainability discourse has begun to critique growth-oriented economic systems, advocating instead for models that promote prosperity without overconsumption (zuhd) . This critique aligns closely with concerns about data overproduction, where excessive data extraction mirrors unsustainable material consumption patterns.

Data as the "New Oil" and the Political Economy of Digital Abundance

Artificial Intelligence (AI) is becoming an important technology in many sectors. It refers to computer systems that can perform tasks normally requiring human intelligence, such as learning, recognizing patterns, and making decisions. With the growth of digital technologies and data availability, AI has developed quickly and is now applied in industries like finance, education, business, and healthcare (Anshari et al; 2021;). One key advantage of AI is its ability to analyze large amounts of data quickly, helping organizations improve efficiency, accuracy, and decision making (Misra et al., 2025). Many organizations are exploring how AI can improve service delivery and overall performance (Aragani & Thirunagalingam, 2025). Implementing AI, however, requires more than technology. Organizations need proper planning, strong data management, and support from stakeholders. AI systems rely on reliable, high-quality data. If data is incomplete or inaccurate, the AI results may also be unreliable. Therefore, proper data governance and employee training are essential.

Ethical and regulatory considerations are also critical. AI often processes sensitive information, so organizations must protect data privacy and cybersecurity (Misra et al., 2025). Transparency and accountability are needed to ensure fair use of AI. Without proper regulation, AI may create risks like privacy violations or biased decisions (Misra et al., 2025).

The expansion of data-driven systems parallels the industrial rise of plastic in both scale and logic. Data is continuously generated through digital interactions, forming the backbone of Industry 4.0 systems characterized by automation, artificial intelligence, and interconnected technologies . These developments have transformed labour markets, resulting in both job displacement of low-skilled workers and creation of high-skilled roles, alongside increased productivity and efficiency.

However, this transformation is not neutral. As highlighted in employability research, the digital economy increasingly demands hybrid competencies combining technical, cognitive, and ethical skills (Azahari et al 2026). This suggests that data is not merely an economic resource but a structural force reshaping human capability systems, influencing how individuals' access and sustain meaningful work. A study connecting the development of future ready human capital calls for more value-based capital components to address future ethical challenges of AI in the future of work. These added value capital components include honesty, trust, spiritual intelligence and soft communication skills (Azahari et al 2026)

From a political economy perspective, data abundance reflects a form of asymmetrical extraction, where individuals generate data while corporations capture and monetize it. This mirrors the plastic economy, where production benefits are concentrated while environmental costs are externalized.

However, this expansion has also exposed significant challenges related to implementation, governance, and sustainability, including issues of trust, data security, and ethical deployment (Nair et al., 2025) .

Much like the historical rise of plastic, which was initially celebrated for its utility before revealing severe environmental consequences (Rhodes, 2018), data is now undergoing a similar trajectory (Couldry & Mejias, 2019). The growing dependence on data-driven technologies risks creating systemic harms if not governed through sustainable and ethical frameworks (Shabana, 2026). Moreover, emerging evidence suggests that such ambitions may generate unintended sustainability risks if pursued through resource-intensive and weakly regulated models. In particular, the rapid expansion of AI infrastructure, including data centres, has introduced significant environmental externalities, especially in relation to water consumption and energy use (Shabana, 2026).

This chapter argues that the plastic–data analogy is not only conceptually insightful but also practically urgent. Based on the previous literature and reports, the need for sustainable digital ecosystems becomes increasingly evident.

Sovereignty in the Age of Data Abundance

Digital systems increasingly generate forms of intangible pollution, including excessive data production, misinformation, surveillance externalities, and algorithmic bias. Although less visible than environmental pollution, these digital externalities can significantly shape cognition, behaviour, institutional legitimacy, and, critically, societal trust. As a result, the erosion of trust in digital systems has placed digital sovereignty at the centre of global policy debates, prompting increasing scrutiny by political leaders and regulatory bodies worldwide.

Digital sovereignty refers to the capacity of a nation, institution, or organisation to control, govern, and safeguard its digital infrastructure, data, and technological systems without excessive dependence on external actors or foreign powers (Misra et al., 2025). It is commonly understood through four interrelated dimensions: data sovereignty, technological autonomy, cybersecurity, and regulatory control. Data sovereignty ensures that data generated within a national territory is stored, processed, and governed under domestic jurisdiction, thereby limiting foreign access and external authority. Technological autonomy reduces reliance on foreign technologies and vendors that may be subject to external legislation, sanctions, or political influence. Cybersecurity focuses on protecting national digital infrastructures from cyberattacks, surveillance, and manipulation, while regulatory control encompasses legal mechanisms for ensuring data privacy, intellectual property protection, and responsible content governance (Misra et al., 2025).

These key aspects have been illustrated in figure 1 to show the various challenges arising from digital sovereignty in Industry 5.0.

Figure 1.

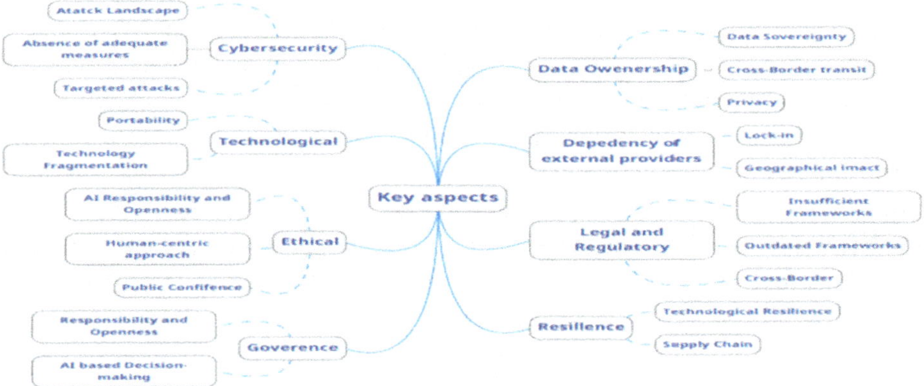

Source: (Misra et al. 2025)

The intensification of digitalization particularly through advances in artificial intelligence (AI) has transformed data into a strategic asset that extends beyond economic value to influence political power, governance capacity, and geopolitical positioning. As digital ecosystems expand, complex networks of public and private actors collect, process, and exchange vast quantities of data to extract value. However, this transformation has heightened concerns surrounding privacy, ownership, and sovereignty, as individuals typically lack meaningful control over the personal data they generate. Consequently, effective data governance, cybersecurity management, and privacy protection frameworks have become essential for safeguarding digital identities, regulating access, and maintaining trust in digital systems (Misra et al., 2025).

These governance challenges are further amplified in the context of Industry 5.0, where autonomous digital architectures and interconnected ecosystems underpin critical sectors such as manufacturing, logistics, and supply chains. Recent studies highlight the need for more comprehensive policy frameworks capable of enhancing trust, accountability, and sovereignty across these mission-critical infrastructures (Misra et al., 2025). Similar concerns extend to the transportation sector, where large-scale citizen data collection is increasingly used to improve mobility services and reduce greenhouse gas emissions. For example, Bokolo (2025) demonstrates how data-driven urban mobility initiatives in Norway rely on local community data while simultaneously raising new sovereignty concerns (Bokolo, 2025). This research identifies emerging dimensions of digital sovereignty, including software sovereignty, operational sovereignty, and contextualised data sovereignty, which are shaped by organisational structures, governance cultures, and institutional norms.

To address these challenges, Bokolo (2025) proposes the deployment of data spaces as a practical mechanism for reinforcing digital sovereignty at the community level. Data spaces provide a structured digital ecosystem in which data owner, such as citizens can define the conditions governing data access, usage, and sharing. This approach enhances transparency, ensures data quality and provenance, and establishes a trusted environment for both data providers and users, including mobility service providers and third parties. By enabling controlled data sharing, data spaces support smarter mobility solutions such as real-time traffic management, intelligent routing, intermodal transport coordination, and on-demand services.

Beyond mobility, both the manufacturing and logistics sectors increasingly require transparent, interoperable, and legally compliant data governance frameworks. Jahnke (2025) proposes an edge-computing-enabled data value chain that spans data acquisition, preparation, information extraction, delivery, and usage. While this framework illustrates how economic value can be systematically derived from data, it also underscores implementation challenges, including skills development, legal compliance, standardisation, and the integration of open-source technologies .

At the macro level, digital sovereignty is closely intertwined with national security, economic resilience, and political stability. Lin (2025) argues that weaknesses in data governance can expose states to risks such as data breaches, misuse, and external control, which may undermine national interests across political, economic, and cultural domains. Addressing these risks requires strengthening domestic data protection regulations, reinforcing technological autonomy, and promoting international cooperation to balance innovation with security. Collectively, these findings underscore the urgency of developing robust, trust-centred digital policy frameworks that recognise data sovereignty as a foundational pillar of sustainable digital transformation.

Through expert consultation and active collaboration, institutions can work together to form a global ethical framework that will guide the decision-making processes of AI and digital integration more smoothly. Global AI policy should exists at all level of management within all sector putting priority of public interest into perspective. Decisions made at global level organizations such as United Nations Sustainable Development Goals can be made to be more inclusive and oriented toward collective well-being. At the individual level, sovereignty involves the capacity to exercise agency over personal data. However, this agency is often constrained by structural factors, including platform dominance and algorithmic control.

As time progresses, technological advancements continue at an unrelenting pace, fundamentally altering the fabric of life as previously known. Traditional social interactions are increasingly supplanted by technological devices, with artificial intelligence and digital media exerting significant influence on the cognitive development of the future generations. This phenomenon gradually erodes the collective human experience once characterized by mutual understandng and trust. The question arises whether it is feasible to restore this way of life or if humanity has already lost sight of its core values. Life encompasses more than mere productivity, ease of access to information, or personalized corporate social responsibility. According to Couldry & Mejas (2019), data-driven digital systems amount to a new form of colonialism, in which everyday human life is continuously extracted, measured, and appropriated for profit. Couldry and Mejias show how this "data colonialism" reshapes power, social relations, and inequality, calling for critical resistance and alternative futures (Couldry & Mejas, 2019).

Reports have shown increasing awareness that the adverse effects of artificial intelligence (AI) will permeate not only economic systems but also social, environmental, cultural, spiritual, and psychological dimensions of life. One of the most pressing concerns is the widening inequality in the workplace, where those with advanced AI skills are rapidly pulling ahead of others. As highlighted by Rebecca Bellan (2026), the emergence of an "AI skills gap" suggests that power users and technologically proficient individuals are able to leverage AI tools to significantly enhance productivity and decision-making, while others are left behind. This creates a stratified labour market in which access to opportunity is increasingly determined by digital and AI literacy rather than traditional qualifications alone.

In higher education, similar disruptions are becoming evident. Michael Scott (2026) notes that universities are being reshaped by multiple converging forces, including AI, which challenge conventional teaching, assessment, and knowledge production practices. The growing use of AI-generated content raises concerns about academic integrity, originality, and the authenticity of learning. This is further reinforced by findings discussed by Julia Krywko (2026), who reports that AI systems have already demonstrated the ability to generate scientific papers capable of passing elements of peer review. Such developments call into question the reliability and value of intellectual capital in an era where machine-generated knowledge may become indistinguishable from human scholarship.

Beyond institutional and economic implications, AI also introduces psychological and cognitive risks. Increased reliance on AI tools may lead to reduced critical thinking, overdependence on automated systems, and a gradual erosion of human intellectual autonomy. From a broader perspective, these trends suggest that AI is not merely a neutral technological advancement but a transformative force that reshapes how knowledge is created, validated, and utilized.

Artificial intelligence, akin to plastic, represents a highly productive innovation that facilitates ease and progress. However, in the long term, it emerges as a disruptive force, supplanting work tasks and employees, replacing repetitive and routine functions, and, in some instances, encroaching upon higher cognitive abilities, thereby significantly undermining human capabilities. If artificial intelligence diminishes our cognitive and productive capacities, what implications does this hold for the sanctity of human intellect in the long term? The sustainability of human thought and ethical considerations are crucial in addressing the ethical challenges posed by artificial intelligence.

Without careful governance, ethical oversight, and inclusive capacity-building, AI risks amplifying existing inequalities across work, education, and intellectual domains. This underscores the urgent need for a holistic and value-driven approach to AI development—one that safeguards not only economic efficiency but also human dignity, social equity, and sustainable knowledge systems.

Across the studies it can be seen that there is a lack of an integrated, cross-sectoral framework that connects digital sovereignty, artificial intelligence adoption, and environmental sustainability. While these studies offer valuable domain-specific insights—ranging from AI implementation challenges in healthcare to plastic waste management and circular economy innovations—they largely remain siloed within technological, environmental, or policy perspectives. There is limited effort to synthesize how digital systems (e.g., AI, data governance) intersect with material sustainability challenges (e.g., plastic waste, energy systems), nor how these interactions impact broader socio-cultural and ethical dimensions. Furthermore, although governance and implementation barriers are discussed, there is insufficient attention to normative and value-based considerations, particularly those addressing long-term human well-being, equity, and moral responsibility.

In light of these gaps, there is a strong need for an ethical framework to govern the implications identified across these studies. Issues of data sovereignty and national security (Li, 2025), as well as digital sovereignty in Industry 5.0 (Misra et al., 2025), highlight the tension between technological advancement and control over data, raising concerns about privacy, autonomy, and geopolitical power imbalances. Similarly, the implementation of AI in healthcare (Nair et al., 2025) underscores ethical challenges related to trust, accountability, and patient safety, particularly when systems are introduced without sufficient transparency or stakeholder readiness. In the environmental domain, studies on plastic waste gasification and recycling (Javed et al., 2025; Massoud & Dsilva, 2025) and the agricultural plastic paradox (Wang et al., 2025) reveal that technological "solutions" may simultaneously generate unintended ecological and health consequences if not governed responsibly. These findings collectively point to the necessity of a comprehensive ethical framework that integrates principles of sustainability, justice, accountability, and responsible stewardship across both digital and environmental systems.

The main concerns arising from these studies revolve around three interconnected issues. First is the risk of unintended consequences, where innovations designed to solve problems such as AI in healthcare or plastic recycling technologies—may introduce new risks, including system inefficiencies, environmental trade-offs, or health hazards. Second is the issue of governance and control, particularly in relation to data sovereignty, where unequal access to digital infrastructure and regulatory capacity may exacerbate global and local inequalities. Third is the challenge of implementation, as barriers such as organizational readiness, lack of trust, and infrastructural limitations hinder the effective and ethical adoption of AI systems. Together, these concerns highlight a broader systemic issue: the acceleration of technological and sustainability innovations without parallel development in ethical governance and holistic oversight. This underscores the urgent need for interdisciplinary and value-driven approaches to ensure that advancements in both digital and environmental domains contribute to genuinely sustainable and equitable outcomes.

Lessons from the Plastic Crisis

Plastic pollution remains one of the most visible consequences of unsustainable production, with profound impacts on marine ecosystems and public health (Rhodes, 2018). The uncontrolled accumulation of plastic waste is widely regarded as one of the most pressing environmental challenges of our time. Plastics are primarily synthesized from hydrocarbon monomers derived from non-renewable fossil fuels, commonly referred to as "virgin" feedstock. As a result, most plastics are non-biodegradable, leading to their long-term accumulation in oceans and terrestrial ecosystems, where they can persist almost indefinitely (Massoud & Dsilva, 2025). According to the United Nations, the global material footprint increased by 70% between 2000 and 2017; approximately one million plastic bottles are purchased every minute, and nearly five trillion single-use plastic bags are discarded annually worldwide (Massoud & Dsilva, 2025). Landfilling, which accounts for more than 60% of global plastic waste disposal, contributes significantly to soil and groundwater contamination through toxic leachates and methane emissions (Javed et al., 2025). In response to these challenges, stakeholders are increasingly urged to adopt the 3R model—Reduce, Reuse, and Recycle—as a key strategy for mitigating the environmental and health risks associated with escalating plastic waste (Massoud & Dsilva, 2025).

Similarly, research examining the use of plastics in agriculture highlights a complex balance between their potential contributions to the Sustainable Development Goals (SDGs) and their associated environmental trade-offs. Identified risks include microplastic contamination of food and soil, increased plastic waste generation, greenhouse gas emissions, water pollution, and long-term degradation of soil quality. Nevertheless, when weighed against these drawbacks, plastics continue to offer cost-effective solutions in agriculture, particularly through the application of plastic film mulching (PFM). Consequently, policy recommendations emphasize the need for a balanced approach that ensures environmental and social costs do not outweigh the economic benefits (Wang et al., 2025).

Another arising issue reported by AI systems, particularly large-scale machine learning models, require substantial cooling mechanisms that depend heavily on freshwater resources. As highlighted by reports in Al-Jazeera by Shabana (2026), major technology firms have reported significant water withdrawals in regions already experiencing water stress. For instance, Microsoft indicated that approximately 41% of its water withdrawals occurred in water-stressed areas, while Google reported that 15% of its water consumption took place in highly water-scarce regions. These patterns suggest that digital sovereignty strategies, if centred on domestic infrastructure expansion, may exacerbate environmental degradation rather than mitigate it (Shabana,

2026). Consequently, while digital sovereignty promises economic and technological empowerment, it may simultaneously generate ecological imbalance and social vulnerability if not governed through a sustainability-oriented framework.

In recognition of these limitations, recent research has increasingly focused on alternative approaches to plastics. Despite their historical significance as a transformative innovation, future research directions prioritize the development of sustainable materials to reduce reliance on conventional, chemically based plastics. This includes growing investments in organic-based bioplastics aimed at addressing the environmental impacts of traditional plastic production (Khan et al., 2025) Additionally, remedial strategies such as gasification have been explored, despite their complexity and high costs. One study, for example, investigates the feasibility of converting non-recyclable plastics into syngas, with potential applications in electricity generation and synthetic fuel production (Javed et al., 2025).

Rhodes (2018), provides a comprehensive overview of the global plastic crisis, detailing the environmental and health impacts of the 8.3 billion tonnes of plastic ever produced and evaluating potential solutions such as recycling, incineration, and the development of sustainable alternatives. This broad challenge is contextualized by Giovannoni and Fabietti (2013), who review the concept of sustainability and explain that it integrates environmental, social, and economic dimensions in order to achieve long-term development. Their study highlights that sustainability requires responsible consumption and behavioral changes in society, which supports initiatives that encourage environmentally friendly practices such as reducing plastic use and adopting reusable products.

From environmental aspect and perspective, Qaisrani et al. (2020) show that plastic debris constitutes most of the waste found on beaches, and it is due to human activities such as tourism and improper disposal practices. This highlights the urgency of implementing effective waste management strategies and promoting sustainable behaviors at the community level.

Finally, to sum up, the synthesis of the literature highlights a recurring paradox: innovations designed to enhance efficiency and productivity often generate unintended environmental and systemic harms. For instance, the "agricultural plastic paradox" identified by Wang et al. demonstrates how plastic use increases food production while simultaneously degrading ecosystems. Similarly, circular solutions such as PET recycling (Massoud & Dsilva, 2025) and biodegradable plastics from marine biomass (Khan et al., 2025) attempt to mitigate waste but remain constrained by scalability, economic feasibility, and lifecycle trade-offs. Even advanced approaches like plastic waste gasification for energy recovery (Javed et al., 2025) reveal tensions between environmental sustainability and resource intensiveness. Collectively, these studies emphasize that sustainability challenges are not solely technological but systemic, involving governance, consumption patterns, and long-term externalities. However, a key research gap lies in the limited translation of these insights into the digital domain, where data—like plastic—has become abundant, extractive, and insufficiently governed. Current discussions on digital sovereignty and data governance rarely draw from sustainability transitions observed in material ecosystems. Bridging this gap, the plastic literature can inform digital sustainability by highlighting the need for lifecycle thinking, circular data practices, ethical stewardship, and anticipatory governance to prevent the emergence of "digital pollution" and ensure that data-driven innovation remains environmentally, socially, and ethically sustainable.

The plastic crisis demonstrates the consequences of ignoring ethical and ecological limits. Islamic sustainability principles reinforce the importance of early intervention (preventing fasād), balanced systems (mīzān) and responsible consumption (avoidance of isrāf). These principles provide a normative foundation for proactive digital governance.

Spiritual and Ethical Dimensions

A key limitation of contemporary digital governance frameworks lies in their insufficient engagement with the spiritual and ethical dimensions of human development. Islamic-based development offers a more holistic framework that integrates both material and non-material aspects of well-being, expanding sustainability beyond purely technical or economic considerations (Al-Jayyousi, 2016; Al-Jayyousi et al., 2022). Within Islamic thought, human development is understood not only in terms of physical and cognitive capacities but also through spiritual intelligence, encompassing self-awareness, ethical reasoning, and transcendental consciousness. These qualities foster resilience, empathy, accountability, and moral responsibility attributes that are increasingly recognized as essential competencies in the AI-driven future of work and ethical technology governance (Al-Jayyousi, 2016; Jobin et al., 2019). Central to this worldview is the concept of *amanah* (trust), which holds that all resources are entrusted to humanity and must be managed responsibly. Applied to digital governance, data can therefore be conceptualized as a moral trust rather than a neutral commodity, reframing data management from a purely technical concern into an ethical obligation that extends accountability beyond regulatory compliance to spiritual and societal responsibility (Al-Jayyousi et al., 2022; Al-Jayyousi et al., 2023).

Viewed through Islamic sustainability principles, the analogy between plastic pollution and digital harm becomes increasingly salient. Digital overproduction reflects *isrāf* (wastefulness), a practice explicitly discouraged in Islamic teachings, as excessive data generation—much like material overconsumption—contributes to cognitive overload, diminished well-being, and systemic imbalance (Al-Jayyousi, 2016). Likewise, algorithmic bias, misinformation, and manipulative digital practices can be understood as contemporary manifestations of *fasād* (corruption), undermining social justice, trust, and institutional legitimacy. This interpretation aligns with the principle of *mīzān* (balance), which emphasizes equilibrium across economic, environmental, and social systems (Al-Jayyousi et al., 2023). Furthermore, the homogenizing effects of global digital platforms threaten cultural diversity and communal identity. Islamic sustainability responds to this challenge by emphasizing the preservation of communities (*umam*) and the cultivation of balanced societies (*ummah wasat*), reinforcing moderation, pluralism, and ethical restraint as essential foundations for sustainable digital futures (Al-Jayyousi, 2016; Al-Jayyousi et al., 2022).

RETHINKING DIGITAL SUSTAINABILITY TOWARDS ETHICAL DATA STEWARDSHIP

The development of ethical data stewardship frameworks requires integrating insights from both sustainability and AI governance literature.

Recent studies emphasize the importance of trustworthy data systems (Marteau et al., 2025), user empowerment in digital systems (Anshari et al., 2021) and AI-informed policymaking (Yar et al., 2024).

To move beyond conventional frameworks, digital sustainability must incorporate multi-dimensional principles derived from Islamic-governance. The most recent developments by Thoha (2026) have ntroduced a framework known as The Green Khalifah Leadership Framework embodies a civilisational response to modernity's ethical vacuum. It reclaims moral coherence where secular modernism produced fragmentation and restores divine intentionality where technocracy bred alienation. By integrating taw īd, adab, maqā id and amānah, it transforms sustainability from managerial rhetoric into sacred stewardship (Thoha 2026). While the GKL-F offers a normatively coherent model grounded in taw īd, moral formation, and maqā id-based governance, its translation into contemporary political reality is neither automatic nor immune to contestation. Any attempt to re-anchor governance in metaphysical principles must confront historical, jurisprudential, and political complexities (Thoha 2026).

This chapter on the other hand contributes a framework based on the analysis of the works of Jayyousi (2016) which can be illustrated in the following framework:

Figure 2. Ethical framework

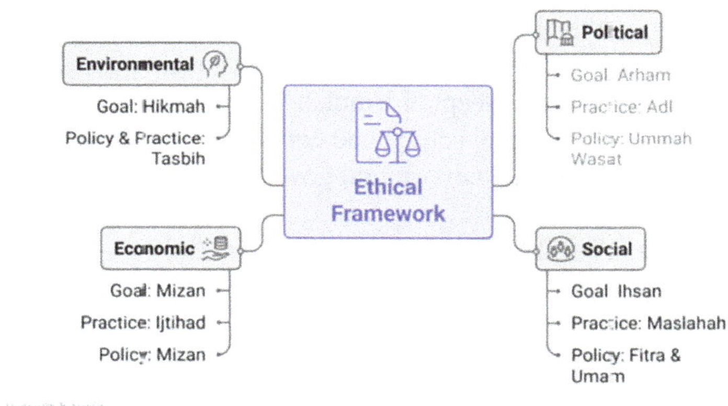

The model illustrated in the figure integrates political, social, economic, and environmental dimensions into the governance of digital sovereignty with the overarching objective of achieving digital sustainability. Unlike conventional sustainability frameworks that predominantly focus on Environmental, Social, and Governance (ESG) indicators, this model explicitly incorporates the political dimension as a foundational element. The inclusion of political ethics is critical, as digital sustainability necessitates responsible collaboration, collective accountability, and trust among diverse actors operating across national and institutional boundaries. Earlier sustainability models often neglect these political responsibilities, thereby limiting their effectiveness in addressing complex digital governance challenges (Al-Jayyousi, 2016; Al-Jayyousi et al., 2022).

Grounded in Islamic worldviews, the framework advances a values-based governance approach that aligns material development with ethical responsibility, spiritual consciousness, and social justice. In doing so, it resonates with Islamic conceptions of sustainable development that emphasize moral purpose (maqasid), balance (mizan), and stewardship (khilafah) as essential principles guiding human interactions with technology, society, and the environment (Al-Jayyousi, 2016).

Political Dimension: Justice and Responsible Collaboration

The political pillar of the framework is oriented toward the goal of Arham, which emphasizes interconnectedness, solidarity, and responsible collaboration among actors. In the context of digital sovereignty, this entails cooperation between states, institutions, and technology stakeholders to ensure ethical data governance and equitable access to digital infrastructure.

The principal practice guiding this dimension is Adl (justice), which serves as an ethical imperative to ensure fairness, transparency, and accountability in digital governance. Justice, within Islamic ethics, is not merely legal compliance but a moral obligation to prevent harm and protect collective rights (Al-Jayyousi et al., 2023). At the policy level, the concept of Ummah Wasat (the balanced or moderate community) encourages tolerance, equity, and cooperation, fostering global alignment toward responsible and inclusive digital governance.

Social Dimension: Welfare, Ethics, and Stewardship

The social dimension is anchored in the goal of Ihsan, which calls for excellence, ethical conduct, and moral intentionality in digital innovation and production. Ethical design, responsible use of digital technologies, and inclusive innovation reflect Ihsan by prioritizing human dignity and societal well-being over purely profit-driven objectives.

The key practice supporting this goal is Maslahah, which prioritizes public interest and collective welfare. In digital contexts, Maslahah demands that technological development enhances social good, reduces harm, and addresses societal vulnerabilities, especially in marginalized communities (Al-Jayyousi et al., 2022).

At the policy level, two complementary concepts are emphasized. Fitra underscores sustainable productivity and the cyclical use of resources, aligning digital systems with natural limits and long-term resilience. Umam emphasizes the preservation of biodiversity and responsible stewardship, extending ethical concern beyond human societies to ecological systems. Together, these policies reinforce a socially responsible framework that embeds sustainability into the cultural and moral fabric of digital governance.

Economic Dimension: Balance and Adaptive Reasoning

Economically, the framework is guided by the goal of Mizan, which represents balance and proportionality in the distribution of wealth and resources. In the digital economy, Mizan implies equitable access to data, fair digital markets, and the avoidance of excessive concentration of digital power.

The practice of Ijtihad plays a central role in this dimension. As a form of continuous ethical reasoning, Ijtihad enables adaptive responses to emerging digital challenges, such as artificial intelligence governance, data monopolies, and cross-border data flows. Through Ijtihad, Islamic ethics remain dynamic and responsive, allowing economic growth to coexist with social justice and ecological sustainability (Al-Jayyousi, 2016).

At the policy level, Mizan again functions as a guiding principle, ensuring that economic progress is balanced with environmental protection and social responsibility. This integrative approach challenges extractive digital economic models and promotes sustainable value creation.

Environmental Dimension: Wisdom and Spiritual Consciousness

The environmental dimension is framed around the goal of Hikmah (wisdom), which calls for ethical consumption and decision-making grounded in knowledge, foresight, and moral responsibility. Hikmah encourages restraint and thoughtful engagement with digital technologies, recognizing their material and environmental footprints.

The associated practices of Tasbih and Tazkiyyah al-Nafs emphasize spiritual consciousness, self-purification, and moderation. These practices cultivate ethical awareness and humility, countering overconsumption and exploitation fostered by unchecked technological growth (Al-Jayyousi et al., 2023).

At the policy level, Tasbih promotes compassion and reverence for creation, reinforcing the understanding that environmental stewardship is a moral and spiritual duty rather than a purely technical obligation.

Interrelationships Among the Dimensions

The strength of this framework lies in the interdependence of its components. Political justice (Adl) underpins social welfare (Maslahah), ensuring that digital policies protect both society and nature. Social aspirations of Ihsan are directly linked to economic Mizan, as ethical innovation must be accompanied by fair distribution and access. Economic Ijtihad provides the adaptive reasoning necessary to balance material growth with ecological limits. Finally, environmental Hikmah and Tasbih ensure that consumption and innovation remain spiritually guided, reinforcing political accountability and social stewardship.

Across diverse socio-economic and geopolitical contexts, governance models may differ in their institutional design. However, one element remains universal: trust. By embedding trust through justice, ethics, balance, and spiritual consciousness, the framework addresses a persistent challenge in digital governance identified within sustainability and climate discourse (Al-Jayyousi et al., 2022; Al-Jayyousi et al., 2023).

Integrated Intended Outcomes of the Model: Islamic Ethics, Digital Sovereignty, and Digital Sustainability

The intended outcomes of this model extend beyond normative ethical guidance and aim to operationalize digital sovereignty as an enabler of digital sustainability. By embedding Islamic ethical principles within contemporary technological and governance frameworks, the model responds directly to emerging challenges in the data economy, Industry 5.0, and smart urban systems, where sovereignty, trust, and sustainability are increasingly interdependent.

1. Ethical Digital Sovereignty for Sustainable Data Infrastructures

First, the model advances a holistic framework for digital sovereignty that aligns technological governance with ethical responsibility. Recent literature highlights that digital sovereignty is no longer limited to control over infrastructure or national data localization but encompasses the ability of societies and organizations to govern data flows responsibly, transparently, and sustainably (Jahnke et al., 2025; Babel, 2025). This framework reinforces that perspective by grounding sovereignty in justice (Adl), balance (Mizan), and public welfare (Maslahah), thereby linking technical control to moral accountability.

In the context of emerging edge computing architectures, the framework complements technical solutions by providing ethical oversight. While edge computing enhances sovereignty by decentralizing data processing and reducing dependency on centralized cloud providers (Jahnke et al., 2025), the Islamic ethical lens ensures that these architectures are governed in ways that protect societal interests, environmental sustainability, and trust. This ethical anchoring responds directly to concerns raised by Babel (2025) regarding data verifiability, accountability, and transparency in digital sustainability infrastructures.

2. Supporting Industry 5.0 and Human-Centric Innovation

Second, the model contributes to Industry 5.0 discourse by reinforcing the shift toward human-centric, sustainable, and resilient digital systems. Misra, Barik, and Kvalvik (2025) emphasize that digital sovereignty in Industry 5.0 must balance advanced automation with human values, social inclusion, and ecological responsibility. The integration of Ihsan (ethical excellence) and Ijtihad (adaptive reasoning) within this framework enables continuous ethical reflection as technologies evolve, ensuring that innovation remains aligned with human dignity and environmental limits.

By positioning Ijtihad as a mechanism for adaptive governance, the model addresses the dynamic challenges posed by artificial intelligence, cyber-physical systems, and autonomous decision-making. This allows organizations and policymakers to interpret ethical principles in response to new technological contexts while maintaining coherence with long-term sustainability objectives (Al-Jayyousi, 2016; Misra et al., 2025).

3. Enhancing Smart Cities and Local Digital Sovereignty

Third, the framework supports localized digital sovereignty initiatives, particularly in smart cities and community-based digital ecosystems. Bokolo (2025) demonstrates that digital sovereignty is essential for enabling smarter mobility solutions and data-driven services that reflect local needs, values, and governance priorities. By emphasizing Maslahah (public interest) and Ummah Wasat (balanced cooperation), the model ensures that smart systems serve communities rather than extract value from them.

This approach reinforces trust between citizens, local authorities, and digital service providers—an issue frequently identified as a barrier to smart city adoption. Ethical governance rooted in social justice and stewardship helps align digital infrastructure investments with societal well-being, environmental sustainability, and participatory governance (Bokolo, 2025; Al-Jayyousi et al., 2023).

4. Building Trust through Verifiability, Balance, and Spiritual Accountability

A fourth key outcome of the model is the institutionalization of trust as a foundational element of digital sustainability. Across diverse governance contexts, trust remains the only truly universal component of digital sovereignty. Babel (2025) emphasizes that digital sustainability infrastructures must reconcile data verifiability with sovereignty, ensuring that data is not only controlled but also auditable, transparent, and credible.

The Islamic ethical emphasis on Hikmah (wisdom) and Tasbih (spiritual consciousness) strengthens this trust by embedding accountability beyond regulatory compliance. Ethical self-restraint, moderation, and reverence for creation ensure that governance decisions are not purely transactional but morally grounded. This reinforces political justice, social stewardship, and responsible economic behavior across borders and institutional settings (Al-Jayyousi et al., 2022; 2023).

5. Harmonizing Human, Technological, and Ecological Systems

Finally, the model promotes systemic harmony between human development, technological progress, ecological preservation, and spiritual growth. Rather than treating digital sovereignty as a technocratic or securitized objective, the framework redefines it as a civilizational responsibility. It integrates political accountability, social welfare, economic balance, and environmental ethics into a unified governance model capable of supporting long-term digital sustainability.

In doing so, the framework aligns with contemporary digital sovereignty scholarship while offering a distinctive normative contribution rooted in Islamic worldviews. It demonstrates that sustainable digital futures require not only advanced technologies and regulatory instruments, but also ethical foundations capable of sustaining trust, cooperation, and responsibility across generations.

CONCLUSION

This chapter has examined the contemporary challenges of digital sovereignty through insights drawn from recent literature. These challenges reveal striking parallels with those historically associated with the rise of plastic—initially celebrated as a symbol of innovation and efficiency, yet later recognized for its unintended long-term consequences. Similarly, while digital technologies have significantly contributed to corporate advancement, productivity, and economic growth, concerns surrounding sustainability and ethical governance have become increasingly prominent.

Digital sovereignty, therefore, should not be understood merely as a governance objective. Rather, it represents a multi-dimensional tension between technological autonomy, economic dependency, and ethical responsibility within a globally interconnected digital ecosystem. This tension is further complicated by competing demands between control and openness, localization and global integration, and independence and structural reliance on dominant technological infrastructures.

In response, this chapter proposes a value-based framework grounded in Islamic principles, which may also be adapted and universalized for broader, non-Islamic contexts. By emphasizing ethical stewardship, accountability, and balance, the framework offers an alternative lens through which digital sovereignty can be pursued in a more sustainable and human-centered manner.

Nevertheless, this chapter has several limitations. Its primary focus has been on data governance and the institutional management of digital infrastructures. Other critical dimensions such as educational systems, intellectual governance, and the role of human capital in shaping digital sovereignty have not been fully explored.

Future research should therefore extend this discussion by examining skills-based frameworks and capacity development strategies that align with the ethical and sustainability challenges of digital sovereignty. Such frameworks could serve as practical guidelines for policymakers, educators, and institutional stakeholders, equipping them with the necessary competencies to anticipate, navigate, and govern the evolving digital landscape in a responsible and sustainable manner.

REFERENCES

Al-Jayyousi, O., Hasan, W. N. W., Mohamed Saniff, S., Sever, S. D., & Tok, E. (2023). A critical discourse analysis on climate change in a globalized world: The nexus of Islam and sustainable development. *Sustainability (Basel)*, *15*(19), 14515. DOI: 10.3390/su151914515

Al-Jayyousi, O., Tok, E., Saniff, S. M., Wan Hasan, W. N., Janahi, N. A., & Yesuf, A. J. (2022). Re-thinking sustainable development within Islamic worldviews: A systematic literature review. *Sustainability (Basel)*, *14*(12), 7300. DOI: 10.3390/su14127300

Al-Jayyousi, O. R. (2016). *Islam and sustainable development: New worldviews*. Gower. DOI: 10.4324/9781315589947

Anshari, M., Almunawar, M. N., Shahrill, M., Wicaksono, D. K., & Huda, M. (2017). Smartphones usage in the classrooms: Learning aid or interference? *Education and Information Technologies*, *22*(6), 3063–3079. DOI: 10.1007/s10639-017-9572-7

Anshari, M., Almunawar, M. N., Younis, M. Z., & Kisa, A. (2021). Modeling users' empowerment in e-health systems. *Sustainability (Basel)*, *13*(23), 12993. DOI: 10.3390/su132312993

Aragani, V. M., & Thirunagalingam, A. (2025). Leveraging advanced analytics for sustainable success. In *Advanced analytics and sustainable business transformation* (pp. 229–248). IGI Global Scientific Publishing., DOI: 10.4018/979-8-3693-9750-3.ch012

Azahari, L. M., Ahmad, F. A., & Mohamed Saniff, S. (2026). *Connecting employability and the future of work: A systematic review of global trends, employer expectations, and evolving recruitment strategies*. IGI Global. DOI: 10.4018/979-8-3373-4450-8.ch005

Bellan, R. (2026, March 26). The AI skills gap is here, says AI company, and power users are pulling ahead. *TechCrunch*. https://techcrunch.com/2026/03/25/the-ai-skills-gap-is-here-says-ai-company-and-power-users-are-pulling-ahead/

Bokolo, A. J. (2025). Implementing digital sovereignty to accelerate smarter mobility solutions in local communities. *Smart Cities*, *8*(4), 1–24. DOI: 10.3390/smartcities8040106

Couldry, N., & Mejias, U. A. (2019). *The costs of connection: How data is colonizing human life and appropriating it for capitalism*. Stanford University Press.

Javed, M. H., Ahmad, A., Rehan, M., Musharavati, F., Nizami, A. S., & Khan, M. I. (2025). Advancing sustainable energy: Environmental and economic assessment of plastic waste gasification for syngas and electricity generation using life cycle modeling. *Sustainability (Basel), 17*(3), 1277. Advance online publication. DOI: 10.3390/su17031277

Jobin, A., Ienca, M., & Vayena, E. (2019). AI ethics guidelines globally. *Nature Machine Intelligence, 1*(9), 389–399. DOI: 10.1038/s42256-019-0088-2

Khan, N., Sudhakar, K., & Mamat, R. (2025). Biodegradable plastics from marine biomass: A solution to marine plastic pollution. *Journal of Hazardous Materials Advances, 17*, 100559. DOI: 10.1016/j.hazadv.2024.100559

Krywko, J. (2026, March 27). AI wrote a scientific paper that passed peer review. *Scientific American*. https://www.scientificamerican.com/article/ai-wrote-a-scientific-paper-that-passed-peer-review/

Marteau, B., ... (2025). Trustworthy AI data systems. *arXiv*. https://doi.org//arXiv.2512.03098DOI: 10.48550

Massoud, T., & Dsilva, J. (2025). Closing the PET plastic recycling loop: A sustainable transformation from plastic to fiber. *Next Sustainability, 6*, 100095. DOI: 10.1016/j.nxsust.2024.100095

Misra, S., Barik, K., & Kvalvik, P. (2025). Digital sovereignty in the era of Industry 5.0: Challenges and opportunities. *Procedia Computer Science, 254*, 108–117. DOI: 10.1016/j.procs.2025.02.069

Nair, M., Nygren, J., Nilsen, P., Gama, F., Neher, M., Larsson, I., & Svedberg, P. (2025). Critical activities for successful implementation and adoption of AI in healthcare: Towards a process framework for healthcare organizations. *Frontiers in Digital Health, 7*, 1550459. Advance online publication. DOI: 10.3389/fdgth.2025.1550459 PMID: 40453810

Rhodes, C. J. (2018). Plastic pollution and solutions. *Science Progress, 101*(3), 207–260. DOI: 10.3184/003685018X15294876706211 PMID: 30025551

Scott, M. (2026, March 16). The three forces writing the future of higher education. *Australian Financial Review*. https://www.afr.com/work-and-careers/education/the-three-forces-writing-the-future-of-higher-education-20260315-p5oalr

Shabana, O. (2026, January 21). AI's growing thirst for water is becoming a public health risk. *Al Jazeera*. https://www.aljazeera.com/opinions/2026/1/21/ais-growing-thirst-for-water-is-becoming-a-public-health-risk

Thoha, A. M. (2026). Green leadership in development management: Synthesizing Islamic ethical paradigms and sustainability science. *AlIrsyad: Journal of Islamic and Contemporary Issues*, *11*(1), 1669–1688. DOI: 10.53840/alirsyad.v11i1.587

Wang, K., Liu, X., Chadwick, D. R., Yan, C., Reay, M., Ge, T., Ding, F., Wang, J., Qi, R., Xiao, M., Jiang, R., Chen, Y., Ma, J., Lloyd, C., Evershed, R. P., Luo, Y., Zhu, Y., Zhang, F., & Jones, D. L. (2025). The agricultural plastic paradox: Feeding more, harming more? *Environment International*, *198*, 109416. Advance online publication. DOI: 10.1016/j.envint.2025.109416 PMID: 40215920

Chapter 5

Developing an Islamic Theory for Managing Data Using Maqasid al-Shariah and Good Governance

Abdur Razzaq
http://orcid.org/0000-0002-8267-5700
Universitas Islam Negeri Raden Fatah Palembang, Indonesia

ABSTRACT

Contemporary data governance discourse is dominated by regulatory compliance models that emphasize procedural adherence over substantive ethical commitment. The study proposes an Islamic theory of data governance anchored in Maqasid al-Shariah, the five higher objectives of Islamic law, and the classical tradition of good governance. By systematically mapping each Maqasid objective to data governance imperatives, the study demonstrates how the protection of religion (Hifz al-Din), life (Hifz al-Nafs), intellect (Hifz al-Aql), lineage (Hifz al-Nasl), and wealth (Hifz al-Mal) can serve as normative pillars for governing the ethical use of personal, public, and sensitive data. The chapter further highlights on the Prophetic governance model and the administrative practices of the Rashidun Caliphate to derive principles of data stewardship, including Amanah (fiduciary responsibility), Musawah (equality of access), Ihsan (excellence and care), and Raqabah (oversight and accountability).

DOI: 10.4018/979-8-2600-2233-7.ch005

1. INTRODUCTION

The governance of data has emerged as one of the most consequential challenges of the contemporary digital era. From biometric surveillance systems deployed by governments to the harvesting of behavioural data by technology corporations, the question of who controls data, under what authority, and in accordance with what values, sits at the heart of twenty-first-century political economy. Yet the frameworks that currently dominate this discourse, ranging from the European Union's General Data Protection Regulation to national data protection statutes across the Global South, share a common architecture: they are fundamentally procedural in character, concerned primarily with compliance, consent mechanisms, and regulatory enforcement rather than with the deeper ethical commitments that ought to animate any serious account of data stewardship.

For Muslim societies in particular, this procedural orientation raises a fundamental problem. The wholesale importation of Western-centric regulatory models into Islamic polities not only bypasses rich traditions of ethical jurisprudence but frequently produces frameworks that are normatively thin, culturally alien, and practically ineffective. This chapter argues that an authentic Islamic theory of data governance must be constructed from within the intellectual tradition of Islamic law and ethics, most prominently from the framework of Maqasid al-Shariah, the higher objectives or purposes of the Shariah, first systematically articulated by the twelfth-century jurist al-Ghazali and further developed by al-Shatibi in the fourteenth century, and subsequently elaborated by contemporary scholars including Jasser Auda (2008, 2022).

The five classical objectives of the Maqasid, the protection of religion (Hifz al-Din), life (Hifz al-Nafs), intellect (Hifz al-Aql), lineage (Hifz al-Nasl), and wealth (Hifz al-Mal), offer a remarkably durable and flexible normative architecture. When mapped systematically onto the domain of data governance, these objectives yield a comprehensive ethical framework capable of addressing the full spectrum of contemporary data challenges: from the surveillance of religious minorities and the commodification of health data, to algorithmic manipulation of public discourse and the exploitation of children's digital identities. The framework is not merely analogical but genuinely normative, grounding specific governance mandates in the teleological structure of Islamic jurisprudence.

Alongside the Maqasid framework, this chapter draws on classical Islamic models of good governance, particularly the administrative practices of the Rashidun Caliphate and the Prophetic model of stewardship, to derive governance principles directly applicable to data management. The concept of Amanah as fiduciary trust, the Hisbah tradition of institutional oversight, and the Shura principle of consultative governance together constitute a rich vocabulary for data governance that predates modern regulatory theory by over a millennium. This legacy represents an intellectual resource of considerable potential for Muslim societies seeking to navigate digital transformation on their own terms.

The chapter is structured as follows. Section 2 situates the argument within existing scholarly literature on data governance and Islamic ethics. Section 3 presents the Maqasid framework and its systematic mapping to data governance imperatives. Section 4 develops the classical governance principles as stewardship norms. Section 5 discusses the practical architecture of an Islamic data governance system, including a visual mapping of the proposed framework. Section 6 addresses the relationship between the proposed theory and existing global frameworks including the GDPR. The chapter concludes with reflections on the broader significance of Islamic data governance for digital transformation in Muslim societies, engaging with the strategic dimensions of resilience in the context of digital ecosystems and economic sustainability (Anshari, 2026).

2. DATA GOVERNANCE BETWEEN PROCEDURE AND ETHICS

2.1 The Limits of Compliance-Based Governance

The dominant paradigm in contemporary data governance is essentially regulatory-procedural. The GDPR, widely considered the gold standard of data protection law, centres on consent, transparency, purpose limitation, data minimisation, and accountability. These are not trivial principles; their adoption represents a substantial improvement over the permissive data practices that preceded them. Nevertheless, as several scholars have noted, the GDPR model conflates legal compliance with ethical governance, producing a form of data protection that can be satisfied through bureaucratic processes without any genuine commitment to the values that motivated the regulation in the first place (Floridi, 2018; Zuboff, 2019).

The problem is not merely procedural but philosophical. Data governance models derived from liberal political philosophy tend to privilege individual consent as the foundational mechanism of data protection. From an Islamic perspective, this individualism is ethically incomplete. Islam understands the human person not as an atomised rights-bearer but as a social being embedded in relations of family, community, and ultimately, before God. Data about a person is simultaneously data about their family, their community, and in the case of sensitive religious or ethnic data, about an entire collectivity. An ethics of data governance that does not account for these collective dimensions is, from an Islamic normative standpoint, structurally deficient (Mohadi & Tarshany, 2023; *cf.* Kamali, 1999).

2.2 Islamic Ethics and Digital Governance

Discussion on Islamic approaches to digital ethics and data governance has increased in recent years. A number of contributions have examined the application of Maqasid al-Shariah to specific domains including Islamic finance (Bashori et al., 2024; Alhammadi et al., 2020), artificial intelligence (Mohadi & Tarshany, 2023; Mustapha, 2025), and fintech regulation (Maulidizen et al., 2024). The intersection of Maqasid with broader data governance questions, however, remains undertheorised.

Auda's (2008) foundational treatment of Maqasid as a systems approach to Islamic law provides the most robust philosophical basis for such an extension. By conceptualising the Maqasid not as a static list of protected goods but as a dynamic, interlocking system of purposive reasoning, Auda opens the way for their application to domains that classical jurists could not have anticipated. More recently, scholarship on Islamic AI ethics has begun to operationalise Maqasid principles as evaluative criteria for technological systems, though as noted by several reviewers, this work remains predominantly declarative rather than institutionally specific (Mustapha, 2025).

The governance dimension has received more attention in the Islamic finance literature, where scholars have examined how Maqasid-aligned institutional frameworks can be developed for Shariah governance boards and regulatory bodies (Ahmad, 2020; Alhammadi et al., 2020). What is notably absent is a systematic attempt to translate these insights into a general theory of data governance applicable across the full spectrum of public and private data practices. The present chapter aims to address that gap.

3. MAQASID AL-SHARIAH AS A FRAMEWORK FOR DATA GOVERNANCE

3.1 The Structure of the Maqasid

The Maqasid al-Shariah are the higher purposes or objectives that Islamic law is understood to serve. In their classical formulation, attributed in systematic form to al-Ghazali and elaborated by al-Shatibi, they comprise five essential human interests that the Shariah is designed to protect and promote: religion (Din), life (Nafs), intellect (Aql), lineage or progeny (Nasl), and wealth or property (Mal). These objectives are further stratified according to the degree of necessity, with the most essential classified as darurat (necessities), followed by hajiyyat (needs), and tahsiniyyat (improvements or refinements).

Contemporary scholars, notably Auda (2008, 2022), have argued persuasively that the Maqasid framework must be understood dynamically rather than statically, as a purposive jurisprudential methodology capable of generating new legal reasoning in response to novel circumstances. On this reading, the application of Maqasid to data governance is not a creative extrapolation but a natural extension of the framework's own logic: if the Shariah's purpose is to protect fundamental human interests, then the protection of those interests in the digital domain must fall within its scope.

3.2 Mapping the Maqasid to Data Governance Imperatives

Table 1 below presents a systematic mapping of each of the five Maqasid objectives to specific data governance imperatives, normative prohibitions or mandates, and practical governance mechanisms. The discussion that follows elaborates each mapping in detail.

Table 1. Mapping Maqasid al-Shariah to Data Governance Imperatives

Maqasid Objective	Data Governance Imperative	Normative Prohibition / Mandate	Practical Mechanism
Hifz al-Din (Protection of Religion)	Safeguard religious identity in digital contexts; prevent algorithmic bias against faith communities	Prohibition of data profiling targeting religious belief; protection of worship data	Faith-neutral AI systems; consent for religious data
Hifz al-Nafs (Protection of Life)	Ensure health and safety data are handled with the utmost care and not weaponized	Privacy of biometric, health, and location data; prohibition of harmful surveillance	Data minimization; purpose limitation
Hifz al-Aql (Protection of Intellect)	Guard cognitive autonomy; prevent algorithmic manipulation of reasoning and opinion	Right to informational autonomy; transparency in algorithmic decision-making	Explainability requirements; anti-manipulation standards
Hifz al-Nasl (Protection of Lineage)	Protect family and genetic data; safeguard children from digital exploitation	Heightened protection for genealogical and children's data; prohibition of kinship profiling	Strict consent for genetic data; children's data protection
Hifz al-Mal (Protection of Wealth)	Secure financial and economic data; prevent data-enabled fraud, exploitation and dispossession	Property rights over personal data; protection from data-driven financial exclusion	Data ownership frameworks; anti-monopoly data regulation

Source: Authors' own elaboration based on Auda (2008) and Mohadi & Tarshany (2023)

3.2.1 Hifz al-Din: The Protection of Religion

The protection of religion represents the first and most fundamental of the Maqasid objectives. In the context of data governance, this imperative translates most directly into the protection of religious identity data from surveillance, profiling, and discriminatory use. The use of algorithmic systems to identify, categorise, or target individuals on the basis of religious affiliation constitutes a direct threat to this objective, as does the collection and retention of data about religious practice, attendance at religious institutions, or consumption of religious content without the freely given and fully informed consent of the individual (Shamdi et al., 2022).

Less obviously but equally importantly, Hifz al-Din requires that digital environments not be designed in ways that systematically disadvantage or marginalise religious communities. Recommendation algorithms that suppress religious content, search engine architectures that demote religious sources, and social media moderation systems that apply differential standards to religious expression all represent forms of digital harm cognisable under this objective. An Islamic data governance framework grounded in this principle would impose strict purpose limitations on the collection of religious data and prohibit its use for any purpose other than that originally consented to by the data subject.

3.2.2 Hifz al-Nafs: The Protection of Life

The protection of life and physical integrity requires, in the data governance context, that health data, biometric data, and location data, which collectively constitute the most intimate and potentially life-affecting categories of personal information, be governed with the highest standard of care. The misuse of health data can directly determine whether an individual obtains insurance, employment, or medical treatment. The misuse of location data can enable intimate partner violence, state persecution, or targeted crime. Biometric data, uniquely, cannot be changed if compromised: its disclosure is permanent.

Hifz al-Nafs therefore supports a regime of heightened protection for these data categories analogous to, but normatively more grounded than, the special categories of personal data recognised in GDPR Article 9. From an Islamic perspective, the prohibition on causing harm (la darar wa la dirar) operates as a direct constraint on data practices that create foreseeable risks to life or physical integrity, whether through data breach, deliberate misuse, or negligent system design.

3.2.3 Hifz al-Aql: The Protection of Intellect

The objective of protecting the intellect has arguably its most important contemporary application in the governance of information systems that shape human cognition, opinion, and decision-making. The deployment of algorithmic systems for targeted manipulation of political opinion, the design of social media platforms to exploit cognitive vulnerabilities for purposes of engagement maximisation, and the use of personalisation algorithms to create epistemic filter bubbles all represent forms of assault on the rational agency of the individual that are cognisable as violations of Hifz al-Aql.

This objective thus provides an Islamic normative basis for requirements of algorithmic transparency, explainability, and anti-manipulation design that go considerably beyond anything currently required by Western data governance regimes. The concept of *gharar*, the prohibition on deceptive uncertainty, which is well-established in Islamic commercial law, can be extended naturally to cover deceptive data practices including dark patterns, hidden tracking, and opaque automated decision-making (Mohadi & Tarshany, 2023; Bashori et al., 2024).

3.2.4 Hifz al-Nasl: The Protection of Lineage

The protection of lineage and progeny translates most directly into heightened governance protections for family data, genetic data, and, critically, children's data. Genealogical and genetic information is not merely personal but familial: the disclosure of an individual's genetic profile necessarily discloses information about their biological relatives who have given no consent. This collective dimension of genetic data is poorly captured by individualist consent models but maps naturally onto the Islamic understanding of Nasl as a collective good to be protected.

Children's data represents a particularly sensitive case. The exploitation of children's digital identities, whether through behavioural profiling, targeted advertising, or the creation of persistent digital profiles that follow individuals from childhood into adulthood, constitutes a serious violation of this Maqasid objective. An Islamic data governance framework would impose strict age verification requirements, prohibit behavioural profiling of minors, and require the deletion of all children's data upon request on reaching adulthood.

3.2.5 Hifz al-Mal: The Protection of Wealth

The objective of protecting wealth addresses the economic dimensions of data governance with particular clarity. In a data-driven economy, personal data has acquired substantial economic value, a fact that sits uneasily with regulatory frameworks that treat data primarily as a privacy concern rather than a property matter. From an Islamic perspective, the appropriation of an individual's data for commercial purposes without fair compensation or meaningful consent represents a form of economic exploitation cognisable as a violation of Hifz al-Mal.

This analysis supports the emerging concept of data ownership and data dividends, the idea that individuals should have property rights over their personal data and should share in the value it generates, while also providing a normative basis for prohibiting data-enabled financial exclusion (Firmansyah et al., 2024). The use of data-driven scoring systems to deny individuals access to credit, insurance, or employment on grounds that reflect historical patterns of discrimination rather than individual risk constitutes a form of economic harm that Islamic jurisprudence, through the prohibition on *zulm* (injustice and oppression), is well-equipped to address (Bashori et al., 2024; Maulidizen et al., 2024).

4. CLASSICAL GOVERNANCE PRINCIPLES

4.1 The Prophetic Model and the Rashidun Tradition

The Islamic intellectual tradition does not confine its governance wisdom to abstract jurisprudential categories. The life of the Prophet Muhammad (peace be upon him) and the administrative practices of his successors, particularly the first four Caliphs, constitute a rich tradition of practical governance from which specific norms of stewardship can be derived. These norms are not merely historical curiosities but carry normative authority within the Islamic tradition, representing the translation of divine guidance into institutional practice.

Several features of early Islamic governance are of particular relevance to contemporary data stewardship. The emphasis on Amanah, or trustworthy stewardship of public resources and information, is perhaps the most directly applicable. The Prophet's well-documented practice of maintaining the confidentiality of personal information entrusted to him, his prohibition on espionage and the invasion of privacy, and his insistence that those in positions of authority act as trustees rather than proprietors of communal resources all speak directly to the ethics of data management (Amiri, 2025).

4.2 Governance Principles for Data Stewardship

Table 2 below maps five classical Islamic governance principles to their data stewardship applications, identifying both their classical sources and their parallels in contemporary Western governance frameworks. The mapping reveals that Islamic governance principles, far from being parochial or archaic, anticipate and in some cases surpass the analytical sophistication of their modern counterparts.

Table 2. Classical Islamic Governance Principles and Their Data Stewardship Applications

Islamic Principle	Classical Source	Data Governance Application	Western Parallel
Amanah (Fiduciary Trust)	Rashidun administration / Prophetic model	Data stewards hold data as a sacred deposit, not a commodity to be monetized or shared without consent	GDPR Article 5(1)(b) purpose limitation; fiduciary data relationships
Musawah (Equality of Access)	Quranic principle of justice (Adl)	Equal rights of access, correction, and deletion of personal data regardless of socioeconomic status	Universal data rights; digital inclusion mandates
Ihsan (Excellence and Care)	Prophetic ethic of beneficence	Data systems must be designed to a standard of excellence; responsible innovation obligations	Privacy by design; proactive disclosure obligations
Raqabah (Oversight and Accountability)	Hisbah institution; Muhtasib oversight	Independent data oversight bodies with enforcement authority; prohibition of regulatory capture	Data Protection Authorities; Shariah-compliant audit
Shura (Consultative Governance)	Caliphal consultative council	Participatory data policy-making involving civil society, scholars, and affected communities	Multi-stakeholder governance forums; public consultation

Source: Authors' own elaboration based on Auda (2008, 2022), Mohadi & Tarshany (2023), and Amiri (2025)

4.2.1 Amanah: Data as a Sacred Deposit

The concept of Amanah, meaning trust or fiduciary obligation, is foundational to Islamic ethics. The Quran (33:72) speaks of humans as having accepted the *amanah*, the trust of moral responsibility, which creation itself refused to bear. In the data governance context, Amanah operates as a principle of fiduciary stewardship: those who collect, process, or store data about others do not become the owners of that data but its trustees. They bear an obligation to manage it solely in the interests of the data subject and the broader community, not for their own commercial or political gain.

This conception of data stewardship as fiduciary responsibility has recently gained traction in Western legal scholarship, with scholars arguing for the recognition of data fiduciaries with legally enforceable duties of loyalty to data subjects (Balkin, 2016; *cf.* Zuboff, 2019). The Islamic framework, however, grounds this obligation not merely in regulatory design but in theological anthropology: the data steward answers ultimately to God, not merely to a regulatory authority. This theological grounding provides a form of motivational force that regulatory compliance frameworks, dependent on external enforcement, systematically lack (Razzaq et al., 2023).

4.2.2 Raqabah and the Hisbah Tradition: Institutional Oversight

The classical Islamic institution of the *Hisbah*, administered by the *Muhtasib*, was a system of market and public conduct oversight charged with ensuring that economic and social activities conformed to Islamic ethical standards. While the institution has been much discussed in the context of Islamic finance, its relevance to data governance has been largely overlooked. The *Hisbah* tradition establishes a clear precedent for independent institutional oversight of powerful economic actors, including the authority to investigate complaints, impose sanctions, and require corrective action.

The principle of Raqabah, meaning oversight, surveillance of conduct, and accountability, translates naturally into the institutional design of data protection authorities. An Islamic framework would insist that such authorities be genuinely independent from both government and industry, possess adequate investigative and enforcement powers, and be staffed by individuals with both technical competence and ethical formation. The Muhtasib model further suggests that oversight functions should be proactive as well as reactive: the data oversight body should not merely respond to complaints but actively monitor data practices for conformity with normative standards.

4.2.3 Shura: Participatory Data Governance

The Shura principle, enshrined in the Quran (42:38) as a fundamental characteristic of the believing community, requires that collective decisions be made through genuine consultation. Applied to data governance, Shura implies a model of participatory policy-making in which the communities most affected by data practices, including civil society organisations, Islamic scholars, technology professionals, and representatives of vulnerable populations, are meaningfully involved in the design and review of governance frameworks (Haidi et al., 2023; Omar & Anshari, 2023).

This principle provides a direct Islamic warrant for the multi-stakeholder governance approaches increasingly favoured in international digital governance discourse, while adding a normatively distinctive requirement: that consultation be genuine rather than perfunctory, and that its outcomes actually shape governance decisions rather than merely legitimating predetermined ones. The participatory dimension of Shura also supports requirements for public consultation before the deployment of high-impact data systems such as automated scoring algorithms or mass biometric surveillance programmes (Hamdan et al., 2023).

5. TOWARD AN ARCHITECTURE OF ISLAMIC DATA GOVERNANCE

5.1 Institutional Design Implications

The normative framework articulated in the preceding sections implies a specific set of institutional design requirements for Islamic data governance. At minimum, it requires the establishment of independent data oversight bodies analogous to but more robustly conceived than existing data protection authorities; the development of Shariah-compliant data audit mechanisms capable of assessing compliance with Maqasid-grounded standards; the creation of data fiduciary frameworks that impose legally enforceable obligations on data processors; and the design of participatory governance processes that give communities genuine influence over data policy.

Beyond these minimum requirements, the framework points toward a more ambitious institutional architecture: one that integrates Islamic ethical expertise into the governance of digital systems through Shariah advisory structures analogous to those already established in the Islamic finance industry. Just as Islamic financial institutions are required to maintain Shariah supervisory boards empowered to evaluate financial products for compliance with Islamic principles, so data-intensive organisations operating in Muslim-majority contexts might be required to maintain data ethics panels with Islamic jurisprudential expertise.

5.2 Connection to Digital Economic Resilience

The governance framework proposed here is not merely an abstract ethical exercise. It has direct practical implications for the digital economic strategies of Muslim-majority states, a connection that deserves explicit attention. As Anshari (2024) has argued in the context of developing digital ecosystems for economic diversification, sustainable digital transformation in Muslim societies requires frameworks that are not only technically sophisticated but normatively grounded in local values and responsive to local vulnerabilities. A digital economy built on imported regulatory templates that sit uneasily with the ethical commitments of the societies they govern is inherently fragile; its legitimacy will always be contested, and its compliance rate likely to be shallow.

An Islamic data governance framework, by contrast, draws on moral resources that command genuine authority within Muslim societies. It can call upon the well-established Islamic obligation of Amanah to motivate genuine data stewardship behaviour, appeal to the Maqasid framework to justify restrictive data practices that might otherwise be resisted as economically inconvenient, and draw on the Shura tradition to build the inclusive stakeholder governance that effective digital policy requires. The normative depth of the Islamic framework is, from this perspective, not merely a philosophical virtue but a practical source of institutional resilience.

Muslim-majority states that have begun to develop comprehensive data protection frameworks, including Saudi Arabia's Personal Data Protection Law and Oman's Personal Data Protection Law of 2022, have largely proceeded by adaptation of Western models rather than by derivation from Islamic normative frameworks. While these efforts represent genuine progress, they miss an opportunity to develop governance architectures that are both effective and authentically grounded. The framework proposed in this chapter offers a constructive alternative: not a rejection of the useful technical insights embedded in Western regulatory models, but their systematic reconception within an Islamic normative architecture that can command genuine moral authority.

5.3 Challenges and Limitations

The framework proposed here faces several substantive challenges that must be acknowledged. The first is the diversity of opinion within Islamic jurisprudence itself: the Maqasid framework, while commanding broad acceptance across the major schools of Islamic law, admits of significant interpretive variation in its application. This variation is not a weakness unique to the Islamic framework, regulatory compliance models face analogous interpretive disputes, but it does mean that the implementation of Maqasid-based governance will require ongoing scholarly consultation and institutional mechanisms for the authoritative resolution of interpretive disputes.

A second challenge concerns the translation of normative principles into operational governance mechanisms. The principles of Amanah, Raqabah, and Shura are normatively rich but institutionally underspecified: they require substantial technical elaboration to be implemented as functional governance frameworks. The field of Islamic governance scholarship has developed considerable expertise in this translation process through the Islamic finance industry, and that expertise can and should be drawn upon. Nevertheless, the extension of these translation practices from financial to data governance is a substantial intellectual undertaking that will require sustained collaborative effort between Islamic scholars, data governance specialists, and technologists.

6. DISCUSSION

The theory of Islamic data governance advanced in this chapter is not proposed as an isolated or narrow alternative to global governance frameworks. On the contrary, it is offered as a contribution to an increasingly global conversation about the values that ought to animate data governance, a conversation that has been impoverished by its almost exclusive reliance on Western liberal and regulatory traditions. Several features of the Islamic framework give it broader potential relevance beyond Muslim-majority contexts.

First, the Maqasid framework's emphasis on substantive ethical outcomes rather than procedural compliance speaks to a widely felt dissatisfaction with governance systems that can be satisfied by form rather than substance. The critique of compliance culture in data governance is not unique to Islamic scholarship: it finds resonance in secular critical scholarship on the GDPR and in the growing literature on privacy washing and ethics washing in AI governance (Floridi, 2018; Zuboff, 2019). The Islamic framework offers a more demanding standard: governance must serve genuine human welfare, not merely satisfy regulatory requirements.

Second, the Islamic framework's attentiveness to collective as well as individual dimensions of data harm anticipates concerns that are increasingly recognised but inadequately addressed by individualist consent models. The protection of family data, community data, and religious community data requires a conception of data governance that goes beyond the bilateral relationship between the data subject and the data processor; it requires, as Islamic jurisprudence has always understood, attention to the relational and communal contexts within which individuals are embedded.

Third, the Islamic governance tradition's long experience with the challenge of creating institutions that can maintain ethical standards in the face of powerful economic and political interests, a challenge crystallised in the Hisbah tradition and the history of Islamic finance governance, provides a reservoir of institutional wisdom that is directly applicable to the governance of powerful technology platforms. The principles of independence, proactive oversight, and accountability to normative standards rather than merely to legal rules are principles of good governance with universal resonance.

The relationship between digital governance and economic resilience deserves particular emphasis in this context. Digital transformation in Muslim-majority states is proceeding rapidly, driven by both economic necessity and strategic ambition. States heavily dependent on hydrocarbon revenues are investing in digital infrastructure and digital industries as essential elements of economic diversification. The quality of the governance frameworks they develop for the data economy will significantly influence both the ethical character and the long-term sustainability of that transformation. Governance frameworks that command genuine moral authority within their societies are more likely to achieve the deep institutional embedding that effective data governance requires.

7. CONCLUSION

The chapter proposes a systematic Islamic theory of data governance grounded in the Maqasid al-Shariah framework and the classical Islamic tradition of good governance. By mapping each of the five Maqasid objectives to specific data governance imperatives and deriving governance principles from the Prophetic model and the Rashidun administrative tradition, it has demonstrated that Islamic jurisprudence possesses the normative resources to generate a comprehensive and genuinely alternative framework for governing the ethical use of data in the digital age. For Muslim societies engaged in digital transformation, the practical implications are significant. Governance frameworks that are authentically grounded in Islamic values rather than imported wholesale from Western regulatory traditions are more likely to achieve genuine compliance, build durable institutional trust, and serve the substantive ethical purposes that data governance ought to serve. The development of such frameworks is an urgent intellectual and institutional challenge. The present chapter offers a systematic theoretical foundation on which such frameworks can be built. Future research should attend to the empirical question of how Maqasid-grounded governance principles can be operationalised in specific regulatory and institutional contexts; to the comparative question of how Islamic data governance frameworks relate to other non-Western governance traditions; and to the political question of how the normative authority of the Islamic framework can be mobilised effectively in the face of the powerful economic interests that benefit from current data governance arrangements. What the present chapter has established is that the intellectual resources for a genuinely Islamic theory of data governance are available and, properly developed, can constitute a significant contribution to global conversations about the ethical governance of the digital world.

REFERENCES

Ahmad, A. A. (2020). Realizing Maqasid al-Shariah in Shariah governance: A case study of Islamic banking institutions Malaysia. *International Journal of Islamic Economics and Finance Research, 3*(2), 39–52. DOI: 10.53840/ijiefer36

Alhammadi, S., Alotaibi, K. O., & Hakam, D. (2020). Analysing Islamic banking ethical performance from Maqasid al-Shariah perspective: Evidence from Indonesia. *Journal of Sustainable Finance & Investment, 10*(4), 321–340. DOI: 10.1080/20430795.2019.1694869

Amiri, S. M. H. (2025). Privacy in Islam: What Muslims should know about data protection. Dhaka College Working Paper. Available at *SSRN*: https://ssrn.com/abstract=5276212

Anshari, M. (2026). Developing a digital ecosystem for economic diversification: A strategic framework for resilience in global uncertainties. International Journal of Policy and Governance Lab Vol. 1 No.3.

Auda, J. (2008). *Maqasid al-Shariah as philosophy of Islamic law: A systems approach.* International Institute of Islamic Thought. DOI: 10.2307/j.ctvkc67tg

Auda, J. (2022). *Re-envisioning Islamic scholarship: Maqasid methodology as a new approach.* Claritas Books.

Bashori, Y. A., Umami, K., & Wahid, S. H. (2024). Maqasid Shariah-based digital economy model: Integration, sustainability and transformation. *Malaysian Journal of Syariah and Law, 12*(2), 405–425. DOI: 10.33102/mjsl.vol12no2.647

Firmansyah, E. A., Masri, M., Anshari, M., & Besar, M. H. A. (2024). Factors influencing SME project returns on Islamic Fintech lending platform. *Journal of Islamic Accounting and Business Research.* Advance online publication. DOI: 10.1108/JIABR-10-2023-0340

Floridi, L. (2018). Soft ethics, the governance of the digital and the General Data Protection Regulation. *Philosophical Transactions. Series A, Mathematical, Physical, and Engineering Sciences, 376*(2133), 20180081. Advance online publication. DOI: 10.1098/rsta.2018.0081 PMID: 30322997

Haidi, H., Anshari, M., Hamdan, M., & Sufian, F. A. (2023). Preserving and Promoting Faith Through a Digital Society: An Islamic Governance Perspective. *Proceedings of the International Conference on Islamic Social Sciences and Humanities.*

Hamdan, M., Anshari, M., Ahmad, N., & Ali, E. (Eds.). (2023). *Public policy's role in achieving sustainable development goals*. IGI Global. DOI: 10.4018/978-1-6684-8903-1

Kamali, M. H. (1999). Maqasid al-Shariah: The objectives of Islamic law. *Islamic Studies, 38*(2), 193–208. DOI: 10.52541/isiri.v38i2.6127

Maulidizen, A., Muchtar, A. H., Salimah, A., & Nugraha, R. (2024). A Maqasid al-Shariah framework for fintech and digital asset regulation in Muslim jurisdictions. *Journal of Islamic Law and Legal Studies, 1*(1). https://mabadiiqtishoda.org/index.php/ShariaLex/article/view/119

Mohadi, M., & Tarshany, Y. (2023). Maqasid al-Shari'ah and the ethics of artificial intelligence: Contemporary challenges. *Journal of Contemporary Maqasid Studies, 2*(2), 79–102. DOI: 10.52100/jcms.v2i2.107

Mustapha, A. (2025). *Maqasid al-Shariah and emerging technologies: Toward an ethical evaluation framework*. International Journal of Islamic Thought and Civilization., DOI: 10.31436/ijtc

Omar, A. M., & Anshari, M. (2023). Super Smart Society 5.0: Innovation in public policy post-industry 4.0. In *Digital Transformation for Business and Society* (pp. 91-110). Routledge.

Razzaq, A., Hutagalung, K. A., & Anshari, M. (2023, September). Modelling Islamic business and online communication ethics: A literature analysis. In *2023 International Conference on Sustainable Islamic Business and Finance (SIBF)* (pp. 1-4). IEEE. DOI: 10.1109/SIBF60067.2023.10379995

Shamdi, W., Lai, D., Aziz, A. A., & Anshari, M. (2022). Artificial intelligence development in Islamic System of Governance: A literature review. *Contemporary Islam, 16*(2), 321–334. DOI: 10.1007/s11562-022-00504-7

Syafrudin, M., Alfian, G., Fitriyani, N. L., & Anshari, M. (2024). Applied artificial intelligence for sustainability. *Sustainability (Basel), 16*(6), 2469. DOI: 10.3390/su16062469

Zuboff, S. (2019). *The age of surveillance capitalism: The fight for a human future at the new frontier of power*. PublicAffairs.

Chapter 6
Financial Reporting, Investor Psychology and the Role of Data Governance in Equity Markets

Annisa Fitri
http://orcid.org/0009-0005-0942-7443
The University of Melbourne, Australia

Hamza Yusuf
RMIT University, Australia

Mujaddid Afkar Izzuddin
Universitas Indonesia, Indonesia

ABSTRACT

The chapter explores the interaction between financial reporting, investor psychology, and data governance in equity markets. Using a bibliometric review of Scopus-indexed publications (1998–2025) and interviews with Indonesia Stock Exchange participants, the study finds that research linking reporting and investor psychology remains limited, fragmented, and largely US-dominated. Keyword mapping highlights a focus on behavioural biases such as confirmation bias, anchoring, recency bias, loss aversion, herd behaviour, and overconfidence, with less attention to report design and data governance. Interviews reveal distinct profiles and decision processes between traders and investors. The chapter argues that strong data governance, ensuring data quality, integrity, accessibility, and ethical use, is

DOI: 10.4018/979-8-2600-2233-7.ch006

essential for financial reports to support credible decision-making and highlights opportunities for interdisciplinary research across accounting, behavioural finance, and governance.

1. INTRODUCTION

Financial markets are often seen as places where investors use information carefully to set fair prices. Financial reports are viewed as neutral and used in a logical way. However, events like the 1987 crash show this view is incomplete. Large price swings during crises and bubbles suggest that behaviour is shaped by psychology as well as data. Behavioural finance explains why investors do not always act rationally. People rely on mental shortcuts and emotions, leading to patterns such as bias, overconfidence, fear of losses and herd behaviour. These affect how investors read reports and can lead to poor decisions and mispriced assets.

Financial reporting remains the main way firms communicate performance and plans. Good reporting reduces information gaps, improves valuation and supports better investment decisions. Presentation also matters. Clear language, structure and balance of information influence how investors understand and respond. The value of reporting depends on the quality of the underlying data. Data governance ensures data is accurate, secure and used properly. As firms rely more on complex systems and AI, trust in reports depends on trust in the data behind them.

Research on reporting and investor psychology has mostly developed separately. Reporting studies focus on transparency and market response, often assuming rational users. Psychology studies focus on behaviour but simplify report content. Few studies link investor biases with responses to financial reports, and even fewer consider the role of data governance. This chapter treats data governance as an important third dimension alongside reporting quality and investor psychology.

Many studies also treat market participants as one group. In reality, traders and investors differ in time horizon, strategy and emotional response. Traders face short term pressure, while investors take a longer view. These differences matter for reporting design, governance and education but are often ignored.

This chapter addresses these gaps in two ways. First, it uses bibliometric analysis of Scopus data to map research on reporting and investor psychology. Second, it uses interviews with traders and investors in the Indonesia Stock Exchange to examine decision making, responses to volatility and emotional factors. A data governance perspective is used throughout to show how data quality, security and ethics affect the usefulness of financial reporting.

2. LITERATURE REVIEW

2.1 The Psychology of Investors

Investor psychology refers to the thoughts, feelings and habits that shape how people make financial decisions. Traditional finance assumes that investors calmly weigh all information and choose the option that gives the best risk-adjusted return (Islam et al., 2024). Many studies show that investors repeatedly make similar mistakes, and these mistakes follow clear patterns rather than being random (Mahmood et al., 2024). These patterns are often called psychological or cognitive biases because they arise from the way people naturally process information. Cognitive biases are mental shortcuts people use to deal with complex problems. They save time and effort but can also lead to poor choices in investing. Instead of carefully weighing every fact in a financial report, investors may focus on a few pieces of information, rely on their first impression, or be guided by emotions. Research in behavioural finance has identified many such biases (Mahmood et al., 2024). For this chapter, eight patterns are especially important because they directly affect how investors read and react to financial reports (see Figure 1).

Confirmation bias means that investors mainly look for information that supports what they already believe and ignore or downplay information that goes against their view (Vafaeimehr et al., 2023). An investor who believes a company is strong may pay close attention to good news in the annual report and skip over warning signs. This can lead them to hold weak stocks for too long or to underestimate risk. Anchoring happens when investors get stuck on a first number or reference point and then judge all later information around it (Mahmood et al., 2024). A simple example is an investor who bought a share at 10 and keeps comparing everything to that price, even when new information clearly suggests the share is now worth much less. Anchoring can affect how investors judge valuations, targets and price movements.

Figure 1. Key Psychological Biases Influencing Investors Based on How Financial Reports

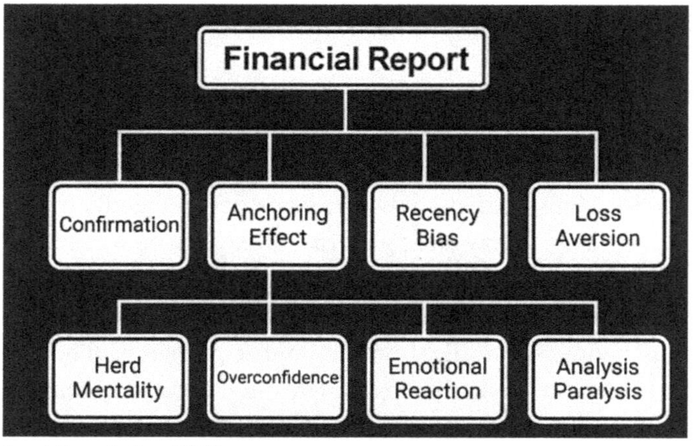

(Source: Authors' Compilation, 2026)

Recency bias occurs when investors put too much weight on recent events and forget about longer-term patterns (Gandre, 2020). After a long rise in prices, investors may assume the good times will continue and increase their risk. After a sharp fall, they may become overly pessimistic and avoid markets even when valuations have improved. This tendency can make investors overreact to short-term earnings or recent news in financial reports. Loss aversion describes the fact that people feel losses more strongly than gains of the same size (Kahneman & Tversky, 1979). Many investors would rather avoid a loss than achieve a similar gain. As a result, they often hold losing stocks for too long because selling would turn the loss into reality, while they sell winning positions too early to lock in profits. This behaviour reduces overall returns and can distort how investors respond to negative information in reports.

Herd mentality means following what other investors are doing instead of relying on one's own analysis (Fei & Liu, 2021). When prices rise and many people are buying, others join in because they do not want to miss out or look different. When prices fall, many sell simply because everyone else is selling. Herding can drive prices far away from what the financial statements would suggest, and it can influence how investors react to widely reported earnings or disclosure events. Overconfidence is the tendency for investors to be too sure about their own knowledge and skills (Inghelbrecht & Tedde, 2024). Overconfident investors often believe they can read reports better than others, spot mispriced stocks or time the market. They trade more frequently, hold less diversified portfolios and pay less attention to information that contradicts their views. Studies show that this extra trading usually reduces net returns once costs are included.

Emotional reactions are another important part of investor psychology (Agarwal & Tewari, 2025). Fear and panic during downturns can cause investors to sell at very low prices, even when fundamentals have not changed much. Greed and excitement during booms can push them into risky or speculative investments. Emotions can easily override a careful reading of financial reports, especially when markets are volatile or media coverage is intense. Analysis paralysis occurs when investors face so much information and so many choices that they feel stuck and delay decisions (Finet et al., 2025). Modern financial reporting provides large amounts of data, notes and narrative sections. For some investors, this volume of information is overwhelming. Instead of making a timely decision, they keep searching, comparing and hesitating. This can mean missing good opportunities or failing to react when reports contain important warnings.

These eight patterns show that investors do not simply read financial reports in a neutral, logical way. Their beliefs, reference points, recent experiences, fear of losses, urge to follow others, confidence in their own skill, emotional swings and sense of overload all influence how they search for information, what they notice and how they act on it. This has direct implications for the design and communication of financial reporting and, as the next sections argue, for the data governance practices that sit behind it.

2.2 Equity Stock Markets

While the terms trader and investor are often used as if they mean the same thing, they refer to two distinct groups of equity market participants with different goals, time horizons and behaviours. A clear distinction between these two groups is important for understanding how psychological factors operate in stock markets, because the pressures and emotional demands they face are quite different. A trader is a market participant who buys and sells stocks over short periods, ranging from minutes to a few weeks. Traders aim to profit from short-term price movements. They rely heavily on technical analysis, chart patterns, price momentum and market timing. Their success depends on making quick decisions and reacting fast to changes in price, volume and market sentiment. Traders typically hold multiple positions at once and adjust them frequently throughout the trading day or week. The key feature of trading is its short time horizon and the need for rapid action (Barber & Odean, 2000; (Greenwald et al., 2020).

An investor, by contrast, is a market participant who buys stocks with the intention of holding them for months or years. Investors focus on the long-term value of a company. They study financial statements, earnings growth, competitive position, management quality and industry outlook before making a purchase (Lo & Repin, 2002). Their goal is to benefit from the company's growth in value over time and from dividends. Investors make fewer transactions and are less concerned with daily or weekly price changes. The key feature of investing is patience and a focus on company fundamentals (Graham & Dodd, 2009).

Table 1 summarises the main differences between traders and investors in equity stock markets.

Table 1. Comparison of traders and investors in equity stock markets

Dimension	Trader	Investor
Time horizon	Minutes to weeks	Months to years
Primary goal	Profit from price movements	Profit from long-term value growth
Analysis method	Technical analysis, charts, momentum	Fundamental analysis, financial reports
Decision speed	Very fast, often within minutes	Slow, deliberate, research-based
Transaction frequency	High, multiple trades per day or week	Low, few transactions per year
View of volatility	Opportunity for short-term gains	Risk, but also accumulation opportunity
Emotional intensity	High, constant pressure	Lower, more measured responses
Relationship with financial reports	Limited direct use; reacts to news flow	Central; reports guide buy, hold and sell decisions

(Source: authors' compilation, 2026)

Understanding the psychological differences between traders and investors is important for two reasons. First, it helps explain why different groups of market participants react differently to the same financial information. A quarterly earnings report that sends traders rushing to sell may prompt investors to review their thesis and potentially buy more. Second, it has practical value for financial regulators, report preparers and educators, who need to recognise that equity market participants are not a uniform group but a mix of people with different goals, emotional profiles and information needs.

2.3 Financial Reporting as Corporate Communication

Financial reporting is the main way companies share information about their performance, financial position and prospects with investors and other parties. Good reporting helps reduce information gaps between managers and outside investors, supports more accurate pricing of securities and allows capital to move towards better projects (Healy & Palepu, 2001). Poor reporting, by contrast, can hide risks, confuse users and contribute to mispricing and loss of trust. Many studies have examined how the quality of financial reporting relates to investment efficiency. Research shows that higher quality reporting is linked to less under-investment by firms with good projects but limited internal funds, and less over-investment by firms with surplus cash that might otherwise be spent on weak projects (Biddle et al., 2009). Clear and reliable reports help investors and lenders assess which projects have positive value and which do not. They also make it easier to monitor managers and reduce problems such as self-interested spending.

Transparency in reporting is closely tied to investor confidence (Hussain et al., 2023). When companies provide timely, accurate and complete information, investors find it easier to judge the health and long-term strength of the business. This tends to support higher valuations and lower costs of capital. In contrast, vague or incomplete reporting increases uncertainty and can make investors demand a higher return or avoid the stock altogether. The global financial crisis of 2008 showed clearly how a lack of clear disclosure about risk exposures can damage trust and cause instability in markets (Avgouleas, 2009).

Recent research has also stressed that the way information is written and presented matters, not just the content itself. Studies on readability show that annual reports written in plain, straightforward language lead to stronger and more consistent investor reactions to both good and bad news (Dau et al., 2024). When information is easy to read, investors are more likely to process it properly and update their views. When reports are very long, full of technical terms or poorly structured, investors may struggle to understand them (Yu & Zhao, 2023). This has been linked to greater mispricing, with some stocks being valued too highly and others too low.

The content of financial disclosures also plays a key role. Analysts and professional investors say that they value both the required numerical information and the voluntary qualitative discussion in reports (Liu, 2023). They want not only past numbers, but also explanations of strategy, risks and factors that could affect future results. Surveys show that many investors would like clearer discussion of management decisions, the reasons behind major changes and the main drivers of performance (Nguyen et al., 2025). This suggests that numbers alone are not enough; context and narrative are also important. At the same time, several studies show that simply providing more or better information does not always change investor behaviour. In some experiments and field studies, even when investors receive clear and simple disclosures about better financial options, only a small share switch (Adams et al., 2021). Many people stay with the status quo because of inattention, procrastination, small switching costs or a general reluctance to act. Psychological frictions such as confirmation bias, habit and the effort required to process information can all limit the real-world impact of disclosure (Loewenstein et al., 2014). The effect of financial reporting on investment decisions therefore depends not only on what is reported and how clearly it is written, but also on how investors think and feel when they use the reports.

2.4 Data Governance and the Trust Architecture of Financial Reports

Four dimensions of data governance are particularly relevant to financial reporting. The first is data quality, which covers accuracy, completeness, timeliness and consistency of records. Weak quality at the data entry stage or during system migrations can produce figures that look precise in the final report but rest on shaky ground. The second is data integrity and security, which includes protection against unauthorised changes, cyber intrusion and insider manipulation. Breaches and leaks can distort reported results, damage investor trust and create legal liability (Anshari et al., 2021). The third is ethical use of data, including respect for privacy, fair handling of customer and employee information and clear limits on how personal data is aggregated and monetised (Sumardi & Anshari, 2020). The fourth is accountability and traceability, which means that every number in a report should be linked back to a clear source, a responsible owner and an audit trail (Sumardi & Anshari, 2020).

These governance concerns have become more urgent as companies adopt artificial intelligence, cloud platforms and large-scale analytics in their reporting workflows. Automated systems can generate earnings estimates, flag unusual transactions or draft narrative sections of reports, but they can also introduce new risks. Opaque algorithms, biased training data and weak human oversight can all feed errors into the reporting process in ways that are hard to detect after the fact (Anshari et al., 2021; Anshari et al., 2023). In emerging market contexts, where data privacy frameworks may still be developing, the absence of clear rules can leave both firms and investors exposed (Sait & Anshari, 2022).

Digital twin concepts and similar models also point to how data governance is moving beyond simple back-office compliance into a strategic concern. Anshari and Hamdan (2022) argue that digital twin arrangements can support innovation management and public service delivery, but only when data flows are trusted, well documented and governed by clear rules. The same logic applies to corporate reporting. When investors read a financial report, they are implicitly relying on a whole set of unseen governance arrangements. If those arrangements are weak, the report may look informative while in fact carrying hidden risks that psychological biases are likely to amplify.

Data governance therefore acts as a trust architecture that sits beneath financial reporting. Strong governance increases the chance that reported numbers reflect reality, that narrative sections are grounded in verifiable evidence and that ethical limits on the use of sensitive information are respected. Weak governance, by contrast, creates conditions where managerial discretion, algorithmic error and outright manipulation can enter the reporting process. Any serious attempt to connect financial reporting with investor psychology must also consider this data governance layer, because even the most psychologically aware reporting design will fail if the data behind it cannot be trusted.

2.5 Bibliometric Analysis as a Review Method

Bibliometric analysis is a set of methods used to study academic literature by looking at publication and citation data (Pessin et al., 2022). Instead of reading each paper in detail, bibliometric studies use information such as author names, journal titles, publication years, references and keywords to identify patterns in a research field. This can show how a topic has grown over time, which countries and institutions contribute most, which journals are central and how ideas are linked through citations and shared concepts. Two broad types of bibliometric techniques are commonly used (Ninkov et al., 2021). Evaluative techniques focus on quantities and performance, such as counting how many papers have been published on a topic, how often they are cited and which authors or journals are most influential. Relational techniques focus on connections, such as which papers are cited together, which authors often publish with each other, or which keywords tend to appear in the same papers. These relational methods help reveal clusters of related work and the structure of research communities (Ninkov et al., 2021).

Several software tools have been developed to support bibliometric work. One widely used tool is VOSviewer, which can read data from major databases such as Scopus and Web of Science and create maps of authors, papers and keywords (Liu et al., 2025). In these maps, items that are strongly connected are placed close to each other. Colours and cluster labels then help identify groups of related topics or research streams. In behavioural finance and investor psychology, bibliometric methods have already been used to review and map the field (Paule-Vianez et al., 2020). Some studies have collected articles with keywords such as overconfidence, herding behaviour or behavioural biases in investment decisions, and then used tools like VOSviewer to identify trends over time, leading journals and main themes. Other work has focused on investor sentiment research, tracking how this concept has developed across many years and how it connects to different models and measures. These studies show that bibliometric analysis can provide a structured overview of complex and fast-growing literatures.

At the same time, bibliometric approaches have limits. Results depend on the coverage and quality of the database used, so relevant work in other languages or in journals not indexed may be missed (Dagli et al., 2025). It can be difficult to separate authors with the same name or to track changes in terminology over time. Citation-based measures also mainly reflect past influence and say less about very recent or still-developing topics. For these reasons, bibliometric findings are usually read alongside more traditional, qualitative reviews of key papers. Despite the growing use of bibliometric methods in behavioural finance, only a small number of studies focus specifically on the link between financial reporting and investor psychology, and fewer still bring in a data governance perspective. This gap motivates the present study.

3. METHODOLOGY

This research uses a mixed-methods approach that combines bibliometric analysis with primary qualitative data collection. The bibliometric component examines and maps the academic literature at the intersection of financial reporting and investor psychology. The qualitative component collects original interview data from traders and investors active in the Indonesian equity stock market. Together, these two approaches provide both a broad view of the field and grounded insights from actual market participants. A data governance lens is then applied during the discussion stage to interpret the findings.

3.1 Bibliometric Analysis

The bibliometric methodology follows standard protocols for this type of research, combining performance analysis to measure publication trends with science mapping techniques to show the structure of the field (Donthu et al., 2021). The data collection process began with a comprehensive search of the Scopus database, which was chosen for its broad coverage of peer-reviewed journals across business, finance, accounting and psychology. Scopus provides standardised and high-quality metadata records, including author details, affiliations, keywords and citation information, which are necessary for reliable bibliometric analysis (Singh et al., 2021).

The search strategy was carefully developed, using specific combinations of keywords to find articles that substantively discuss both financial reporting and disclosure on one hand, and investor psychology and behavioural biases on the other. To ensure the search was sufficiently targeted, the keywords were looked for in the article titles, abstracts and author keywords sections of each record. Several criteria were applied to refine the dataset and ensure its quality and relevance. The search was limited to peer-reviewed journal articles, conference papers and review articles, which excluded non-academic sources such as trade magazines and editorials. While no initial restrictions were placed on language or country of origin, the final dataset was composed almost entirely of English-language publications. The search covered publications from 1998 to 2025.

After these filters were applied, the remaining documents underwent a manual screening process. The titles and abstracts of each document were carefully read to confirm that the study genuinely examined the link between financial reporting and investor psychology. Studies that focused only on financial reporting without a behavioural dimension, or only on behavioural finance without a clear connection to reporting practices, were excluded from the final sample. This screening process resulted in a final dataset of highly relevant documents, confirming that explicit integration of the two fields remains limited.

The bibliographic data for selected documents were exported from Scopus in CSV format. This file contained all the necessary information for the analysis, including authors, publication years, source titles, subject areas and reference lists. The analysis was conducted using VOSviewer, a specialised software tool designed for constructing and showing bibliometric networks. VOSviewer was used to perform two main types of analysis. The first was a performance analysis, which involved examining descriptive statistics to characterise the field (Pessin et al., 2022). This included analysing publication trends over time, breaking down the documents by subject area and identifying the geographical distribution by country. The second type was a keyword co-occurrence analysis, a network technique used to map the conceptual structure of the literature (Thakur et al., 2024). VOSviewer identified the most frequently used keywords and created a visual map where keywords that often appear together in the same documents are placed near each other. The software also applied a temporal overlay to the map, using colours to distinguish between older, more established themes and newer, emerging topics.

3.2 Primary Interviews with Traders and Investors

To supplement the bibliometric findings with real-world evidence, this study collected primary data through semi-structured interviews with equity market participants in Indonesia. The interviews aimed to explore how traders and investors differ in their psychological responses, decision-making behaviour and emotional intensity when they engage with the stock market, and how they perceive the trustworthiness of the financial information they rely on.

Participants were selected through purposive sampling. The criteria required that each participant had at least two years of active experience in the Indonesia Stock Exchange (IDX) and could be clearly classified as either a trader (holding stocks for days to weeks, relying on technical analysis) or an investor (holding stocks for months to years, relying on fundamental analysis). The final sample included participants from both categories, representing a range of experience levels and portfolio sizes.

Each interview lasted between 30 and 60 minutes and was conducted in Bahasa Indonesia, with key terms in English retained where commonly used by participants. The interview guide covered four main areas: how participants define their own approach to the stock market, how they make buying and selling decisions, how they respond emotionally to market volatility and price movements, and how they use or react to financial reports and market news. Informed consent was obtained from all participants. All interviews were recorded with consent, transcribed and analysed using thematic analysis. The analysis focused on identifying patterns and differences between traders and investors across two key dimensions, decision-making processes and emotional intensity, and also looked for any spontaneous comments about trust in company data and disclosures.

4. ANALYSIS

The analysis is presented in two parts. The first part reports findings from the bibliometric analysis. The second part presents findings from the interviews with traders and investors in the Indonesian equity market.

4.1 Bibliometric Findings

4.1.1 Research Activity over Time

The chart shows several peak periods of activity. The highest spikes appear in 2003 and 2022, with two documents published in each of these years. Single documents were published in several years including 1998, 1999, 2008, 2011, 2019, 2020, 2021 and 2025. Multiple years show zero publications on this specific topic, including the entire period from 2000 to 2002 and from 2004 to 2007, as well as 2009, 2010, 2013 through 2018, and 2023 and 2024 (see Figure 2).

Figure 2. Documents by subject area per year

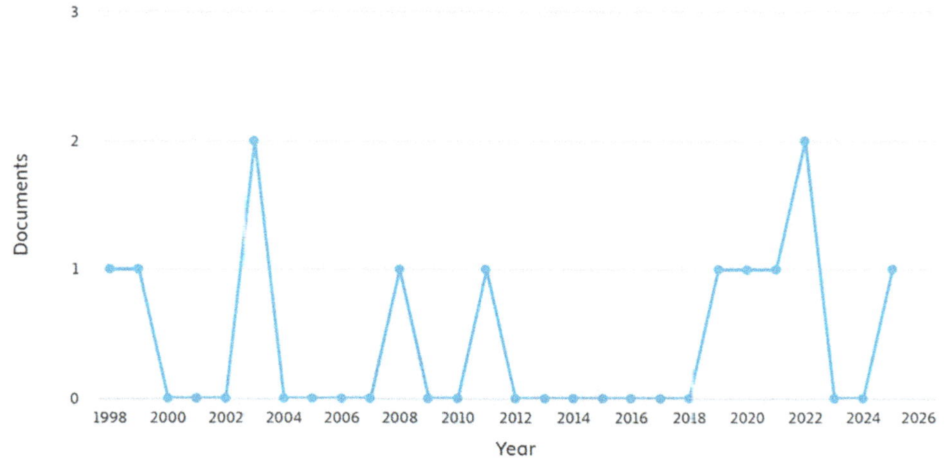

(Source: authors' compilation, 2026)

This irregular publication pattern suggests that while some researchers have examined how investor psychology influences the processing of financial reporting, this has not been a sustained research stream but rather an area that remains under-researched. The discontinuous publication activity may reflect the interdisciplinary challenges that exist in combining accounting and behavioural finance perspectives (Anderson & Chang, 2019). Researchers in accounting and financial reporting may lack familiarity with psychological theories and methods, while behavioural finance scholars may focus more on trading behaviour and market patterns than on information disclosure mechanisms. The peaks in 2003 and 2022 may correspond to periods when methodological advances or theoretical developments made cross-disciplinary work more feasible, or when practical concerns about market functioning increased interest in understanding psychological factors affecting financial information use (Alam et al., 2025).

4.1.2 Distribution by Subject Area

The pie chart shows that Business, Management and Accounting represents the largest category at 44.4 per cent of documents, showing that business school scholars have been the primary contributors to this literature. Economics, Econometrics and Finance accounts for 33.3 per cent of documents, reflecting strong representation from finance and economics departments. Social Sciences make up 11.1 per cent of publications, suggesting some contributions from scholars examining behavioural and social dimensions of financial markets. Decision Sciences represents 7.4 per cent of documents, showing involvement from scholars studying judgment and decision-making processes. Finally, Arts and Humanities accounts for 3.7 per cent of publications, likely representing work examining interpretive and cultural aspects of financial communication (see Figure 3).

Figure 3. Distribution of Documents by Subject Area (Source: Authors' Compilation, 2026)

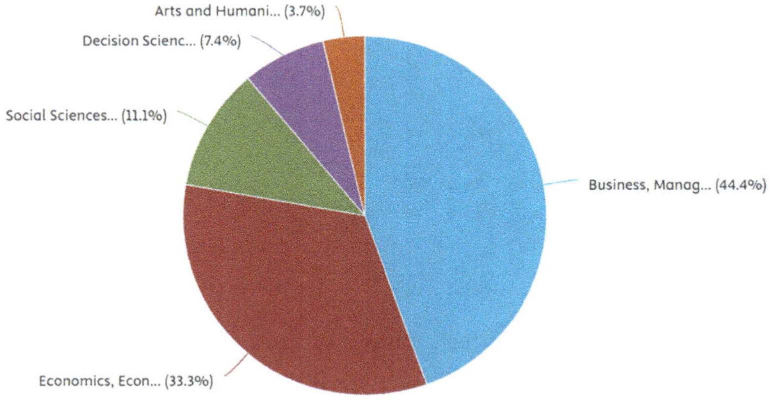

This distribution shows that research on financial reporting and investor psychology spans traditional business disciplines, economics and social sciences. The dominance of business and finance categories is expected given that financial reporting and investment decisions fall within these domains. However, the presence of social sciences and decision sciences shows contributions from psychology and behavioural research. The relatively small humanities contribution suggests opportunities for interpretive and qualitative approaches to understanding how investors make sense of financial narratives. What is almost entirely absent in this subject distribution is work from information systems, computer science or data science, which is where much of the current literature on data governance and algorithmic accountability sits. This absence underlines how isolated the current body of work remains from the data infrastructure questions raised in section 2.4.

4.1.3 Geographical Distribution

The bar chart shows that the United States accounts for approximately ten documents, representing the majority of research output on this topic. Canada and the United Kingdom each contribute approximately one document. No other countries appear in the chart, suggesting that research explicitly examining financial reporting and investor psychology together has been mainly produced by scholars in these three English-speaking countries with developed capital markets. This geographical concentration likely reflects several factors. The United States has the largest financial markets and most extensive research infrastructure in accounting and finance, allowing for substantial scholarly output on specialised topics (Mosteanu, 2017). The prevalence of behavioural finance research in US business schools provides both theoretical foundations and methodological expertise for investigating psychological aspects of financial decisions. Canada and the United Kingdom similarly have strong traditions in accounting scholarship and behavioural economics research. The absence of contributions from emerging markets is notable given that behavioural factors may be particularly important in contexts with less developed information infrastructures and lower financial literacy. The same absence is visible from a data governance angle: emerging economies are still building their national data policy frameworks (Sait & Anshari, 2022), yet their experiences are hardly reflected in the bibliometric record. This geographical limitation points to opportunities for expanding research to examine how cultural contexts, institutional environments and data governance regimes affect the relationship between financial reporting and investor psychology (see Figure 4).

Figure 4. Documents by country (Source: authors' compilation, 2026)

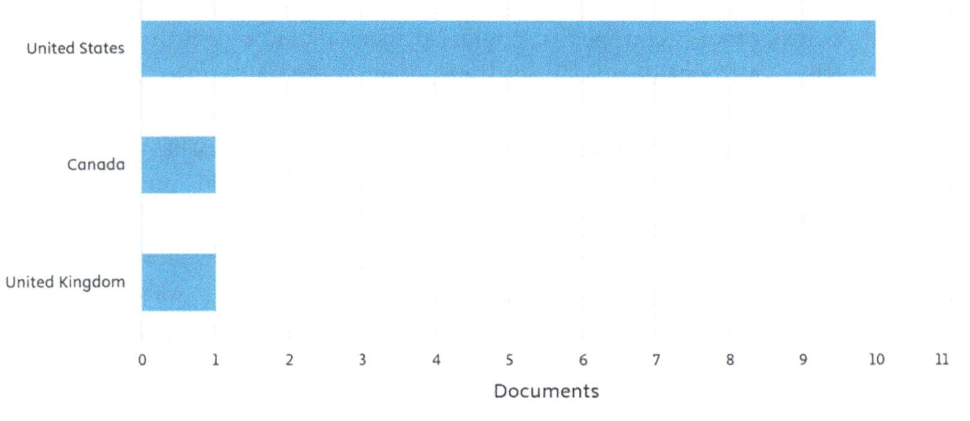

4.1.4 Conceptual Structure and Thematic Clusters

Figure 5 shows the overlay visualisation with frequently occurring keywords as nodes and connections showing co-occurrence patterns. The colour gradient from purple to yellow represents the shift from older to more recent research. Several distinct thematic clusters emerge. One cluster centres on behavioural finance concepts including behavioural finance, investor psychology and capital markets. These terms appear in purple tones, which means they represent more established themes in earlier research. Their central positioning and multiple connections suggest these concepts serve as foundational elements linking various research streams.

Figure 5. Bibliometric overlay visualisation by topic year (Source: authors' compilation, 2026)

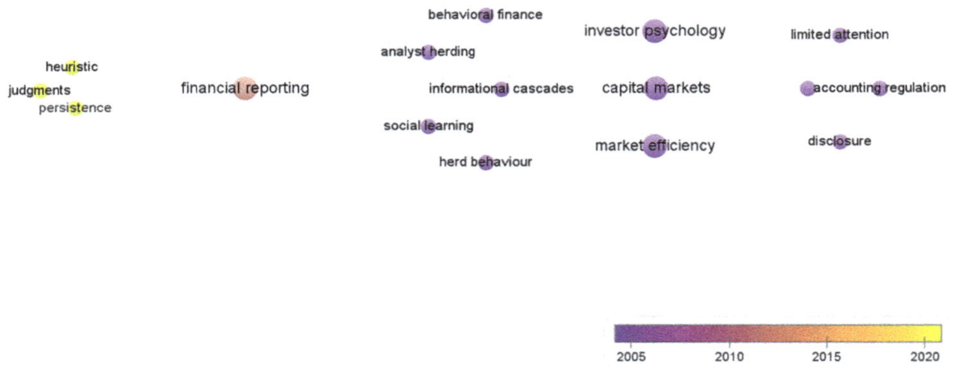

Another cluster focuses on specific cognitive biases including confirmation bias, anchoring effect, overconfidence and herd behaviour. These terms reflect the specific psychological mechanisms investigated in studies of investor decision making. The importance of these biases in the keyword network shows that they have been focal concerns in research examining how investors process financial information. A third cluster covers information and disclosure themes including financial reporting, information cascades, disclosure and accounting regulation. These terms connect behavioural concepts to reporting practices and regulatory contexts. A fourth cluster relates to market efficiency and investor behaviour, including market efficiency and limited attention. These terms reflect theoretical concerns about whether markets efficiently take in information when investors have cognitive constraints and behavioural tendencies.

Several keywords appear in warmer yellow and orange tones, which indicates more recent research emphasis. These include heuristic, judgments and persistence, suggesting that contemporary work is examining the heuristic processes behind biased judgments and the persistence of poor decision patterns. The term social learning also appears in warmer tones, pointing to growing interest in how investors learn from others and how social dynamics spread behavioural tendencies.

The keyword analysis reveals that research has examined multiple specific biases and their consequences for financial decision making. However, relatively fewer keywords relate to specific financial reporting characteristics, disclosure formats or data governance constructs such as data quality, data ethics, audit trails or algorithmic accountability. This pattern suggests that while substantial work has documented how various biases affect investor behaviour, less research has investigated how reporting design and the governance of underlying data might reduce or strengthen those psychological factors. This represents an important research gap.

4.1.5 The Eight Key Psychological Patterns

The analysis of the eight key psychological patterns, including confirmation bias, anchoring effect, recency bias, loss aversion, herd mentality, overconfidence, emotional reactions and analysis paralysis, provides a framework for understanding how cognitive and emotional factors systematically influence investor responses to financial reporting.

Confirmation bias causes investors to selectively process financial information in ways that support their existing beliefs about companies or market trends. When reviewing annual reports or earnings releases, investors influenced by confirmation bias focus too much on data that supports their existing positions while dismissing contradictory evidence. This selective attention prevents accurate updating of beliefs in response to new information. Financial reporting, regardless of quality, becomes filtered through biased lenses that distort its informational value (Armansyah, 2022).

Anchoring effect leads investors to fix on particular reference points when evaluating financial information. Common anchors include historical stock prices, analyst estimates or prior earnings figures. These initial data points have too much influence on later judgments about value and prospects. For example, investors may judge current earnings as disappointing relative to an anchored expectation even when the absolute performance is strong. Financial reporting inherently provides many potential anchors including prior period comparisons, guidance figures and industry benchmarks. Understanding which information serves as anchors and how this influences interpretation is critical for effective disclosure design (Mardiana et al., 2025).

Recency bias causes investors to give too much weight to recent financial results while overlooking longer-term patterns and fundamentals. Quarterly earnings reports that show recent strong performance receive too much attention even when underlying business trends are weakening. Temporary setbacks cause excessive pessimism that ignores sustained historical success. This distortion in how people process information over time reduces the effectiveness of financial reporting that focuses on long-term value creation over short-term results.

Loss aversion makes investors very sensitive to information suggesting potential losses while relatively less sensitive to equivalent gain prospects. Financial disclosures revealing risks or declines in performance cause strong negative reactions that are out of proportion. Investors hold losing positions to avoid making the loss real, even when financial information clearly shows that fundamentals are weakening. The uneven emotional response to gains and losses means that balanced financial reporting that covers both positives and negatives may be perceived as mostly negative by loss-averse investors.

Herd mentality causes investors to follow the decisions of others rather than conducting independent analysis of financial information. When many investors are buying a stock, others join in despite what financial reports may say about valuation. Selling pressure similarly leads to further selling as investors rush for the exits. This collective behaviour can overwhelm the informational content of financial reporting, as social influences take over rational assessment of disclosed data. Herd behaviour contributes to momentum effects and bubbles that continue despite warning signs visible in financial statements.

Overconfidence leads investors to overestimate their ability to interpret financial information and predict outcomes. Overconfident investors believe they understand financial reports better than they actually do and can forecast future performance more accurately than is objectively possible. This inflated self-assessment reduces careful analysis of disclosed information and increases trading frequency based on false pattern recognition. Financial reporting complexity may, in a paradoxical way, feed overconfidence by providing more data that investors believe they are uniquely capable of interpreting.

Emotional reactions cause fear and panic to override rational assessment during market stress. When portfolio values decline, emotional pain causes selling to find relief even when financial fundamentals remain sound. Excitement during bull markets similarly causes excessive risk taking that is disconnected from sober analysis of financial reports. These emotional extremes reduce the influence of informational disclosure on actual decisions. Even investors who have carefully studied financial statements may abandon reasoned conclusions when strong emotions take hold.

Analysis paralysis occurs when investors become overwhelmed by the volume and complexity of financial information. Rather than helping with decisions, extensive disclosure can freeze investors who are unable to process and bring together large amounts of data. The fear of making mistakes when faced with many alternatives leads to decision avoidance. While transparency advocates assume more information improves decisions, psychological research reveals that too much choice and information can reduce decision quality and satisfaction. Financial reporting must balance thoroughness with clarity to avoid overwhelming users.

Confirmation bias and anchoring both involve selective attention to information but operate through different mechanisms. Recency bias and loss aversion both distort how people evaluate events over time but reflect different underlying causes. Herd behaviour amplifies individual biases through social pressure. Overconfidence prevents recognition of other biases. Emotional reactions and analysis paralysis represent extremes of engagement with information, from emotional override to cognitive overload. Understanding these patterns and how they interact is essential for designing financial reporting and data governance arrangements that work with actual human psychology rather than assume perfect rational processing.

4.2 Interview Findings from Indonesian Equity Market Participants

The interviews with traders and investors in the Indonesia Stock Exchange revealed clear and consistent differences in how the two groups respond to market conditions, make decisions and experience emotions when dealing with equity stocks. The findings are organised around two key dimensions: decision-making processes and emotional intensity. A secondary theme, trust in company information, emerged from both groups and is reported at the end of this section.

4.2.1 Decision-Making Processes

Traders described their decision making as fast-paced and heavily dependent on reading price charts, candlestick patterns and trading volume. Most traders said they make buying or selling decisions within minutes or, at most, hours. They look for short-term signals such as breakout points, support and resistance levels and momentum shifts. One trader explained that he watches the order book and price action closely throughout the trading session and acts as soon as he sees a pattern forming. Several traders mentioned that they rarely look at company financial statements in detail. Instead, they rely on market sentiment, news headlines and social media discussion to inform their actions.

Investors described a much slower and more structured decision-making process. Most investors said they spend days or weeks researching a company before buying shares. They read annual reports, quarterly earnings and analyst commentaries. They evaluate financial ratios such as price to earnings, debt to equity and return on equity. Several investors stressed that they try to understand the business behind the stock, including the company's competitive position, management team and growth prospects. One long-term investor said he only buys when he is confident that the company's intrinsic value is higher than the current market price, and that he is willing to wait years for the market to reflect that value.

The difference in decision-making speed and information sources between the two groups has clear implications for how financial reports are used. For traders, financial reports are secondary to price action. For investors, financial reports are the primary basis for making decisions. This means that the design and clarity of financial reporting matter more directly to investors, while traders are more influenced by how information flows through market sentiment channels.

4.2.2 Emotional Intensity and Response to Volatility

The most striking difference between traders and investors was in the level of emotional intensity they reported. Traders consistently described their emotional experience as intense and closely tied to every price movement. Several traders used words like adrenaline, rush and pressure when talking about their daily trading experience. One trader said that losing money on a trade feels like a physical blow, while winning a trade gives a high that is hard to describe. Traders reported that they sometimes feel anxiety even when they are not actively trading, because they worry about positions they hold overnight or about missing an opportunity.

Traders also described volatility as their main source of profit. When asked how they respond to sudden market drops, most traders said they see falling prices as an opportunity to enter short positions or to buy at lower levels for a quick bounce. One trader explained that without volatility, there is no money to be made in trading. However, several traders also admitted that high volatility can lead to impulsive decisions, emotional overtrading and significant losses when the market moves against their expectations. The emotional cycle of excitement, fear and regret was a common theme among traders.

Investors reported a very different emotional experience. Most described themselves as calm or patient when discussing market movements. When asked about market crashes or sharp drops, several investors said they feel concerned but do not panic. Their first response is to check whether the company's fundamentals have changed. If the business remains strong, they see falling prices as a buying opportunity rather than a threat. One investor described a market crash as a sale where good companies become available at lower prices. Another investor said that he has trained himself not to check stock prices every day because it creates unnecessary emotional noise.

However, investors were not entirely free from emotional responses. Several admitted that holding a stock that keeps falling for months can test their patience and confidence, especially when friends or family members question their decisions. A few investors mentioned experiencing doubt during prolonged market downturns, even when they believe in the company's long-term value. One investor said that the hardest part of investing is doing nothing when every headline tells you to sell.

4.2.3 Trust in Company Information

A further theme that emerged across both groups was trust in the quality of company disclosures. Several investors described moments when they stopped believing in a particular company's reports after noticing unusual patterns in earnings, frequent restatements or governance scandals. In these cases, the investors said they no longer relied on the reported numbers even when the figures looked attractive, and some exited their positions entirely. Traders were less focused on report content, but a number of them mentioned that they pay attention to rumours of data manipulation and regulatory actions, because such events can trigger sharp price movements that are profitable or dangerous depending on how quickly traders react. These comments suggest that data governance concerns, even when not named explicitly, already shape how Indonesian market participants treat the information firms publish.

Table 2 summarises the key findings from the interviews, comparing traders and investors across decision making, emotional intensity and trust-related responses.

Table 2. Summary of interview findings: traders and investors in Indonesian equity markets

Dimension	Traders	Investors
Decision speed	Fast; decisions made in minutes to hours	Slow; decisions made over days to weeks
Information sources	Charts, price action, news headlines, social media	Financial reports, annual reports, analyst commentary, financial ratios
Use of financial reports	Minimal; secondary to price signals	Central; primary basis for decisions
View of volatility	Opportunity for short-term profit	Risk, but also accumulation opportunity when fundamentals are strong
Emotional intensity	High; described as intense, adrenaline driven	Lower; described as calm, patient, measured
Response to market drops	See as trading opportunity; may short-sell or buy for quick bounce	Check fundamentals first; if strong, may buy more at lower prices
Common emotional traps	Impulsive decisions, overtrading, regret after losses	Doubt during prolonged declines, reluctance to sell losers
Psychological biases most visible	Overconfidence, herding, anchoring	Confirmation bias, loss aversion, analysis paralysis
Data trust concerns	Alert to rumours of manipulation or regulatory action as trade triggers	Reduce or exit positions when report credibility is questioned

(Source: primary data, 2026)

5. DISCUSSION

The findings from both the bibliometric analysis and the primary interviews offer a more complete picture of how financial reporting, investor psychology and data governance interact in equity stock markets. The bibliometric analysis confirms that research on the first two topics remains limited. Only a small number of documents in the Scopus database address financial reporting and investor psychology together, despite large literatures in each field considered separately. This small body of work shows that the connection between how firms communicate financial information and how psychological factors shape investor responses is still under-explored. The governance of the data that feeds those reports is almost entirely missing from the current bibliometric picture, which suggests an even more fundamental blind spot.

The irregular pattern of publications shows that, although some studies have examined how investor psychology affects the use of financial reporting, the topic has not developed into a sustained line of research. Individual contributions have provided useful insights, but they have not grown into a continuous body of inquiry. This fragmented pattern is consistent with the idea that institutional and intellectual boundaries between accounting, behavioural finance and information systems make sustained collaboration difficult. Accounting scholars tend to focus on information production and disclosure, behavioural finance researchers often concentrate on trading behaviour and price dynamics, and information systems scholars work on data quality, algorithmic accountability and ethical data use in relative isolation from financial market questions. Building a more connected field will require researchers who are comfortable working across these traditions.

The disciplinary profile of the documents shows that most studies come from business, management, accounting, economics and finance, with smaller contributions from social sciences, decision sciences and the humanities. This is understandable given that financial reporting and capital markets are core concerns of business and economics departments. At the same time, the modest representation of psychology, sociology and related fields, and the near absence of information systems and data science perspectives, suggests that many relevant theories and methods have not yet been fully used. Greater engagement with perspectives on judgment under uncertainty, social influence, information processing and data governance could deepen understanding of how investors actually work with financial reports (Sumardi & Anshari, 2020).

The majority of documents come from the United States, with only a small number from Canada and the United Kingdom and none from other countries. This geographical concentration reflects the scale of US capital markets and the strength of its research infrastructure in accounting and finance, but it also means that most findings come from a narrow institutional context. Investor behaviour, reporting practices and data governance regimes in emerging markets or civil law countries may differ in important ways. Expanding research coverage to a wider set of countries would help clarify how legal systems, regulatory environments, cultural norms and data governance arrangements influence the relationship between financial reporting and investor psychology.

The keyword co-occurrence analysis highlights the conceptual focus of the existing literature. Many studies investigate specific psychological tendencies such as confirmation bias, anchoring, recency bias, loss aversion, herd behaviour and overconfidence, as well as broader notions of limited attention and investor sentiment. These constructs are well established as drivers of departures from fully rational behaviour. However, the same analysis shows less systematic attention to how particular features of financial reports, such as language complexity, narrative structure, presentation format or the use of visual elements, interact with these biases, and almost no attention to data governance variables such as data quality controls, audit trails, cyber security, algorithmic oversight and ethical use of personal data. In other words, research has documented that investors are subject to biases, but has given less effort to examining how the design of reporting and the governance of underlying data can either reduce or strengthen those tendencies (Loewenstein et al., 2014; Sumardi & Anshari, 2020).

The primary interview data from Indonesian equity market participants adds an important layer to these findings. The interviews confirm that traders and investors are distinct groups with different psychological profiles, and that treating all market participants as a uniform category overlooks meaningful differences. Traders experience higher emotional intensity because their short time horizon and reliance on price movements create constant psychological pressure. Every trade carries the weight of a quick decision made under uncertainty, and the emotional cycle of excitement, anxiety and regret repeats many times each day. This level of intensity makes traders especially vulnerable to biases such as overconfidence, where they believe they can read the market better than others, herding, where they follow what other traders are doing, and anchoring, where they get stuck on a particular price level (Anshari et al., 2026).

Investors experience a different type of psychological challenge. Their emotional intensity is lower on a daily basis, but they face sustained pressure over longer periods. Holding a stock that drops 30 per cent over several months requires a different kind of emotional discipline than managing a losing trade for a few hours (Ridzuan et al., 2026). The interviews showed that investors are more likely to fall into confirmation bias, where they focus on information that supports their existing view of a company, and loss aversion, where they refuse to sell a declining stock because they hope it will recover. Several investors also reported experiencing analysis paralysis, especially when faced with large amounts of financial data and conflicting analyst opinions (Yusuf et al., 2026).

The interview finding that traders see volatility as opportunity while investors see volatility as risk and also as a chance for accumulation when fundamentals are strong is particularly important. It suggests that the same market event can trigger completely different psychological and behavioural responses depending on whether the participant is a trader or an investor. A sharp market drop that sends traders looking for short-term profit may cause investors to review their analysis and potentially increase their holdings. These different responses mean that financial reporting and disclosure may need to serve multiple audiences with different information needs and different psychological profiles (Aliakhbar et al., 2026).

The trust-related comments from both groups tie these findings back to data governance. Investors who stopped relying on a company's reports after noticing restatements or governance scandals were, in effect, responding to a perceived failure of data governance. Traders who tracked rumours of manipulation or regulatory action were doing the same thing through a different lens. In both cases, the credibility of the information ecosystem shaped market behaviour as strongly as the content of any individual disclosure. This pattern is consistent with arguments in the broader governance literature that trust in data and its handling is a precondition for trust in any communication built on that data (Sumardi & Anshari, 2020; Anshari et al., 2021).

The findings also carry implications for practice and policy. Standard setters and regulators often assume that improvements in disclosure quantity and quality will translate directly into more efficient markets. The evidence reviewed here suggests that this assumption is incomplete. If investors rely on mental shortcuts, focus on recent information or follow the crowd, then even well-designed reporting regimes may not deliver their intended benefits (Hussain et al., 2023). If, in addition, the underlying data suffers from weak quality, poor security or ethical lapses, then reported numbers can be wrong in ways that amplify rather than correct psychological biases. Regulators and professional bodies may therefore need to complement traditional disclosure rules with two kinds of additional guidance. The first would explicitly recognise behavioural constraints, for example through recommendations on plain language, balanced narratives, or the presentation of key metrics in formats that reduce common interpretive errors (Bai et al., 2018). The second would strengthen data governance standards around how firms produce, store, audit and secure the data that flows into their reports, including how AI-based tools are monitored within reporting pipelines (Anshari et al., 2021; Anshari et al., 2023).

The Indonesian context adds a further consideration. In emerging markets where retail participation is growing rapidly, many new participants enter the market with limited financial literacy and high exposure to social media-driven sentiment.

Financial literacy programmes in such settings could benefit from recognising the different emotional and cognitive profiles of traders and investors and providing targeted guidance for each group, along with basic education on how to assess the credibility of company disclosures and the governance behind them (Sait & Anshari, 2022; Anshari & Hamdan, 2022).

For corporate managers and investor relations teams, the findings stress the importance of thinking about reports not only as legal compliance documents but also as communication tools that interact with psychological tendencies and rest on data governance foundations. Decisions about narrative emphasis, ordering of information and the use of summaries can alter how investors perceive risk and performance (Liu, 2023). Decisions about data quality controls, audit trails, access rights and ethical use of customer and employee data shape whether the numbers underneath those narratives can be trusted in the first place (Sumardi & Anshari, 2020). Awareness of common biases and of data governance risks can help preparers anticipate how disclosures might be received and adjust their communication and control strategies accordingly, within the boundaries of fair and balanced reporting.

Future research could extend the bibliometric analysis to additional databases and languages, which would provide a more complete map of global scholarship in this area. Empirical and experimental studies could then test specific hypotheses about how reporting design and data governance arrangements affect biased judgments in realistic decision settings. Longitudinal analyses might explore whether regulatory changes, such as new disclosure requirements, readability guidelines or data protection rules, influence the prevalence of particular biases in market reactions. Future studies should also expand primary data collection to include larger samples of traders and investors from different country contexts, and could use survey instruments alongside interviews to allow for quantitative comparison. By moving beyond documentation of biases toward evaluation of concrete reporting and governance solutions, and by recognising the different psychological profiles of market participants, researchers can help build a more practical and more relevant understanding of how financial information and investor psychology interact in contemporary capital markets.

6. CONCLUSION

This chapter examined how financial reporting, investor psychology and data governance intersect in the academic literature and in the real experience of equity market participants. By mapping Scopus-indexed documents published between 1998 and 2025, the analysis showed that research explicitly linking financial reporting and investor psychology is limited and under-explored. These publications are concentrated in business and finance journals and are mainly produced in the United States, with smaller contributions from Canada and the United Kingdom. As a result, current knowledge is shaped by a narrow disciplinary and geographical base, and data governance considerations are almost entirely absent from the bibliometric record.

The conceptual mapping highlighted strong interest in well-known psychological tendencies such as confirmation bias, anchoring, recency bias, loss aversion, herd behaviour, overconfidence, emotional reactions and analysis paralysis. However, there is much less systematic work on how specific features of financial reports, including language, structure and presentation, interact with these tendencies, and still less on how the data governance arrangements behind reports shape the credibility of the information investors receive. The findings therefore suggest that existing research has focused more on documenting investor biases than on understanding how disclosure design and data governance practices might reduce or strengthen them.

The primary interview data from Indonesian equity market participants adds a new contribution by showing that traders and investors are distinct groups with different psychological responses. Traders experience higher emotional intensity and make faster decisions under pressure, seeing volatility as their main source of opportunity. Investors experience lower but more sustained emotional demands, and they see volatility as risk but also as a chance for accumulation when company fundamentals remain strong. Both groups, in their own way, also respond to signals about the trustworthiness of company data, which points back to the importance of sound data governance. These differences mean that financial reporting, investor education and market regulation would benefit from treating traders and investors as separate audiences with different information needs and psychological profiles, and from strengthening the data governance foundations on which all corporate disclosures rest (Sumardi & Anshari, 2020; Anshari et al., 2021; Sait & Anshari, 2022). By combining bibliometric evidence with field data from an emerging market setting, this chapter offers a broader and more grounded view of how financial information, investor psychology and data governance interact in equity stock markets.

REFERENCES

Adams, P., Hunt, S., Palmer, C., & Zaliauskas, R. (2021). Testing the effectiveness of consumer financial disclosure: Experimental evidence from savings accounts. *Journal of Financial Economics, 141*(1), 122–147. DOI: 10.1016/j.jfineco.2020.05.009

Agarwal, S., & Tewari, R. (2025). *Role of emotions in investment decision-making: A systematic review*. Qualitative Research in Financial Markets., DOI: 10.1108/QRFM-01-2025-0001

Alam, M. R., Ahmad, A., Akhter, J., & Aziz, T. (2025). Mapping the field of behavioral finance: A systematic review and bibliometric analysis. Asian Education and Development Studies, 1–23. DOI: 10.1108/AEDS-07-2024-0162

Aliakhbar, I. H., Anshari, M., & Masri, M. (2026). Digital wallets as enablers of sustainable digital finance for ESG integration and global sustainability goals. *South Asian Journal of Business Studies*, 1-22.

Anderson, H. D., & Chang, Y. Y. (2019). Interdisciplinary finance. *Managerial Finance, 45*(1), 85–87. DOI: 10.1108/MF-01-2019-537

Anshari, M., Almunawar, M. N., Masri, M., & Hamdan, M. (2021). Financial technology with AI-enabled and ethical challenges. *Society, 58*(3), 189–195. DOI: 10.1007/s12115-021-00592-w

Anshari, M., Almunawar, M. N., Masri, M., Ordoñez, D. E., & Pablos, P. (2026). Industry 4.0 and the sustainable business model for the digital marketplace. *International Journal of Innovation Science*, •••, 1–28. DOI: 10.1108/IJIS-02-2025-0092

Anshari, M., & Hamdan, M. (2022). Enhancing e-government with a digital twin for innovation management. *Journal of Science and Technology Policy Management, 13*(4), 940–959. DOI: 10.1108/JSTPM-11-2021-0176

Anshari, M., Hamdan, M., Ahmad, N., Ali, E., & Haidi, H. (2023). COVID-19, artificial intelligence, ethical challenges and policy implications. *AI & Society, 38*(2), 707–720. DOI: 10.1007/s00146-022-01471-6

Armansyah, R. F. (2022). Herd instinct bias, emotional biases, and information processing biases in investment decisions. Jurnal Manajemen dan Kewirausahaan, 24(2), 105–117.

Avgouleas, E. (2009). The global financial crisis and the disclosure paradigm in European financial regulation: The case for reform. *European Company and Financial Law Review, 6*(4). Advance online publication. DOI: 10.1515/ECFR.2009.440

Bai, X., Dong, Y., & Hu, N. (2018). Financial report readability and stock return synchronicity. *Applied Economics*, *51*(4), 346–363. DOI: 10.1080/00036846.2018.1495824

Barber, B. M., & Odean, T. (2000). Trading is hazardous to your wealth: The common stock investment performance of individual investors. *The Journal of Finance*, *55*(2), 773–806. DOI: 10.1111/0022-1082.00226

Biddle, G. C., Hilary, G., & Verdi, R. S. (2009). How does financial reporting quality relate to investment efficiency? *Journal of Accounting and Economics*, *48*(2–3), 112–131. DOI: 10.1016/j.jacceco.2009.09.001

Dagli, N., Haque, M., & Kumar, S. (2025). Bibliometric analysis in scientific research: Applications, limitations, and key considerations for authors. *Bangladesh Journal of Medical Science*, *24*(1), 7–10. DOI: 10.3329/bjms.v24i1.78602

Dau, N. H., Nguyen, D. V., & Thi, H. (2024). Annual report readability and firms' investment decisions. *Cogent Economics & Finance*, *12*(1), 2296230. Advance online publication. DOI: 10.1080/23322039.2023.2296230

Donthu, N., Kumar, S., Mukherjee, D., Pandey, N., & Lim, W. M. (2021). How to conduct a bibliometric analysis: An overview and guidelines. *Journal of Business Research*, *133*, 285–296. DOI: 10.1016/j.jbusres.2021.04.070

Fei, T., & Liu, X. (2021). Herding and market volatility. *International Review of Financial Analysis*, *78*, 101880. DOI: 10.1016/j.irfa.2021.101880

Finet, A., Kristoforidis, K., & Laznicka, J. (2025). Negative emotions and decision-making paralysis among individual investors: A qualitative approach. *Risks*, *13*(11), 209. DOI: 10.3390/risks13110209

Gandre, P. (2020). US stock prices and recency-biased learning in the run-up to the Global Financial Crisis and its aftermath. *Journal of International Money and Finance*, *104*, 102165. DOI: 10.1016/j.jimonfin.2020.102165

Graham, B., & Dodd, D. (2009). *Security analysis* (6th ed.). McGraw-Hill.

Greenwald, B. C., Kahn, J., Bellissimo, E., Cooper, M. A., & Santos, T. (2020). *Value investing: From Graham to Buffett and beyond* (2nd ed.). Wiley.

Healy, P. M., & Palepu, K. G. (2001). Information asymmetry, corporate disclosure, and the capital markets: A review of the empirical disclosure literature. *Journal of Accounting and Economics*, *31*(1–3), 405–440. DOI: 10.1016/S0165-4101(01)00018-0

Hussain, S. M., Alaya, A., & Azizi, T. A. (2023). The impact of financial accounting disclosures on investors' reactions towards bad news: The moderating role of investors' sentiments. *Cogent Economics & Finance*, *11*(2), 2228087. Advance online publication. DOI: 10.1080/23322039.2023.2228087

Inghelbrecht, K., & Tedde, M. (2024). Overconfidence, financial literacy and excessive trading. *Journal of Economic Behavior & Organization*, *219*, 152–195. DOI: 10.1016/j.jebo.2024.01.010

Islam, K. U., Bhat, S. A., Lone, U. M., Darzi, M. A., & Malik, I. A. (2024). Financial risk propensity and investment decisions: An empirical analysis using behavioural biases. *IIMB Management Review*, *36*(3), 213–229. Advance online publication. DOI: 10.1016/j.iimb.2024.06.004

Kahneman, D., & Tversky, A. (1979). Prospect theory: An analysis of decision under risk. *Econometrica*, *47*(2), 263–292. DOI: 10.2307/1914185

Liu, B. (2023). Share pledge and qualitative information disclosures: Evidence from the tone of management discussion and analysis. *Economic Analysis and Policy*, *78*, 1342–1358. DOI: 10.1016/j.eap.2023.05.010

Liu, Q., Ali, N. L., & Lee, H. Y. (2025). Applying VOSviewer in a bibliometric review on English language teacher education research: An analysis of narratives, networks and numbers. *Cogent Education*, *12*(1), 2449728. Advance online publication. DOI: 10.1080/2331186X.2025.2449728

Lo, A. W., & Repin, D. V. (2002). The psychophysiology of real-time financial risk processing. *Journal of Cognitive Neuroscience*, *14*(3), 323–339. DOI: 10.1162/089892902317361877

Loewenstein, G., Sunstein, C. R., & Golman, R. (2014). Disclosure: Psychology changes everything. *Annual Review of Economics*, *6*(1), 391–419. DOI: 10.1146/annurev-economics-080213-041341

Mahmood, F., Arshad, R., Khan, S., Afzal, A., & Bashir, M. (2024). Impact of behavioral biases on investment decisions and the moderation effect of financial literacy: An evidence of Pakistan. *Acta Psychologica*, *247*, 104303. DOI: 10.1016/j.actpsy.2024.104303

Mardiana, R., Yossinomita, Y., Saputra, M. H., Mandasari, R., & Kartika, Y. D. (2025). Behavioral bias (availability, representativeness, anchoring, and confirmation) toward investment decision-making. [SMEs]. *Journal of Management: Small and Medium Enterprises*, *18*(1), 399–412.

Mosteanu, N. R.Narcisa Roxana Mosteanu. (2017). The influence of financial markets on countries' economic life. *Economics World, 5*(3). Advance online publication. DOI: 10.17265/2328-7144/2017.03.007

Nguyen, T. H., Vu, L. P. T., Mai, A. N., & Tran, T. Q. (2025). Do narrative-related disclosures in the annual report enhance firm value? New evidence from an emerging market. *International Review of Financial Analysis, 102*, 104077. DOI: 10.1016/j.irfa.2025.104077

Ninkov, A., Frank, J. R., & Maggio, L. A. (2021). Bibliometrics: Methods for studying academic publishing. *Perspectives on Medical Education, 11*(3), 173–176. DOI: 10.1007/S40037-021-00695-4

Paule-Vianez, J., Gomez-Martinez, R., & Prado-Roman, C. (2020). A bibliometric analysis of behavioural finance with mapping analysis tools. *European Research on Management and Business Economics, 26*(2), 71–77. Advance online publication. DOI: 10.1016/j.iedeen.2020.01.001

Pessin, V. Z., Yamane, L. H., & Siman, R. R. (2022). Smart bibliometrics: An integrated method of science mapping and bibliometric analysis. *Scientometrics, 127*(6), 3695–3718. DOI: 10.1007/s11192-022-04406-6

Ridzuan, N. N., Masri, M., & Anshari, M. (2026). Exploratory Study of the Fintech Regulative Sandbox: Opportunities and Challenges. *Promoting Inclusivity and Accessibility With FinTech*, 395-414.

Sait, M. A., & Anshari, M. (2022). Assessing Brunei Darussalam public and private sector readiness towards big data application. *International Journal of Asian Business and Information Management, 13*(2), 1–22. DOI: 10.4018/IJABIM.20220701.oa7

Singh, V. K., Singh, P., Karmakar, M., Leta, J., & Mayr, P. (2021). The journal coverage of Web of Science, Scopus and Dimensions: A comparative analysis. *Scientometrics, 126*(6), 5113–5142. DOI: 10.1007/s11192-021-03948-5

Sumardi, W. H., & Anshari, M. (2020). Employing big data in business organisation and business ethics. *International Journal of Business Governance and Ethics, 14*(3), 181–205. DOI: 10.1504/IJBGE.2020.106349

Thakur, K. K., Lekurwale, R., Pansare, R., & Bansode, S. (2024). Bibliometric analysis on bioprinting: Mapping co-occurrence of keywords and future research direction using VOSviewer. 78–92. DOI: 10.1201/9781003596707-9

Vafaeimehr, A., Ansari, S., & Rahmani, M. (2023). Confirmation bias in investment decisions: A behavioural finance review. *Journal of Behavioural Finance Studies, 8*(2), 45–62.

Yu, X., & Zhao, L. (2023). Textual disclosure complexity and analysts' weighting of information. *Journal of Contemporary Accounting & Economics, 100395*. Advance online publication. DOI: 10.1016/j.jcae.2023.100395

Yusuf, H., Fitri, A., & Razzaq, A. (2026). Using artificial intelligence for human-AI collaboration in knowledge management systems to improve organizational efficiency and learning. In *Driving Organizational Transformation Through Human-Robotic Collaboration* (pp. 35–48). IGI Global Scientific Publishing.

Chapter 7
Governing Financial Data in the FinTech Era:
Digital Sovereignty, Gender Inequality, and Consumer Protection in Emerging Economies

Wahyu Wibowo
http://orcid.org/0009-0000-5176-7103
Sunan Kalijaga State Islamic University, Yogyakarta, Indonesia

Bagas Noval Ramadhani
http://orcid.org/0009-0006-2783-5851
Jurai Siwo Islamic State University, Lampung, Indonesia

Taufikur Rohman
http://orcid.org/0009-0003-2231-0739
Sunan Kalijaga State Islamic University, Yogyakarta, Indonesia

Nasrudin Nasrudin
http://orcid.org/0009-0008-2215-6192
Universitas Islam Kalimantan Muhammad Arsyad Al Banjary Banjarmasin, Indonesia

Nofriansyah Nofriansyah
http://orcid.org/0009-0001-5150-6082
Indonesia University of Education, Bandung, Indonesia

ABSTRACT

This study examines financial data governance in the fintech era by linking digital sovereignty, gender inequality, and consumer protection in emerging economies.

DOI: 10.4018/979-8-2600-2233-7.ch007

Fintech is understood not only as a tool of financial inclusion but also as a datafied infrastructure that transforms transactions, identities, and behaviors into governable and monetizable assets. The discussion shows how platform power, cross-border data dependence, and algorithmic decision-making reshape state authority and deepen user vulnerability, especially for women and digitally less literate groups. It also highlights how opaque credit scoring, weak accountability, and limited regulatory capacity may reproduce exclusion under the language of innovation. A more inclusive governance framework therefore requires data justice, algorithmic accountability, secure interoperability, and stronger consumer protection.

INTRODUCTION

The last decade has witnessed a fundamental shift in the financial technology (fintech) sector, especially in developing countries where digitalization has become a key shortcut to financial inclusion. Digital payments, online loans, machine learning-based credit scoring, and open banking systems now rely not only on traditional banking history but on large-scale extraction, integration, and analysis of transaction data, behavioral data, and user identity data. As a result, financial data can no longer be viewed as a mere administrative record; it is now a form of power infrastructure that determines who is visible to the system, who qualifies for financial services, and who can be monetized through advanced data processing (Hanisch et al., 2023; Purtova & van Maanen, 2024; Tigges et al., 2024; Babina et al., 2025).

The common narrative often presents fintech as a progressive tool for increasing financial access for the unbanked and underbanked (Afjal, 2023; Kishor et al., 2024; Dao Ha et al., 2025). While this view holds some truth, emerging evidence shows that access to customer data through platforms like open banking can not only encourage new fintech players but also expand the options available for financial services (He et al., 2023; Dinçkol et al., 2023; Casolaro et al., 2024; Akyildirim et al., 2025). However, this expansion of access has simultaneously shifted control away from traditional financial institutions to data platforms, digital infrastructure providers, and cloud ecosystems, many of which operate across borders. Therefore, the central issue of fintech in developing countries is not simply whether digital services can reach the underserved, but who controls the data architecture that makes such inclusion possible. At this juncture, digital sovereignty becomes critical—not just as a discourse of data nationalism, but as the real capability of the state to regulate the storage, transfer, interoperability, auditability, and inferential use of its citizens' financial data.

The problem is that much of the discussion surrounding fintech governance still centers on privacy in a narrow sense, focusing only on data breaches or weak user consent. In fact, recent developments indicate that the more profound risk lies in the power of inference: the platform's ability to transform transaction and behavioral data into automated assessments of creditworthiness, risk profiles, and commercial strategies that users cannot easily review (Ayari et al., 2025; Farahani et al., 2025). In the digital economy, consumers not only submit data, but also provide the potential meanings that can be inferred from that data. In this context, consent often becomes a formality, lacking real substance; users click "agree" but have no power over the analytical models, scoring algorithms, or the distribution of economic benefits derived from their data. Therefore, consumer protection in fintech must evolve from a notice-and-consent model to one based on contestability, explainability, and accountability for automated decisions (Aldboush & Ferdous, 2023; Ahnert et al., 2025; Sargeant, 2026).

These concerns become even more pressing when viewed from a gender perspective. Emerging research highlights that fintech does not automatically close the gender gap; in fact, in many contexts, the gender gap in fintech usage can be wider than in traditional bank account ownership (Chen et al., 2023; Galindo-Manrique & Rojas-Vargas, 2025). Cross-country studies by Chen et al. (2023) indicate a persistent fintech gender gap in digital financial service usage, while more recent studies in emerging markets and low-income countries show that the evolving fintech environment has not always been followed by equitable distribution of benefits for women, especially in access to digital credit and the utilization of data-driven financial services (Ogawa et al., 2022; Özşuca, 2024; Khan et al., 2026). These findings are significant because they reveal that digital exclusion is not only about lack of access but also about how the system reads female subjects through data that may be incomplete, unstable, or shaped by unequal socio-economic positions (Magwedere & Marozva, 2025).

This gap has largely been overlooked. While many studies have addressed digital financial inclusion as a matter of expanding access, fewer have explored the inclusion-extraction paradox: groups previously invisible to formal financial systems can only be included once they become highly readable by data systems (Omotubora, 2024; Tigges et al., 2024; Sargeant, 2026). For women in developing countries, this situation creates a double burden: on one hand, fintech promises faster and more flexible access, but on the other hand, alternative data-based models and behavioral scoring have the potential to translate structural constraints—such as informal income, unstable device ownership, consumption patterns shaped by domestic responsibilities, and thin transaction histories—into individual risk signals. Inferentially, social inequality can be embedded into data models and later reappear as seemingly neutral credit decisions. Studies on AI for women's financial inclusion in Nigeria (Omotubora, 2024), research on alternative data in credit scoring (Tigges et al., 2024), and debates surrounding explainability in credit decisions (Sargeant,

2026) emphasize that product design, data proxy selection, and regulatory frameworks determine whether fintech is truly inclusive or simply replicates old biases in more sophisticated forms.

Policy challenges in developing countries are more complex than just a lack of regulation. The deeper issue lies in the combination of reliance on foreign digital infrastructure, limited algorithmic audit capabilities, fragmented data protection regimes, and the pressure to remain innovation-friendly. As a result, states may be strong in rhetoric around sovereignty but weak in their ability to enforce control over financial data flows and digital scoring practices. In such contexts, open banking and interoperability may lead to two diverging outcomes. If designed with data reciprocity, security standards, and strong objection rights, these frameworks can foster competition and increase consumer choice. However, without these principles, they can further concentrate power in the hands of those who are most capable of integrating data, building predictive models, and controlling user interfaces. The latest literature on open banking, platform power, and the political economy of fintech regulation highlights the interconnectedness of competition, data protection, and consumer rights (Babina et al., 2025; Zhang & Zhang, 2025; Graef & Bostoen, 2026).

The paper argues that financial data governance in the fintech era must be understood as a multi-layered issue, interrelating digital sovereignty over infrastructure and data flows, gender inequality in the datafication of financial services, and consumer protection against inferential risks and automated decisions. This perspective offers a novel contribution compared to previous studies that often compartmentalize these issues into separate domains, such as gender-neutral privacy, inclusion without platform power, or innovation without data sovereignty. In developing countries, the interplay of these three factors determines whether digital transformation will enhance citizens' capabilities or deepen new dependencies.

Thus, the conceptual contribution of this paper is not merely to assert that financial data needs regulation—something widely acknowledged—but to highlight that what truly needs regulation are the social and political conditions of digital readability itself. The focus shifts from the question, "How does fintech expand access?" to "Under what conditions is data granted, who benefits from the analytics, and what mechanisms exist when inference harms already vulnerable groups?" From this perspective, consumer protection must go beyond cybersecurity or consent for data usage and encompass the right to understand, challenge, and limit the impact of automated decisions. Likewise, digital sovereignty should not be limited to server localization, but must include the state's ability to set standards for interoperability, algorithmic auditing, and cross-border governance that prioritizes data fairness. This framework makes the study of fintech, gender inequality, and consumer protection in emerging economies not only relevant but urgently important, both theoretically and in terms of policy.

CONCEPTUAL FRAMEWORK

The conceptual framework presented in this paper builds on the premise that fintech cannot merely be understood as an innovation in financial services; rather, it should be viewed as an arena of financial datafication. This term refers to the process in which users' transactions, identities, behaviors, and economic habits are transformed into data that can be processed, exchanged, and monetized. Within this framework, fintech goes beyond accelerating services such as payments, lending, or investments—it also creates a new social classification infrastructure. This infrastructure determines who is deemed viable, risky, trustworthy, or profitable in the digital financial ecosystem (Hanisch et al., 2023). Thus, fintech governance cannot solely focus on operational efficiency; it must also be understood as an issue of control, trust, and the distribution of power in a society that increasingly depends on data-driven decisions.

Financial data, from this perspective, is no longer simply an administrative trace of economic activity; it has become a strategic asset that enables platforms and financial institutions to assess, predict, and influence user behavior. This shift is crucial because it alters the relationship between citizens, markets, and states. While in the traditional financial model, risk assessment primarily relied on formal credit history, the fintech model increasingly depends on alternative data, transaction patterns, device usage, and other behavioral information (Ahnert et al., 2025; Babina et al., 2025). As a result, financial access is now more determined by the system's ability to interpret subjects through data, rather than simply by the economic needs of users. This is a critical point often overlooked: digital inclusion is frequently hailed as the expansion of access, but in parallel, it also represents an expansion of citizens' visibility by digital systems. In other words, fintech creates what can be called the inclusion-extraction paradox: the more someone desires to be included in digital financial services, the more they must expose themselves to data extraction and inference.

A central concept in this framework is digital sovereignty. Digital sovereignty is not simply about the localization of servers or the nationalization of data; it refers to a state's capacity to establish conditions for how financial data is collected, stored, transferred, processed, shared, and audited, particularly in an environment where infrastructure is often controlled by cross-border actors (Belli et al., 2024). Recent literature shows that data sovereignty is intricately tied to issues such as cross-border data transfers, reliance on cloud services and global platforms, and the ability of states to maintain policy autonomy amid technological and market asymmetries (Belli et al., 2024; Scherenberg et al., 2024; Santaniello, 2025). Therefore, in the context of developing countries, the key issue is not merely whether the state has regulations in place, but whether it has the institutional and technological capacity to enforce those regulations against actors who control the infrastructure, interoperability standards, and computing architecture.

This framework positions fintech as a meeting point for sovereignty, platform power, and the governance gap. On the one hand, policies such as open banking promise data portability, enhanced competition, and broader service innovation. Early evidence suggests that access to customer data can facilitate the entry of new fintech players, expand credit offerings, and enhance financial service relationships for consumers and small businesses (Akyildirim et al., 2025; Babina et al., 2025; Zhang & Zhang, 2025). On the other hand, interoperability and data sharing do not automatically lead to a more equitable distribution of power. If technical standards, objections, and algorithmic accountability mechanisms are weak, then data disclosure can amplify the concentration of power in the hands of those most capable of integrating data, constructing predictive models, and controlling user interfaces. As such, this framework views fintech governance as a struggle over who has the right to access data, for what purpose, under what form of supervision, and with what recourse for affected parties.

In this context, gender inequality is not treated as a mere side effect, but as a structural dimension of financial datafication. While many discussions still view gender inequality in fintech as being limited to issues such as device access, literacy, or account ownership, recent studies show that the gender gap in fintech usage is far more profound. Chen et al. (2023) reveal that women are not only less likely to use fintech services across many countries, but are also more vulnerable to being disadvantaged in data-driven classification processes. Omotubora (2024) found that the gender gap in fintech usage is even larger than the gap in traditional bank account ownership. Other studies show that a stronger fintech environment can reduce disparities, but such progress heavily depends on supportive factors such as women's literacy, workforce participation, institutional quality, and access to digital infrastructure (Khan et al., 2026; Sargeant, 2026). This indicates that fintech is not inherently inclusive—it only becomes inclusive if the social and regulatory environment ensures that old biases do not simply resurface as digital risk scores and profiles.

This framework sharpens the analytical lens on gendered datafication, which is not merely a digital divide but a manifestation of how social inequality is ingrained in fintech systems. Women in developing countries often operate in informal economies, have limited credit histories, share devices within households, and exhibit transaction patterns shaped by domestic responsibilities. In machine-learning-based credit systems, these conditions are often read not as social contexts that need to be understood, but as individual signals of uncertainty or risk. Consequently, structural bias can subtly infiltrate the models, appearing as neutral indicators of creditworthiness. Research by Omotubora (2024) underscores that technological innovation alone is insufficient; product design, data proxies, and transparency policies are crucial in determining whether women are genuinely included or merely used as new objects for analysis. Therefore, gender must not be treated as an additional variable but as a critical lens through which we understand how social inequalities are embedded in fintech's data infrastructure.

The third component of this framework is consumer protection, which must be understood in broader terms than just privacy protection. In the fintech ecosystem, consumer vulnerability stems not only from data leaks or weak cybersecurity measures but also from inferential harm—the harm that occurs when user data is used to generate profiles, predictions, and automated decisions that are opaque and difficult to contest. This is where the concepts of explainability, contestability, and algorithmic accountability become crucial. Sargeant (2026) suggests that algorithm-based credit decisions weaken accountability when the basis for their inferences cannot be adequately explained to consumers. At the same time, research by Ahnert et al. (2025) on digital payment privacy and cybersecurity in the banking sector shows that digital efficiency often comes at the cost of increased data observability, monitoring, and exposure. Therefore, consumer protection in fintech must evolve from the logic of mere notice-and-consent to the right to understand, challenge, and limit the inferential use of personal data.

This framework also acknowledges the importance of digital financial literacy as a conditioning factor, but not as a comprehensive solution. While digital financial literacy is essential for understanding digital transactions, recognizing fraud, and improving financial well-being, relying solely on literacy to protect consumers oversimplifies the issue. The power asymmetry between platforms and users is so vast that even digitally savvy consumers often lack the tools to assess how their data is profiled, how their risk is calculated, or how automated decisions affect their financial opportunities. Therefore, literacy should be viewed as an initial layer of protection, but substantive protection must come from system design, regulatory standards, and effective audit mechanisms. Research on the relationship between literacy, financial well-being, and fraud vulnerability supports the view that individual capabilities are important but cannot replace the need for robust structural governance (Choung et al., 2023; Isaia et al., 2024; Ibrushi et al., 2026).

Based on this framework, the paper proposes that fintech should be seen as an arena for financial datafication, digital sovereignty as the capacity to control data architecture, and gender inequality and consumer protection as the two primary areas where the impact of data power distribution is most evident. The relationship between these elements is interdependent: the weaker a country's digital sovereignty, the more likely platform dominance will prevail over financial data flows; the greater the platform dominance, the more likely that credit, payment, and financial service mechanisms will deepen gender bias and undermine consumer positions; and the weaker the algorithmic accountability, the harder it will be for the benefits of digital inclusion to translate into social justice. Thus, the theoretical contribution of this framework is to shift the focus from the old question of whether fintech improves inclusion to a more fundamental question: under what governance conditions does that inclusion occur, who bears the costs of datafication, and who benefits from the resulting digital readability?

FINANCIAL DATA GOVERNANCE IN THE FINTECH ECOSYSTEM

Financial data governance cannot be understood as just an administrative matter regarding who keeps the data and how long it is retained. In the fintech ecosystem, governance is really about setting the upper end of the data lifecycle: how data is collected, what categories are formed from it, who can access it, under what conditions it can be exchanged, and how the results of its processing are used to make decisions that have a direct impact on the economic lives of users (Purtova & van Maanen, 2024; Tigges et al., 2024). When financial data is viewed as an economic asset, the conversation shifts from mere information management to regulating power dynamics. Ultimately, those who control the data also control the ability to interpret behavior, predict needs, and influence users' financial decisions. In this sense, financial data governance represents the governance of citizens' economic visibility within the system.

Practically, the issue becomes more complex because fintech platforms not only collect data directly provided by users but also extract value from seemingly trivial traces. These include transaction frequency, payment patterns, cash flow stability, app usage habits, and interactions that are indirectly interpreted as risk signals (Egbert & Ulbricht, 2024). As a result, users don't simply submit data; they also open themselves to the creation of digital profiles that will be used to determine service eligibility, pricing, and access limits to financial products. A significant inequality arises when service providers understand far more about users than users understand about how these systems function (Aldboush & Ferdous, 2023). In such instances, consent becomes a mere formality, while substantive control remains in the hands of the platform that manages the analytical model, computing infrastructure, and classification logic.

This shift marks a fundamental change in financial risk assessment. Traditionally, credit decisions relied on relatively limited financial histories and recognizable data sources. However, fintech increasingly uses a combination of alternative data, predictive modeling, and automated systems, which work in layers that are not always easy to monitor. While this brings greater efficiency, it also alters the way individuals are recognized by the financial system (Tigges et al., 2024). Individuals are no longer judged solely based on what they own or formally do; they are assessed based on predicted behaviors derived from the data model. The problem arises when these decisions—such as credit access, interest rates, or service denial—are made without users fully understanding the basis of their judgments. In such cases, data governance should encompass transparency, traceability, and the ability to challenge automated decisions, not just the legality of data collection at the outset (Sargeant, 2026).

Moreover, platformization deepens the dominance of service providers. These platforms not only offer financial products but also determine the pathways through which data flows (Egbert & Ulbricht, 2024). The platform becomes a nexus between users, financial institutions, third parties, and analytics tools, expanding its power beyond service provision to control the very architecture of the market itself. They define technical standards, interfaces, and interoperability formats that ultimately decide who enters the market and who is excluded. In certain contexts, open banking schemes can foster competition and provide users with more choices. However, without strong regulation, the opening of data access can lead to new forms of dependency, as the greatest value is captured by those who are most adept at consolidating, interpreting, and monetizing data at scale (Babina et al., 2025; Graef & Bostoen, 2026)Therefore, financial data governance must not only ensure protection but also guarantee that the benefits of interoperability are equitably distributed, rather than monopolized by a few digital giants.

The sensitivity of this issue becomes more pronounced because financial data is deeply intimate. It reflects not only an individual's ability to pay but also the rhythm of their life, social networks, economic activity locations, vulnerability levels, and even crisis patterns they may be facing. From seemingly simple transaction data, systems can infer income regularity, debt dependence, consumption preferences, and the likelihood of default. Therefore, data breaches or misuse of financial data should not be seen as ordinary technical incidents, but as potentially catastrophic events with lasting consequences on a user's economic reputation, bargaining position, and access to other services. In the digital payments ecosystem, even the choice of payment methods can create a trade-off between efficiency and privacy, as digital transactions leave traces that can be used for further analysis (Ahnert et al., 2025). This is why cybersecurity, internal access controls, and clarity about data processing purposes must be central to governance, rather than being mere compliance requirements.

From these points, we can see that adequate financial data governance must be built on several interrelated principles. First, data should not be excessively collected without a clear connection to the service's purpose. Second, users should be informed not just that their data is being processed, but also how that processing affects the outcomes they receive. Third, there must be an audit trail and accountability mechanisms to address automated decisions that cause harm or discrimination. Fourth, interoperability must be opened securely, ensuring that data does not become a closed monopoly. However, this openness must be limited by security, proportionality, and user control principles. In other words, good governance does not equate to complete restrictions, but rather to setting boundaries that allow innovation to thrive without sacrificing consumers' dignity, privacy, and bargaining power (Purtova & van Maanen, 2024; Babina et al., 2025; Perdana et al., 2025).

Ultimately, the issue of financial data governance in fintech comes down to one fundamental question: Is data being used to enhance users' economic capabilities, or is it deepening their dependence on non-transparent systems? As long as data is viewed only as a raw material for platform growth, user protection will always be subordinated to the logic of market expansion. However, when governance is framed as regulating power relations in data processing, fintech can evolve from a mere tool for efficiency to a fairer digital financial infrastructure. This is the point at which discussions about digital sovereignty, gender inequality, and consumer protection become critical—not as add-on issues, but as direct consequences of how financial data is governed from the very beginning.

DIGITAL SOVEREIGNTY AND CONTROL OVER FINANCIAL DATA

Digital sovereignty in the fintech ecosystem refers to the capacity of states to determine the conditions under which citizens' financial data is collected, stored, transferred, processed, shared, and used for economic decision-making. In the digital economy, sovereignty is not limited to the physical location of servers or the formal jurisdiction under which data is stored. It involves a deeper question of control: who owns or manages the computing infrastructure, who sets interoperability standards, who governs cross-border data transfers, and who benefits from the economic value generated by financial data. Therefore, control over financial data is not merely an administrative or technical concern. It is part of the state's broader ability to preserve policy autonomy within a digital architecture increasingly shaped by platform companies, cloud providers, financial technology firms, and global data regimes that may not always align with domestic public interests. Belli et al. (2024) emphasize that data sovereignty and data transfers are fundamental elements of digital transformation, while Santaniello (2025) conceptualizes digital sovereignty as a contested political resource that is continuously reshaped by global power relations.

In developing countries, the significance of digital sovereignty becomes particularly visible when governments seek to expand financial inclusion through fintech while relying on infrastructures that they do not fully control. Digital payment systems, e-wallets, open banking platforms, digital credit scoring, and app-based lending depend on cloud computing, application programming interfaces, cybersecurity systems, data storage facilities, and analytics tools that are often operated, owned, or standardized by cross-border actors (Mayer & Lu, 2025; Santaniello, 2025). As a result, a state may formally exercise jurisdiction over its citizens and financial markets, but it may not have substantive control over the data engines that mediate those activities. This creates a fundamental tension. On the one hand, digital transformation promises efficiency, reach, competition, and broader financial access. On the other hand, it may place countries in a position of growing dependence on external infrastructures to perform functions that are central to public policy, financial supervision, and consumer protection.

This dependence is not neutral. Mayer & Lu (2025) show that the global digital order is structured around unequal patterns of dependence, dominated by major "technopoles," especially the United States and China, which possess extensive capacity to control digital infrastructure, platforms, standards, and technological ecosystems. When this structure intersects with digital finance, the financial data of citizens in developing countries becomes more than an object of domestic legal protection. It becomes part of a wider geography of digital power. The question of where data is stored is therefore inseparable from questions about who has the computing capacity to process it, who can set the access protocols, who can audit the systems, and who captures the greatest value from data circulation. For this reason, control over financial data contains regulatory, technological, economic, and geopolitical dimensions at the same time (Santaniello, 2025). Countries with weak digital infrastructure may appear to regulate fintech formally, while the core processes of data processing, scoring, and platform governance remain shaped by external technical standards and commercial interests.

This condition explains why digital sovereignty cannot be reduced to data localization alone. Requiring financial data to be stored domestically may strengthen formal jurisdiction, but it does not automatically give the state the ability to understand, audit, restrict, or correct how data is processed and used to generate financial decisions. A server located within national territory may still operate through proprietary software, opaque algorithms, foreign cloud dependencies, or cross-border analytics arrangements. Santaniello (2025) shows that digital sovereignty is multi-layered and politically contested, while Belli et al. (2024) highlight that data transfers are a crucial site where domestic interests and global digital regimes are continuously negotiated. In fintech, this means that the state must do more than require data to remain within its territory. It must also regulate interoperability standards, third-party access, data-sharing permissions, audit obligations, cybersecurity requirements, and limits on the inferential use of citizens' financial data. Without these capacities, sovereignty risks becoming a fragile legal symbol rather than an operational capacity to govern digital financial systems.

The issue becomes more complex because fintech architectures are often promoted through the language of openness, innovation, competition, and consumer empowerment. Open banking, for example, is commonly presented as a mechanism that allows consumers to share transaction data with authorized third-party providers, thereby increasing competition and broadening access to financial products. Babina et al. (2025) show that open banking policies have been adopted in many countries and can encourage the entry of new fintech players, expand access to financial advice and credit, and create new financing relationships for consumers and small businesses. However, the opening of data flows is never free from power relations. The more data circulates, the more valuable it becomes for actors that are able to aggregate datasets, build predictive models, control user interfaces, and convert behavioral information into commercial advantage. Thus, without strong institutional safeguards, data portability may shift from an instrument of empowerment into a new pathway for platform dependency and digital power concentration.

For this reason, digital sovereignty must include governance over openness itself. Open banking and interoperability should not be understood simply as technical arrangements that allow data to move between institutions. They should be designed with clear principles of reciprocity, proportionality, security, auditability, and user control. Data-sharing frameworks should specify not only who can access data, but also for what purposes, under what security conditions, for how long, and with what mechanisms for revocation, correction, complaint, and redress. In addition, states must ensure that data portability does not benefit only large platforms that already possess superior analytics capacity. If smaller financial institutions and consumers lack meaningful bargaining power, open data regimes may reproduce inequality rather than correct it. In this sense, digital sovereignty is not the opposite of openness. Rather, it is the capacity to define the terms under which openness serves public interest, fair competition, and consumer protection.

At this point, control over financial data should be understood not only as a privacy issue, but also as a matter of governing economic classification. Graef & Bostoen (2026) map platform power into three forms of control: control over markets, control over individuals, and control over society. This typology is highly relevant to fintech because financial data allows platforms not only to compete in financial markets but also to build asymmetric knowledge about individuals and influence broader social structures. When platforms know more about users' risk profiles, consumption patterns, borrowing needs, repayment capacity, and economic vulnerabilities than users or regulators do, their power is no longer merely commercial. It becomes epistemic power: the power to define how individuals are seen, ranked, priced, and treated by the financial system. In such circumstances, state control over financial data becomes necessary to ensure that the classification of citizens does not occur entirely outside public supervision.

The digitization of payments and credit also creates a persistent trade-off between efficiency and privacy. Ahnert et al. (2025) show that digital payments can improve efficiency in economic transactions, but they also reveal information to financial actors, while more anonymous instruments such as cash provide stronger privacy protection but may reduce certain forms of efficiency. In fintech, this trade-off is especially important because financial inclusion is often pursued through systems that require continuous identification, transaction recording, behavioral monitoring, and automated assessment. The more digital financial systems depend on constantly readable identities and transaction histories, the greater the need for rules that determine who may observe what, for what purpose, and with what consequences for users. Digital sovereignty, therefore, should not be framed only as a state project against foreign actors. It should also be understood as a normative framework for limiting excessive economic observability and protecting citizens from disproportionate forms of data extraction.

For developing countries, this issue is particularly urgent because digital financial inclusion can easily become digital dependency if it is pursued without adequate control over data infrastructure. A country may successfully increase the number of digital payment users or online borrowers, while at the same time losing control over the systems that process financial behavior, evaluate risk, and determine future access. In such a situation, inclusion may expand numerically but weaken sovereignty structurally. The state becomes responsible for the social consequences of fintech systems, including exclusion, discrimination, fraud, and consumer harm, while lacking the technical and institutional capacity to inspect or correct the systems that produce those outcomes. This is why digital sovereignty must be connected to regulatory capacity, not only regulatory aspiration.

A more substantive approach to digital sovereignty in fintech should therefore include several elements. First, states must develop clear rules on cross-border data transfers, including safeguards for sensitive financial data and obligations for accountability when data is processed outside national jurisdiction. Second, they must strengthen institutional capacity for algorithmic audits, cybersecurity supervision, and technical assessment of data-driven financial services. Third, data-sharing frameworks such as open banking must include meaningful user rights, including the right to withdraw consent, challenge harmful outcomes, and receive explanations of automated decisions. Fourth, interoperability standards should be designed to prevent both data monopolies and unsafe data circulation. Finally, financial data governance should be aligned with consumer protection and gender-sensitive inclusion, because weak data control often affects vulnerable groups most severely.

In sum, digital sovereignty in fintech should not be understood as a defensive attempt to block data flows or isolate national markets. It is better understood as the capacity of the state to guide digital financial transformation so that it remains accountable to public interest. A country that controls financial data is not necessarily one that closes data circulation entirely, but one that can set fair conditions for openness, impose accountability on data processors, supervise cross-border data practices, and prevent digital infrastructure from hollowing out policy sovereignty from within. In developing countries, this is crucial because fintech can expand access while simultaneously creating new forms of dependence, extraction, and classification. From this perspective, the discussion of gender inequality and consumer protection becomes inseparable from digital sovereignty. When control over financial data is weak, the groups with the least bargaining power—women, low-income users, informal workers, and consumers with limited digital literacy—are often the first to bear the consequences.

GENDER INEQUALITY IN ACCESS TO AND UTILIZATION OF FINTECH

Gender inequality in the fintech ecosystem demonstrates that the digitalization of financial services does not automatically lead to equal inclusion. Women's access to digital payments, online loans, and app-based financial services is still heavily influenced by factors such as device ownership, internet connectivity, digital and financial literacy, job market participation, and social norms that restrict their control over economic resources. Thus, while fintech is often promoted as a fast track to financial inclusion, the real question is not only how broadly these services reach new users, but who can actually utilize them safely, consistently, and profitably. Cross-border evidence reveals a clear fintech gender gap: women's use of fintech products continues to lag behind men's, and this gap is, in many cases, even larger than the traditional gender gap in bank account ownership (Chen et al., 2023; Choung et al., 2023; Omotubora, 2024).

This gender gap is further complicated by barriers that go beyond initial access. While many women have successfully entered the digital ecosystem as users, they often remain in weaker positions when it comes to utilizing higher-value services, particularly digital credit (Khan et al., 2026). The impact of a stronger fintech environment in narrowing these gender disparities is highly contingent on supporting factors such as women's literacy, workforce participation, institutional quality, internet access, and basic infrastructure (Choung et al., 2023). In other words, fintech does not operate in a vacuum. It tends to increase opportunities when the socio-economic foundations are supportive, but it can also perpetuate existing inequalities when it enters environments that are inherently unequal.

The issue becomes even more pressing in digital lending services and data-driven credit scoring, where systems often appear neutral due to their reliance on statistical models and automated processing. However, the data used to assess users' economic viability is never entirely free of context. For example, when transaction histories, consumption patterns, income stability, and device usage patterns are used as key data points for credit assessments, women—who are more likely to work in informal sectors, have fixed incomes, or share devices within households—are often categorized as higher risk. As a result, social inequalities that were previously structural can resurface as objective-sounding scores, recommendations, or denials of service. Studies show that women are less likely to apply for digital loans, and even when they do, their approval rate is lower than men's, while similar gender disparities are not as pronounced in traditional bank loan systems (Oluoch & Alhassan, 2026).

This highlights the need to view gender inequality in fintech not only as a digital divide but as a fundamental issue of how data systems recognize and classify female subjects. In many cases, the barriers women face are not simply a matter of access, but stem from a mismatch between the design of digital products and the realities of their lives. For instance, an analysis of AI services for women's financial inclusion in Nigeria reveals that technological innovation alone is insufficient to bridge this gap. The design of fintech products, the assumptions made about ideal users, the transparency of the models used, and how these systems respond to social barriers all determine whether fintech is truly inclusive or simply expands the market without addressing existing inequalities (Omotubora, 2024).

At this juncture, gender issues cannot be treated as an afterthought or an additional variable. Instead, they should be the primary lens through which we assess whether fintech governance prioritizes access fairness or merely the efficiency of expansion. This is crucial because the expansion of fintech can only be deemed inclusive if it does more than open up access. It must also change the conditions that have historically made women more vulnerable to exclusion in the use of digital financial services. Without addressing issues such as literacy, product design, informal work contexts, and biases in data classification, fintech risks perpetuating a more subtle form of exclusion: appearing modern and efficient while still placing women in a disadvantaged position within the system.

In conclusion, the inclusivity of new fintech solutions depends not only on their ability to expand access but also on their capacity to rectify the social and structural factors that have historically marginalized women. Without significant attention to the gendered dimensions of digital financial services, the digital economy risks reinforcing rather than challenging traditional gender inequalities.

USER VULNERABILITY AND DIGITAL FINANCIAL LITERACY

User vulnerability in fintech services arises from the intersection of technological complexity and the limitations of users' understanding of how these systems function. Many users engage with digital payment services, online loans, or investment platforms through seemingly simple interfaces. However, behind this convenience lies a complex process of data collection, consent for information usage, profiling, and automated decision-making, all of which are not always easy for users to comprehend. In such cases, consent often becomes a formality rather than a genuine understanding of the implications. Users may click the "agree" button to access a service, but they rarely know what types of data are being collected, how that data is being analyzed, or how the results of that analysis impact their access to financial services. The ethics and privacy discussions in fintech highlight the core issues of bias, discrimination, transparency, data ownership, and control over personal information, which are fundamental to building trust within this ecosystem (Aldboush & Ferdous, 2023; Choung et al., 2023; Ibrushi et al., 2026).

In this context, digital financial literacy plays a critical role, as it extends beyond simply understanding how to use financial applications. It also involves recognizing the hidden risks embedded in the ease and convenience of digital services. Digital financial literacy includes the ability to comprehend digital transactions, account security, data footprints, terms of service, and potential risks such as fraud, which often exploits user negligence. Research by Choung et al. (2023) shows that digital financial literacy is closely linked to financial well-being, and that this relationship is largely shaped by financial knowledge and the ability to protect oneself from digital fraud. These findings underscore the importance of literacy not just as technical proficiency, but as a key element in safeguarding users' economic positions in the digital space. In essence, the less a person understands the digital financial ecosystem, the greater their vulnerability to harm—whether from poor financial decisions, exposure to fraud, or inadvertently agreeing to unfavorable terms.

However, focusing solely on literacy as the solution oversimplifies the problem—a tendency that many public policymakers gravitate toward, often because it is less costly than addressing structural issues. In fintech services, user vulnerability is not solely a result of a lack of knowledge; it is also driven by significant information asymmetry between platforms and consumers. Platforms have in-depth knowledge about how their models work, the purpose of data processing, and the economic value of the data they collect. In contrast, users typically only see the surface of the service (Egbert & Ulbricht, 2024). Even when users possess basic knowledge about security, they often lack the ability to assess how their data is being profiled, how their risk is calculated, or how automated decisions impact their pricing, credit scores, and access to financial opportunities. Therefore, while digital literacy is an essential first layer of protection, more substantive safeguards must come from system transparency, data usage restrictions, and platform accountability. Ethical critiques of fintech based on big data and AI emphasize that trust cannot rest solely on user intelligence; it must also be supported by governance mechanisms that limit the abuse of data power.

This vulnerability also manifests in the relationship between digital finance and fraud. Evidence from Ibrushi et al. (2026) highlights the real connection between financial knowledge and vulnerability to fraud in digital finance, though the effects vary across user groups. The findings suggest that participation in higher-risk digital assets can reduce the effectiveness of financial literacy in protecting users from fraud. This observation offers an important insight: users' vulnerabilities are not isolated but are influenced by the digital environment they engage with, the types of products they use, and the complexity of the decisions they face. The more complex the product and the more aggressively a platform utilizes data, the less likely it is that basic literacy alone can protect users from harm.

From this, it becomes clear that user protection in fintech must be approached on two levels. On one hand, users need to be empowered through digital financial literacy, enabling them to recognize risks, maintain security, and understand the basic consequences of engaging in digital financial activities. On the other hand, the system itself must be constrained by regulations that make consent more meaningful, ensure data usage is proportionate, and require automated decisions to be explainable and subject to challenge. Models of payments and privacy in the digital economy show that while digital transactions offer greater efficiency, they also come at the cost of increased visibility of user information to third parties. Therefore, as financial services become more integrated into the digital space, it is crucial to ensure that users are not forced to trade their privacy and bargaining power just to gain access to these services. In this framework, digital literacy should not be seen as a substitute for governance; rather, it complements the protection that should be embedded within the system itself.

CONSUMER PROTECTION IN DIGITAL FINANCIAL SERVICES

Consumer protection in digital financial services can no longer be confined to traditional notions of transaction security or clear contract terms. In the fintech ecosystem, consumers' vulnerabilities have grown substantially, as their interactions with service providers are increasingly mediated by data, digital interfaces, and automated decisions—systems whose functioning is often opaque to users. In this context, consumers do not merely purchase or use services; they continuously generate data that is used to assess risk profiles, determine product offerings, and, in many cases, influence credit decisions. This shift makes consumer protection a more fundamental issue, extending beyond concerns about data leaks to the broader question of how to ensure that consumers are not harmed by systems that know too much about them, while consumers themselves understand too little about the system. Ahnert et al. (2025) highlight that while digital payments enhance economic efficiency, they also come with the trade-off of privacy, as digital transactions expose information to lenders. Anonymity, while offering protection, reduces certain economic efficiencies. This illustrates the inherent trade-off in digital finance: convenience and visibility are intertwined, and consumer protection must start with the understanding that financial data is not just a service complement—it is a source of power.

Consumer vulnerability intensifies when decisions affecting access to credit or service terms are driven by algorithmic models that are difficult to explain. In these scenarios, consumers can face significant economic outcomes such as credit denials, higher interest rates, or restricted access, without receiving adequate explanations for these decisions. Sargeant (2026) argues that legal safeguards based on data protection alone are insufficient to guarantee meaningful explanations or accountability for automated credit decisions. This insight is critical because it suggests that the core issue is not simply the presence of automation, but whether consumers have a legitimate right to understand, challenge, and question the outcomes of these systems. Without such rights, transparency becomes a hollow formality, leaving the power asymmetry intact and potentially exacerbating consumer vulnerability.

Consumer protection is also deeply reliant on the security of the digital infrastructure that underpins financial services. Wang et al. (2024) emphasize that the banking sector views data privacy and cybersecurity as central to regulatory compliance, competitive advantage, and user trust. Strategies for maintaining security include access control, threat monitoring, training, governance compliance, and encryption. For consumers, this means that protection should not merely consist of lengthy terms of service or consent notifications, but should be embedded in systems designed to prevent data misuse and reduce the risk of leaks. When technical protections are weak, the entire burden of risk falls on consumers, who have the least control over the underlying system architecture.

To ensure effective consumer protection in digital financial services, several elements must be integrated. First, data usage should be subject to proportionate restrictions. Second, the terms of service should be clear and understandable to users, ensuring that they can make informed decisions. Third, there must be meaningful explanations of automated decisions, with mechanisms for challenging these decisions when they result in harm. Fourth, there should be effective complaint mechanisms that allow consumers to voice grievances and seek redress. Finally, regulatory oversight must be able to penetrate the technical layers of the platform, ensuring that platforms are held accountable not only for what they do with the data, but also for how they design and implement their systems. Without these components, financial digitalization will only refine existing vulnerabilities—users will remain at their most vulnerable, but now those vulnerabilities will be obscured by sleeker interfaces and faster processes.

Ultimately, consumer protection in the digital financial services ecosystem must evolve from reactive measures to proactive, system-wide safeguards. This includes a robust legal framework, clear regulatory standards, and transparency in decision-making processes. Only by addressing these elements can fintech become a truly equitable space where consumers are not simply subject to data-driven decisions but are empowered to understand and influence those decisions for their benefit.

POWER RELATIONS AND POLICY CHALLENGES IN THE FINTECH ECOSYSTEM

In the fintech ecosystem, digital transformation is fundamentally a transformation in the distribution of power. While innovation often brings faster, cheaper, and more accessible services, it also leads to a concentration of control over critical aspects such as data, user interfaces, and analytical capabilities. The platform is not just an intermediary for transactions but also the entity that possesses the most comprehensive knowledge about the economic behavior of users, making it best positioned to turn this knowledge into business decisions (Egbert & Ulbricht, 2024). In this regard, the power of platforms extends beyond the marketplace; it reaches into the very mechanisms by which individuals are read, classified, and directed within the digital financial system. Graef & Bostoen (2026) map platform power into three forms of control: over the market, over individuals, and over society. This framework helps explain why platform dominance in fintech should not be understood simply as a success of innovation but as an exercise in power.

On the other hand, the state must continue to assert its regulatory authority, but it often faces significant challenges in doing so under less-than-ideal conditions. Global digital infrastructure reliance, limited audit capabilities, and the speed of innovation outpacing rule-making have left many developing countries in a reactive position. The global structure of digital dependence is highly unbalanced, dominated by two technopoles—the United States and, to a lesser extent, China—that possess far greater autonomy than other actors (Mayer & Lu, 2025). In the context of fintech, this imbalance means that while states may have formal jurisdiction over digital economy activities, they do not always maintain substantive control over the technological infrastructure that supports them. This is where the regulatory and enforcement gaps arise—not simply because the state is slow, but because technological and market power are unevenly distributed from the outset.

Policy challenges are compounded by the fact that fintech regulation is not simply about adding new rules. In the case of China, for instance, the effectiveness of fintech regulation, especially in investment-oriented sectors, is significantly influenced by the economic conditions and maturity of investors (Zhang & Zhang, 2025). This provides a valuable lesson for developing countries: effective policies are not just those written on paper, but those that align with institutional capacity, market readiness, and enforcement capabilities. In an increasingly algorithm-driven environment, the need for rigorous data governance, system resilience, and cross-sector collaboration is emphasized in the study of algorithmic trust and regulation in Indonesia. Therefore, the main challenge in fintech policy is not choosing between innovation or protection, as some regulators may assume, but rather designing oversight that limits platform dominance while preserving the social benefits of innovation.

The consequences of this unequal power dynamic are most acutely experienced by users. When platforms have an advantage in data control and the state has not fully penetrated the technical layers of digital decision-making, users find themselves in the weakest position. They are subjected to unbalanced terms of service, non-transparent classifications, and often ineffective objection mechanisms. As a result, the discussion of power in fintech must be seen as central to policy issues, not merely as theoretical concerns. As long as the distribution of power over data and infrastructure remains uneven, digital transformation will continue to offer surface-level convenience while leaving deep vulnerabilities at the structural level.

DIRECTION OF INCLUSIVE AND RESPONSIBLE FINANCIAL DATA GOVERNANCE

Inclusive financial data governance cannot simply be built by adding more rules or tightening formal approval processes. What is needed is a framework that balances innovation, user rights, and digital accountability. In the fintech ecosystem, data indeed facilitates faster, more precise, and more competitive services. However, it also opens up new possibilities for surveillance, classification, and decision-making that users may not fully understand or control. Therefore, responsible governance must begin with the principle that financial data is not just raw material for market efficiency, but a sensitive asset that can determine one's economic bargaining power.

Policies such as open banking suggest that providing broader access to data can encourage the entry of new actors and expand service options. However, these benefits are only valid if data disclosure is accompanied by strong safeguards to prevent the concentration of power in the hands of the most technologically dominant players.

Data sharing, if not properly regulated, risks reinforcing existing power imbalances rather than leveling the playing field.

From this foundation, several core principles emerge. First, data minimization should be a guiding principle to prevent platforms from over-collecting data simply because it is technically feasible. Platforms must collect only the data that is strictly necessary for providing the service. Second, informed consent should be understood as a meaningful understanding, not just as a click on an agreement forced by interface design. Users must be genuinely informed about the data being collected, how it will be used, and the consequences of that use. Third, algorithmic accountability must ensure that automated decisions, particularly those involving credit and risk assessments, can be explained, audited, and contested when they harm users. Without these three elements, public trust in fintech will remain superficial, as mere transparency will not eliminate the underlying asymmetry between platforms and consumers. The framework for algorithmic trust in Indonesia emphasizes that algorithmic governance must consider the ethical, legal, and social dimensions simultaneously, not as an afterthought once the system is already operational (Perdana et al., 2025).

Furthermore, inclusive governance must be responsive to the existing inequalities within society. This means that while interoperability should be expanded, it must be done safely, without exacerbating biases against women, vulnerable groups, and those with limited access to tools, digital literacy, or formal financial histories. At the same time, complaint mechanisms, regulatory audits, and data security oversight must be fully operational. Merely stating protections in policy documents is insufficient if they do not translate into real-world safeguards for users who are harmed by the system (Babina et al., 2025; Perdana et al., 2025). The challenges facing fintech regulation show that success depends not only on the rigor of regulations but also on how well policy design aligns with institutional capacity and the market environment.

Therefore, responsible financial data governance must be directed not just at fostering innovation, but also at ensuring that digital transformation operates under principles of data fairness, public accountability, and real protection for the most vulnerable. It is not enough for the digital financial ecosystem to be efficient and innovative; it must also be equitable and just for all users.

IMPLICATIONS, CONCLUSIONS, AND FUTURE RESEARCH DIRECTION

Financial data governance in the fintech ecosystem must be understood not just as a technical issue related to data storage, processing, or security, but as a broader issue involving the distribution of power, protection of user rights, and the capacity of states to guide digital transformation. In developing countries, fintech offers significant opportunities for expanding financial inclusion, enhancing service efficiency, and increasing access to financial products that were previously difficult to reach. However, this expansion also introduces significant risks, particularly in relation to control over financial data, privacy, cybersecurity, algorithmic biases, and access inequalities that could worsen the vulnerability of certain groups, including women and individuals with limited digital literacy.

As a result, strengthening governance should not focus solely on promoting innovation. It must be underpinned by regulations that are transparent, accountable, gender-responsive, and oriented toward consumer protection. Inclusive governance should ensure that the benefits of financial digitalization are not solely concentrated in the hands of platforms and infrastructure providers but also serve to empower society, particularly as consumers of digital financial services. The need for inclusive regulation becomes clear, as governance must ensure that the economic benefits of fintech are distributed fairly, with particular attention to preventing the exploitation of vulnerable groups.

For future research, there is a need to explore the relationship between data sovereignty, digital financial literacy, user trust, algorithmic bias, and policy design that balances innovation, interoperability, and justice. Understanding these interconnections will help in designing regulatory frameworks that can effectively manage the tensions between technological advancement and social inclusion. Future studies should also investigate how financial data governance models can be adapted to protect vulnerable groups and promote gender equity in the fintech sector. Thus, the study of fintech should not be limited to questions of market efficiency but should also contribute to the creation of a fairer, more secure, and responsible digital financial system that truly serves all users.

REFERENCES

Afjal, M. (2023). Bridging the Financial Divide: A Bibliometric Analysis on The Role of Digital Financial Services Within Fintech in Enhancing Financial Inclusion and Economic Development. *Humanities and Social Sciences Communications 2023 10:1, 10*(1), 645-. DOI: 10.1057/s41599-023-02086-y

Ahnert, T., Hoffmann, P., & Monnet, C. (2025). Payments and Privacy in the Digital Economy. *Journal of Financial Economics, 169*, 104050. DOI: 10.1016/j.jfineco.2025.104050

Akyildirim, E., Corbet, S., Mukherjee, A., & Ryan, M. (2025). Global Perspectives on Open Banking: Regulatory Impacts and Market Response. *Journal of International Financial Markets, Institutions and Money, 101*(2), 102159. DOI: 10.1016/j.intfin.2025.102159

Aldboush, H. H. H., & Ferdous, M. (2023). Building Trust in Fintech: An Analysis of Ethical and Privacy Considerations in the Intersection of Big Data, AI, and Customer Trust. *International Journal of Financial Studies 2023, Vol. 11, 11*(3). DOI: 10.3390/ijfs11030090

Ayari, H., Guetari, P. R., & Kraïem, P. N. (2025). Machine Learning Powered Financial Credit Scoring: A Systematic Literature Review. *Artificial Intelligence Review 2025 59:1, 59*(1), 13-. DOI: 10.1007/s10462-025-11416-2

Babina, T., Bahaj, S., Buchak, G., De Marco, F., Foulis, A., Gornall, W., Mazzola, F., & Yu, T. (2025). Customer Data Access and Fintech Entry: Early Evidence from Open Banking. *Journal of Financial Economics, 169*(2), 103950. DOI: 10.1016/j.jfineco.2024.103950

Belli, L., Gaspar, W. B., & Singh Jaswant, S. (2024). Data Sovereignty and Data Transfers as Fundamental Elements of Digital Transformation: Lessons from the BRICS Countries. *Computer Law & Security Review, 54*, 106017. DOI: 10.1016/j.clsr.2024.106017

Casolaro, A. M. B., Rauber, G. N., & de Lima, U. S. M. (2024). Open Banking: A Systematic Literature Review. *Journal of Banking Regulation 2024 26:3, 26*(3), 340–355. DOI: 10.1057/s41261-024-00262-x

Chen, S., Doerr, S., Frost, J., Gambacorta, L., & Shin, H. S. (2023). The Fintech Gender Gap. *Journal of Financial Intermediation, 54*, 101026. DOI: 10.1016/j.jfi.2023.101026

Choung, Y., Chatterjee, S., & Pak, T. Y. (2023). Digital Financial Literacy and Financial Well-Being. *Finance Research Letters*, *58*, 104438. DOI: 10.1016/j.frl.2023.104438

Dinçkol, D., Ozcan, P., & Zachariadis, M. (2023). Regulatory standards and consequences for industry architecture: The case of UK Open Banking. *Research Policy*, *52*(6), 104760. DOI: 10.1016/j.respol.2023.104760

Egbert, S., & Ulbricht, L. (2024). Data Integration and Analysis Platforms as Digital Platforms: A Conceptual Proposal. *Information Communication and Society*, 1–22. Advance online publication. DOI: 10.1080/1369118X.2024.2442394

Farahani, M. S., Mahmoudi, G., & Ghasemi, G. (2025). Credit Rating in the Age of Artificial Intelligence. *FinTech and Sustainable Innovation*, *1*, A9–A9. DOI: 10.47852/bonviewFSI52025716

Galindo-Manrique, A. F., & Rojas-Vargas, N. P. (2025). The Role of Digital Financial Services in Narrowing the Gender Gap in Low–Middle-Income Economies: A Bayesian Machine Learning Approach. *Risks 2025, Vol. 13, 13*(5). DOI: 10.3390/risks13050096

Graef, I., & Bostoen, F. (2026). A Typology of Platform Power and Its Regulation. *Information Communication and Society*, *29*(1), 324–338. Advance online publication. DOI: 10.1080/1369118X.2025.2512972

Ha, D., Le, P., & Nguyen, D. K. (2025). Financial Inclusion and Fintech: A State-of-the-Art Systematic Literature Review. *Financial Innovation*, *11*(1), 1–42. DOI: 10.1186/s40854-024-00741-0

Hanisch, M., Goldsby, C. M., Fabian, N. E., & Oehmichen, J. (2023). Digital Governance: A Conceptual Framework and Research Agenda. *Journal of Business Research*, *162*(1), 113777. DOI: 10.1016/j.jbusres.2023.113777

He, Z., Huang, J., & Zhou, J. (2023). Open Banking: Credit Market Competition When Borrowers Own the Data. *Journal of Financial Economics*, *147*(2), 449–474. DOI: 10.1016/j.jfineco.2022.12.003

Ibrushi, D., Palacios Diaz, M., & Wang, S. (2026). Financial Literacy and Fraud Vulnerability in Digital Finance: Evidence from the 2024 NFCS. *Finance Research Letters*, *94*, 109674. DOI: 10.1016/j.frl.2026.109674

Isaia, E., Oggero, N., & Sandretto, D. (2024). Is Financial Literacy a Protection Tool from Online Fraud in the Digital Era? *Journal of Behavioral and Experimental Finance*, *44*, 100977. DOI: 10.1016/j.jbef.2024.100977

Khan, H. H., Khan, S., Akhtar, T., Anwar, A., & Ahmad, M. R. (2026). Fintech Environment and Gender Disparity in Financial Inclusion: Empirical Evidence from Emerging Markets. *Borsa Istanbul Review*, *26*(2), 100787. DOI: 10.1016/j.bir.2026.100787

Kishor, K., Bansal, S. K., & Kumar, R. (2024). The Role of Fintech in Promoting Financial Inclusion to Achieve Sustainable Development: An Integrated Bibliometric Analysis and Systematic Literature Review. *Journal of the Knowledge Economy 2024 16:1, 16*(1), 5664–5692. DOI: 10.1007/s13132-024-02168-5

Magwedere, M. R., & Marozva, G. (2025). Financial Technology and Income Inequality: An Empirical Investigation. *Discover Global Society 2025 3:1, 3*(1), 68-. DOI: 10.1007/s44282-025-00198-1

Mayer, M., & Lu, Y. C. (2025). Global Structures of Digital Dependence and the Rise of Technopoles. *New Political Economy*, *30*(5), 755–774. DOI: 10.1080/13563467.2025.2497766

Ogawa, S., Khera, P., Vasishth, M., & Sahay, R. (2022). Women in Fintech: As Leaders and Users. *IMF Working Paper*, *2022*(140), 1. DOI: 10.5089/9798400215384.001

Oluoch, W., & Alhassan, A. L. (2026). Bridging the Gender Credit Gap in Low-Income Countries: The Impact of Digital Financial Inclusion. *Emerging Markets Review*, *70*(1), 101389. DOI: 10.1016/j.ememar.2025.101389

Omotubora, A. (2024). AI For Women's Financial Inclusion—Analysis of Product Design and Policy Approaches in Nigeria. *Data & Policy*, *6*, e66. DOI: 10.1017/dap.2024.62

Özşuca, E. A. (2024). Gender Gap in Digital Financial Inclusion Across Generations. *Empirica 2024 52:2, 52*(2), 197–210. DOI: 10.1007/s10663-024-09641-z

Perdana, A., Arifin, S., & Quadrianto, N. (2025). Algorithmic Trust and Regulation: Governance, Ethics, Legal, and Social Implications Blueprint for Indonesia's Central Banking. *Technology in Society*, *81*, 102838. DOI: 10.1016/j.techsoc.2025.102838

Purtova, N., & van Maanen, G. (2024). Data as an Economic Good, Data as a Commons, and Data Governance. *Law, Innovation and Technology*, *16*(1), 1–42. DOI: 10.1080/17579961.2023.2265270 PMID: 39634789

Santaniello, M. (2025). Attributes of Digital Sovereignty: A Conceptual Framework. *Geopolitics*. Advance online publication. DOI: 10.1080/14650045.2025.2521548

Sargeant, H. (2026). Mind the Gap: Securing Algorithmic Explainability for Credit Decisions Beyond the UK GDPR. *Computer Law & Security Review*, *60*, 106247. DOI: 10.1016/j.clsr.2025.106247

Scherenberg, F. von, Hellmeier, M., & Otto, B. (2024). Data Sovereignty in Information Systems. *Electronic Markets 2024 34:1, 34*(1), 15-. DOI: 10.1007/s12525-024-00693-4

Tigges, M., Mestwerdt, S., Tschirner, S., & Mauer, R. (2024). Who Gets the Money? A Qualitative Analysis of Fintech Lending and Credit Scoring Through the Adoption of AI and Alternative Data. *Technological Forecasting and Social Change*, *205*, 123491. DOI: 10.1016/j.techfore.2024.123491

Wang, S., Asif, M., Shahzad, M. F., & Ashfaq, M. (2024). Data Privacy and Cybersecurity Challenges in the Digital Transformation of the Banking Sector. *Computers & Security*, *147*, 104051. DOI: 10.1016/j.cose.2024.104051

Zhang, M., & Zhang, C. (2025). The Political Economy of the Fintech Regulation in China and Its Implications. *Computer Law & Security Review*, *56*, 106089. DOI: 10.1016/j.clsr.2024.106089

Chapter 8
Financial Data Governance in Digital Lending:
A Case Study of Consumer Protection Challenges in FinTech Platforms in Emerging Markets

K. Balaji
http://orcid.org/0000-0002-3065-3294
CHRIST University, Bengaluru, India

ABSTRACT

The rapid expansion of digital lending platforms in emerging markets has transformed access to credit while simultaneously raising critical concerns around data governance and consumer protection. This study examines the role of financial data governance in digital lending ecosystems, with a specific focus on consumer protection challenges in FinTech platforms across emerging markets. Adopting a qualitative case study approach, the research draws on secondary data sources including regulatory reports, policy documents, and case evidence from leading digital lending platforms in India and comparable emerging economies. The study employs thematic analysis and comparative regulatory assessment as key analytical tools to identify patterns in data usage, governance practices, and consumer risk. The findings reveal significant gaps in data governance, including opaque algorithmic credit scoring, unauthorized data sharing, and inadequate disclosure mechanisms, which heighten consumer vulnerability.

DOI: 10.4018/979-8-2600-2233-7.ch008

1. INTRODUCTION

In emerging markets, the financial landscape has drastically changed, with an increasing number of digital lending platforms rising to the surface. Digital lending through financial technology (FinTech) has fostered faster, more data-driven and accessible credit delivery to marginalized groups, driving a shift to financial inclusion in response to the need. Recently, digital lending has been propelled by financial technology (FinTech), rapid uptake in smartphones and the desire to achieve financial inclusion by enabling faster and more data-driven credit delivery to underserved populations. Such services as peer-to-peer (P2P) lending, Buy Now Pay Later (BNPL), and instant personal loans have experienced exponential growth, especially in countries like India, Brazil and the economies of Southeast Asia. These advancements have enhanced the availability of credit but have also brought about fresh challenges around data utilisation, risk management, and regulatory compliance. These improvements have made credit more available, yet they've likewise raised fresh difficulties in regards to information use, dangers, and the regulation (Agarwal & Zhang, 2020).

Financial data governance has become an essential component in this dynamic context to guarantee transparency, accountability, and trust in the digital financial ecosystem. The use of this personal data, transactional data and behavioural data is essential for FinTech platforms to evaluate the creditworthiness of customers, automate processes and improve the customer experience. Strengthening data governance frameworks is crucial to ensure data is collected, processed, stored and shared effectively and safely, which can reduce the risk of data misuse, breach and opacity of algorithms. Effective governance models ensure adherence to regulatory requirements and help to ensure sustainable innovation in the FinTech industry (Agoraki et al., 2011).

But the growing digital lending market has also raised consumer protection issues. Consumers, especially vulnerable segments, are exposed to high risks through issues of unauthorised access to data, informed consent issues or predatory lending practices or opaque algorithmic decision processes. Many emerging markets have evolving regulatory frameworks, with enforcement and oversight issues. These are all challenges that highlight the need to blend innovation with strong data protection regulations, and financial data governance is a key priority in the digital lending landscape. In this context the present study seeks to explore how financial data governance affects digital lending practices; it aims to highlight some of the most pressing consumer protection issues related to data-driven lending models; to assess the quality of the existing regulatory frameworks; to identify key gaps in governance where consumers may be subject to financial and informational risks; and to recommend management and policy strategies that can help improve governance and consumer protection outcomes in emerging market FinTech's.

2. CONCEPTUAL BACKGROUND

The study has been developed underpinned by the conceptualization of „financial data governance in the context of the quickly growing digital lending segment, with a special focus on the implications for consumer protection. Financial Data Governance: A set of policies, standards and institution-based arrangements for achieving the accuracy, integrity, security and ethical use of the financial data. Its implications, in a digital finance context, span beyond data management to algorithmic accountability, interoperability of data, regulatory adherence and inter-platform data sharing. The digital lending landscape has become a revolution in lending intermediation with the formation of digital intermediaries like NBFCs, P2P lending, and Buy Now Pay Later (BNPL) companies. They utilise high-tech tools such as artificial intelligence, machine learning, and big data analysis to evaluate and process creditworthiness as well as speed up the loan disbursement process and boost customer interaction. Such innovations have improved financial inclusion and cut down transaction expenses, but have also ushered in novel challenges in systemic risk—including regarding data management, transparency, and rules. Such innovations have increased financial inclusion and lowered transaction costs, but also brought an additional layer of systematic risk related to data management, transparency and rules (Albertazzi & Gambacorta, 2009).

Consumer protection continues to be a key issue in this dynamic framework. As digital platforms gain importance, problems of lack of information visibility, bias in algorithmic results, hidden costs, excessive recovery methods and lack of grievance redress mechanisms have been growing in scope. In addition, personal and alternative data have significant issues of informed consent, privacy of data, and freedom of choice (Allen & Gale, 2000).

2.1. Theoretical Foundations

To grasp the intricacies of financial data governance and consumer protection in the digital lending space, it is necessary to have a strong theoretical foundation. The framework for this study is positioned around three beneficial theoretical perspectives – the Information Asymmetry Theory, the Agency Theory and Data Privacy and Protection Frameworks – all of which offer a multidimensional perspective for understanding the various elements and dynamics between financial institutions, platforms, regulators and consumers.

2.1.1 Information Asymmetry Theory

Information Asymmetry Theory is the theory developed first by George Akerlof, Michael Spence and Joseph Stiglitz as the explanation for the occurrence of situations where one party in a transaction has more or better information than the other party. This imbalance is especially noticeable in financial markets between lenders and borrowers. Historically, lenders were exposed to a variety of difficulties, including measuring borrowers' creditworthiness given the lack of or imperfect information, which resulted in adverse selection and moral hazard issues (F. Allen & Gale, 2004).

2.1.2. Agency Theory

The theory emphasises the natural and unavoidable conflicts of interests, of principals which require agents' action to be in their best interest, but can be in pursuit of their own best interests (L. Allen et al., 2022). In the digital lending environment, the occurrence of multiple middlemen role players such as third-party service providers, data aggregators, NBFCs and fintech service providers magnifies agency risks. For example, digital lending platforms (agents) may be more focused on providing the customer with a loan sooner than they would otherwise be able to provide the loan, get the customer to sign the agreement or deliver a loan to the customer at any cost instead of being responsible for ensuring they are providing a loan to a consumer. This can result in pushy marketing, failure to sufficiently inform borrowers about the conditions of their loan, or dependence on those high-risk borrowers.

2.1.3. Data Privacy and Protection Frameworks

Data Privacy and Protection Frameworks are the normative and regulatory frameworks for handling personal and financial data in the digital society. The principles of these frameworks include individual autonomy, informed consent, transparency, accountability and purpose limitation. Enhanced global and emerging national regulations, like the General Data Protection Regulation (GDPR), are making it important to guard user knowledge while additionally permitting innovation. (Ampudia et al., 2021). In digital lending, this data is gathered in large quantities, ranging from personal and behavioural to transactional information, and used to evaluate creditworthiness and tailor financial services and products to individual needs. As it improves efficiency and financial access, it also introduces dangers to consumers, like systems staging data breaches, unauthorised sharing and systems engaging with profiling or surveillance. To address these concerns, data privacy frameworks introduce data minimisation, specify the data processing purpose, introduce the concept of consent, and offer persons rights over their data, such as access, correction, and erasure. Moreover, they place requirements on data processors with regard to the security of data and accountability in processing data.

But there are some hurdles in putting such schemes into practice in the digital lending ecosystem. Among these are a lack of consumer awareness, the complexity of consent agreements, cross-border data transfers and the ability to regulate algorithmic decision-making processes. Thus, embedding robust data protection principles alongside financial data governance is essential for fostering trust, transparency and responsible data practices in the digital financial landscape.

2.1.4. Synthesis of Theoretical Perspectives

The three theoretical frameworks are linked together and can be used to analyse digital lending systems comprehensively. The information asymmetry theory emphasises the information gap that exists in financial transactions, and Agency Theory identifies the potential conflicts of interest between parties. Data Privacy and Protection Frameworks set out the ethical and regulatory parameters around the use of data. They convey a clear message of the importance of adopting a balanced approach, supporting innovation and accountability, transparency and consumer protection in the digital financial ecosystem (Anginer et al., 2014). To truly capture the governance dynamics of financial information in digital lending contexts, it is important to combine various theories that account for interactions between fintech platforms, consumers and regulatory institutions. In the proposed theoretical framework, financial data governance is seen as the pivotal element that connects technological innovation to financial consumer protection outcomes (Balyuk et al., 2020).

Figure 1. Integrated Theoretical Framework of Financial Data Governance in Digital Lending

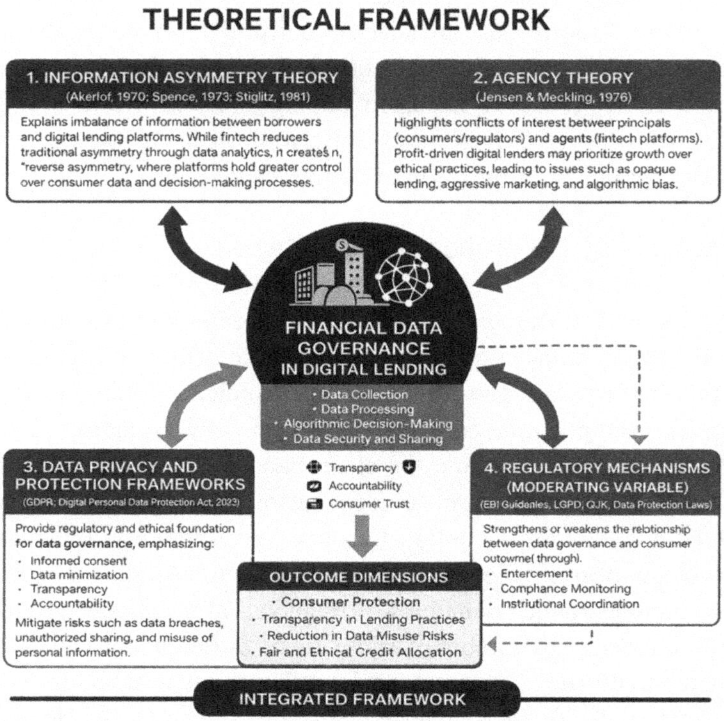

Source: Author's own work.

Figure 1 contains the financial data governance presentation, which includes the theory of how financial data governance works in digital lending ecosystems, as well as the impact on consumer protection as a result. The adoption of IAT also indicates that, while it diminishes the unauthorised information gap of the traditional financial service layer, it simultaneously introduces a new information gap in the form of being dominated and opaque by algorithms. The agency theory also suggests that the internal conflicts between profit-driven fintech companies and consumer welfare are best understood, highlighting a need for accountability and ethical practices. (Balaji, K. 2025f),(Banna et al., 2021).

2.2. Conceptual Framework of the Study

The conceptual design of this research is designed to analyse the interactions between financial data governance, digital lending and their regulations and the outcomes of consumer protection in the financial services sector in emerging markets'

FinTech platforms. The framework is rooted in Information Asymmetry Theory, Agency Theory, and Data Privacy and Protection, offering a structured view of the relationship between governance gaps and consumer risks and the potential of regulations to address these issues (Banna et al., 2021). Financial data governance is the heart of the framework, involving data collection, storage, processing, and sharing policies, processes, and institutional mechanisms on digital lending platforms. Good data governance will lead to transparency, accountability, data security and ethical handling of customer data. Yet, in a variety of emerging markets, weaknesses in governance, including poor consent building, limited standardisation, and poor monitoring, also impact consumers' rights.

The framework defines the digital lending ecosystem that involves NBFCs, P2P platforms, and BNPL providers as the market space where financial data is proactively used. They extensively use alternative data and algorithmic models to evaluate creditworthiness and provide financial services. This not only increases financial inclusion and efficiency in operations, but also expands the risks involved of algorithmic bias, lack of transparency in decision-making and over-collection of data. These outcomes are reflected in key challenges such as data privacy violations, lack of transparency in loan terms, discriminatory lending practices, predatory behaviour, and cybersecurity threats (Bao & Huang, 2021).

Regulators, by policies, guidance, and regulation, seek to promote compliance, increase transparency and help protect consumer interests. Effective and cohesive regulatory structures can reduce the risks involved by making sure that data protection requirements are adhered to, lending practices are treated fairly and more accountability is put in place. In addition, the framework acknowledges the importance of behaviour and institutional practices of these companies themselves, which is called an intervening variable. Data utilization, transparency, and ethical principles are crucial factors that shape the effectiveness of firms' strategies and affect governance structures. By embracing responsible data practices, explaining the data, and adopting advanced security measures, businesses can minimise risks, while superficial practices driven by profit increase the potential for consumers to be exploited (Beck et al., 2013). The detailed is shown below.

Figure 2. Conceptual Framework of the Study

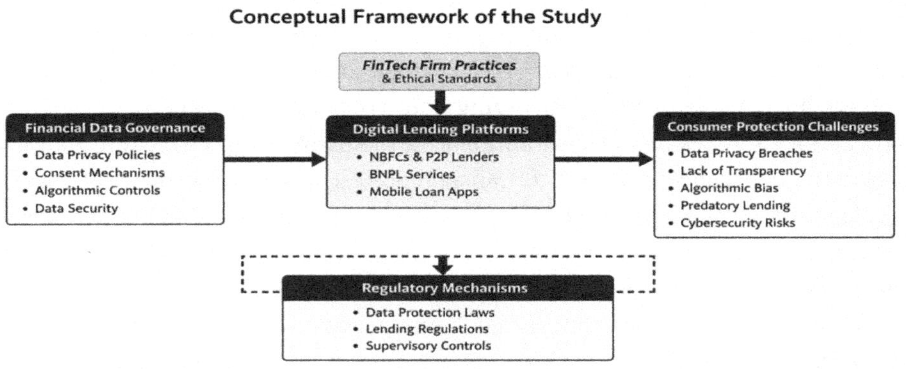

Source: Author's own work.

The conceptual framework (Figure 2) foretells a causal connection with financial data governance affecting financial consumer protection outcomes through an indirect way of fintech operational practices, which is, in turn, moderated by regulatory effectiveness

3. LITERATURE REVIEW

Financial Technology (FinTech) and digital lending are topics endlessly discussed by professors over the last twenty years, especially in the developing world. The initial research conducted between 2000 and 2010 was mostly on banking services and electronic payment systems' digitisation, which would form the basis of how the fintech ecosystem evolved into what it is today. With a financial crisis as its catalyst, scholars like(Beck, Cecchetti, et al., 2022), hailed FinTech's emergence as a game-changer in financial intermediation using technology. Further studies went on to demonstrate the advantages of mobile banking, digital wallets, and online lending for increasing access to financial services, especially for underserved populations in developing economies (Balaji, K. 2025e).

Literature in the post-2015 period focused more on digital lending and new lending models, such as peer-to-peer (P2P) lending, marketplace lending, and Buy Now, Pay Later (BNPL), (Beck, Gambacorta, et al., 2022) In Brazil, the researchers analysed the consumer adoption of fintech loan products and concluded that several factors, including convenience, speed and the lack of documentation, had a significant impact on the borrower's preferences. Similarly, (Bellardini et al., 2022) examined 'Digital lending in emerging economies' and emphasised the role of the automation of 'Credit scoring systems based on alternative information' that leverages transaction history and mobile usage as a substitute for traditional credit history. All these developments have helped to enhance financial inclusion but also introduced concerns around transparency and data management, along with system risk.

More recent studies (2024-2025) have taken a more holistic view and examined relations between fintech developments and financial and economic inclusion (Berg et al., 2022). The University of Berkeley's website, an exhaustive bibliometric study of fintech studies performed, identified digital lending, mobile banking, and blockchain technologies as some of the core ideas leading the way in the measurement of financial inclusion in emerging markets. Their research also uncovered research gaps in the areas of long-term financial stability, regulatory issues, and vulnerable populations. Similarly, (Bertsch et al., 2020), A systematic review of literature on 185 science papers focused on the pivotal role of fintech in expanding financial inclusion and highlighted the importance of creating inclusive and responsible innovation frameworks.

In Brazil, the researchers analysed the consumer adoption of fintech loan products and concluded that several factors, including convenience, speed and the lack of documentation, had a significant impact on the borrower's preferences (BIS, 2017) emphasised the importance of regulatory frameworks in addressing risks associated with data-driven financial services, including issues of transparency, accountability, and systemic stability (Balaji, K. 2025d). More recent research has explored the intersection of data governance and fintech innovation. Acosta-(BIS, 2018), identified cybersecurity risks and data protection challenges as key emerging concerns in fintech-driven digital banking environments. Similarly, (Boot et al., 2021), examined 'Digital lending in emerging economies' and emphasised the role of the automation of 'Credit scoring systems based on alternative information' that leverages transaction history and mobile usage as a substitute for traditional credit history. All these developments have helped to enhance financial inclusion but also introduced concerns around transparency and data management, along with system risk.

More recent studies (2024-2025) have taken a more holistic view and examined relations between fintech developments and financial and economic inclusion. The (Chen et al., 2022) An exhaustive bibliometric study of fintech studies performed identified digital lending, mobile banking, and blockchain technologies as some of the core ideas leading the way in the measurement of financial inclusion in emerging markets. Their research also uncovered research gaps in the areas of long-term financial stability, regulatory issues, and vulnerable populations. A systematic review of literature on 185 science papers focused on the pivotal role of fintech in expanding financial inclusion and highlighted the importance of creating inclusive and responsible innovation frameworks (Cornelli et al., 2021) .

Trust in digital financial services and cybersecurity is also getting attention in the literature, as it is also important. Also, trust in digital financial services and cybersecurity are becoming key fields of interest in the literature. (Cruz-García et al., 2021) Carried out a comprehensive review of cybersecurity risks in fintech services and found several vulnerabilities such as phishing, malware and data breaches, which damage consumer confidence and raise the threat of systemic risk.(Cubillas et al., 2021) the addition of third-party fintech solutions also brings with it its own set of security implications and demands for robust regulatory protocols and cutting-edge technological security measures. These insights highlight the importance of data governance in creating safe and authentic digital lending ecosystems. The impact of AI and the emerging field of data analytics on shaping consumer experience and risk management for digital lending is another key aspect of the literature study. (Delis, 2012) Software developed with AI can also increase customer engagement and make credit risk management more efficient; however, it should also reduce issues related to safeguarding data and personal information, which may be used in the wrong manner. The research revealed an incomplete current research on the dimensions of explainability and fairness in AI models used in credit scoring, prompting the call for the development and integration of more transparent and accountable credit scoring systems (Balaji, K. 2025c).

Though there is a vast amount of literature available, there seems to be a number of research gaps, especially pertaining to emerging markets. Firstly, there is a lack of studies that focus on the governance of financial data on digital lending platforms, and the field of fintech adoption and financial inclusion has received many studies. There has been limited research on the governance of financial data in digital lending platforms, while there are many studies on fintech adoption and financial inclusion. Current research tends to overlook data governance as merely a back-bone topic that is not first priority to analyse. Second, there is a lack of in-depth empirical studies that investigate the complex relationship between data governance, consumer protection and regulatory effectiveness within the framework of emerging economies. Most of the studies conducted are conceptual or specific to a particular region; these studies are not easily generalizable to other regions (Balaji, K. 2025b). Third, these literature surveys show that there is a lack of understanding of longer-term consequences of digital lending to financial stability and consumer welfare. The short-term benefits of greater access to credit are well-established, but the consequences of over-indebtedness or algorithmic bias and data misuse need to be further explored . (Degryse & Ongena, 2007) specifically call, outline, and emphasize the importance of future research studying these areas as well as building enhanced theoretical and empirical understanding of fintech ecosystems (Cubillas & González, 2014).

Though there has been significant work undertaken on fintech adoption and financial inclusion, the findings show some discrepancies. Alternative data can help make credit more accessible, some argue, while some feel that over-reliance on algorithmic decision making can perpetuate discrimination and exclusion. In addition, most studies are based on conceptual or region-specific analyses; they therefore lack generalizability to the emerging markets. Consumer protection and regulatory effectiveness – and the relationship between the two and data governance – have largely been overlooked in practice, leaving a great need for theoretical and methodological research.

3.1. Regulatory Landscape in Emerging Markets

In emerging countries, financial sector regulations and data protection laws play more and more determining roles for the regulatory landscape of digital lending and financial data governance. The goal of these laws and frameworks is to promote transparency and accountability, protect consumers and spur innovation in FinTech ecosystems. Case studies of important key legislation in large emerging markets offer a deeper understanding of the evolution of regulatory frameworks to rise to the challenges posed by digital finance.

3.1.1. India: Digital Lending and Data Protection Frameworks

India has become a model for regulation's response to "digital finance. The enactment of the Digital Personal Data Protection Act, 2023 (DPDP Act), is one of the key milestones towards an all-encompassing data governance framework. Principles highlighted in the Act include lawful processing, purpose limitation, data minimisation and informed consent. It also defines the term "data fiduciary," thus, the entities in possession of personal data, such as digital lending platforms, should have personal data security standards and make them transparent. On the other hand, the Reserve Bank of India (RBI) has introduced Digital Lending Guidelines (2022) to govern what fintech lenders lend. Unsolicited intermediaries are not allowed in these guidelines; the repayment and disbursal of these loans should happen between the borrower and regulated entities directly. They also want transparency in loan terms, no collecting excessive data and explicit consent to share personal data with borrowers. In addition, the Information Technology Act, 2000 and the Rules in its Rules include a basis for cybersecurity and protection of information. Put together, they are meant to achieve a balance as regards innovation and consumer protection in India's fast-growing digital lending sector.

3.1.2. Brazil: General Data Protection and Financial Regulation

The LGPD follows, eminently, principles adopted by other countries, like GDPR, and introduces thorough guidance on data processing, mandatory consent and the rights of the data subject, along with penalties for failing to comply with it. The LGPD sets strict requirements for the collection, storage and sharing of consumer financial information for fintech companies. At the same time, the Central Bank of Brazil (BCB) has taken steps to regulate digital lending and foster financial innovation. Notably, Brazil has an Open Banking (Open Finance) approach with security and customers' approval to share their information with other banks. This effort will increase competition and better credit access, while also adopting an established and accepted standard for data governance.

3.1.3. Indonesia: Consumer Protection and FinTech Regulation

There has been a surge in the number of P2P lending solutions in Indonesia, leading to the development of specific regulatory guidelines. The regulation regulated fintech lending is Regulation No. 77/POJK.01/2016 about P2P lending activities issued by Otoritas Jasa Keuangan (OJK). This regulation includes the lender's obligations to obtain licenses, equity, and risk management standards, and to ensure transparency in lending activities. In response to worries regarding the Hawkins of the personal data, Indonesia has enacted the Personal Data Protection Law, 2022, which provides far-ranging direction for personal data processing, consisting of consent, the security of the personal data and restrictions on cross-border transfer of personal data. The law also instils consumer confidence in digital financial services through penalties for data breaches and unauthorized use of personal data.

3.1.4. Kenya: Digital Credit and Data Protection Laws

Mobile-based digital lending in Africa is a notable example, with Kenya's digital lending platform, integrated with mobile money services, standing out. The Central Bank of Kenya (CBK) published the Digital Credit Providers Regulations (2022) to oversee hitherto unregulated digital credit providers. These rules are licensed, adhere to information disclosure requirements, and place restrictions on unethical practices, like harassment and utilization of borrower data. The enactment of the Data Protection Act of 2019 in Kenya mirrors the regional and international privacy laws and legislations and introduces the office of the Data Protection Commissioner. The Act provides for the important principles of lawful processing, minimisation of data and data subject rights and ensures compliance with strict data governance norms in fintech.

3.1.5. Philippines: FinTech Oversight and Data Privacy

In the Philippines, digital lending is under regulatory authority of the Securities and Exchange Commission (SEC), which regulates lending companies and online digital lending platforms. The SEC has made very clear rules that mandate a registration process, rate transparency during registration, and minimum disclosure of fair collection practices. The Data Privacy Act of 2012 is enforced by the National Privacy Commission and regulates data privacy. Consent-based data processing, data security rules, and accountability guidelines are imposed on data handlers in this Act. It is a key factor in mitigating threats to privacy with digital lending apps. A clear trend in emerging markets is the overlapping regulatory frameworks surrounding financial regulation and data protection provisions in order to tackle the challenges of digital lending. Although these acts set high legal ground, there are a number of problems that remain. These include: limited enforcement capability, consumer unawareness, regulatory fragmentation and challenges related to the cross-border activity of fintech. Furthermore, advancements in technology are occurring at a pace that exceeds regulatory changes, and various aspects like algorithm transparency, AI-driven credit scoring, and platform accountability are areas where issues are felt. Yet, despite all these obstacles, the shifting regulatory context also shows an increasing recognition of the need for integrated frameworks that merge the processes of financial stability, data governance and consumer protection into one (Balaji, K. 2025a).

4. RESEARCH METHODOLOGY

This research is of a qualitative nature with a multiple case study design to analyse financial data governance and consumer protection in digital lending ecosystems in emerging markets. The qualitative method fits for the fact that it allows the understanding of regulatory, technological and institutional issues, with an approach which goes beyond a quantitative description. The research discards from one angle how fintech platforms handle financial data and their impact on consumer safeguards and from another angle how their governance practices affect consumer safeguards outcomes. Markets that were considered for inclusion were those identified as being important, the presence of diverse lending models such as mobile lending, buy now pay later (BNPL) and peer-to-peer (P2P) lending, relevance of regulation, and public information availability. Taking into consideration these, four representative cases have been chosen: Ant Group (China); Lending Club (USA); Tala (Kenya/Global); and Paytm (India) for their diverse governance structures and/or regulatory contexts.

The study was conducted mainly about the secondary qualitative information, which is gathered from regulatory reports, company annual reports, privacy policies, policy documents, peer reviewed articles, industry reports, and official documents from regulatory bodies like RBI, BIS, World Bank etc. A pluralistic use of more than one source facilitated the reliability and validity of the results, by data triangulation. Thematic analysis and comparative case analysis are the main techniques used in the study. A cross-case comparison was also conducted to highlight commonalities and governance gaps and good practices across the platforms and countries selected. The study has certain limitations. Primarily relies on secondary and public information that does not comprehensively represent the internal governance systems of fintech companies. Furthermore, the study is qualitative and this provides a restriction for statistics generalisation. However, the study sheds light on financial data governance and consumer protection issues in digital lending marketplaces.

4.1. Case Studies of Companies Promoting Real-World Applications of Financial Data Governance in Digital Lending

4.1.1. Ant Group (China): Data-Driven Credit Ecosystem and Governance Challenges

Dubbed one of the world's top fintech ecosystems, Ant Group is part of Alibaba Group since it was founded in 2014 and operates its flagship platform, Alipay. By offering lending products like Huabei (consumer credit) and Jiebei (microloans), backed by huge quantities of user data to gauge consumer creditworthiness, the company was a force that was changing the face of online lending in China. Its own credit scoring system called Sesame Credit, uses alternative data such as payment behaviours, e-commerce transactions, behavioural analytics, and more. This information-based model greatly lowered information asymmetry and gave another million or more people who were not previously banked the ability to access credit for their needs, which helped achieve financial inclusion on a large scale.

Finance Data Government, Ant Group performed with superior danger administration frameworks powered by artificial intelligence and machine learning. The platform additionally facilitated quick and convenient loan disbursements, providing a much better customer experience for the end user because of its capacity to handle large-scale information. But there were huge concerns about data privacy, market power and systemic risk caused by the same approach. The main problems concerning consumer protection that arose here were transparency and over-indebtedness. Credit became integrated into daily activities, enabling unrestrained borrowing and possibly failing to disclose clearly the risks. Also, there were some ethical queries concerning data possession and users' permission to use behavioural data. To respond, the regulators gave Ant Group new bylaws and governance rules as it would have for a bank, which, along with tightened banking legislation, also imposes tougher data privacy rules on financial firms. The Ant case is a good example of the opportunities and dangers of data-driven digital loans. The platform's ability to open up credit and create efficiency was matched, however, by the need for comprehensive legislative and policy frameworks to increase transparency, achieve accountability, and protect consumers. Lessons learned from this case study are of special interest to EM emerging markets grappling with the need to innovate while also abiding by ethical data governance.

4.1.2. Lending Club (USA): Marketplace Lending and Transparency Reforms

Lending Club was founded in 2006 and is one of the first peer-to-peer (P2P) lending sites, acting as a marketplace and placing borrowers and investors together. It is headquartered in the United States, but its model has had an impact on digital lending around the world, including in developing countries. In large part, Lending Club relies on data analytics and algorithmic credit scoring to assess the risk of loans, in a way that decreases the need for traditional bank middlemen to approve them. This unique feature allowed for quicker approvals, lower interest rates and credit availability to underserved market segments. Throughout the audit, Lending Club has adopted structured data governance by ensuring that credit assessment best practices are standardised, loan terms are clearly communicated, and there are robust sell-side notification practices. The platform focuses on data integrity, verification, and regulation, aligning with consumer protection considerations.

Unfortunately, the company had high governance issues throughout the year of 2016 because of the embezzlement of loan data. The breach revealed the vulnerabilities in the internal control and data integrity systems used by the company, which caused investors' trust to be lost and resulted in the intervention of regulators. To counteract this, Lending Club has undergone a number of changes, such as a more robust governance framework, improved transparency, and compliance systems. Lending Club has been working on issues of consumer protection by increasing consumer awareness and supporting equal lending practices. The platform offers comprehensive loan details, interest rates, and repayment terms, aiding in informed decision-making. What's more, with its data analytics, you can also reduce risks of default while fairly rewarding the creditworthy borrower with its risk-based pricing. The Lending Club case demonstrates how these essential elements—transparency, accountability, and strong internal controls—are essential in both financial data governance. Trust and ethical practice hinge on effective governance mechanisms that enhance efficiency and access with technological innovation. This case serves as a good reminder for emerging markets of the need for regulatory oversight and institutional accountability across the digital lending ecosystem.

4.1.3. Tala (Kenya/Global): Financial Inclusion through Alternative Data

Established in 2011, Tala is an international fintech firm operating in the sector of microloans to underserved segments of emerging markets, such as Kenya, India, the Philippines and Mexico. Using data from the smartphone, the company examines purchasing patterns, device usage, and other behavioural metrics to determine someone's creditworthiness when they don't have a credit plan or bill history. Tala's mobile lending application provides access to small loans in "real-time" within minutes, making a huge difference in financial inclusion. At the heart of Tala's financial datasets governance are ways in which the companies utilize alternative credit data and machine learning algorithms in credit scoring. The platform focuses on responsible data use, including consent and user education to improve transparency. Tala's non-bank source data helps lower information asymmetry, thereby providing credit to the differently-abled, such as the informal sector workers and small entrepreneurs.

Although it is beneficial, Tala's model poses significant consumer protection issues. There are discussions going on about privacy, consent and ethical usage of personal and behavioural data. There are discussions about privacy, consent and ethical usage of personal and behavioural data. In other cases, digital lenders in comparable markets have come under fire for the data collection they are allowed to access as well as the rigorous methods used to recover payment. To address these concerns, Tala has taken steps to improve its data governance policies and practices, such as restricting access to data, implementing security protocols, and complying with local data protection regulations. Tala's efforts to enhance the financial capabilities of those outside the formal financial system, particularly through its capacity to provide loans, have been significant in terms of its impact on economic empowerment. The platform helps small businesses, generates income and fosters financial resilience. With AI-powered analytics, it streamlines the lending process, providing real-time solutions to boost efficiency. This is the power of fintech to facilitate financial inclusion, and how crucial the ethical stewardship of data is. In the case of emerging markets, the lesson is that while innovation is vital to digital lending, consumer protection must be considered to ensure that the advantages are not counterbalanced by privacy threats and abusive practices.

4.1.4. Paytm (India): Integrated Digital Ecosystem and Regulatory Compliance

Founded in 2010, Paytm is one of India's top fintech companies providing a variety of services such as wallet, digital lending, and digital payments. Banking fintech Paytm offers a variety of personal loans, merchant loans and Buy Now Pay Later (BNPL) through its lending platform, partnering with government-regulated financial institutions. On the financial data governance part, Paytm is in a highly regulated environment that is governed by the Reserve Bank of India (RBI) and data protection laws. The platform also follows stringent policies regarding data privacy, consent, and transparency, ensuring that users are kept up to date on how their data is being utilised and the terms of their loan. By leveraging India's digital public infrastructure, such as Aadhaar and Unified Payments Interface (UPI), Paytm has improved the accuracy and interoperability of data while ensuring compliance with regulatory standards.

Paytm has made Consumer Protection one of its primary growth areas, and with regulatory bodies targeting digital lending in India, it seems to be a very judicious decision on their part. The platform demonstrates transparency with regard to interest rates, fees and repayment terms, and has established grievance redressal mechanisms to handle customer grievances. Along with this, adherence to the RBI's digital lending guidelines will help the distribution of loans happen via a controlled body, thereby minimising the danger of an illegal transaction. But there are issues to ensure transparency and oversight over drafting, especially in BNPL, which offers credit as a seamless element in consumption. To address these concerns, Paytm has made efforts to update its compliance procedures and adhere to regulatory requirements. On value generation grounds, Paytm has performed a remarkable ride in the direction of financial incorporation in India by making financially inclusive financial products and services accessible and convenient. It offers real-time lending solutions, promoting economic growth and digital connectivity in the process, benefiting both consumers and small businesses.

This Paytm case offers valuable insights into the need for regulatory harmony, technology integration, and customer-focused practices in the digital lending landscape. It provides an example of the power of data governance basics to support innovation while protecting consumer interests in emerging markets. These case studies highlight the different ways financial data governance informs digital lending practice across the various regions. On the one hand, companies like Ant Group and Tala do data-driven innovation and financial inclusion, while others like Lending Club and Paytm champion transparency, regulatory adherence and consumer safety. They highlight the importance of having a balance between governance structures that allow innovation and ethics, and responsible use of financial data.

4.1.5. Cross-Case Thematic Analysis of Financial Data Governance and Consumer Protection

Cross case thematic analysis is used to deliver a comparative perspective on our understanding of the outcomes of financial data governance practices on consumer protection across top digital lending application platforms in both emerging and advanced markets. The research looks at specific instances such as Ant Group, Lending Club, Tala, and Paytm and highlights commonalities in the usage of data, transparency, regulatory adherence, and risk exposure. The next table outlines the systemically identified themes based on the cross-case comparison, including the similarities, differences, and general themes that were observed related to financial data governance and consumer protection. It's a forward-thinking overview of innovative digital lending practices and their level of accountability—and an identification of key governance omissions that heighten the risks that domestic consumers face to their financial and informational interests.

Table 1. Cross-Case Thematic Analysis of Financial Data Governance and Consumer Protection

Theme	Ant Group (China)	Lending Club (USA)	Tala (Kenya/ Global)	Paytm (India)	Cross-Case Insight
Data-Driven Innovation	Extensive use of AI, big data, and Sesame Credit	Algorithmic credit scoring using structured financial data	Uses alternative mobile and behavioural data	Uses ecosystem data (UPI, wallet, transactions)	Data-driven models enhance financial inclusion but create data dependency and asymmetry
Transparency & Algorithmic Opacity	Low transparency in proprietary scoring	Improved transparency after governance reforms	Limited explainability in AI models	Moderate transparency due to RBI norms	Algorithmic opacity increases information asymmetry and reduces accountability
Data Privacy & Consent	Concerns over extensive data collection and usage	Stronger governance post-2016 misconduct	Relies on sensitive personal/mobile data	Operates under stricter consent frameworks (DPDP Act)	Weak consent mechanisms lead to privacy risks and unethical data usage

continued on following page

Table 1. Continued

Theme	Ant Group (China)	Lending Club (USA)	Tala (Kenya/ Global)	Paytm (India)	Cross-Case Insight
Regulatory Environment	Strong intervention (IPO halt, restructuring)	Mature regulatory oversight (SEC)	Evolving regulatory frameworks	Strong RBI and data protection regulations	Strong regulation improves governance, but enforcement gaps persist
Consumer Protection Risks	Over-indebtedness, hidden risks	Data misrepresentation (historical issue)	Risk of debt cycles among low-income users	BNPL-driven impulsive borrowing	Digital lending increases financial vulnerability and exploitation risks
Predatory Practices	Seamless credit encourages excessive borrowing	Controlled environment, fewer predatory issues	Potential aggressive recovery in similar ecosystems	BNPL may encourage overuse of credit	Profit-driven models may lead to predatory lending behaviour
Governance Maturity	Advanced technology but initially weak oversight	Strong governance after reforms	Developing governance structures	High compliance with regulatory standards	Governance maturity determines trust, stability, and compliance
Financial Inclusion Impact	High inclusion through digital ecosystem	Expands access to credit markets	Strong inclusion for unbanked populations	Enhances inclusion via digital infrastructure	Inclusion benefits are significant but come with consumer protection trade-offs
Cybersecurity Risks	High due to large-scale data processing	Managed through regulatory compliance	Vulnerable due to mobile-based lending	Stronger security due to regulatory standards	Cyber risks threaten data integrity and consumer trust
Theoretical Linkages	Information asymmetry is reduced but a reversed imbalance emerges	Agency issues addressed through reforms	High asymmetry and privacy concerns	Balanced approach due to regulation	Supports Information Asymmetry, Agency Theory, and Data Privacy frameworks

Source: Author's own work.

The cross-case analysis shows that, generally, digital lending platforms work more towards innovation through data and less towards mature financial data governance frameworks. On the one hand, all platforms make important progress in tackling financial inclusion issues via the use of advanced analytics and alternative data; on the other hand, they share certain common issues such as algorithmic transparency, inadequate consent procedures and heightened vulnerability of consumers. The results demonstrate that the relationship of asymmetrical information has shifted rather than vanished, and that the consumer end-user is held mostly responsible for data sharing and transaction decision-making with the help of fintech platforms. Moreover, the study highlights the importance of the effectiveness of regulation to the governance results. The level of transparency and accountability of platforms under strong regulatory frameworks like Paytm and Lending Club is relatively high, while platforms operating in more developed or less coordinated regulatory systems are more likely to be subject to a lack of governance or to experience a consumer exploitation incident. Agency conflicts can be seen in all cases: there may be conflicts with the principle of fair and ethical lending, because profitable business models may have a greater interest in conflict with the principles (K. Balaji, 2023).

4.1.6. Comparative Regulatory Analysis of Digital Lending Frameworks in Emerging Markets

This table provides a comparison of digital lending and financial data governance regulations in selected emerging markets. It sheds light on salient differences in regulatory focus, regulatory strengths, and regulatory enforcement problems that affect consumer protection results.

Table 2. Comparative Regulatory Analysis of Digital Lending Frameworks in Emerging Markets

Country	Key Regulatory Frameworks	Regulatory Focus	Strengths	Challenges	Comparative Insight
India	DPDP Act (2023), RBI Digital Lending Guidelines (2022), IT Act (2000)	Data privacy, consent, transparency, lending regulation	Strong integration of financial and data governance; clear disclosure norms; consumer-centric policies	Enforcement gaps; rapid fintech growth challenges oversight	Highly proactive and integrated framework with strong consumer protection focus
Brazil	LGPD (2020), Open Banking Framework	Data protection, open finance, interoperability	Strong data governance aligned with global standards; promotes innovation and competition	Supervisory challenges; balancing innovation with consumer protection	Data-centric and innovation-friendly model
Indonesia	OJK Regulation No. 77/2016, Personal Data Protection Law (2022)	Licensing, risk management, data protection	Emerging legal framework; improved focus on privacy and fintech regulation	Weak enforcement; fragmented regulatory coordination	Evolving but partially fragmented system
Kenya	Digital Credit Providers Regulations (2022), Data Protection Act (2019)	Consumer protection, mobile lending regulation, data privacy	Rapid regulatory response to fintech growth; improved licensing and disclosure norms	Limited enforcement capacity; institutional constraints	Reactive but fast-developing regulatory model
Philippines	SEC Guidelines, Data Privacy Act (2012)	Transparency, registration, data protection	Clear compliance requirements; structured oversight by SEC and NPC	Moderate enforcement; regulatory fragmentation	Compliance-oriented but moderately effective framework

Source: Author's own work.

Based on the Table 2 comparison, the countries with integrated, well-enforced regulatory systems perform better on the key governance effectiveness and consumer protection measures. While fragmented and evolving structures, on the other hand, are very difficult to enforce and are more subject to misuse of data and financial risks (K. Balaji and P. S. Rao,2024).

4.2. Key Consumer Protection Challenges

Digital lending platforms in emerging markets have grown exceedingly fast, providing many benefits in terms of financial inclusion and efficiency. It has also created several consumer protection issues that call for adequate regulation and institutional development measures. The profound adoption of financial data, the widespread practice of algorithmic decision-making, and the continuously changing structure of fintech business models are the vital factors that contribute to these challenges.

4.2.1. Data Privacy and Unauthorized Data Access

Customer data security is one of the most essential issues of the digital lending process. FinTech platforms may gather a huge quantity of personal, financial and behavioural information, such as mobile usage data, location and transaction history. This information may improve credit evaluation, but it can also lead to unauthorised use, data breaches, misuse, jeopardise security, and negatively impact customer privacy and protection. Consumers, in many instances, are not fully aware of the degree of data that is collected or how it is used. Consumers in emerging markets are especially susceptible to exploitation and identity theft because data protection regulations are still being developed in those areas, and there are gaps in enforcement.

4.2.2. Lack of Transparency in Loan Terms

Numerous loan platforms have complex pricing, featuring hidden fees, excessive processing fees, and unclear interest calculations. Digital interfaces usually create information that is broken down or disjointed, making it difficult for consumers to understand the cost of borrowing. Plus, the applicant may not read the terms and conditions carefully due to instant loan approvals and less paperwork. This situation of opacity might cause borrowers to make decisions on finance without receiving detailed information, thereby causing them to jump into financial trouble and get into over-indebtedness.

4.2.3 Algorithmic Bias and Discrimination

The growing use of AI and machine learning in the credit scoring process has raised concerns about algorithmic bias and discrimination. Due to their use of non-traditional data sources, digital lending platforms can assess whether a person is more or less likely to pay back their loan, albeit these data components might show how social and economic inequalities already exist. This can lead to algorithmic discrimination against particular groups, where those who are excluded aren't offered out or may face additional rates on account. Consequently, some groups may be unfairly excluded or charged additional interest rates because of biased algorithms. This situation is exacerbated by the lack of explanation around automated decision-making, where consumers may struggle to comprehend or question the justification behind credit decisions. This poses pertinent ethical and regulatory issues regarding equality, accountability and inclusiveness of digital finance.

4.2.4. Predatory Lending Practices

In the unregulated or loosely regulated digital lending scenario, predatory lending practices have become common. One type of platform is referred to as an aggressive platform as it targets users who are less affluent and less capable of repaying the loans, and charges high interest rates and penalties. However, when it gets to the extreme, it has been reported that the lenders attempt recovery tactics – harassment, public shaming by going through borrowers' contact lists. Credit is also being integrated into everyday use of digital transactions - online BNPL - further adding to the likelihood of impulsive borrowing and debt. Such practices should be viewed as a slap on the face of the consumers and the demand for better regulations and lending ethics has risen.

4.2.5. Cybersecurity Risks

Cybersecurity is doing much harm to consumers and digital lending institutions. Financial services digitisation has left fintech systems with varying levels of vulnerability – especially to phishing, malware, ransomware and data breaches. Financial data can be susceptible to loss, which can cause serious harm to the reputation and finances of an organisation due to one security However, emerging markets may be plagued with other problems, including inadequately developed cybersecurity infrastructure, lack of cybersecurity professionals and lack of consumer awareness about digital risks. Strong cyber security measures, such as robust encryption methods, erudition, multiple factor authentication and persistent monitoring, are crucial for protecting the customer's data and ensuring trust when using digital financial services.

The challenges point to the tension between innovation and risk in digital lending ecosystems, from a consumer protection perspective. Regulators, fintech companies, and consumers need to cooperate to tackle problems with data security, safety and protection, fairness of algorithms, predatory practices and transparency. Increasing legal resilience, improving technical protection and fostering financial literacy are essential to fostering a safe, transparent and inclusive digital financial system in emerging markets.

5. ANALYSIS AND DISCUSSION

The analysis shows strong evidence that there is a clear correlation between the extent of a consumer's risk within an emerging market's digital lending ecosystem and the lack of financial data governance. Such weak governance structures – inadequate consent mechanisms, weak data security policies and transparency – create enormous vulnerabilities for consumers. These gaps allow fintech platforms to take advantage of the disparity in knowledge by engaging in lending practices that are difficult to understand, mismanagement of personal information, and low accountability. Consumers therefore face threats such as identity theft, data misrepresentation and unfair credit (quotas, denial of credit, etc.), especially in areas where regulatory regulation is developing. While many emerging markets have progressive laws and policies, there is considerable variation in their effectiveness: in some countries, there are difficulties in enforcing the laws. One of the key constraints in regulations is inherent institutional capacity weaknesses and weak institutional governance, and the speed of technological change. The difficulties of coordination and inefficiency of enforcement arise in several instances due to overlapping tasks across regulatory bodies, including regulatory agencies like the central bank, data protection authorities and consumer protection authorities. Additionally, the innovation of fintech products has often outrun the ability of regulators to adapt, resulting in regulatory omissions like real-time tracking of digital lending transactions and the responsibility for algorithmic accountability.

The relationship between fintech companies and regulators is an important aspect of the governance structure. FinTech firms, being the most innovative businesses, have a crucial role to play in safeguarding consumers' privacy interests and upholding ethical data use. But there can be a conflict between their profit motives and the dictates of the need for transparency and fairness. Regulators, however, have to balance innovation and the protection of consumer interests. This is where the joint frameworks of co-regulation, regulatory sandboxes and industry self-governance are needed. Fintech companies must embrace proactive measures of responsibility and exert accountability, while the regulators must mature their technological capabilities and oversight systems. In a sustainable ecosystem, it becomes crucial for fintech companies to take proactive steps in both accountability measures and, at the same time, for regulators to advance their technology skills and supervision processes. Compare across countries for useful learnings on governance and system gaps for digital lending. A sound regulatory system and effective enforcement foster more consumer confidence and confidence in the market. On the other hand, jurisdictions with disjointed or less-developed regulatory frameworks have higher rates of consumer exploitation, data breaches, and predatory lending. The comparative findings underscore the need for coordinated and coherent actions in the field of fintech, such as regulatory initiatives, institutional capacity development, and international collaboration to meet the global and connected nature of fintech operations.

6. IMPLICATIONS

6.1 Policy Implications

The results of this research stress the pressing significance of enhancing regulatory enforcement in developing countries. Ensuring that countries successfully implement and monitor data protection laws and digital lending regulations is essential. There is a need for a new integrated regulatory approach that involves integrated regulations that incorporate financial supervision and principles of data governance. To achieve this, it is necessary to invest in the creation of data governance structures that use consistent data collection, processing, and sharing. They should also provide a focus on transparency, accountability, and consumer rights that improve market confidence in digital financial systems.

6.2 Managerial Implications

For managers, ethical data governance must not just be a compliance issue, but a strategic approach to making the most of this treasure trove of data. There is a need to embrace transparency in data practices, communicating with consumers about the collection and use of their data. To improve accountability and minimise bias from algorithms, explainable artificial intelligence models could be implemented. Further, companies should make good efforts to implement strong cybersecurity protocols and robust grievance redressal processes. Establishing consumer trust will need the focus to change toward responsible lending, communication and fairness as well as transparency.

6.3 Academic Implications

The study brings together theoretical and practical approaches and enriches new knowledge in the areas of consumer protection, data governance, and fintech, while complementing the growing literature on these topics. In this regard, it identifies the necessity of inter-disciplinary research that incorporates the lessons drawn from financial, information systems, legal and behavioural studies to gain a deeper understanding of the complexities of digital lending environments. Future empirical studies examining the effect of data governance practices on customer experience and financial stability will have great potential. In addition, comparative research around a number of regions can give deeper insights into context-specific challenges, and they can contribute to the development of globally relevant frameworks.

7. RECOMMENDATIONS

The study proposes several key recommendations to enhance financial data governance and consumer protection in digital lending. Improvements are needed to consumer consent options, which must be streamlined and made clear to consumers so they can make informed choices about sharing their data. It is also crucial to improve the transparency of algorithms, and fintech companies should be encouraged to use explainable artificial intelligence systems that enable stakeholders to be informed and assess credit decisions. Educating consumers about financial literacy and awareness is essential for ensuring they use digital financial services in a responsible and conscious way and identify potential risks. Moreover, the cross-border coordination of Data Governance mechanisms should be emphasised to tackle challenges from the cross-border activities of fintech entities. Standardised regulations to enhance the effectiveness of data governance frameworks and the encouragement of international cooperation can help.

8. CONCLUSION

To sum up, this paper emphasises the ambivalence of digital lending in emerging markets, which has increased financial access for the consumer while giving rise to new problems for consumer protection. The findings highlight that consumer financial data governance issues, including in the areas of privacy, transparency, and accountability, are at the heart of consumer risks. Despite the evolving rules, they need to be implemented well, which is not always possible in practice because of enforcement problems, institutional obstacles and other factors. Moving forward, digital lending governance will depend on the stakeholders' having a balanced and collaborative stance. The role of regulators must be expanded to closely monitor and regulate fintech practices, and firms should demonstrate ethical and transparent practices. As the financial landscape continues to change, let's embrace new technologies and prepare responsive and anticipatory governance models. Going forward, empirical testing, advanced technologies to improve governance and the establishment of globally inter-standardised regulatory frameworks are important for a safe, inclusive and sustainable DFE to be realised.

REFERENCES

Agarwal, S., & Zhang, J. (2020). FinTech, Lending and Payment Innovation: A Review. *Asia-Pacific Journal of Financial Studies*, *49*(3), 353–367. DOI: 10.1111/ajfs.12294

Agoraki, M.-E.-K., Delis, M. D., & Pasiouras, F. (2011). Regulations, competition and bank risk-taking in transition countries. *Journal of Financial Stability*, *7*(1), 38–48. DOI: 10.1016/j.jfs.2009.08.002

Albertazzi, U., & Gambacorta, L. (2009). Bank profitability and the business cycle. *Journal of Financial Stability*, *5*(4), 393–409. DOI: 10.1016/j.jfs.2008.10.002

Allen, F., & Gale, D. (2000). Financial Contagion. *Journal of Political Economy*, *108*(1), 1–33. DOI: 10.1086/262109

Allen, F., & Gale, D. (2004). Competition and Financial Stability. *Journal of Money, Credit and Banking*, *36*(Jun), 453–480. DOI: 10.1353/mcb.2004.0038

Allen, L., Shan, Y., & Shen, Y. (2022). Do FinTech Mortgage Lenders Fill the Credit Gap? Evidence from Natural Disasters. *Journal of Financial and Quantitative Analysis*. Advance online publication. DOI: 10.1017/S002210902200120X

Ampudia, M., Beck, T., & Popov, A. (2021). *Out with the New, In with the Old?* Bank Supervision and the Composition of Firm Investment. [Unpublished manuscript]

Anginer, D., Demirguc-Kunt, A., & Zhu, M. (2014). How does competition affect bank systemic risk? *Journal of Financial Intermediation*, *23*(1), 1–26. DOI: 10.1016/j.jfi.2013.11.001

Balaji, K. "Exploring the Drivers and Effects on Supply Chain Resilience and Performance in an Emerging Market Using Artificial Intelligence," *2023 3rd International Conference on Smart Generation Computing, Communication and Networking (SMART GENCON)*, Bangalore, India, 2023, pp. 1-6, DOI: 10.1109/SMARTGENCON60755.2023.10442071

Balaji, K. (2025). Harnessing AI and Blockchain in Sustainability Assurance: Trends Shaping the Future of Verification. In Khatib, S., & Abbas, A. (Eds.), *Navigating Trust in Sustainability Reporting and Assurance* (pp. 215–242). IGI Global Scientific Publishing., DOI: 10.4018/979-8-3373-0117-4.ch007

Balaji, K. (2025). Revolutionizing High-Frequency Trading: The Impacts of Financial Technology and Data Science Innovations. In Chen, H. (Ed.), *Machine Learning and Modeling Techniques in Financial Data Science* (pp. 103–124). IGI Global Scientific Publishing., DOI: 10.4018/979-8-3693-8186-1.ch004

Balaji, K. (2025). Neuromarketing and Sustainable Finance: Real-World Case Studies of Green Investment Promotions. In Taneja, S., Chahal, B., Johri, A., Ozen, E., & Kumar, P. (Eds.), *Neuromarketing's Role in Sustainable Finance* (pp. 169–204). IGI Global Scientific Publishing., DOI: 10.4018/979-8-3693-9117-4.ch010

Balaji, K. (2025). AI as a Game Changer: How Digital Entrepreneurs Are Redefining Business Practices. In Tunio, M. (Ed.), *Improving Entrepreneurial Processes Through Advanced AI* (pp. 21–48). IGI Global Scientific Publishing., DOI: 10.4018/979-8-3693-1495-1.ch002

Balaji, K. (2025). IoT in Financial Services Innovations in Banking and Insurance. In Ho, R., Song, B., & Tee, P. (Eds.), *Managing Customer-Centric Strategies in the Digital Landscape* (pp. 75–104). IGI Global Scientific Publishing., DOI: 10.4018/979-8-3693-5668-5.ch004

Balaji, K. (2025). Human-Centric Innovation: Building Sustainable Organizations for Industry 5.0. In Erturk, A., Özşahin, M., & Simovic, V. (Eds.), *Human-Centric, Sustainable, and Resilient Organizations in the Digital Age* (pp. 101–124). IGI Global Scientific Publishing., DOI: 10.4018/979-8-3693-8181-6.ch005

Balaji, K., & Rao, P. S. "Artificial Intelligence and Chatbots: Transforming User Experience in E-tailing," *2024 9th International Conference on Communication and Electronics Systems (ICCES)*, Coimbatore, India, 2024, pp. 1375-1379, DOI: 10.1109/ICCES63552.2024.10859474

Balyuk, T., Berger, A. N., & Hackney, J. (2020). *What is Fueling FinTech Lending? The Role of Banking Market Structure*. DOI: 10.2139/ssrn.3633907

Banna, H., Hassan, M. K., & Rashid, M. (2021). Fintech-based financial inclusion and bank risk-taking: Evidence from OIC countries. *Journal of International Financial Markets, Institutions and Money*, *75*, 101447. Advance online publication. DOI: 10.1016/j.intfin.2021.101447

Bao, Z., & Huang, D. (2021). Shadow Banking in a Crisis: Evidence from FinTech during COVID-19. *Journal of Financial and Quantitative Analysis*, *56*(7), 2320–2355. Advance online publication. DOI: 10.1017/S0022109021000430

Beck, T., Cecchetti, S., Grothe, M., Kemp, M., Pelizzon, L., & Sánchez-Serrano, A. (2022). Will video kill the radio star? *Digitalisation and the future of banking* (No. 12; pp. 1–64). ESRB.

Beck, T., De Jonghe, O., & Schepens, G. (2013). Bank competition and stability: Cross-country heterogeneity. *Journal of Financial Intermediation*, *22*(2), 218–244. DOI: 10.1016/j.jfi.2012.07.001

. Beck, T., Gambacorta, L., Huang, Y., Li, Z., & Qiu, H. (2022). *Big techs, QR code payments and financial inclusion* [Unpublished manuscript].

Bellardini, L., Del Gaudio, B. L., Previtali, D., & Verdoliva, V. (2022). How do banks invest in fintechs? Evidence from advanced economies. *Journal of International Financial Markets, Institutions and Money*, *77*, 101498. Advance online publication. DOI: 10.1016/j.intfin.2021.101498

Berg, T., Fuster, A., & Puri, M. (2022). FinTech Lending. *Annual Review of Financial Economics*, *14*(1), 187–207. DOI: 10.1146/annurev-financial-101521-112042

Bertsch, C., Hull, I., Qi, Y., & Zhang, X. (2020). Bank misconduct and online lending. *Journal of Banking & Finance*, *116*, 105822. Advance online publication. DOI: 10.1016/j.jbankfin.2020.105822

. BIS. (2017). *Sound Practices: Implications of fintech developments for banks and bank supervisors.*

. BIS. (2018). *Implications of fintech developments for banks and bank supervisors.*

Boot, A., Hoffmann, P., Laeven, L., & Ratnovski, L. (2021). Fintech: What's old, what's new? *Journal of Financial Stability*, *53*, 100836. Advance online publication. DOI: 10.1016/j.jfs.2020.100836

Chen, T., Huang, Y., Lin, C., & Sheng, Z. (2022). Finance and Firm Volatility: Evidence from Small Business Lending in China. *Management Science*, *68*(3), 2226–2249. DOI: 10.1287/mnsc.2020.3942

. Cornelli, G., Doerr, S., Franco, L., & Frost, J. (2021). Funding for fintechs: Patterns and drivers. *BIS Quarterly Review*, 31–43.

Cruz-García, P., Fernández de Guevara, J., & Maudos, J. (2021). Bank competition and multimarket contact intensity. *Journal of International Money and Finance*, *113*, 102338. Advance online publication. DOI: 10.1016/j.jimonfin.2020.102338

Cubillas, E., Ferrer, E., & Suárez, N. (2021). Does investor sentiment affect bank stability? International evidence from lending behavior. *Journal of International Money and Finance*, *113*, 102351. Advance online publication. DOI: 10.1016/j.jimonfin.2020.102351

Cubillas, E., & González, F. (2014). Financial liberalization and bank risk-taking: International evidence. *Journal of Financial Stability*, *11*(1), 32–48. DOI: 10.1016/j.jfs.2013.11.001

Degryse, H., & Ongena, S. (2007). The impact of competition on bank orientation. *Journal of Financial Intermediation*, *16*(3), 399–424. DOI: 10.1016/j.jfi.2007.03.002

Delis, M. D. (2012). Bank competition, financial reform, and institutions: The importance of being developed. *Journal of Development Economics*, *97*(2), 450–465. DOI: 10.1016/j.jdeveco.2011.05.012

Reserve Bank of India. (2022). *Guidelines on digital lending*. RBI Publications.

Reserve Bank of India. (2023). *Report on trend and progress of banking in India*. RBI Publications.

World Bank. (2020). *Consumer risks in fintech: New manifestations of consumer risks and emerging regulatory approaches*. World Bank Publications.

KEY TERMS AND DEFINITIONS

Algorithmic Bias: When AI systems make unfair or discriminatory decisions based on biased data.

Algorithmic Controls: Rules and systems that manage how AI and algorithms make lending decisions, ensuring fairness and accuracy.

BNPL (Buy Now, Pay Later): A service that allows consumers to purchase goods immediately and pay later in instalments.

Consent Mechanisms: Processes through which users agree to share their data, ideally with full understanding and transparency.

Cybersecurity Risks: Threats such as hacking or fraud that can compromise financial and personal data.

Data Privacy Breaches: Situations where personal data is accessed or shared without permission.

Ethical Standards: Principles that ensure fintech firms operate in a fair, transparent, and responsible manner.

Financial Data Governance: The system of rules and practices that ensures financial data is collected, used, stored, and shared safely and ethically.

FinTech Firm Practices: The strategies and operational methods used by fintech companies, including data usage, lending policies, and customer handling.

NBFCs (Non-Banking Financial Companies): Financial institutions that provide loans and financial services without being traditional banks.

P2P (Peer-to-Peer) Lending: A system where individuals lend money directly to other individuals through online platforms.

Predatory Lending: Unethical lending practices that exploit borrowers, often with high interest rates and hidden costs.

Chapter 9
Governance of Financial Market Data as a Determinant of Regulatory Compliance and Investor Confidence in Global Capital Markets

Hamza Yusuf
http://orcid.org/0009-0007-8029-5660
RMIT University, Australia

ABSTRACT

Financial markets rely on accurate, transparent, and consistently governed data across institutions and jurisdictions. Yet financial market data governance remains underexamined as a determinant of regulatory credibility and investor confidence. This chapter argues that data governance is a foundational institutional system shaping compliance with international standards and inclusion in global financial benchmarks. Using a qualitative case study of the 2026 Indonesia episode, where MSCI flagged concerns over ownership transparency and free float reliability, the study shows how data governance failures triggered index freezes, capital outflows, and regulatory leadership changes. The findings position data governance as a legitimacy mechanism central to market stability, transparency, and global capital integration.

DOI: 10.4018/979-8-2600-2233-7.ch009

1. INTRODUCTION

In modern financial markets, a single warning from a global index provider can erase billions of dollars in market value within hours, as the 2026 MSCI-Indonesia incident demonstrated (Bloomberg, 2026). Not because of an economic downturn or a geopolitical crisis, but because of concerns about how a country's financial data is governed. Trading halts, foreign capital withdrawals, and currency pressure can all follow from a signal that ownership data is unreliable, that disclosure practices are inconsistent, or that free-float calculations cannot be verified. The system does not run on economic performance alone. It runs on data, and when confidence in that data breaks down, markets respond immediately. These are not hypothetical risks. Recent incidents in emerging markets, including the 2026 MSCI index freeze on Indonesian securities, have demonstrated that data governance failures can trigger rapid, measurable disruptions to capital flows and market stability (MSCI, 2026a).

Here lies a structural problem. Financial markets depend on data at every level of their operation. Regulatory enforcement relies on reported data to monitor compliance. Investors rely on disclosed data to assess risk. Index providers rely on standardized data to construct benchmarks that guide trillions of dollars in investment. The governance of this data, meaning the standards, validation processes, and controls that ensure its quality throughout its lifecycle, is the foundation on which all these functions rest. Yet in many markets, the systems responsible for producing and maintaining financial data remain fragmented, inconsistently enforced, or misaligned with international expectations. The problem is not that data exists but that the governance surrounding it is often too weak to guarantee its reliability.

It matters because the global financial system has become structurally sensitive to data quality. Trillions of dollars are benchmarked to indices maintained by providers such as MSCI and FTSE Russell (Robertson, 2019), who evaluate markets not only on economic fundamentals but on whether the underlying data environment meets specific transparency and consistency standards. Rating agencies incorporate data transparency into sovereign and corporate assessments (SEC, 2024; UNCTAD, 2024). In this environment, data governance is no longer an internal administrative concern. It is a gatekeeper that determines whether a market can participate in global capital flows on favourable terms. A failure in data governance triggers repricing, reallocation, and reputational damage that can take years to reverse.

Despite this practical importance, the governance of financial market data remains underdeveloped as a subject of study across several dimensions. Conceptually, the field lacks a clear conceptual basis that integrates technical data governance principles with the operational realities of financial markets. Most financial market scholarship treats data as a background input to analysis rather than as a governed asset with its own lifecycle, oversight structures, and failure modes (Abraham et al.,

2019). Information governance literature, conversely, has developed robust approaches to data quality, stewardship, and lifecycle management, but has rarely applied these to contexts where governance failures carry systemic financial consequences. Empirically, there is limited research examining how specific data governance deficiencies, such as weak ownership disclosure, inconsistent reporting standards, or poor system interoperability, translate into observable market outcomes like capital withdrawal, index reclassification, or volatility. Normatively, the question of who should set and enforce data governance standards in global finance, whether domestic regulators, international bodies, or private actors like index providers, remains largely unaddressed. The result is a fragmented understanding in which the technical, organisational, and market dimensions of financial data governance are studied in isolation rather than as an interconnected system.

Existing theoretical approaches offer useful but incomplete explanations. Governance theory contributes an understanding of how accountability structures operate over shared systems. This theory is relevant but haven't been systematically applied to the governance of financial market data as a distinct domain of practice. Governance theory addresses structural accountability but has not been extended to the challenges of governing financial data across multiple institutions, jurisdictions, and technology platforms simultaneously.

Against this background, the chapter addresses these gaps by asking how does the governance of financial market data function as a driver of regulatory compliance and investor confidence in modern financial markets? It examines data governance as a distinct system and develops an analytical structure connecting technical components, including reporting standards, validation processes, disclosure infrastructure, and system interoperability, to outcomes such as regulatory compliance, investor confidence, and market stability. Drawing on governance theory and grounded in an empirical case from an emerging market context, the study argues that data governance is not a background function but a core determinant of whether financial markets can sustain credibility, attract capital, and operate with stability.

2. LITERATURE REVIEW

The section that follows reviews the existing scholarship and conceptual foundations relevant to the governance of financial market data, its role in regulatory compliance and investor confidence, and the theoretical foundations that help explain its significance. The review is organized into five areas. It begins with the foundational principles of data governance as a discipline, then examines how these principles apply specifically within financial markets. It moves to the role of external benchmarking actors in shaping compliance standards, followed by the relationship between data quality, information asymmetry, and investor behaviour. It concludes with the governance theory perspective that underpins the analytical approach of this study. Together, these bodies of literature establish the conceptual basis for understanding why the governance of market data is not a peripheral concern but a structural determinant of how financial markets function and how they are perceived by global participants.

2.1. Data Governance: Foundations and Core Principles

Data governance, broadly defined, refers to the system of standards, roles, processes, and controls that determine how data is collected, validated, stored, and made available within an organization or across institutions (DAMA International, 2017). In information management literature, it is understood not simply as a technical function but as a structural system that assigns accountability for data quality and ensures that data serves its intended purposes reliably. Core principles include accuracy, consistency, timeliness, accessibility, and auditability (Al-Ruithe et al., 2019). These principles apply regardless of the domain in which data operates, but their significance varies depending on the stakes attached to data quality in each context.

In financial markets, these stakes are exceptionally high. The data that circulates through stock exchanges, regulatory bodies, custodian banks, and index providers is not passive information. It functions as infrastructure. Ownership records, free-float calculations, settlement data, trading volumes, and corporate disclosures all feed into models and systems that determine how capital is allocated across markets and jurisdictions (MSCI, 2025; Petry et al., 2021). If any part of this data environment is unreliable, the downstream effects extend beyond individual transactions. They affect the perceived integrity of entire markets.

What distinguishes data governance from related concepts such as data management or data analytics is its focus on accountability. Data management is concerned with the operational handling of data. Data governance asks who is responsible for ensuring that data meets defined standards, what processes exist to detect and correct errors, and how conflicts between different data sources or reporting standards are resolved (Abraham et al., 2019). In financial markets, this distinction is critical because the effects of poor governance are not limited to internal inefficiencies. They are externally visible and externally punished.

2.2. Financial Market Data and the Architecture of Transparency

Financial markets depend on transparency, and transparency depends on data. This relationship, while intuitive, involves a more complex set of mechanisms than is often acknowledged. Transparency in financial markets is not achieved simply by making data available (Bushman et al., 2004). It requires that data is structured in standardized formats, disclosed within predictable timeframes, verified through independent or regulatory processes, and accessible to all relevant market participants on equal terms.

Several categories of data are particularly central to market transparency (Bushman et al., 2004; MSCI, 2025). Corporate financial reporting, including earnings, liabilities, and capital structure, provides the basis for valuation. Ownership data, including shareholder breakdowns, beneficial ownership, and free-float calculations, determines how tradable and accessible a stock is to different classes of investors. Operational data, including settlement records, trading volumes, and clearing information, ensures that market infrastructure functions predictably. Each of these categories involves its own governance challenges. Corporate reporting depends on accounting standards and audit processes. Ownership data depends on disclosure thresholds and registry systems. Operational data depends on the technical interoperability of systems maintained by exchanges, custodians, and regulators.

When these data systems work in coordination, markets create an information environment where participants can make decisions based on comparable and verifiable inputs. When coordination breaks down, or when one category of data is governed less rigorously than others, the resulting inconsistencies create openings for information asymmetry. Investors who cannot verify ownership structures, for example, face uncertainty about the true liquidity of a stock. Regulators who receive inconsistent reporting across listed firms face difficulty enforcing standards uniformly. These are governance failures with direct implications for how a market is perceived and how capital flows into or out of it.

2.3. External Benchmarking and Private Regulatory Authority

One of the distinctive features of modern financial markets is that compliance is not determined solely by domestic regulators. A parallel layer of governance exists through external actors, most notably global index providers, rating agencies, and large institutional investors, who evaluate markets against their own standards and methodologies.

MSCI is among the most influential of these actors (Petry et al., 2021). It classifies national equity markets into categories including Developed, Emerging, Frontier, and Standalone. These classifications are not honorary labels. They directly shape the flow of global capital because trillions of dollars in institutional investment are benchmarked to MSCI indices (Robertson, 2019). When a country is classified as an Emerging Market, it becomes eligible for inclusion in funds that track Emerging Market indices. When that classification is threatened or downgraded, fund managers who track these benchmarks are obligated to reduce exposure, regardless of their own assessment of the market's fundamentals.

MSCI's classification criteria are heavily data dependent. They evaluate markets based on the size and liquidity of listed companies, the accessibility of the market to foreign investors, and critically, the transparency and reliability of the data that underpins these assessments. Requirements related to free-float accuracy, foreign ownership limit transparency, disclosure quality, and settlement systems are, at their core, tests of data governance. A market may have strong economic fundamentals and many listed firms, but if the data environment surrounding those firms is opaque or inconsistent, MSCI's methodology will reflect that as a governance risk (Anshari & Hamdan, 2023).

In effect, this places index providers in a position that resembles regulatory authority, even though they hold no legislative power (Petry et al., 2021). When MSCI freezes index upgrades, places a market on review, or signals potential re-classification, it imposes discipline through capital allocation channels rather than legal enforcement. The effect, however, can be equally consequential. Markets that fail to meet MSCI's data governance expectations face not only the direct impact of reduced index weighting but also the reputational signal that their information environment is not trusted by one of the most widely followed benchmarks in global finance (Ridzuan et al., 2024).

What emerges is something that can be understood as private regulatory power in financial markets. Domestic regulators set rules for reporting and disclosure, but external benchmarking actors determine whether the outputs of those rules meet the standards required for international participation. The gap between what domestic regulation requires and what international benchmarking demands often reveals the true state of a country's data governance capacity (Shamdi et al., 2022; Yar et al., 2024).

2.4. Information Asymmetry, Investor Confidence, and Market Stability

The relationship between data governance and investor confidence operates primarily through the mechanism of information asymmetry (Akerlof, 1970; Healy & Palepu, 2001). When data governance is strong, all market participants have access to comparable, timely, and reliable information. This reduces uncertainty and allows investors to price risk based on observable fundamentals. When data governance is weak, certain participants may have better information than others, or the available information may be too unreliable to support confident assessment. In either case, the result is increased uncertainty.

For foreign institutional investors, this uncertainty carries weight. Unlike domestic participants who may have informal channels of information or contextual familiarity with market conditions, foreign investors depend almost entirely on formally disclosed and publicly available data. If that data is inconsistent, delayed, or difficult to verify, foreign investors face a choice between accepting higher risk or reducing exposure. In practice, many institutional mandates resolve this choice automatically. Funds with governance screens or compliance thresholds will reduce allocation to markets where data quality falls below defined standards (Leuz et al., 2009).

The effects of reduced investor confidence extend beyond portfolio rebalancing. When foreign capital exits or slows, liquidity declines. Reduced liquidity increases volatility, which further discourages investment. This creates a feedback loop in which data governance weaknesses lead to capital withdrawal, which feeds market instability, which reinforces the perception that the market is risky. Breaking this cycle requires addressing the root cause, which is the governance of the data itself, rather than responding to the symptoms of volatility or capital flight (Anshari et al., 2025a).

Market stability, in this sense, is not only a function of macroeconomic conditions or monetary policy. It is also a function of informational stability. When the data environment of a market is perceived as credible, shocks tend to be absorbed more smoothly because participants trust the information available to them (Anshari et al., 2025b). When the data environment is perceived as fragile, even relatively minor signals, such as a warning from an index provider, can trigger disproportionate market reactions because participants interpret the signal as confirmation of deeper governance problems.

2.5. Governance Theory

Governance theory provides the analytical foundation for understanding financial market data as a system of structured accountability rather than merely a technical resource (Rhodes, 1997; Bevir, 2013). At its core, governance theory examines how authority, responsibility, and oversight are distributed across multiple actors within complex systems. This perspective is particularly relevant to financial markets, where data is produced, verified, and circulated through networks that include regulators, exchanges, listed firms, custodians, auditors, and external benchmarking institutions.

Modern governance arrangements are rarely centralized. Instead, they operate through coordinated relationships across public and private actors (Rhodes, 1997). In the context of financial market data, no single institution controls the entire data lifecycle. Reporting standards, validation processes, disclosure mechanisms, and enforcement practices are distributed across institutions and, often, across jurisdictions. The effectiveness of the system therefore depends not only on the existence of rules but on the coherence and coordination of those rules across actors (Ahmad et al., 2024).

Legitimacy and accountability are equally central to governance theory. Markets function sustainably only when participants recognize regulatory and disclosure systems as credible and consistently enforced. If accountability for data accuracy is unclear, or if validation processes are weak, formal regulations alone are insufficient to sustain investor confidence. Legitimacy arises from predictable enforcement, transparent standards, and visible oversight.

Applied to financial market data, governance theory clarifies that regulatory compliance and investor confidence are outcomes generated by coordinated oversight structures (Anshari et al., 2022). Data governance is therefore not simply a technical matter of information management. It is a governance arrangement that determines whether financial markets can maintain credibility within an interconnected global system.

3. METHODOLOGY

The chapter uses qualitative research grounded in the analysis of secondary data. The methodological approach is shaped by the nature of the research question, which asks how the governance of financial market data functions as a driver of regulatory compliance and investor confidence, and by the characteristics of the empirical context, which involves a high-profile, rapidly evolving event in an emerging market. Because the goal is to understand how governance works in practice, not to measure statistical relationships, a qualitative approach fits. It allows for close examination of how governance structures operate, how failures in those structures produce specific market consequences, and how different actors interpret and respond to data governance deficiencies.

A single case study strategy is used here, focusing on the incident that occurred in early 2026 in which MSCI flagged concerns over ownership transparency, free-float data reliability, and potential coordinated trading behaviour in Indonesia (MSCI, 2026a)'s equity market. The case is selected based on its analytical significance rather than its statistical representativeness. The MSCI-Indonesia incident is particularly instructive because it condenses a wide range of data governance issues, including disclosure failures, validation weaknesses, and accountability gaps, into a single observable sequence of events with clearly traceable market consequences. The index freeze, the immediate and severe market selloff (Bloomberg, 2026), the leadership changes that followed (The Jakarta Post, 2026), and the broader reputational effects on Indonesia's capital market collectively provide a rich empirical setting in which the relationship between data governance capacity and market outcomes can be examined in concrete terms. A case study approach works well here because it makes it possible to trace processes, identify causal links, and examine how governance structures interact with external pressures within a specific, bounded context (Yin, 2018).

The data used for this study is entirely from secondary sources. These include official statements and publications from MSCI, regulatory communications from Indonesian financial authorities, market data from recognised financial information providers, policy documents, and reporting from established financial media. Academic literature on data governance, governance theory, financial regulation, and information asymmetry provides the conceptual foundation against which the empirical evidence is interpreted. Using secondary data is a deliberate choice. The incident under examination is extensively documented through publicly available materials, and the key actions taken, including MSCI's communications, market responses, and regulatory interventions, are recorded in official and independently verifiable sources. For system-level phenomena like this one, where the relevant evidence takes the form of organisational outputs, regulatory decisions, and market indicators rather than individual accounts, secondary data is the right fit.

In terms of analytical approach, the study follows a structured thematic process. The secondary data is first organised chronologically to establish the factual sequence of events, from MSCI's initial flagging of concerns through to the market and regulatory responses that followed. It is then examined thematically against the conceptual groundwork established in the literature review, with particular attention to how the evidence reflects the operation or failure of specific data governance mechanisms, including reporting standards, validation processes, disclosure infrastructure, and system interoperability. The analysis traces how deficiencies in these mechanisms produced observable consequences across three outcome dimensions: regulatory compliance, investor confidence, and market stability. The point is to move beyond descriptive narration and to draw out the analytical connections between governance inputs and market outcomes.

The analysis is guided by governance theory, as established in the literature review. Governance theory directs attention to how authority, responsibility, and oversight are distributed across different actors, and how the coordination or fragmentation of these arrangements determines system-level outcomes. Applied to the empirical case, this lens enables the study to interpret specific data governance failures not as isolated technical errors but as symptoms of deeper structural misalignment between domestic governance capacity and the expectations of international evaluative actors. Under this lens, MSCI is positioned not merely as a market actor but as a mechanism of discipline, one that translates data governance performance into tangible market effects through classification decisions, index composition changes, and reputational signalling.

There are several methodological limitations worth noting. The study relies on a single case, which limits the generalisability of its findings across different market contexts. However, the purpose of the case study is analytical rather than statistical. The aim is to develop and illustrate a conceptual argument about the role of data governance, not to produce findings that are directly transferable to all markets. Additionally, the reliance on secondary data means that the study does not capture the internal deliberations of MSCI, Indonesian regulators, or market participants. That said, the publicly available record is rich and diverse enough to mitigate this, which includes official communications from relevant authorities, market performance data, and extensive reporting from multiple independent sources. Finally, because the period examined occurred in 2026 and its longer-term consequences are still unfolding, the study captures a defined period of response rather than a fully resolved outcome. The analysis is upfront about this boundary, and it does not prevent the study from examining how data governance failures produce market disruptions.

What this approach allows is an examination of financial market data governance as a system with observable consequences, grounded in a well-documented case that has broader relevance for understanding how markets build and sustain credibility within the global financial system.

4. FINDINGS

What follows presents the findings of the study, organised around the three outcome dimensions identified in the methodology which are regulatory compliance, investor confidence, and market stability. The analysis traces how specific data governance deficiencies in Indonesia's equity market were identified and acted upon by MSCI and examines the sequence of consequences that followed. Rather than narrating events in purely chronological terms, the findings are structured to show the mechanisms through which data governance failures produced observable market outcomes.

4.1. Data Governance Deficiencies and the Triggering of External Scrutiny

On 27 January 2026, MSCI announced a temporary freeze on certain index changes for Indonesian securities (MSCI, 2026a), effective immediately and covering the February 2026 rebalancing period. The announcement followed a global consultation in which MSCI solicited feedback from institutional investors on the quality and reliability of data governing Indonesian equities. The concerns that emerged from this consultation were not peripheral or isolated. They centred on three interconnected data governance failures: insufficient transparency in shareholding structures, unreliable free-float data, and indications of coordinated trading behaviour that could undermine fair price formation. Each one reflects a breakdown in a component of the data governance system identified in the literature review as essential to market transparency and credibility.

On ownership transparency, MSCI's consultation revealed that many institutional investors lacked confidence in the accuracy of reported ownership structures for Indonesian listed companies. While the Indonesia Central Securities Depository (KSEI) published monthly holding composition reports, MSCI received substantial feedback from global investors questioning the reliability of KSEI's shareholder classification system. The issue was not that ownership data was unavailable. It was that the categories used to classify shareholders did not consistently reflect the true nature of ownership relationships. In several cases, shares classified as publicly held were effectively controlled by parties affiliated with majority shareholders, creating a discrepancy between reported and actual ownership structures. For international investors, this opacity made it hard to tell who controlled listed companies, and whether the market was really as deep and liquid as its headline data suggested. The limited disclosure of ultimate beneficial owners compounded this problem, particularly for large-capitalisation and conglomerate-linked stocks that carried significant weight in major indices.

Free-float data reliability was the second area of concern. Free float, defined as the proportion of a company's shares that are genuinely available for public trading, is a critical input for index construction. MSCI acknowledged that minor improvements had been made to the Indonesia Stock Exchange's (IDX) free-float data feed but concluded that these enhancements were insufficient to resolve the fundamental investability concerns raised by market participants. The core of the problem was structural. Indonesia's regulatory framework required only a 7.5 percent minimum free float for listed companies, meaning that up to 92.5 percent of a firm's shares could remain concentrated in the hands of controlling shareholders. In practice, even the shares classified as freely traded were not always genuinely accessible to public investors, as high ownership concentration among a small number of wealthy families and conglomerates limited the actual liquidity available in the market. For an index provider whose methodology depends on accurate assessments of investability, these discrepancies between reported and actual free float constituted a serious data governance failure.

Coordinated trading behaviour was the third issue flagged. MSCI flagged that patterns of trading activity in certain heavily weighted Indonesian stocks raised questions about whether price formation was occurring through genuine market mechanisms or was being influenced by coordinated action among affiliated parties. Several stocks had experienced sharp and unexplained price increases that were inconsistent with their underlying fundamentals, pushing the Jakarta Composite Index higher without corresponding improvements in corporate earnings or economic conditions. This issue had drawn regulatory attention prior to MSCI's intervention. In October 2025, Indonesia's Finance Minister had announced intensified efforts to address market manipulation (Kompas.id, 2026), and the IDX had previously flagged unusual activity in certain counters. However, the persistence of these patterns into early 2026 indicated that existing surveillance and enforcement arrangements had not been sufficient to address the problem. The concealment of broker codes and domicile codes during trading hours further reduced the visibility of trading patterns (Kompas.id, 2026), making it more difficult for both regulators and market participants to assess whether price movements reflected legitimate market activity (see Figure 1 for a comparison of Indonesia's pre-crisis standards against international benchmarks).

Figure 1. Indonesia's Data Governance Standards vs International Benchmarks (Pre-Crisis)

Governance Dimension	Indonesia (Pre-Crisis)	MSCI / International Standard	Gap / Risk Assessment
Minimum Free-Float	7.5%	15-25% (common in peer markets)	Severe: Inflated index weights; liquidity risk
Ownership Transparency	KSEI categories (limited granularity)	Beneficial ownership disclosure required	Critical: Cannot verify true public float
Trading Surveillance	Broker/domicile codes concealed during hours	Real-time surveillance with full visibility	High: Coordinated trading undetectable
Corporate Disclosure	Inconsistent timeframes	Standardised, periodic, independently verified	Moderate: Reduces comparability

These three deficiencies were not independent of one another. Opaque ownership structures made it difficult to calculate accurate free-float figures, and the combination of concentrated ownership and unreliable free-float data created conditions in which coordinated trading could occur without effective detection. The interconnection of these failures illustrates a central finding of this study: data governance operates as a system, and a weakness in one component, such as disclosure infrastructure, can compromise the integrity of the entire chain, including validation processes and market surveillance capacity. Figure 2 illustrates the chronological sequence of events from the initial warning signals through to the institutional response.

Figure 2. Timeline of the MSCI-Indonesia Crisis (October 2025 – May 2026)

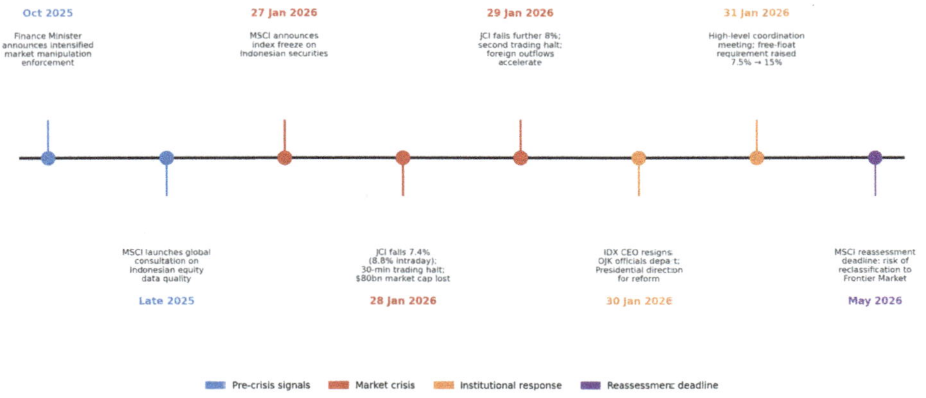

4.2. MSCI's Response as an Exercise of Private Regulatory Authority

MSCI's response to these governance deficiencies took the form of a series of immediate restrictions that functioned, in effect, as disciplinary measures imposed through capital market mechanisms rather than legal authority. The index provider froze all increases in Foreign Inclusion Factors and the Number of Shares for Indonesian securities. It halted the addition of any Indonesian stocks to MSCI's Investable Market Indexes. It suspended all upward size-segment migrations, including promotions from the Small Cap to the Standard Index. These measures were applied immediately and covered the February 2026 rebalancing period, effectively removing Indonesia from the normal cycle of index updates that drives passive capital allocation across global markets.

Critically, MSCI accompanied these restrictions with an explicit warning: if significant transparency improvements were not achieved by May 2026, the index provider would reassess Indonesia's market accessibility status. The potential consequences of such a reassessment included a reduction in Indonesia's weighting within the MSCI Emerging Markets Index and, in a more severe scenario, the reclassification of Indonesia from Emerging Market to Frontier Market status. Given that Indonesia accounted for approximately one percent of the MSCI Emerging Markets Index, which tracks roughly ten trillion dollars in global investments (SCMP, 2026; MSCI, 2025), even a modest weighting reduction would carry significant capital flow implications. A full reclassification to Frontier Market status, which would place Indonesia alongside economies such as Bangladesh, Pakistan, and Sri Lanka, would represent a far more consequential institutional judgment, one that would fundamentally alter how the global investment community perceives and allocates capital to the Indonesian market.

What matters about MSCI's actions for this study is not only their content but their character. MSCI holds no legislative or regulatory authority over Indonesia. It is a private actor operating in the global financial infrastructure. Yet its intervention produced consequences that, in terms of their market impact, far exceeded what most domestic enforcement actions could have achieved. The freeze was not a legal sanction but a market signal, one that communicated to the global investment community that Indonesia's data governance capacity did not meet the standards required for full participation in the index ecosystem. What this confirms is the literature review's framing of index providers as actors exercising private regulatory authority, disciplining markets not through legal enforcement but through capital allocation channels that are no less consequential.

What followed confirmed this dynamic through contagion. Within two weeks of MSCI's announcement, FTSE Russell, another major global index provider, separately postponed its planned March 2026 index review for Indonesian securities (FTSE Russell, 2026). FTSE Russell cited similar concerns about the difficulty of determining accurate free-float levels and adopted a parallel freeze on index additions, deletions, weighting changes, and investability updates for domestically listed Indonesian stocks. The convergence of action by two of the world's most influential index providers reinforced the severity of the governance signal and compounded the pressure on Indonesian authorities. It also demonstrated that data governance deficiencies, once identified by one evaluative actor, can rapidly cascade across the global benchmarking ecosystem, amplifying the consequences for the affected market.

4.3. Immediate Market Consequences and the Collapse of Investor Confidence

The market response to MSCI's announcement was immediate and severe, which is consistent with what one would expect when data governance signals from global evaluative actors are interpreted as evidence of deeper governance failures. On 28 January 2026, the benchmark Jakarta Composite Index fell 7.4 percent, the largest single-day decline in over nine months, before plunging as much as 8.8 percent intraday and triggering a thirty-minute trading halt (Bloomberg, 2026). The following day, selling pressure continued, with the index falling a further eight percent before a second trading halt was imposed. Over the course of two trading sessions, an estimated eighty billion dollars in market capitalisation was erased (SCMP, 2026; see Figure 3). Foreign investors engaged in heavy net selling, with outflows of approximately 6.17 trillion rupiah on 28 January and a further 4.63

trillion rupiah on 29 January (IDNFinancials, 2026), accelerating a trend of foreign capital withdrawal that had already seen cumulative outflows of 13.96 trillion rupiah throughout 2025 (IDX, 2026).

Figure 3. Jakarta Composite Index Performance and Foreign Capital Outflows (27–31 January 2026)

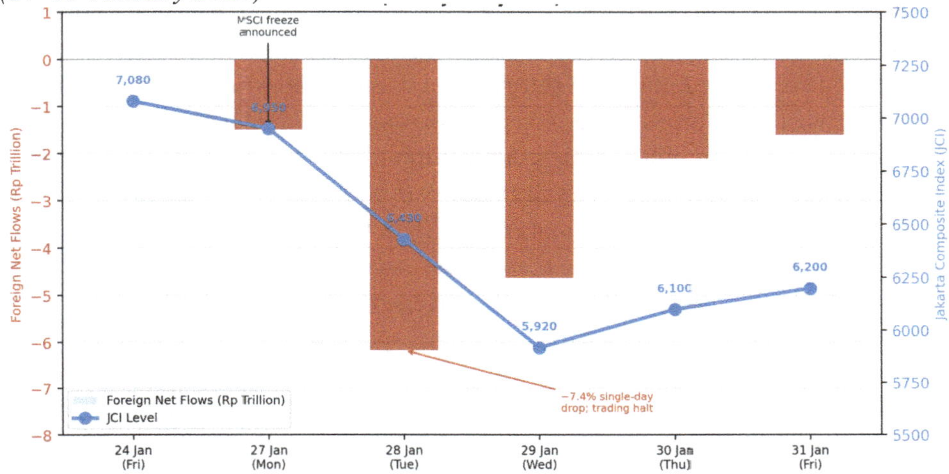

In terms of what drove the selloff, the speed and scale of it closely reflected the information asymmetry dynamics described in the literature review. For foreign institutional investors, who depend almost entirely on formally disclosed and publicly available data to assess market conditions, MSCI's warning functioned as a definitive signal that the data environment in Indonesia could not be trusted. The response was not measured or graduated. It was what market participants described as a sell-first ask-later reaction, driven by the recognition that data governance failures carry forward-looking implications for investability and that the risks of remaining exposed to a market under index scrutiny outweigh the costs of exit. This dynamic was compounded by the mechanical operation of passive investment. Index-tracking funds and exchange-traded funds benchmarked to MSCI indices faced the prospect of forced selling in the event of a reclassification, creating incentives for early exit. Goldman Sachs estimated that passive outflows alone could reach between 2.2 billion and 7.8 billion dollars (Goldman Sachs, 2026) in the event of a downgrade, with a further 5.6 billion dollars at risk if FTSE Russell were to make a similar classification change.

Nor was the confidence crisis confined to passive funds. Active fund managers and major global investment banks responded with their own reassessments. On 29 January, Goldman Sachs downgraded Indonesian equities to underweight, citing not only the MSCI risk but also broader macroeconomic vulnerabilities including soft private consumption, slowing credit growth, and a fiscal deficit approaching the legal three percent of GDP limit. UBS similarly lowered its recommendation on Indonesian equities to neutral from overweight, citing concerns over free float, liquidity, and regulatory certainty. These downgrades carried independent significance because they reflected a judgment by sophisticated institutional actors that Indonesia's data governance problems were not merely technical but symptomatic of broader systemic weaknesses. The feedback loop described in the literature review, in which data governance failures produce capital withdrawal, which produces market instability, which reinforces perceptions of risk, was clear in this sequence of events.

A structural vulnerability in the composition of Indonesia's investor base was also laid bare. While domestic retail participation had grown substantially, with Single Investor Identification accounts reaching 21.04 million by end-January 2026 (IDX, 2026), retail investors lacked the volume and capital depth to absorb the scale of institutional selling that MSCI's warning triggered. The market's dependence on foreign institutional capital meant that any event capable of shaking the confidence of international investors had the potential to produce outsized market disruption. What this makes clear is that data governance capacity is not only a matter of regulatory quality but also a determinant of the structural resilience of a market's investor base.

4.4. Institutional Disruption and Regulatory Accountability

The fallout from the data governance failures extended beyond market losses to produce disruption at the highest levels of Indonesia's financial regulatory architecture. On 30 January 2026, IDX President Director Iman Rachman resigned, citing personal responsibility for the extreme market turbulence (IDNFinancials, 2026). His resignation was followed on the same day by the departure of several senior officials from the Financial Services Authority (OJK), including Chairman of the Board of Commissioners Mahendra Siregar, Deputy Chairman Mirza Adityaswara, and the Chief Executive for Capital Market Supervision Inarno Djajadi (ANTARA, 2026). These resignations were subsequently confirmed to have been made at the direction of President Prabowo Subianto (see Figure 4 for the full institutional cascade), who, according to his special envoy Hashim Djojohadikusumo, was angered by the absence of transparency (Tempo.co, 2026) and by the fact that MSCI had sent multiple communications to Indonesian authorities prior to the public announcement without receiving an adequate response.

Analytically, the leadership changes carried significant weight. From a governance theory perspective, the forced departures signalled that accountability for data governance failures had escalated from the technical domain to the political level. Data governance, which had previously been treated as an operational matter delegated to the exchange and the securities depository, was now being recognised as an issue with direct consequences for national economic credibility and political authority. Replacement officials were appointed with a clear mandate: address MSCI's concerns and implement structural reforms. Jeffrey Hendrik, appointed as acting IDX President Director, was immediately tasked with engaging directly with MSCI and articulating Indonesia's reform agenda. Friderica Widyasari Dewi was named acting OJK chairwoman with a mandate to prioritise market stability through regulatory reform. These appointments reflected a recognition that data governance capacity required dedicated leadership rather than diffuse administrative oversight.

Beyond the personnel changes, the response extended to substantive regulatory commitments. The Coordinating Minister for Economic Affairs convened a high-level meeting on 29 January, attended by the Central Bank Governor, the OJK Chairman, the State Secretary, and the Finance Minister, to coordinate the government (The Jakarta Post, 2026)'s response to the crisis. Among the reform measures announced were a commitment to increase the minimum free-float requirement from 7.5 percent to 15 percent (Jakarta Globe, 2026), the introduction of enhanced disclosure requirements for ultimate beneficial ownership, the acceleration of IDX's structural demutualization to reduce conflicts of interest between exchange management and market members, and increased allocation limits for pension and insurance funds in high-capitalisation equities. The OJK set a March 2026 deadline for the announcement of detailed regulatory reforms, with the May 2026 MSCI reassessment serving as the overarching pressure point. It represented a fundamental shift. The previous approach had relied on voluntary compliance incentives and incremental disclosure improvements. What replaced it was a mandated reform programme driven directly by external pressure from global index providers.

Figure 4. Institutional Cascade: From Data Governance Failure to Systemic Institutional Response

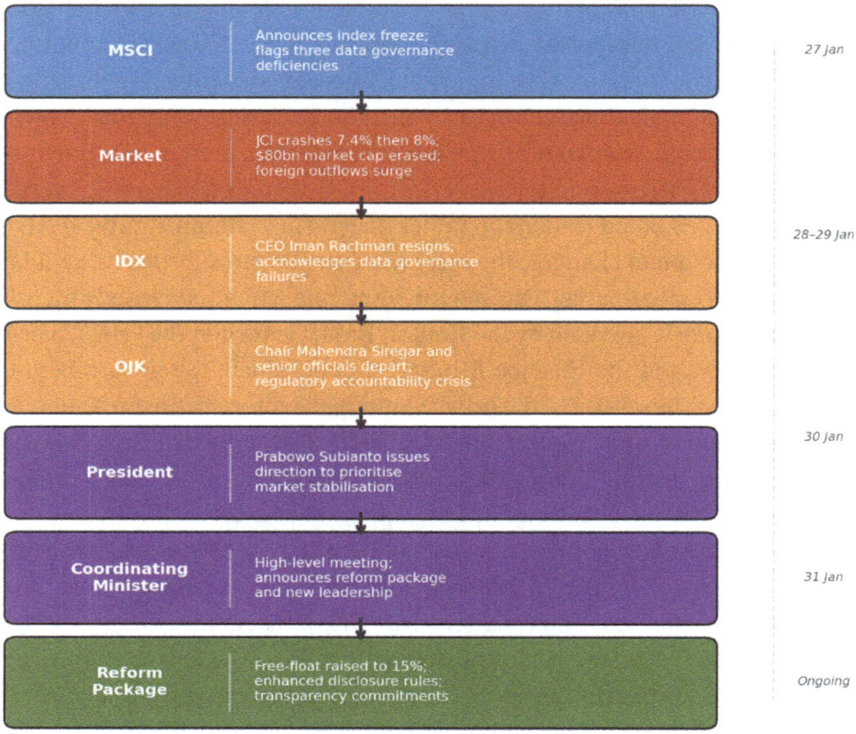

4.5. Data Governance as a Legitimacy Mechanism

When the findings are considered as a whole, a clear pattern emerges data governance functions as the mechanism through which a financial market's legitimacy is ultimately assessed and maintained within the global system. The MSCI-Indonesia event did not involve a failure of economic fundamentals in the conventional sense. Indonesia's equity market had reached an all-time high in January 2026 prior to the intervention. The crisis was not triggered by a recession, a sovereign debt problem, or a geopolitical shock. It was triggered by a judgment about the quality of the data environment, specifically, the reliability of ownership disclosures, the accuracy of free-float calculations, and the integrity of price formation mechanisms (see Figure 5 for the conceptual framework). A data governance signal from a private actor produced an eighty-billion-dollar market contraction, forced five senior financial officials to resign (The Jakarta Post, 2026), prompted the intervention of the President (Tempo.co, 2026), and catalysed a comprehensive regulatory overhaul. That alone demonstrates that data governance is not a background administrative function. It is the infrastructure through which markets are evaluated, and its failure carries consequences that are organisational, financial, and political in nature.

Figure 5. Conceptual Framework: Data Governance as a Legitimacy Mechanism in Global Financial Markets

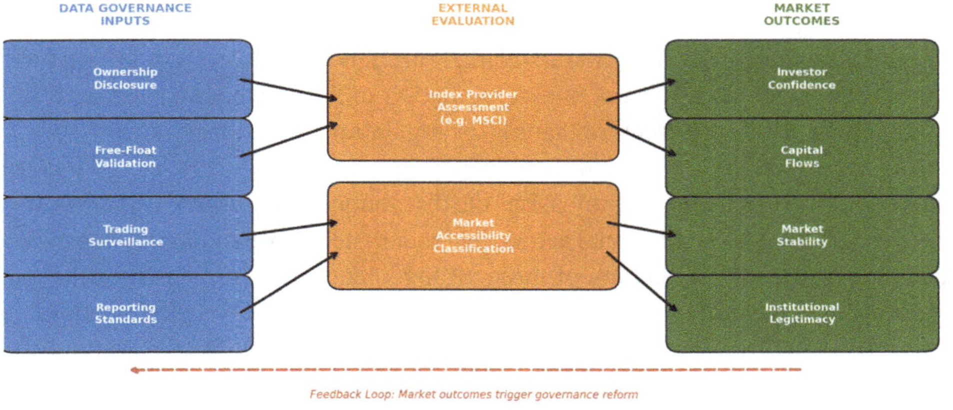

It also becomes clear from this incident how data governance deficiencies produce consequences that extend well beyond their technical scope. The initial governance failures were specific and identifiable: opaque ownership classification, unreliable free-float calculations, and insufficient trading surveillance. But the effects that followed, including mass capital withdrawal, leadership collapse, contagion across index providers, and the threat of international reclassification, were systemic in character. This amplification effect is a central finding of the study. Data governance failures do not produce proportionate responses. They produce cascading disruptions because they undermine the informational foundation on which all other market functions depend. When investors can no longer trust the data, they do not simply adjust their models. They withdraw, and the withdrawal itself generates further instability, further reputational damage, and further pressure on the structures that failed to maintain data integrity in the first place.

4.6. Theoretical Implications of Repositioning Data Governance in Financial Market Scholarship

What emerges from the analysis carries several implications for how data governance is understood within financial market scholarship. The existing literature, as reviewed in this chapter, has tended to treat data governance as a technical or administrative concern, distinct from the institutional and regulatory structures that shape market outcomes. The MSCI-Indonesia incident challenges this separation. What the case demonstrates is that data governance is not simply an input to regulatory compliance or investor confidence but the mechanism through which both are produced and sustained. When ownership disclosures are unreliable, compliance with transparency standards cannot be verified. When free-float data is inaccurate, the evaluative criteria on which global index providers depend become meaningless. When trading surveillance is inadequate, the integrity of price formation, which is the most fundamental expression of market efficiency, is called into question. In each instance, the failure is not one of regulation in the conventional sense. It is a failure of the data infrastructure that makes regulation operational.

There are broader implications here for governance theory as applied to financial markets. Governance theory emphasises the distribution of authority, responsibility, and oversight across institutional actors, and that system-level outcomes depend on the coherence and coordination of these arrangements. The findings bear this out while pushing the argument further (cf. Rhodes, 1997). What the MSCI-Indonesia case reveals is that governance coordination is not only a matter of aligning rules and enforcement across domestic institutions but also of aligning the outputs of domestic governance systems with the evaluative standards of international actors. Indonesia's regulatory framework was not, in a narrow legal sense, deficient. Rules for disclosure, reporting, and listing existed. The problem was that the data produced under these rules did not meet the quality and reliability standards that global index providers required for their own assessments. The gap was not between the presence and absence of regulation but between the outputs of domestic data governance and the expectations of international evaluative standards. The distinction between regulatory existence and governance effectiveness is one that governance theory has acknowledged in principle but that the financial market literature has not systematically explored.

The analysis also adds depth to how information asymmetry in financial markets is understood. The literature review established that weak data governance produces information asymmetry, which in turn undermines investor confidence (Akerlof, 1970; Healy & Palepu, 2001). What the Indonesian case shows is not only that this relationship holds, but how fast and how forcefully it operates in an environment of globally integrated capital markets and passive investment. The market did not gradually reprice Indonesian equities over a period of weeks or months. Within forty-eight hours of MSCI's announcement, eighty billion dollars in value had been destroyed. The rapidity is explained by the structural dependence of modern capital markets on index-mediated allocation. When an index provider signals that a market's data environment is unreliable, the signal does not merely inform. It compels action, because the mechanical rules governing passive funds and institutional mandates translate governance judgments into immediate capital flow consequences. What this points to is that information asymmetry in the context of data governance operates not as a gradual friction but as a threshold effect: once the credibility of data is questioned by a recognised evaluative authority, the market response is abrupt and disproportionate to the technical scope of the underlying deficiency.

4.7. Policy Implications for Emerging Markets

Beyond the theoretical dimension, there are direct policy implications for emerging economies seeking to integrate more fully into global capital markets. The Indonesian case illustrates a pattern that is not unique to Indonesia but is characteristic of the structural position that many emerging markets occupy within the global financial system (Petry et al., 2021; UNCTAD, 2024). These markets are increasingly subject to evaluation by international actors whose methodologies are data dependent (MSCI, 2025; Robertson, 2019), yet their domestic governance systems have often evolved to serve domestic purposes without systematic attention to whether their data outputs are compatible with international standards. The result is a vulnerability that remains latent until an external review event, such as an index review, a rating assessment, or an institutional investor consultation, exposes the gap between domestic governance capacity and international expectations.

What this means in practice is that emerging market regulators should treat data governance not as a subordinate function of market operations but as strategic infrastructure that requires dedicated institutional attention, sustained investment, and proactive alignment with the standards of global evaluative actors. Indonesia's pre-crisis approach, which relied on voluntary compliance incentives, incremental improvements to data feeds, and a minimum free-float threshold well below international norms, proved insufficient to withstand external scrutiny. The reactive nature of the subsequent reform programme, which was driven by the threat of reclassification rather than by proactive institutional planning, itself illustrates the cost of treating data governance as an afterthought. Markets that invest in data governance systems in advance of external pressure, rather than in response to it, are better positioned to sustain the confidence of international investors and to avoid the cascading institutional disruptions that reactive reform inevitably produces. Emerging research also suggests that AI-driven tools may enhance the inclusivity and responsiveness of policy development in such contexts (Asfand yar et al., 2026), pointing to opportunities for technology-enabled governance reform in financial markets.

There is also the matter of the growing power of private evaluative actors in shaping the governance priorities of sovereign financial systems. MSCI and FTSE Russell are not international organisations with formal regulatory mandates. They are private firms whose classification decisions carry consequences that rival or exceed those of formal regulatory interventions. This dynamic raises important questions about sovereignty, accountability, and the distribution of governance authority in global finance. While these questions fall outside the primary scope of this chapter, the findings make clear that any serious policy response to data governance challenges must account for the reality that compliance is no longer defined solely by domestic rules. It is defined, in practice, by the capacity of domestic data systems to satisfy the standards of private actors whose decisions control the flow of global capital.

5. CONCLUSION

The chapter set out to examine how the governance of financial market data functions as a driver of regulatory compliance and investor confidence in global capital markets. Using the 2026 MSCI–Indonesia incident as its empirical context, it argued that data governance is not a background administrative function but a foundational institutional system through which markets produce transparency, sustain investor trust, and secure their position within global financial benchmarks. What the analysis shows is that when data governance fails, the consequences go far beyond the technical deficiencies that triggered them.

The empirical case made this dynamic visible in concrete terms. When MSCI flagged concerns over ownership transparency, free-float data reliability, and potential coordinated trading behaviour in Indonesia's equity market, what followed was not a measured correction. Within forty-eight hours, approximately eighty billion dollars in market capitalisation was wiped out (SCMP, 2026). Trading was halted multiple times. Foreign investors pulled capital at an accelerating pace. Major international investment banks downgraded their recommendations on Indonesian equities. FTSE Russell followed with its own index review postponement, compounding the governance signal across the global benchmarking infrastructure. The leadership of both the Indonesia Stock Exchange and the Financial Services Authority resigned, and a comprehensive programme of regulatory reform was announced under direct presidential instruction. None of this was caused by an economic downturn or a geopolitical crisis. It was caused by a judgment, made by a private actor with no formal regulatory mandate, that the data environment governing Indonesia's equity market could not be trusted.

Three main contributions come out of this chapter. The first is a repositioning of data governance within financial market scholarship, from a technical or administrative concern to a central institutional determinant of market outcomes. The literature on financial regulation, investor confidence, and market stability has traditionally treated data as a background input rather than as a governed asset with its own institutional architecture and failure modes. What this chapter shows is that the governance of data is the mechanism through which regulatory compliance is made verifiable, investor confidence is sustained, and market legitimacy is produced. Without reliable data governance, the formal architecture of regulation and disclosure is an empty structure, incapable of generating the trust on which market participation depends.

The second contribution is an extension of governance theory to the specific domain of financial market data. The MSCI–Indonesia case showed that a market can have formal rules for disclosure, reporting, and listing and still fail the governance test imposed by global index providers. The critical gap was not between the presence and absence of regulation but between the quality of data produced under domestic governance arrangements and the reliability standards required by international evaluative infrastructure. Governance theory has long recognised the distinction between regulatory existence and governance effectiveness in conceptual terms, but this chapter demonstrates what that distinction looks like in practice within financial markets, and what it costs when the gap is left unaddressed.

The third contribution is practical. The Indonesian experience showed that reactive governance reform, undertaken under the threat of reclassification and at speed, is vastly more costly and institutionally disruptive than proactive investment in data governance infrastructure (cf. Rhodes, 1997). Emerging markets that treat data governance as strategic infrastructure, and that work to align their disclosure systems, validation mechanisms, and surveillance capacity with international standards before external scrutiny forces them to, are in a far better position to sustain investor confidence, avoid cascading institutional disruptions, and hold their standing within global financial benchmarks.

That said, the study is not without limitations. It relies on a single case, which limits how far its findings can be generalised, though the analytical depth afforded by the case study design allows for a more rigorous examination of institutional mechanisms than a comparative approach would have. The use of secondary data, while appropriate for studying institutional-level phenomena, does not capture the internal deliberations of key actors. And because the events examined occurred in 2026 and their longer-term consequences are still playing out, the analysis captures a defined period of institutional response rather than a fully resolved outcome. These limitations do not weaken the core argument, but they define the scope of what can be claimed and point towards where further work is needed.

On that point, several directions for future research emerge. Comparative work examining how different emerging markets have responded to similar data governance pressures from global index providers would test whether the mechanisms identified here hold across different contexts. Longitudinal studies tracking the outcomes of Indonesia's post-crisis governance reforms would show whether reactive reform programmes can achieve durable institutional change. Research into the accountability structures of index providers themselves, how their evaluative criteria are developed, how their classification decisions are contested, and whether their growing influence introduces new forms of systemic risk, would pick up questions that this chapter has raised but not fully explored. And the intersection of data governance with technological developments, including digital infrastructure, automated reporting systems, and real-time data validation, is an increasingly important frontier for both scholarship and policy (Anshari et al., 2026).

At its core, the lesson of what happened between MSCI and Indonesia is both specific and general. It is specific in that it exposes the vulnerabilities of a market whose data governance systems had not kept pace with the expectations of global benchmarking actors. It is general in that it demonstrates a structural principle applicable to any financial market operating within the contemporary global system: the credibility of a market is, in the final analysis, the credibility of its data. Markets that cannot govern their data reliably cannot sustain the trust of investors, cannot satisfy the standards of international benchmarking actors, and cannot secure the capital flows on which their growth and stability depend. Data governance is not the backdrop against which financial markets operate. It is the foundation on which they stand.

REFERENCES

Abraham, R., Schneider, J., & vom Brocke, J. (2019). Data governance: A conceptual framework, structured review, and research agenda. *International Journal of Information Management*, *49*, 424–438. DOI: 10.1016/j.ijinfomgt.2019.07.008

Ahmad, N., Anshari, M., Hamdan, M., & Ali, E. (2024). ETHICS AND PUBLIC TRUST IN AI GOVERNANCE: A. *International Journal of Law. Government & Communication*, *9*, 37. DOI: 10.35631/IJLGC.936003

Akerlof, G. A. (1970). The market for "lemons": Quality uncertainty and the market mechanism. *The Quarterly Journal of Economics*, *84*(3), 488–500. DOI: 10.2307/1879431

Al-Ruithe, M., Benkhelifa, E., & Hameed, K. (2019). A systematic literature review of data governance and cloud data governance. *Personal and Ubiquitous Computing*, *23*(5–6), 839–859. DOI: 10.1007/s00779-017-1104-3

Anshari, M., Almunawar, M. N., & Ordóñez de Pablos, P. (Eds.). (2025). *Multi-industry Digitalization and Technological Governance in the AI Era*. IGI Global. DOI: 10.4018/979-8-3373-1681-9

Anshari, M., & Hamdan, M. (2023). Enhancing e-government with a digital twin for innovation management. *Journal of Science and Technology Policy Management*, *14*(6), 1055–1065. DOI: 10.1108/JSTPM-11-2021-0176

Anshari, M., Hamdan, M., Ahmad, N., & Ali, E. (2025). Public service delivery, artificial intelligence and the sustainable development goals: Trends, evidence and complexities. *Journal of Science and Technology Policy Management*, *16*(1), 163–181. DOI: 10.1108/JSTPM-07-2023-0123

Anshari, M., Ordóñez de Pablos, P., & Almunawar, M. N. (Eds.). (2026). *Emerging AI, governance, and digital innovations for sustainable organizations*. IGI Global. DOI: 10.4018/979-8-3373-8607-2

Anshari, M., Syafrudin, M., Fitriyani, N. L., & Razzaq, A. (2022). Ethical responsibility and sustainability (ERS) development in a metaverse business model. *Sustainability (Basel)*, *14*(23), 15805. DOI: 10.3390/su142315805

ANTARA. (2026, January 31). Indonesia's OJK reshuffles leadership after board resignations. https://en.antaranews.com/news/402390/indonesias-ojk-reshuffles-leadership-after-board-resignations

Asfand yar, M., Hamdan, M., & Anshari, M. (2026). AI integration enhancing inclusivity and responsiveness in public policy development. In M. Anshari, P. Ordóñez de Pablos, & M. N. Almunawar (Eds.), Governance, and digital innovations for sustainable organizations (pp. 1–18). IGI Global. DOI: 10.4018/979-8-3373-8607-2.ch001

Bevir, M. (2013). A theory of governance. University of California Press. https://escholarship.org/uc/item/2qs2w3rb

Bloomberg. (2026, January 28). MSCI halts Indonesia index changes, flags transparency risks. https://www.bloomberg.com/news/articles/2026-01-28/msci-halts-indonesia-index-changes-flags-transparency-risks

Bursa Efek Indonesia, P. T. (2026). Indonesia stock exchange monthly statistical report: January 2026. https://www.idx.co.id

Bushman, R. M., Piotroski, J. D., & Smith, A. J. (2004). What determines corporate transparency? *Journal of Accounting Research*, *42*(2), 207–252. DOI: 10.1111/j.1475-679X.2004.00136.x

DAMA International. (2017). DAMA-DMBOK: Data management body of knowledge (2nd ed.). Technics Publications. https://www.dama.org/cpages/body-of-knowledge

Goldman Sachs. (2026, January 29). Indonesia equities: Downgrade to underweight. Goldman Sachs Global Investment Research.

Healy, P. M., & Palepu, K. G. (2001). Information asymmetry, corporate disclosure, and the capital markets: A review of the empirical disclosure literature. *Journal of Accounting and Economics*, *31*(1–3), 405–440. DOI: 10.1016/S0165-4101(01)00018-0

IDNFinancials. (2026, January 28). MSCI Indonesia stocks slump, JCI plunges 7.35%. https://www.idnfinancials.com/news/60831/msci-indonesia-stocks-slump-jci-plunges-7-35

Jakarta Globe. (2026, January 30). Indonesia to raise minimum free float requirement to 15% after MSCI review. https://jakartaglobe.id/business/indonesia-to-raise-minimum-free-float-requirement-to-15-after-msci-review

Kompas.id. (2026, January 28). Why did MSCI's policy cause the JCI to collapse? https://www.kompas.id/artikel/en-menilik-kebijakan-msci-yang-buat-ihsg-ambrol

Leuz, C., Lins, K. V., & Warnock, F. E. (2009). Do foreigners invest less in poorly governed firms? *Review of Financial Studies*, *22*(8), 3245–3285. DOI: 10.1093/rfs/hhn089

MSCI. (2025). MSCI global market accessibility review: June 2025. https://www.msci.com/indexes/index-resources/market-classification

MSCI. (2026a, January 27). Results of consultation on free float assessment of Indonesian securities. https://www.msci.com/indexes/index-resources/market-classification

MSCI. (2026b). MSCI market classification framework. https://www.msci.com/indexes/index-resources/market-classification

Petry, J., Fichtner, J., & Heemskerk, E. M. (2021). Steering capital: The growing private authority of index providers in the age of passive asset management. *Review of International Political Economy*, *28*(1), 152–176. DOI: 10.1080/09692290.2019.1699147

Rhodes, R. A. W. (1997). *Understanding governance: Policy networks, governance, reflexivity and accountability*. Open University Press.

Ridzuan, N. N., Masri, M., Anshari, M., Fitriyani, N. L., & Syafrudin, M. (2024). AI in the financial sector: The line between innovation, regulation and ethical responsibility. *Information (Basel)*, *15*(8), 432. DOI: 10.3390/info15080432

Robertson, A. (2019). Passive in name only: Delegated management and "index" investing. *Yale Journal on Regulation*, *36*(2), 795–851. https://openyls.law.yale.edu/handle/20.500.13051/7793

Russell, F. T. S. E. (2026). FTSE Russell postpones March 2026 index review for Indonesian securities. https://www.ftserussell.com

SCMP. (2026, January 29). Indonesia scrambles to halt US$80 billion market crash as rupiah hits record low. https://www.scmp.com/news/asia/southeast-asia/article/3341716/indonesia-scrambles-halt-us80-billion-market-crash-rupiah-hits-record-low

Shamdi, W., Lai, D., Aziz, A. A., & Anshari, M. (2022). Artificial intelligence development in Islamic System of Governance: A literature review. *Contemporary Islam*, *16*(2), 321–334. DOI: 10.1007/s11562-022-00504-7

Tempo.co. (2026, January 31). IHSG plunge explained: What happened, why it matters, and what followed. https://en.tempo.co/read/2084169/ihsg-plunge-explained-what-happened-why-it-matters-and-what-followed

The Jakarta Post. (2026, January 31). Heads roll at IDX, OJK, as govt vows to fix stock market. https://www.thejakartapost.com/business/2026/01/31/heads-roll-at-idx-ojk-as-govt-vows-to-fix-stock-market.html

United Nations Conference on Trade and Development. (2024). Credit rating agencies, developing countries and bias: Policy review (UNCTAD/GDS/2024/3). https://unctad.org/publication/credit-rating-agencies-developing-countries-and-bias

Yar, M. A., Hamdan, M., Anshari, M., Fitriyani, N. L., & Syafrudin, M. (2024). Governing with intelligence: The impact of artificial intelligence on policy development. *Information (Basel)*, *15*(9), 556. DOI: 10.3390/info15090556

Yin, R. K. (2018). *Case study research and applications: Design and methods* (6th ed.). Sage Publications., https://opac.atmaluhur.ac.id/uploaded_files/temporary/DigitalCollection/YTE3NDlmYTY0ZjE2MDA5ODE4NGI1Y2FhMjdkMjRmYWNkMDA2MTVhOQ==.pdf

Compilation of References

A. V. S. K., Rautrao, R. R., Suseelan, S. T., S., N. B., K. R. S., S. R., & Ganaie, N. A. (2026). Gamification Learning for Urban Educational Challenges: A Mixed-Methods Quasi-Experimental Study in PGDM Programs. In A. C. Ocaña & J. F. Molina (Eds.), *Transforming Teaching with AI and Digital Tools: Methods, Platforms, and Classroom Innovations* (pp. 265–298). IGI Global Scientific Publishing. DOI: 10.4018/979-8-2600-1568-1.ch013

Abdelilah, C., Ahriz, S., El Guemmat, K., & Mansouri, K. (2024). Implementation of suitable information technology governance frameworks for Moroccan higher education institutions. *International Journal of Electrical and Computer Engineering*, *14*(3), 3116. Advance online publication. DOI: 10.11591/ijece.v14i3.pp3116-3126

Abraham, R., Schneider, J., & vom Brocke, J. (2019). Data governance: A conceptual framework, structured review, and research agenda. *International Journal of Information Management*, *49*, 424–438. DOI: 10.1016/j.ijinfomgt.2019.07.008

Adams, P., Hunt, S., Palmer, C., & Zaliauskas, R. (2021). Testing the effectiveness of consumer financial disclosure: Experimental evidence from savings accounts. *Journal of Financial Economics*, *141*(1), 122–147. DOI: 10.1016/j.jfineco.2020.05.009

Afjal, M. (2023). Bridging the Financial Divide: A Bibliometric Analysis on The Role of Digital Financial Services Within Fintech in Enhancing Financial Inclusion and Economic Development. *Humanities and Social Sciences Communications 2023 10:1*, *10*(1), 645-. DOI: 10.1057/s41599-023-02086-y

Agarwal, S., & Tewari, R. (2025). *Role of emotions in investment decision-making: A systematic review*. Qualitative Research in Financial Markets., DOI: 10.1108/QRFM-01-2025-0001

Agarwal, S., & Zhang, J. (2020). FinTech, Lending and Payment Innovation: A Review. *Asia-Pacific Journal of Financial Studies*, *49*(3), 353–367. DOI: 10.1111/ajfs.12294

Agoraki, M.-E.-K., Delis, M. D., & Pasiouras, F. (2011). Regulations, competition and bank risk-taking in transition countries. *Journal of Financial Stability*, *7*(1), 38–48. DOI: 10.1016/j.jfs.2009.08.002

Ahmad, A. A. (2020). Realizing Maqasid al-Shariah in Shariah governance: A case study of Islamic banking institutions Malaysia. *International Journal of Islamic Economics and Finance Research*, *3*(2), 39–52. DOI: 10.53840/ijiefer36

Ahmad, N., Anshari, M., Hamdan, M., & Ali, E. (2024). ETHICS AND PUBLIC TRUST IN AI GOVERNANCE: A. *International Journal of Law. Government & Communication*, *9*, 37. DOI: 10.35631/IJLGC.936003

Ahnert, T., Hoffmann, P., & Monnet, C. (2025). Payments and Privacy in the Digital Economy. *Journal of Financial Economics*, *169*, 104050. DOI: 10.1016/j.jfineco.2025.104050

Aisy, F. R., Maskur, M. A., & Amiruddin, A. M. A. (2025). Establishing Indonesia's Personal Data Protection Agency: Comparative Administration Sanctions Enforcement from Ireland, Australia, and Singapore. *Journal of Indonesian Legal Studies*, *10*(1), 431–482. DOI: 10.15294/jils.v10i1.13755

Akdogan, O., Uyar, G. C., Yesilbas, E., Baskurt, K., Malkoc, N. A., Ozdemir, N., Yazici, O., Oksuzoglu, B., Uner, A., Ozet, A., & Sutcuoglu, O. (2025). Effect of a ChatGPT-based digital counseling intervention on anxiety and depression in patients with cancer: A prospective, randomized trial. *European Journal of Cancer : Official Journal for European Organization for Research and Treatment of Cancer (EORTC) [and] European Association for Cancer Research (EACR)*, *221*, 115408. Advance online publication. DOI: 10.1016/j.ejca.2025.115408 PMID: 40215593

Akerlof, G. A. (1970). The market for "lemons": Quality uncertainty and the market mechanism. *The Quarterly Journal of Economics*, *84*(3), 488–500. DOI: 10.2307/1879431

Akyildirim, E., Corbet, S., Mukherjee, A., & Ryan, M. (2025). Global Perspectives on Open Banking: Regulatory Impacts and Market Response. *Journal of International Financial Markets, Institutions and Money*, *101*(2), 102159. DOI: 10.1016/j.intfin.2025.102159

Al-Afeef, M. A. M., Ali, O. A. M., Al-Tahat, S., Malkawi, A. F., Kalbounhe, N. Y., & Al-Azzam, Z. F. (2023). The effect of big data governance on financial technology in Jordanian commercial banks: The mediation role of organisational culture. *International Journal of Data and Network Science*, *7*(3), 1283–1294. Advance online publication. DOI: 10.5267/j.ijdns.2023.4.010

Alam, M. R., Ahmad, A., Akhter, J., & Aziz, T. (2025). Mapping the field of behavioral finance: A systematic review and bibliometric analysis. Asian Education and Development Studies, 1–23. DOI: 10.1108/AEDS-07-2024-0162

Alanazi, A., & Altukhys, A. (2025). Mapping the impact: A systematic review of the psychological and social repercussions of technostress. *American Journal of Applied Scientific Research*, *11*(4), 203–210. DOI: 10.11648/j.ajasr.20251104.13

Albertazzi, U., & Gambacorta, L. (2009). Bank profitability and the business cycle. *Journal of Financial Stability*, *5*(4), 393–409. DOI: 10.1016/j.jfs.2008.10.002

Aldboush, H. H. H., & Ferdous, M. (2023). Building Trust in Fintech: An Analysis of Ethical and Privacy Considerations in the Intersection of Big Data, AI, and Customer Trust. *International Journal of Financial Studies 2023, Vol. 11, 11*(3). DOI: 10.3390/ijfs11030090

Alghamdi, A. A. (2025). University students' perceptions of generative AI for critical thinking and creativity: The influence of self-efficacy and disciplinary differences. *Innovations in Education and Teaching International*, •••, 1–15. DOI: 10.1080/14703297.2025.2600476

Alhammadi, S., Alotaibi, K. O., & Hakam, D. (2020). Analysing Islamic banking ethical performance from Maqasid al-Shariah perspective: Evidence from Indonesia. *Journal of Sustainable Finance & Investment*, *10*(4), 321–340. DOI: 10.1080/20430795.2019.1694869

Aliakhbar, I. H., Anshari, M., & Masri, M. (2026). Digital wallets as enablers of sustainable digital finance for ESG integration and global sustainability goals. *South Asian Journal of Business Studies*, 1-22.

Al-Jayyousi, O. R. (2016). *Islam and sustainable development: New worldviews*. Gower. DOI: 10.4324/9781315589947

Al-Jayyousi, O., Hasan, W. N. W., Mohamed Saniff, S., Sever, S. D., & Tok, E. (2023). A critical discourse analysis on climate change in a globalized world: The nexus of Islam and sustainable development. *Sustainability (Basel)*, *15*(19), 14515. DOI: 10.3390/su151914515

Al-Jayyousi, O., Tok, E., Saniff, S. M., Wan Hasan, W. N., Janahi, N. A., & Yesuf, A. J. (2022). Re-thinking sustainable development within Islamic worldviews: A systematic literature review. *Sustainability (Basel)*, *14*(12), 7300. DOI: 10.3390/su14127300

Allen, F., & Gale, D. (2000). Financial Contagion. *Journal of Political Economy*, *108*(1), 1–33. DOI: 10.1086/262109

Allen, F., & Gale, D. (2004). Competition and Financial Stability. *Journal of Money, Credit and Banking*, *36*(Jun), 453–480. DOI: 10.1353/mcb.2004.0038

Allen, L., Shan, Y., & Shen, Y. (2022). Do FinTech Mortgage Lenders Fill the Credit Gap? Evidence from Natural Disasters. *Journal of Financial and Quantitative Analysis*. Advance online publication. DOI: 10.1017/S002210902200120X

Al-Qatanani, K. M. (2025). The impact of implementing information technology governance based on the COBIT-2019 framework on institutional performance. *Edelweiss Applied Science and Technology*, *9*(3), 84–95. Advance online publication. DOI: 10.55214/25768484.v9i3.5117

Alqhatani, A. (2026). Exploring Privacy in Digital Mental Health: User and Psychotherapist Perspectives. In Applied Human Factors and Ergonomics International (Vol. 200, pp. 140–147). DOI: 10.54941/ahfe1007073

Al-Ruithe, M., Benkhelifa, E., & Hameed, K. (2019). A systematic literature review of data governance and cloud data governance. *Personal and Ubiquitous Computing*, *23*(5–6), 839–859. DOI: 10.1007/s00779-017-1104-3

Aminah, S., Hidayah, N., Hanurawan, F., Indreswari, H., & Rangka, I. B. (2023). Career adaptability to prevent unexpected careers and burnout for woman employees in the remote work era. *Journal of Public Health (Oxford, England)*, *45*(4), e795–e796. DOI: 10.1093/pubmed/fdad080 PMID: 37286530

Amiri, S. M. H. (2025). Privacy in Islam: What Muslims should know about data protection. Dhaka College Working Paper. Available at *SSRN*: https://ssrn.com/abstract=5276212

Ampudia, M., Beck, T., & Popov, A. (2021). *Out with the New, In with the Old?* Bank Supervision and the Composition of Firm Investment. [Unpublished manuscript]

Anderson, H. D., & Chang, Y. Y. (2019). Interdisciplinary finance. *Managerial Finance*, *45*(1), 85–87. DOI: 10.1108/MF-01-2019-537

Anginer, D., Demirguc-Kunt, A., & Zhu, M. (2014). How does competition affect bank systemic risk? *Journal of Financial Intermediation*, *23*(1), 1–26. DOI: 10.1016/j.jfi.2013.11.001

Anser, M. K., Nabi, A. A., Ahmad, I., Abro, M. M. Q., & Zaman, K. (2025). Advancing Mental Health Care: A Comprehensive Review of Digital Tools and Technologies for Enhancing Diagnosis, Treatment, and Wellness. *Health Care Science*, *4*(3), 163–178. DOI: 10.1002/hcs2.70018 PMID: 40568629

Anshari, M. (2026). Developing a digital ecosystem for economic diversification: A strategic framework for resilience in global uncertainties. International Journal of Policy and Governance Lab Vol. 1 No.3.

Anshari, M., Almunawar, M. N., Masri, M., & Hamdan, M. (2021). Financial technology with AI-enabled and ethical challenges. *Society*, *58*(3), 189–195. DOI: 10.1007/s12115-021-00592-w

Anshari, M., Almunawar, M. N., Masri, M., Ordoñez, D. E., & Pablos, P. (2026). Industry 4.0 and the sustainable business model for the digital marketplace. *International Journal of Innovation Science*, 1–28. DOI: 10.1108/IJIS-02-2025-0092

Anshari, M., Almunawar, M. N., & Ordóñez de Pablos, P. (Eds.). (2025). *Multi-industry Digitalization and Technological Governance in the AI Era*. IGI Global. DOI: 10.4018/979-8-3373-1681-9

Anshari, M., Almunawar, M. N., Shahrill, M., Wicaksono, D. K., & Huda, M. (2017). Smartphones usage in the classrooms: Learning aid or interference? *Education and Information Technologies*, *22*(6), 3063–3079. DOI: 10.1007/s10639-017-9572-7

Anshari, M., Almunawar, M. N., Younis, M. Z., & Kisa, A. (2021). Modeling users' empowerment in e-health systems. *Sustainability (Basel)*, *13*(23), 12993. DOI: 10.3390/su132312993

Anshari, M., & Hamdan, M. (2022). Enhancing e-government with a digital twin for innovation management. *Journal of Science and Technology Policy Management*, *13*(4), 940–959. DOI: 10.1108/JSTPM-11-2021-0176

Anshari, M., Hamdan, M., Ahmad, N., & Ali, E. (2025). Public service delivery, artificial intelligence and the sustainable development goals: Trends, evidence and complexities. *Journal of Science and Technology Policy Management*, *16*(1), 163–181. DOI: 10.1108/JSTPM-07-2023-0123

Anshari, M., Hamdan, M., Ahmad, N., Ali, E., & Haidi, H. (2023). COVID-19, artificial intelligence, ethical challenges and policy implications. *AI & Society*, *38*(2), 707–720. DOI: 10.1007/s00146-022-01471-6

Anshari, M., Ordóñez de Pablos, P., & Almunawar, M. N. (Eds.). (2026). *Emerging AI, governance, and digital innovations for sustainable organizations*. IGI Global. DOI: 10.4018/979-8-3373-8607-2

Anshari, M., Syafrudin, M., Fitriyani, N. L., & Razzaq, A. (2022). Ethical responsibility and sustainability (ERS) development in a metaverse business model. *Sustainability (Basel)*, *14*(23), 15805. DOI: 10.3390/su142315805

ANTARA. (2026, January 31). Indonesia's OJK reshuffles leadership after board resignations. https://en.antaranews.com/news/402390/indonesias-ojk-reshuffles-leadership-after-board-resignations

Aragani, V. M., & Thirunagalingam, A. (2025). Leveraging advanced analytics for sustainable success. In *Advanced analytics and sustainable business transformation* (pp. 229–248). IGI Global Scientific Publishing., DOI: 10.4018/979-8-3693-9750-3.ch012

Armansyah, R. F. (2022). Herd instinct bias, emotional biases, and information processing biases in investment decisions. Jurnal Manajemen dan Kewirausahaan, 24(2), 105–117.

Asfand yar, M., Hamdan, M., & Anshari, M. (2026). AI integration enhancing inclusivity and responsiveness in public policy development. In M. Anshari, P. Ordóñez de Pablos, & M. N. Almunawar (Eds.), Governance, and digital innovations for sustainable organizations (pp. 1–18). IGI Global. DOI: 10.4018/979-8-3373-8607-2.ch001

Ashforth, B. E., Kreiner, G. E., & Fugate, M. (2000). All in a day's work: Boundaries and micro role transitions. *Academy of Management Review*, *25*(3), 472–491. DOI: 10.2307/259305

Auda, J. (2008). *Maqasid al-Shariah as philosophy of Islamic law: A systems approach*. International Institute of Islamic Thought. DOI: 10.2307/j.ctvkc67tg

Auda, J. (2022). *Re-envisioning Islamic scholarship: Maqasid methodology as a new approach*. Claritas Books.

Avgouleas, E. (2009). The global financial crisis and the disclosure paradigm in European financial regulation: The case for reform. *European Company and Financial Law Review*, *6*(4). Advance online publication. DOI: 10.1515/ECFR.2009.440

Ayari, H., Guetari, P. R., & Kraïem, P. N. (2025). Machine Learning Powered Financial Credit Scoring: A Systematic Literature Review. *Artificial Intelligence Review 2025 59:1*, *59*(1), 13-. DOI: 10.1007/s10462-025-11416-2

Azahari, L. M., Ahmad, F. A., & Mohamed Saniff, S. (2026). *Connecting employability and the future of work: A systematic review of global trends, employer expectations, and evolving recruitment strategies*. IGI Global. DOI: 10.4018/979-8-3373-4450-8.ch005

Babina, T., Bahaj, S., Buchak, G., De Marco, F., Foulis, A., Gornall, W., Mazzola, F., & Yu, T. (2025). Customer Data Access and Fintech Entry: Early Evidence from Open Banking. *Journal of Financial Economics*, *169*(2), 103950. DOI: 10.1016/j.jfineco.2024.103950

Bai, X., Dong, Y., & Hu, N. (2018). Financial report readability and stock return synchronicity. *Applied Economics*, *51*(4), 346–363. DOI: 10.1080/00036846.2018.1495824

Baj-Rogowska, A. (2023). Antecedents and outcomes of social media fatigue. *Information Technology & People*, *36*(8), 226–254. DOI: 10.1108/ITP-03-2022-0207

Balaji, K. "Exploring the Drivers and Effects on Supply Chain Resilience and Performance in an Emerging Market Using Artificial Intelligence," *2023 3rd International Conference on Smart Generation Computing, Communication and Networking (SMART GENCON)*, Bangalore, India, 2023, pp. 1-6, DOI: 10.1109/SMARTGENCON60755.2023.10442071

Balaji, K., & Rao, P. S. "Artificial Intelligence and Chatbots: Transforming User Experience in E-tailing," *2024 9th International Conference on Communication and Electronics Systems (ICCES)*, Coimbatore, India, 2024, pp. 1375-1379, DOI: 10.1109/ICCES63552.2024.10859474

Balaji, K. (2025). AI as a Game Changer: How Digital Entrepreneurs Are Redefining Business Practices. In Tunio, M. (Ed.), *Improving Entrepreneurial Processes Through Advanced AI* (pp. 21–48). IGI Global Scientific Publishing , DOI: 10.4018/979-8-3693-1495-1.ch002

Balaji, K. (2025). Harnessing AI and Blockchain in Sustainability Assurance: Trends Shaping the Future of Verification. In Khatib, S., & Abbas, A. (Eds.), *Navigating Trust in Sustainability Reporting and Assurance* (pp. 215–242). IGI Global Scientific Publishing., DOI: 10.4018/979-8-3373-0117-4.ch007

Balaji, K. (2025). Human-Centric Innovation: Building Sustainable Organizations for Industry 5.0. In Erturk, A., Özşahin, M., & Simovic, V. (Eds.), *Human-Centric, Sustainable, and Resilient Organizations in the Digital Age* (pp. 101–124). IGI Global Scientific Publishing., DOI: 10.4018/979-8-3693-8181-6.ch005

Balaji, K. (2025). IoT in Financial Services Innovations in Banking and Insurance. In Ho, R., Song, B., & Tee, P. (Eds.), *Managing Customer-Centric Strategies in the Digital Landscape* (pp. 75–104). IGI Global Scientific Publishing., DOI: 10.4018/979-8-3693-5668-5.ch004

Balaji, K. (2025). Neuromarketing and Sustainable Finance: Real-World Case Studies of Green Investment Promotions. In Taneja, S., Chahal, B., Johri, A., Ozen, E., & Kumar, P. (Eds.), *Neuromarketing's Role in Sustainable Finance* (pp. 169–204). IGI Global Scientific Publishing., DOI: 10.4018/979-8-3693-9117-4.ch010

Balaji, K. (2025). Revolutionizing High-Frequency Trading: The Impacts of Financial Technology and Data Science Innovations. In Chen, H. (Ed.), *Machine Learning and Modeling Techniques in Financial Data Science* (pp. 103–124). IGI Global Scientific Publishing., DOI: 10.4018/979-8-3693-8186-1.ch004

Balkin, J. M. (2016). Information fiduciaries and the first amendment. *U.C. Davis Law Review*, *49*(4), 1183–1234.

Balyuk, T., Berger, A. N., & Hackney, J. (2020). *What is Fueling FinTech Lending? The Role of Banking Market Structure*. DOI: 10.2139/ssrn.3633907

Banerjee, S., & Gupta, R. (2024). Managing technostress in the digital era. *Journal of Organizational Behavior*, *45*(3), 412–430.

Bangun, C. S., Hetilaniar, H., Faturahman, A., Jackson, S., Anjani, S. A., & Natasya, E. A. (2025). Analyzing Opportunities and Challenges of Artificial Intelligence Integration in Indonesian Innovation and Education. Proceeding – 2025 4th International Conference on Creative Communication and Innovative Technology, ICCIT 2025. DOI: 10.1109/ICCIT65724.2025.11167011

Banna, H., Hassan, M. K., & Rashid, M. (2021). Fintech-based financial inclusion and bank risk-taking: Evidence from OIC countries. *Journal of International Financial Markets, Institutions and Money*, *75*, 101447. Advance online publication. DOI: 10.1016/j.intfin.2021.101447

Bao, Z., & Huang, D. (2021). Shadow Banking in a Crisis: Evidence from FinTech during COVID-19. *Journal of Financial and Quantitative Analysis*, *56*(7), 2320–2355. Advance online publication. DOI: 10.1017/S0022109021000430

Barber, B. M., & Odean, T. (2000). Trading is hazardous to your wealth: The common stock investment performance of individual investors. *The Journal of Finance*, *55*(2), 773–806. DOI: 10.1111/0022-1082.00226

Bashori, Y. A., Umami, K., & Wahid, S. H. (2024). Maqasid Shariah-based digital economy model: Integration, sustainability and transformation. *Malaysian Journal of Syariah and Law*, *12*(2), 405–425. DOI: 10.33102/mjsl.vol12no2.647

Bećirović, S., Polz, E., & Tinkel, I. (2025). Exploring students' AI literacy and its effects on their AI output quality, self-efficacy, and academic performance. *Smart Learning Environments*, *12*(1), 29. DOI: 10.1186/s40561-025-00384-3

Beck, T., Cecchetti, S., Grothe, M., Kemp, M., Pelizzon, L., & Sánchez-Serrano, A. (2022). Will video kill the radio star? *Digitalisation and the future of banking* (No. 12; pp. 1–64). ESRB.

Becker, J., Derra, N. D., Regal, C., & Kühlmann, T. M. (2021). Mitigating the negative consequences of ICT use: The moderating effect of active-functional and dysfunctional coping. *Journal of Decision Systems*, *31*(4), 374–406. DOI: 10.1080/12460125.2021.1901337

Becker, W. J., Belkin, L. Y., Conroy, S. A., & Tuskey, S. (2019). Killing me softly: Organizational e-mail monitoring expectations' impact on employee and significant other well-being. *Journal of Management*, *47*(4), 848–884. DOI: 10.1177/0149206319890655

Beck, T., De Jonghe, O., & Schepens, G. (2013). Bank competition and stability: Cross-country heterogeneity. *Journal of Financial Intermediation*, *22*(2), 218–244. DOI: 10.1016/j.jfi.2012.07.001

Bellan, R. (2026, March 26). The AI skills gap is here, says AI company, and power users are pulling ahead. *TechCrunch*. https://techcrunch.com/2026/03/25/the-ai-skills-gap-is-here-says-ai-company-and-power-users-are-pulling-ahead/

Bellardini, L., Del Gaudio, B. L., Previtali, D., & Verdoliva, V. (2022). How do banks invest in fintechs? Evidence from advanced economies. *Journal of International Financial Markets, Institutions and Money*, *77*, 101498. Advance online publication. DOI: 10.1016/j.intfin.2021.101498

Belli, L., Gaspar, W. B., & Singh Jaswant, S. (2024). Data Sovereignty and Data Transfers as Fundamental Elements of Digital Transformation: Lessons from the BRICS Countries. *Computer Law & Security Review*, *54*, 106017. DOI: 10.1016/j.clsr.2024.106017

Berg, T., Fuster, A., & Puri, M. (2022). FinTech Lending. *Annual Review of Financial Economics*, *14*(1), 187–207. DOI: 10.1146/annurev-financial-101521-112042

Bertsch, C., Hull, I., Qi, Y., & Zhang, X. (2020). Bank misconduct and online lending. *Journal of Banking & Finance*, *116*, 105822. Advance online publication. DOI: 10.1016/j.jbankfin.2020.105822

Bevir, M. (2013). A theory of governance. University of California Press. https://escholarship.org/uc/item/2qs2w3rb

Bicudo, E., Morrison, M., Li, P., Faulkner, A., Webster, A., Mourby, M., & Kaye, J. (2022). Patent power in biomedical innovation: Technology governance in biomodifying technologies. *The Journal of World Intellectual Property*, *25*(2), 473–494. Advance online publication. DOI: 10.1111/jwip.12237

Biddle, G. C., Hilary, G., & Verdi, R. S. (2009). How does financial reporting quality relate to investment efficiency? *Journal of Accounting and Economics*, *48*(2–3), 112–131. DOI: 10.1016/j.jacceco.2009.09.001

Bloomberg. (2026, January 28). MSCI halts Indonesia index changes, flags transparency risks. https://www.bloomberg.com/news/articles/2026-01-28/msci-halts-indonesia-index-changes-flags-transparency-risks

Bokolo, A. J. (2025). Implementing digital sovereignty to accelerate smarter mobility solutions in local communities. *Smart Cities*, *8*(4), 1–24. DOI: 10.3390/smartcities8040106

Bondanini, G., Giorgi, G., Ariza-Montes, A., Vega-Muñoz, A., & Andreucci-Annunziata, P. (2023). Technostress at work during the COVID-19 lockdown phase (2020–2021): A systematic review. *Frontiers in Psychology*, *14*, 1173425. Advance online publication. DOI: 10.3389/fpsyg.2023.1173425 PMID: 37179875

Boot, A., Hoffmann, P., Laeven, L., & Ratnovski, L. (2021). Fintech: What's old, what's new? *Journal of Financial Stability*, *53*, 100836. Advance online publication. DOI: 10.1016/j.jfs.2020.100836

Bouguettaya, A., Stuart, E. M., & Aboujaoude, E. (2025). Racial bias in AI-mediated psychiatric diagnosis and treatment: A qualitative comparison of four large language models. npj. *Digital Medicine*, *8*(1), 332. Advance online publication. DOI: 10.1038/s41746-025-01746-4 PMID: 40467886

Brod, C. (1984). *Technostress: The human cost of the computer revolution*. Addison-Wesley.

Bursa Efek Indonesia, P. T. (2026). Indonesia stock exchange monthly statistical report: January 2026. https://www.idx.co.id

Bushman, R. M., Piotroski, J. D., & Smith, A. J. (2004). What determines corporate transparency? *Journal of Accounting Research*, *42*(2), 207–252. DOI: 10.1111/j.1475-679X.2004.00136.x

Bussy, A., & Zheng, H. (2023). Responses of FDI to geopolitical risks: The role of governance, information, and technology. *International Business Review*, *32*(4), 102136. Advance online publication. DOI: 10.1016/j.ibusrev.2023.102136

Califf, C. B., Sarker, S., & Sarker, S. (2020). The bright and dark sides of technostress: A mixed-methods study involving healthcare IT. *Management Information Systems Quarterly*, *44*(2), 809–856. DOI: 10.25300/MISQ/2020/14818

Casolaro, A. M. B., Rauber, G. N., & de Lima, U. S. M. (2024). Open Banking: A Systematic Literature Review. *Journal of Banking Regulation 2024 26:3, 26*(3), 340–355. DOI: 10.1057/s41261-024-00262-x

Cavoukian, A. (2012). *Privacy by design: The 7 foundational principles*. Information and Privacy Commissioner of Ontario.

Chan, C. K. Y. (2025). AI as the Therapist: Student Insights on the Challenges of Using Generative AI for School Mental Health Frameworks. *Behavioral Sciences (Basel, Switzerland)*, *15*(3), 287. Advance online publication. DOI: 10.3390/bs15030287 PMID: 40150182

Chen, S., Doerr, S., Frost, J., Gambacorta, L., & Shin, H. S. (2023). The Fintech Gender Gap. *Journal of Financial Intermediation*, *54*, 101026. DOI: 10.1016/j.jfi.2023.101026

Chen, T., Huang, Y., Lin, C., & Sheng, Z. (2022). Finance and Firm Volatility: Evidence from Small Business Lending in China. *Management Science*, *68*(3), 2226–2249. DOI: 10.1287/mnsc.2020.3942

Cho, J., Ramgolam, D. I., Schaefer, K. M., & Sandlin, A. N. (2020). The rate and delay in overload: An investigation of communication overload and channel synchronicity on identification and job satisfaction. *Journal of Applied Communication Research*, *39*(2), 113–131.

Choung, Y., Chatterjee, S., & Pak, T. Y. (2023). Digital Financial Literacy and Financial Well-Being. *Finance Research Letters*, *58*, 104438. DOI: 10.1016/j.frl.2023.104438

Colledani, D., Capozza, D., & Falvo, R. (2025). Measuring technostress in everyday life: Development and validation of an assessment scale. Human Behavior and Emerging Technologies. *Human Behavior and Emerging Technologies*, *5793644*(1), 5793644. Advance online publication. DOI: 10.1155/hbe2/5793644

Couldry, N., & Mejias, U. A. (2019). *The costs of connection: How data is colonizing human life and appropriating it for capitalism*. Stanford University Press.

Couldry, N., & Mejias, U. A. (2023). The decolonial turn in data and technology research: What is at stake and where is it heading? *Information Communication and Society*, *26*(4), 786–802. DOI: 10.1080/1369118X.2021.1986102

Cruz-García, P., Fernández de Guevara, J., & Maudos, J. (2021). Bank competition and multimarket contact intensity. *Journal of International Money and Finance, 113*, 102338. Advance online publication. DOI: 10.1016/j.jimonfin.2020.102338

Cubillas, E., Ferrer, E., & Suárez, N. (2021). Does investor sentiment affect bank stability? International evidence from lending behavior. *Journal of International Money and Finance, 113*, 102351. Advance online publication. DOI: 10.1016/j.jimonfin.2020.102351

Cubillas, E., & González, F. (2014). Financial liberalization and bank risk-taking: International evidence. *Journal of Financial Stability, 11*(1), 32–48. DOI: 10.1016/j.jfs.2013.11.001

Dagli, N., Haque, M., & Kumar, S. (2025). Bibliometric analysis in scientific research: Applications, limitations, and key considerations for authors. *Bangladesh Journal of Medical Science, 24*(1), 7–10. DOI: 10.3329/bjms.v24i1.78602

DAMA International. (2017). DAMA-DMBOK: Data management body of knowledge (2nd ed.). Technics Publications. https://www.dama.org/cpages/body-of-knowledge

Dang, C. (2025). Public Opinion and Its Influence on Technology Governance in the Age of Digital Transformation. *International Journal of Computational and Experimental Science and Engineering, 11*(2). Advance online publication. DOI: 10.22399/ijcesen.1406

Dau, N. H., Nguyen, D. V., & Thi, H. (2024). Annual report readability and firms' investment decisions. *Cogent Economics & Finance, 12*(1), 2296230. Advance online publication. DOI: 10.1080/23322039.2023.2296230

Degryse, H., & Ongena, S. (2007). The impact of competition on bank orientation. *Journal of Financial Intermediation, 16*(3), 399–424. DOI: 10.1016/j.jfi.2007.03.002

Delis, M. D. (2012). Bank competition, financial reform, and institutions: The importance of being developed. *Journal of Development Economics, 97*(2), 450–465. DOI: 10.1016/j.jdeveco.2011.05.012

Dinçkol, D., Ozcan, P., & Zachariadis, M. (2023). Regulatory standards and consequences for industry architecture: The case of UK Open Banking. *Research Policy, 52*(6), 104760. DOI: 10.1016/j.respol.2023.104760

Dogruel, L., Masur, P., & Joeckel, S. (2022). Development and Validation of an Algorithm Literacy Scale for Internet Users. *Communication Methods and Measures, 16*(2), 115–133. DOI: 10.1080/19312458.2021.1968361

Donthu, N., Kumar, S., Mukherjee, D., Pandey, N., & Lim, W. M. (2021). How to conduct a bibliometric analysis: An overview and guidelines. *Journal of Business Research, 133*, 285–296. DOI: 10.1016/j.jbusres.2021.04.070

Egbert, S., & Ulbricht, L. (2024). Data Integration and Analysis Platforms as Digital Platforms: A Conceptual Proposal. *Information Communication and Society*, 1–22. Advance online publication. DOI: 10.1080/1369118X.2024.2442394

Eppler, M. J., & Mengis, J. (2004). The concept of information overload: A review of literature from organization science, accounting, marketing, MIS, and related disciplines. *The Information Society*, *20*(5), 325–344. DOI: 10.1080/01972240490507974

Estrada-Muñoz, C., Castillo, D., Vega-Muñoz, A., & Boada-Grau, J. (2022). Teacher technostress in the Chilean school system. *International Journal of Environmental Research and Public Health*, *17*(15), 5280. DOI: 10.3390/ijerph17155280 PMID: 32707973

Farahani, M. S., Mahmoudi, G., & Ghasemi, G. (2025). Credit Rating in the Age of Artificial Intelligence. *FinTech and Sustainable Innovation*, *1*, A9–A9. DOI: 10.47852/bonviewFSI52025716

Farzan, M., Ebrahimi, H., Pourali, M., & Sabeti, F. (2025). Artificial Intelligence-Powered Cognitive Behavioral Therapy Chatbots, a Systematic Review. *Iranian Journal of Psychiatry*, *20*(1), 100–108. DOI: 10.18502/ijps.v20i1.17395 PMID: 40093525

Fei, T., & Liu, X. (2021). Herding and market volatility. *International Review of Financial Analysis*, *78*, 101880. DOI: 10.1016/j.irfa.2021.101880

Finet, A., Kristoforidis, K., & Laznicka, J. (2025). Negative emotions and decision-making paralysis among individual investors: A qualitative approach. *Risks*, *13*(11), 209. DOI: 10.3390/risks13110209

Firmansyah, E. A., Masri, M., Anshari, M., & Besar, M. H. A. (2024). Factors influencing SME project returns on Islamic Fintech lending platform. *Journal of Islamic Accounting and Business Research*. Advance online publication. DOI: 10.1108/JIABR-10-2023-0340

Flix-Valle, A., Medina, J. C., Souto-Sampera, A., Arizu-Onassis, A., Juan-Linares, E., Serra-Blasco, M., Ciria-Suárez, L., Feixas, G., & Ochoa-Arnedo, C. (2025). Therapeutic alliance in a stepped digital psychosocial intervention for breast cancer patients: Findings from a multicentre randomised controlled trial. *BJPsych Open*, *11*(1), e23. Advance online publication. DOI: 10.1192/bjo.2024.844 PMID: 39865983

Floridi, L. (2018). Soft ethics, the governance of the digital and the General Data Protection Regulation. *Philosophical Transactions. Series A, Mathematical, Physical, and Engineering Sciences, 376*(2133), 20180081. Advance online publication. DOI: 10.1098/rsta.2018.0081 PMID: 30322997

Galindo-Manrique, A. F., & Rojas-Vargas, N. P. (2025). The Role of Digital Financial Services in Narrowing the Gender Gap in Low–Middle-Income Economies: A Bayesian Machine Learning Approach. *Risks 2025, Vol. 13, 13*(5). DOI: 10.3390/risks13050096

Ganaie, N. A. A. V., S. K., Mir, T. A., Jan, I., S., N. B., & K. R. S., S. R. (2026). Smart Learning and Smart Schools: Transforming Indian Education Through AI-Enabled NEP 2020 Implementations. In *Human-AI Leadership for Transforming Schools* (pp. 223–258). DOI: 10.4018/979-8-2600-0388-6.ch009

Ganaie, N. A. (2015). Sikh socio-religious reform movements in Jammu and Kashmir from 1900 to 1947. *Journal of Interdisciplinary and Multidisciplinary Research, 2*(8).

Ganaie, N. A. (2026). The role of artificial intelligence in radicalisation, recruitment and terrorist propaganda: Deconstructing violent extremism and reimagining counterterrorism in contemporary digital ecosystems. *Frontiers in Political Science, 7*, 1718396. DOI: 10.3389/fpos.2025.1718396

Ganaie, N. A., Mir, T. A., Jaysingh, M., & Rath, D. M. (2026). Algorithmic governance and surveillance federalism: Transforming the digital state in India and ASEAN. *Frontiers in Political Science, 8*, 1757636. DOI: 10.3389/fpos.2026.1757636

Ganaie, N. A., Saikia, T., Mir, T. A., & Jan, I. (2025). *Dynamics of Public Policy and Good Governance in India: The Road to Viksit Bharat* (First). Authors Click Publishing. DOI: 10.5281/ZENODO.15870017

Ganaie, N. A., Takri, K. K., Raviteja, Y., Sahu, D., Rout, B., & Islam, B. (2026). Digital governance and poverty alleviation mechanisms: Lessons from the public distribution system in Kashmir and Kerala. *ShodhKosh: Journal of Visual and Performing Arts, 7*(7s), 25–39. DOI: 10.29121/shodhkosh.v7.i7s.2026.7009

Gandre, P. (2020). US stock prices and recency-biased learning in the run-up to the Global Financial Crisis and its aftermath. *Journal of International Money and Finance, 104*, 102165. DOI: 10.1016/j.jimonfin.2020.102165

Ganesh, M. S., & Venkateswaramurthy, N. (2025). Artificial Intelligence (AI) Generated Health Counseling For Mental Illness Patients. *Current Psychiatry Research and Reviews, 21*(3), 269–283. DOI: 10.2174/0126660822277500240109050359

Girardi, P., & Temporelli, A. (2017). Smartainability: A Methodology for Assessing the Sustainability of the Smart City. *Energy Procedia, 111*, 810–816. DOI: 10.1016/j.egypro.2017.03.243

Goldman Sachs. (2026, January 29). Indonesia equities: Downgrade to underweight. Goldman Sachs Global Investment Research.

Gong, X., Liu, W., & Shang, Z. (2025). Ethical challenges in artificial intelligence-based mental health interventions. *Academic Journal of Naval Medical University*, *46*(8), 970–976. DOI: 10.16781/j.CN31-2187/R.20250449

Graef, I., & Bostoen, F. (2026). A Typology of Platform Power and Its Regulation. *Information Communication and Society*, *29*(1), 324–338. Advance online publication. DOI: 10.1080/1369118X.2025.2512972

Graham, B., & Dodd, D. (2009). *Security analysis* (6th ed.). McGraw-Hill.

Gray, C. (2023). More than Extraction: Rethinking Data's Colonial Political Economy. *International Political Sociology*, *17*(2), olad007. Advance online publication. DOI: 10.1093/ips/olad007

Greenwald, B. C., Kahn, J., Bellissimo, E., Cooper, M. A., & Santos, T. (2020). *Value investing: From Graham to Buffett and beyond* (2nd ed.). Wiley.

Guenduez, A. A., Mergel, I., Schedler, K., Fuchs, S., & Douillet, C. (2024). Institutional work in smart cities: Interviews with smart city managers. *Urban Governance*, *4*(1), 80–90. Advance online publication. DOI: 10.1016/j.ugj.2024.01.003

Habib Saragih, A., Ali, S., Suwardi, E., & Utomo, H. (2024). Finding the missing pieces to an optimal corporate tax savings: Information technology governance and internal information quality. *International Journal of Accounting Information Systems*, *52*, 100665. Advance online publication. DOI: 10.1016/j.accinf.2023.100665

Ha, D., Le, P., & Nguyen, D. K. (2025). Financial Inclusion and Fintech: A State-of-the-Art Systematic Literature Review. *Financial Innovation*, *11*(1), 1–42. DOI: 10.1186/s40854-024-00741-0

Haidi, H., Anshari, M., Hamdan, M., & Sufian, F. A. (2023). Preserving and Promoting Faith Through a Digital Society: An Islamic Governance Perspective. *Proceedings of the International Conference on Islamic Social Sciences and Humanities*.

Hamdan, M., Anshari, M., Ahmad, N., & Ali, E. (Eds.). (2023). *Public policy's role in achieving sustainable development goals*. IGI Global. DOI: 10.4018/978-1-6684-8903-1

Hanisch, M., Goldsby, C. M., Fabian, N. E., & Oehmichen, J. (2023). Digital Governance: A Conceptual Framework and Research Agenda. *Journal of Business Research, 162*(1), 113777. DOI: 10.1016/j.jbusres.2023.113777

Hariyadi, S., Antika, E. R., & Prabawa, A. F. (2025). Digital evolutions: Analysis of self-talk transformation among Generation Z and its impact on counseling services. *Multidisciplinary Science Journal, 8*(4), 2026225. Advance online publication. DOI: 10.31893/multiscience.2026225

Healy, P. M., & Palepu, K. G. (2001). Information asymmetry, corporate disclosure, and the capital markets: A review of the empirical disclosure literature. *Journal of Accounting and Economics, 31*(1–3), 405–440. DOI: 10.1016/S0165-4101(01)00018-0

He, Z., Huang, J., & Zhou, J. (2023). Open Banking: Credit Market Competition When Borrowers Own the Data. *Journal of Financial Economics, 147*(2), 449–474. DOI: 10.1016/j.jfineco.2022.12.003

Hidayat, H., Hidayah, N., Rusmana, N., Hariko, R., & Tririzky, R. (2024). The Effect of Using Smart Application on Critical Literacy of Engineering Education Students. *International Journal of Information and Education Technology (IJIET), 14*(6), 834–844. DOI: 10.18178/ijiet.2024.14.6.2109

Hulus, A. (2026). A systematic response to ethical blind spots in AI education: Cross-cultural insights and the role of digital literacy. *Smart Learning Environments, 13*(1), 11. Advance online publication. DOI: 10.1186/s40561-026-00437-1

Hussain, S. M., Alaya, A., & Azizi, T. A. (2023). The impact of financial accounting disclosures on investors' reactions towards bad news: The moderating role of investors' sentiments. *Cogent Economics & Finance, 11*(2), 2228087. Advance online publication. DOI: 10.1080/23322039.2023.2228087

Ibrushi, D., Palacios Diaz, M., & Wang, S. (2026). Financial Literacy and Fraud Vulnerability in Digital Finance: Evidence from the 2024 NFCS. *Finance Research Letters, 94*, 109674. DOI: 10.1016/j.frl.2026.109674

IDNFinancials. (2026, January 28). MSCI Indonesia stocks slump, JCI plunges 7.35%. https://www.idnfinancials.com/news/60831/msci-indonesia-stocks-slump-jci-plunges-7-35

Inghelbrecht, K., & Tedde, M. (2024). Overconfidence, financial literacy and excessive trading. *Journal of Economic Behavior & Organization, 219*, 152–195. DOI: 10.1016/j.jebo.2024.01.010

Isaia, E., Oggero, N., & Sandretto, D. (2024). Is Financial Literacy a Protection Tool from Online Fraud in the Digital Era? *Journal of Behavioral and Experimental Finance*, *44*, 100977. DOI: 10.1016/j.jbef.2024.100977

Islam, B., & Guha, P. (2020). Impact of occupational migration of unskilled labourers from domestic agriculture on farm business income in source households of Assam, India. *International Journal of Social Economics*, *47*(12), 1561–1576. DOI: 10.1108/IJSE-05-2020-0296

Islam, K. U., Bhat, S. A., Lone, U. M., Darzi, M. A., & Malik, I. A. (2024). Financial risk propensity and investment decisions: An empirical analysis using behavioural biases. *IIMB Management Review*, *36*(3), 213–229. Advance online publication. DOI: 10.1016/j.iimb.2024.06.004

Jain, L. R., & Menon, V. (2023). AI Algorithmic Bias: Understanding its Causes, Ethical and Social Implications. Proceedings – International Conference on Tools with Artificial Intelligence, ICTAI, 460–467. DOI: 10.1109/ICTAI59109.2023.00073

Jakarta Globe. (2026, January 30). Indonesia to raise minimum free float requirement to 15% after MSCI review. https://jakartaglobe.id/business/indonesia-to-raise-minimum-free-float-requirement-to-15-after-msci-review

Javed, M. H., Ahmad, A., Rehan, M., Musharavati, F., Nizami, A. S., & Khan, M. I. (2025). Advancing sustainable energy: Environmental and economic assessment of plastic waste gasification for syngas and electricity generation using life cycle modeling. *Sustainability (Basel)*, *17*(3), 1277. Advance online publication. DOI: 10.3390/su17031277

Jobin, A., Ienca, M., & Vayena, E. (2019). AI ethics guidelines globally. *Nature Machine Intelligence*, *1*(9), 389–399. DOI: 10.1038/s42256-019-0088-2

Johnston, M. P. (2017). Secondary data analysis: A method of which the time has come. *Qualitative and Quantitative Methods in Libraries*, *3*(3), 619–626.

Kahneman, D., & Tversky, A. (1979). Prospect theory: An analysis of decision under risk. *Econometrica*, *47*(2), 263–292. DOI: 10.2307/1914185

Kamali, M. H. (1999). Maqasid al-Shariah: The objectives of Islamic law. *Islamic Studies*, *38*(2), 193–208. DOI: 10.52541/isiri.v38i2.6127

Khalid, M., Khan, R. A., Khushnood, M., Aslam, S., Khattak, Z. Z., & Abbas, S. (2022). An Empirical Analysis of the Influence of Project Governance and Information Technology Governance on Project Delay. *Global Business Review*, 09721509221121179. Advance online publication. DOI: 10.1177/09721509221121179

Khan, H. H., Khan, S., Akhtar, T., Anwar, A., & Ahmad, M. R. (2026). Fintech Environment and Gender Disparity in Financial Inclusion: Empirical Evidence from Emerging Markets. *Borsa Istanbul Review*, *26*(2), 100787. DOI: 10.1016/j.bir.2026.100787

Khan, N., Sudhakar, K., & Mamat, R. (2025). Biodegradable plastics from marine biomass: A solution to marine plastic pollution. *Journal of Hazardous Materials Advances*, *17*, 100559. DOI: 10.1016/j.hazadv.2024.100559

Khedhaouria, A., Montani, F., & Lam, W. (2024). Technology-driven work pressure and technostress: Examining the role of automation in employee well-being. *Computers in Human Behavior*, *150*, 107998.

Kishor, K., Bansal, S. K., & Kumar, R. (2024). The Role of Fintech in Promoting Financial Inclusion to Achieve Sustainable Development: An Integrated Bibliometric Analysis and Systematic Literature Review. *Journal of the Knowledge Economy 2024 16:1*, *16*(1), 5664–5692. DOI: 10.1007/s13132-024-02168-5

Kompas.id. (2026, January 28). Why did MSCI's policy cause the JCI to collapse? https://www.kompas.id/artikel/en-menilik-kebijakan-msci-yang-buat-ihsg-ambrol

Kowalczyk, M., & Napiecek, R. (2023). E-governance and blockchain technology in local government. *Zeszyty Teoretyczne Rachunkowosci*, *47*(3), 221–238. Advance online publication. DOI: 10.5604/01.3001.0053.7703

Krywko, J. (2026, March 27). AI wrote a scientific paper that passed peer review. *Scientific American*. https://www.scientificamerican.com/article/ai-wrote-a-scientific-paper-that-passed-peer-review/

Kuhlmann, S., Stegmaier, P., & Konrad, K. (2019). The tentative governance of emerging science and technology—A conceptual introduction. *Research Policy*, *48*(5), 1091–1097. Advance online publication. DOI: 10.1016/j.respol.2019.01.006

Kupersmith, J. (1992). Technostress and the reference librarian. *RSR. Reference Services Review*, *20*(2), 7–14. DOI: 10.1108/eb049150

Lazarus, R. S., & Folkman, S. (1984). *Stress, appraisal, and coping*. Springer.

Leuz, C., Lins, K. V., & Warnock, F. E. (2009). Do foreigners invest less in poorly governed firms? *Review of Financial Studies*, *22*(8), 3245–3285. DOI: 10.1093/rfs/hhn089

Liando, D. M., Ganaie, N. A., & Yuslaini, N. (2026). Smart City 2.0 governance policy model: Institutional configurations and the politics of urban inclusion in India, Singapore, and Indonesia. *Frontiers in Political Science*, *8*, 1730870. DOI: 10.3389/fpos.2026.1730870

Liu, B. (2023). Share pledge and qualitative information disclosures: Evidence from the tone of management discussion and analysis. *Economic Analysis and Policy*, *78*, 1342–1358. DOI: 10.1016/j.eap.2023.05.010

Liu, B., You, Z., & Jiang, F. (2024). Research on ethical governance technology of biological identification technology based on the technology track theory. *Chinese Medical Ethics*, *37*(10). Advance online publication. DOI: 10.12026/j.issn.1001-8565.2024.10.01

Liu, Q., Ali, N. L., & Lee, H. Y. (2025). Applying VOSviewer in a bibliometric review on English language teacher education research: An analysis of narratives, networks and numbers. *Cogent Education*, *12*(1), 2449728. Advance online publication. DOI: 10.1080/2331186X.2025.2449728

Lo, A. W., & Repin, D. V. (2002). The psychophysiology of real-time financial risk processing. *Journal of Cognitive Neuroscience*, *14*(3), 323–339. DOI: 10.1162/089892902317361877

Loewenstein, G., Sunstein, C. R., & Golman, R. (2014). Disclosure: Psychology changes everything. *Annual Review of Economics*, *6*(1), 391–419. DOI: 10.1146/annurev-economics-080213-041341

Maestre-Góngora, G., & Aponte, D. (2023). Dataset about information technology governance: A survey in Colombian enterprises. *Data in Brief*, *50*, 109480. Advance online publication. DOI: 10.1016/j.dib.2023.109480

Magwedere, M. R., & Marozva, G. (2025). Financial Technology and Income Inequality: An Empirical Investigation. *Discover Global Society 2025 3:1, 3*(1), 68-. DOI: 10.1007/s44282-025-00198-1

Mahmood, F., Arshad, R., Khan, S., Afzal, A., & Bashir, M. (2024). Impact of behavioral biases on investment decisions and the moderation effect of financial literacy: An evidence of Pakistan. *Acta Psychologica*, *247*, 104303. DOI: 10.1016/j.actpsy.2024.104303

Malgieri, G. (2023). *Vulnerability and data protection law*. Oxford University Press. DOI: 10.1093/oso/9780192870339.001.0001

Manggalasari, L. C., Rosdiana, W., Lestari, Y., Narot, P., & Kiettikunwong, N. (2025). From Centralized Control to Co-Creation: Rethinking Educational Governance in the Digital Era. *Educational Process: International Journal, 17*(1). Advance online publication. DOI: 10.22521/edupij.2025.17.321

Mardiana, R., Yossinomita, Y., Saputra, M. H., Mandasari, R., & Kartika, Y. D. (2025). Behavioral bias (availability, representativeness, anchoring, and confirmation) toward investment decision-making. [SMEs]. *Journal of Management: Small and Medium Enterprises, 18*(1), 399–412.

Marteau, B., ... (2025). Trustworthy AI data systems. *arXiv*. https://doi.org//arXiv.2512.03098DOI: 10.48550

Martha, A. S. D., Widowati, S., & Rahayu, D. P. (2025). Assessing Student Readiness and Perceptions of ChatGPT in Learning: A Case Study in Indonesian Higher Education. *Journal of Information Technology Education, 24*, 023. Advance online publication. DOI: 10.28945/5599

Massoud, T., & Dsilva, J. (2025). Closing the PET plastic recycling loop: A sustainable transformation from plastic to fiber. *Next Sustainability, 6*, 100095. DOI: 10.1016/j.nxsust.2024.100095

Mattern, J., Tarafdar, M., Klein, S., & Schellhammer, S. (2024). Thriving in a bruising job: How high achieving IT professionals can cope with occupational demands. *Information Systems Journal, 34*(6), 2045–2096. DOI: 10.1111/isj.12513

Maulidizen, A., Muchtar, A. H., Salimah, A., & Nugraha, R. (2024). A Maqasid al-Shariah framework for fintech and digital asset regulation in Muslim jurisdictions. *Journal of Islamic Law and Legal Studies, 1*(1). https://mabadiiqtishoda.org/index.php/ShariaLex/article/view/119

Mayer, M., & Lu, Y. C. (2025). Global Structures of Digital Dependence and the Rise of Technopoles. *New Political Economy, 30*(5), 755–774. DOI: 10.1080/13563467.2025.2497766

Mazmanian, M., Orlikowski, W. J., & Yates, J. (2013). The autonomy paradox: The implications of mobile email devices for knowledge professionals. *Organization Science, 24*(5), 1337–1357. DOI: 10.1287/orsc.1120.0806

Merchán-Rodríguez, V., & Juiz, C. (2024). Governance of Technologies and Information Systems for Higher Education: Systematic Mapping of Studies. *Journal of Computer Science and Technology (Argentina), 24*(1), e05. Advance online publication. DOI: 10.24215/16666038.24.e05

Mir, S. A., Saini, N., Senthil Kumar, A. V., Ganaie, N. A., Rautrao, R. R. R., Choudhary, A., Sehgal, S., & Khandelwal, A. R. R. (2025). GenAI: Opportunities, Disruptions, and the New Learning Paradigm. In *New Media Applications in Digital Education* (pp. 339–362). IGI Global Scientific Publishing. DOI: 10.4018/979-8-3373-5157-5.ch012

Mirbabaie, M., Stieglitz, S., & Marx, J. (2022). Digital detox. *Business & Information Systems Engineering*, *64*(2), 239–246. DOI: 10.1007/s12599-022-00747-x

Mishra, P. K., & Rašticová, M. (2024). Role and status of biomarkers in technostress research: A systematic review. *Psychology Research and Behavior Management*, *17*, 1961–1972. DOI: 10.2147/PRBM.S446782 PMID: 38751567

Misra, S., Barik, K., & Kvalvik, P. (2025). Digital sovereignty in the era of Industry 5.0: Challenges and opportunities. *Procedia Computer Science*, *254*, 108–117. DOI: 10.1016/j.procs.2025.02.069

Mohadi, M., & Tarshany, Y. (2023). Maqasid al-Shari'ah and the ethics of artificial intelligence: Contemporary challenges. *Journal of Contemporary Maqasid Studies*, *2*(2), 79–102. DOI: 10.52100/jcms.v2i2.107

Mohamed, A. M. E., Alnor, N. H. A., Mohammed, O. A. A., Al-Matari, E. M., Alhebri, A., & Ahmed, A. (2024). The impact of information technology governance according to the COBIT on performance. *International Journal of Advanced and Applied Sciences*, *11*(3), 127–136. Advance online publication. DOI: 10.21833/ijaas.2024.03.014

Molino, M., Ingusci, E., Signore, F., Manuti, A., Giancaspro, M. L., Russo, V., Zito, M., & Cortese, C. G. (2020). Wellbeing costs of technology use during Covid-19 remote working: An investigation using the Italian translation of the technostress creators scale. *Sustainability (Basel)*, *12*(15), 5911. DOI: 10.3390/su12155911

Mosteanu, N. R.Narcisa Roxana Mosteanu. (2017). The influence of financial markets on countries' economic life. *Economics World*, *5*(3). Advance online publication. DOI: 10.17265/2328-7144/2017.03.007

Moylan, R., & Code, J. (2024). Algorithmic futures: An analysis of teacher professional digital competence frameworks through an algorithm literacy lens. *Teachers and Teaching*, *30*(4), 452–470. DOI: 10.1080/13540602.2023.2263732

MSCI. (2025). MSCI global market accessibility review: June 2025. https://www.msci.com/indexes/index-resources/market-classification

MSCI. (2026a, January 27). Results of consultation on free float assessment of Indonesian securities. https://www.msci.com/indexes/index-resources/market-classification

MSCI. (2026b). MSCI market classification framework. https://www.msci.com/indexes/index-resources/market-classification

Mumford, D. (2022). Data colonialism: Compelling and useful, but whither epistemes? *Information Communication and Society*, *25*(10), 1511–1516. DOI: 10.1080/1369118X.2021.1986103

Murphy, R., Kettner, H., Zeifman, R., Giribaldi, B., Kartner, L., Martell, J., Read, T., Murphy-Beiner, A., Baker-Jones, M., Nutt, D., Erritzoe, D., Watts, R., & Carhart-Harris, R. (2022). Therapeutic Alliance and Rapport Modulate Responses to Psilocybin Assisted Therapy for Depression. *Frontiers in Pharmacology*, *12*, 788155. Advance online publication. DOI: 10.3389/fphar.2021.788155 PMID: 35431912

Mustapha, A. (2025). *Maqasid al-Shariah and emerging technologies: Toward an ethical evaluation framework*. International Journal of Islamic Thought and Civilization., DOI: 10.31436/ijtc

Nair, M., Nygren, J., Nilsen, P., Gama, F., Neher, M., Larsson, I., & Svedberg, P. (2025). Critical activities for successful implementation and adoption of AI in healthcare: Towards a process framework for healthcare organizations. *Frontiers in Digital Health*, *7*, 1550459. Advance online publication. DOI: 10.3389/fdgth.2025.1550459 PMID: 40453810

Nandyala, S., Borse, L. B., Gayatri, A. P., & Bonthu, M. G. (2025). Artificial intelligence applications in patient counseling: Latest research, developments, and practical insights for beginners and advanced professionals. In Artificial Intelligence in Patient Counselling (pp. 385–402). DOI: 10.1016/B978-0-443-43823-3.00017-0

Nastjuk, I., Trang, S., Grummeck-Braamt, J.-V., Adam, M. T. P., & Tarafdar, M. (2024). Integrating and synthesising technostress research: A meta-analysis on technostress creators, outcomes, and IS usage contexts. *European Journal of Information Systems*, *33*(3), 361–382. DOI: 10.1080/0960085X.2022.2154712

Newport, C. (2019). *Digital minimalism: Choosing a focused life in a noisy world*. Portfolio/Penguin.

Ngoveni, M. (2025). Bridging the AI Knowledge Gap: The Urgent Need for AI Literacy and Institutional Support. *International Journal of Technologies in Learning*, *32*(2), 83–100. DOI: 10.18848/2327-0144/CGP/v32i02/83-100

Nguyen, T. H., Vu, L. P. T., Mai, A. N., & Tran, T. Q. (2025). Do narrative-related disclosures in the annual report enhance firm value? New evidence from an emerging market. *International Review of Financial Analysis*, *102*, 104077. DOI: 10.1016/j.irfa.2025.104077

Ninkov, A., Frank, J. R., & Maggio, L. A. (2021). Bibliometrics: Methods for studying academic publishing. *Perspectives on Medical Education, 11*(3), 173–176. DOI: 10.1007/S40037-021-00695-4

Ogawa, S., Khera, P., Vasishth, M., & Sahay, R. (2022). Women in Fintech: As Leaders and Users. *IMF Working Paper, 2022*(140), 1. DOI: 10.5089/9798400215384.001

Oluoch, W., & Alhassan, A. L. (2026). Bridging the Gender Credit Gap in Low-Income Countries: The Impact of Digital Financial Inclusion. *Emerging Markets Review, 70*(1), 101389. DOI: 10.1016/j.ememar.2025.101389

Omar, A. M., & Anshari, M. (2023). Super Smart Society 5.0: Innovation in public policy post-industry 4.0. In *Digital Transformation for Business and Society* (pp. 91-110). Routledge.

Omotubora, A. (2024). AI For Women's Financial Inclusion—Analysis of Product Design and Policy Approaches in Nigeria. *Data & Policy, 6*, e66. DOI: 10.1017/dap.2024.62

Özşuca, E. A. (2024). Gender Gap in Digital Financial Inclusion Across Generations. *Empirica 2024 52:2, 52*(2), 197–210. DOI: 10.1007/s10663-024-09641-z

Pampus, J., & Heisel, M. (2025). A Delimitation of Data Sovereignty From Privacy. In *Empowering Digital Sovereignty* (pp. 1–24). Balancing Privacy and Global Connectivity., DOI: 10.4018/979-8-3693-9137-2.ch001

Patne, A. Y., & Suryawanshic, M. (2025). Ethical considerations in artificial intelligence-powered patient counseling. In Artificial Intelligence in Patient Counselling (pp. 195–232). DOI: 10.1016/B978-0-443-43823-3.00011-X

Paule-Vianez, J., Gomez-Martinez, R., & Prado-Roman, C. (2020). A bibliometric analysis of behavioural finance with mapping analysis tools. *European Research on Management and Business Economics, 26*(2), 71–77. Advance online publication. DOI: 10.1016/j.iedeen.2020.01.001

Pavlopoulos, A., Rachiotis, T., & Maglogiannis, I. (2024). An Overview of Tools and Technologies for Anxiety and Depression Management Using AI. *Applied Sciences (Basel, Switzerland), 14*(19), 9068. Advance online publication. DOI: 10.3390/app14199068

Perdana, A., Arifin, S., & Quadrianto, N. (2025). Algorithmic Trust and Regulation: Governance, Ethics, Legal, and Social Implications Blueprint for Indonesia's Central Banking. *Technology in Society, 81*, 102838. DOI: 10.1016/j.techsoc.2025.102838

Perlis, R. H. (2026). Artificial Intelligence and the Potential Transformation of Mental Health. *JAMA Psychiatry, 83*(4), 409. Advance online publication. DOI: 10.1001/jamapsychiatry.2025.4116 PMID: 41533367

Pessin, V. Z., Yamane, L. H., & Siman, R. R. (2022). Smart bibliometrics: An integrated method of science mapping and bibliometric analysis. *Scientometrics, 127*(6), 3695–3718. DOI: 10.1007/s11192-022-04406-6

Petry, J., Fichtner, J., & Heemskerk, E. M. (2021). Steering capital: The growing private authority of index providers in the age of passive asset management. *Review of International Political Economy, 28*(1), 152–176. DOI: 10.1080/09692290.2019.1699147

Pirkkalainen, H., & Salo, M. (2016). Two decades of the dark side in the information systems basket: Suggesting five areas for future research. In *Proceedings of the 24th European Conference on Information Systems (ECIS 2016).*

Prashad, D. (2018). Urban sustainability in practice: Priorities in India. *Lecture Notes in Civil Engineering, 3*, 1483–1493. Advance online publication. DOI: 10.1007/978-3-319-57937-5_154

Prianto, A. L., & Amalia, A. A. (2019). Combatting Slums, Sustaining Poverty: Dynamic Urban Governance in Makassar, Indonesia. *Otoritas : Jurnal Ilmu Pemerintahan, 9*(1), 28–41. Advance online publication. DOI: 10.26618/ojip.v9i1.2008

Purtova, N., & van Maanen, G. (2024). Data as an Economic Good, Data as a Commons, and Data Governance. *Law, Innovation and Technology, 16*(1), 1–42. DOI: 10.1080/17579961.2023.2265270 PMID: 39634789

Putri Syarifa, D. F., Krisna Moeljono, A. A., Hidayat, W. N., Shafelbilyunazra, A., Abednego, V. K., & Prasetya, D. D. (2024). Development of a Micro Counselling Educational Platform Based on AI and Face Recognition to Prevent Students Anxiety Disorder. Proceedings – IEIT 2024 – 2024 International Conference on Electrical and Information Technology, 1–6. DOI: 10.1109/IEIT64341.2024.10763282

Radtke, T., Apel, T., Schenkel, K., Keller, J., & von Lindern, E. (2022). Digital detox: An effective solution in the smartphone era? A systematic literature review. *Mobile Media & Communication, 10*(2), 190–215. DOI: 10.1177/20501579211028647

Ragu-Nathan, T. S., Tarafdar, M., Ragu-Nathan, B. S., & Tu, Q. (2008). The consequences of technostress for end users in organizations: Conceptual development and empirical validation. *Information Systems Research, 19*(4), 417–433. DOI: 10.1287/isre.1070.0165

Rasool, T., Warraich, N. F., & Sajid, M. (2022). Examining the impact of technology overload at the workplace: A systematic review. *SAGE Open*, *12*(3), 215824402211143. DOI: 10.1177/21582440221114320

Ravid, D. M., Tomczak, D. L., White, J. C., & Behrend, T. S. (2023). EPM 20/20: A review, framework, and research agenda for electronic performance monitoring. *Journal of Management*, *46*(1), 100–126. DOI: 10.1177/0149206319869435

Razzaq, A., Hutagalung, K. A., & Anshari, M. (2023, September). Modelling Islamic business and online communication ethics: A literature analysis. In *2023 International Conference on Sustainable Islamic Business and Finance (SIBF)* (pp. 1-4). IEEE. DOI: 10.1109/SIBF60067.2023.10379995

Reijers, W., O'Brolcháin, F., & Haynes, P. (2016). Governance in Blockchain Technologies & Social Contract Theories. *Ledger*, *1*, 134–151. Advance online publication. DOI: 10.5195/ledger.2016.62

Reserve Bank of India. (2022). *Guidelines on digital lending*. RBI Publications.

Reserve Bank of India. (2023). *Report on trend and progress of banking in India*. RBI Publications.

Rhodes, C. J. (2018). Plastic pollution and solutions. *Science Progress*, *101*(3), 207–260. DOI: 10.3184/003685018X15294876706211 PMID: 30025551

Rhodes, R. A. W. (1997). *Understanding governance: Policy networks, governance, reflexivity and accountability*. Open University Press.

Ridzuan, N. N., Masri, M., & Anshari, M. (2026). Exploratory Study of the Fintech Regulative Sandbox: Opportunities and Challenges. *Promoting Inclusivity and Accessibility With FinTech*, 395-414.

Ridzuan, N. N., Masri, M., Anshari, M., Fitriyani, N. L., & Syafrudin, M. (2024). AI in the financial sector: The line between innovation, regulation and ethical responsibility. *Information (Basel)*, *15*(8), 432. DOI: 10.3390/info15080432

Robertson, A. (2019). Passive in name only: Delegated management and "index" investing. *Yale Journal on Regulation*, *36*(2), 795–851. https://openyls.law.yale.edu/handle/20.500.13051/7793

Robles, P., & Mallinson, D. J. (2025). Artificial intelligence technology, public trust, and effective governance. *The Review of Policy Research*, *42*(1), 11–28. Advance online publication. DOI: 10.1111/ropr.12555

Russell, F. T. S. E. (2026). FTSE Russell postpones March 2026 index review for Indonesian securities. https://www.ftserussell.com

Saikia, B. (2019). New mode of governance: Governance through technology. *International Journal of Recent Technology and Engineering*, *8*(3), 4052–4055. Advance online publication. DOI: 10.35940/ijrte.C5392.098319

Sait, M. A., & Anshari, M. (2022). Assessing Brunei Darussalam public and private sector readiness towards big data application. *International Journal of Asian Business and Information Management*, *13*(2), 1–22. DOI: 10.4018/IJABIM.20220701.oa7

Saly, J. N., & Sulthanah, L. T. (2023). Pelindungan Data Pribadi dalam Tindakan Doxing Berdasarkan Undang-Undang Nomor 27 Tahun 2022. *Jurnal Kewarganegaraan*, *7*(2), 1708–1713.

Santaniello, M. (2025). Attributes of Digital Sovereignty: A Conceptual Framework. *Geopolitics*. Advance online publication. DOI: 10.1080/14650045.2025.2521548

Sargeant, H. (2026). Mind the Gap: Securing Algorithmic Explainability for Credit Decisions Beyond the UK GDPR. *Computer Law & Security Review*, *60*, 106247. DOI: 10.1016/j.clsr.2025.106247

Saritha, B. (2025). Smart City 2.0: Evaluating Citizen-Centric Digital Governance and Urban Sustainability in India. *International Journal of Research Publication and Reviews*, (6).

Scherenberg, F. von, Hellmeier, M., & Otto, B. (2024). Data Sovereignty in Information Systems. *Electronic Markets 2024 34:1, 34*(1), 15-. DOI: 10.1007/s12525-024-00693-4

Schraggeová, M.. (2025). The effect of digital detox through digital minimalism using the MinimalistPhone app on the behavior of young users and their emotional experience. Computers in Human Behavior Reports. *Article, 100579*. Advance online publication. DOI: 10.1016/j.chbr.2025.100579

Schwinghammer, R., Neuburger, R., & Hess, T. (2025). Power as the Secret Ingredient: First Insights into the Governance of Personal Data in Digital Platforms. *Americas Conference on Information Systems, AMCIS 2025*, 1, 116–125.

SCMP. (2026, January 29). Indonesia scrambles to halt US$80 billion market crash as rupiah hits record low. https://www.scmp.com/news/asia/southeast-asia/article/3341716/indonesia-scrambles-halt-us80-billion-market-crash-rupiah-hits-record-low

Scott, M. (2026, March 16). The three forces writing the future of higher education. *Australian Financial Review*. https://www.afr.com/work-and-careers/education/the-three-forces-writing-the-future-of-higher-education-20260315-p5oalr

Shabana, O. (2026, January 21). AI's growing thirst for water is becoming a public health risk. *Al Jazeera*. https://www.aljazeera.com/opinions/2026/1/21/ais-growing-thirst-for-water-is-becoming-a-public-health-risk

Shamdi, W., Lai, D., Aziz, A. A., & Anshari, M. (2022). Artificial intelligence development in Islamic System of Governance: A literature review. *Contemporary Islam*, *16*(2), 321–334. DOI: 10.1007/s11562-022-00504-7

Sharma, S. K., Seetharaman, A., & Maddulety, K. (2021). Framework for Sustainable Urban Water Management in the Context of Governance, Infrastructure, Technology and Economics. *Water Resources Management*, *35*(12), 3903–3913. Advance online publication. DOI: 10.1007/s11269-021-02916-1

Shelton, T., Zook, M., & Wiig, A. (2015). The "actually existing smart city.". *Cambridge Journal of Regions, Economy and Society*, *8*(1), 13–25. Advance online publication. DOI: 10.1093/cjres/rsu026

Singh, V. K., Singh, P., Karmakar, M., Leta, J., & Mayr, P. (2021). The journal coverage of Web of Science, Scopus and Dimensions: A comparative analysis. *Scientometrics*, *126*(6), 5113–5142. DOI: 10.1007/s11192-021-03948-5

Sirisomboonsuk, P., Gu, V. C., Cao, R. Q., & Burns, J. R. (2018). Relationships between project governance and information technology governance and their impact on project performance. *International Journal of Project Management*, *36*(2), 287–300. Advance online publication. DOI: 10.1016/j.ijproman.2017.10.003

Soltanzadeh, S. (2025). A metaphysical account of agency for technology governance. *AI & Society*, *40*(3), 1723–1734. Advance online publication. DOI: 10.1007/s00146-024-01941-z

Stokols, A. (2025). The insurgent smart city: How a social movement created an alternative imaginary of the smart city. *Journal of Urban Affairs*, *47*(4), 1149–1166. Advance online publication. DOI: 10.1080/07352166.2023.2216887

Sumardi, W. H., & Anshari, M. (2020). Employing big data in business organisation and business ethics. *International Journal of Business Governance and Ethics*, *14*(3), 181–205. DOI: 10.1504/IJBGE.2020.106349

Sun, H., Zhang, Z., & Liu, Z. (2022). Does air pollution collaborative governance promote green technology innovation? Evidence from China. *Environmental Science and Pollution Research International*, *29*(34), 51609–51622. Advance online publication. DOI: 10.1007/s11356-022-19535-x

Syafhendry, S., Ganaie, N. A., & Yama, A. (2025). Smart elections or rigged algorithms: The rise of artificial intelligence in electoral governance in Southeast Asia. *Frontiers in Political Science*, *7*, 1672310. Advance online publication. DOI: 10.3389/fpos.2025.1672310

Syafrudin, M., Alfian, G., Fitriyani, N. L., & Anshari, M. (2024). Applied artificial intelligence for sustainability. *Sustainability (Basel)*, *16*(6), 2469. DOI: 10.3390/su16062469

Tarafdar, M., Cooper, C. L., & Stich, J.-F. (2019). The technostress trifecta—Techno eustress, techno distress and design: Theoretical directions and an agenda for research. *Information Systems Journal*, *29*(1), 6–42. DOI: 10.1111/isj.12169

Tarafdar, M., Tu, Q., Ragu-Nathan, B. S., & Ragu-Nathan, T. S. (2007). The impact of technostress on role stress and productivity. *Journal of Management Information Systems*, *24*(1), 301–328. DOI: 10.2753/MIS0742-1222240109

Tempo.co. (2026, January 31). IHSG plunge explained: What happened, why it matters, and what followed. https://en.tempo.co/read/2084169/ihsg-plunge-explained-what-happened-why-it-matters-and-what-followed

ten Brummelhuis, L. L., & Bakker, A. B. (2012). A resource perspective on the work–home interface: The work–home resources model. *The American Psychologist*, *67*(7), 545–556. DOI: 10.1037/a0027974 PMID: 22506688

Thakur, K. K., Lekurwale, R., Pansare, R., & Bansode, S. (2024). Bibliometric analysis on bioprinting: Mapping co-occurrence of keywords and future research direction using VOSviewer. 78–92. DOI: 10.1201/9781003596707-9

The Jakarta Post. (2026, January 31). Heads roll at IDX, OJK, as govt vows to fix stock market. https://www.thejakartapost.com/business/2026/01/31/heads-roll-at-idx-ojk-as-govt-vows-to-fix-stock-market.html

Thoha, A. M. (2026). Green leadership in development management: Synthesizing Islamic ethical paradigms and sustainability science. *AlIrsyad: Journal of Islamic and Contemporary Issues*, *11*(1), 1669–1688. DOI: 10.53840/alirsyad.v11i1.587

Thomas, J., & Harden, A. (2008). Methods for the thematic synthesis of qualitative research in systematic reviews. *BMC Medical Research Methodology*, *8*(1), 45. DOI: 10.1186/1471-2288-8-45 PMID: 18616818

Tian, N., & Wang, W. (2025). Innovative Pathways for Collaborative Governance in Technology-Driven Smart Communities. *Sustainability (Basel)*, *17*(1), 98. Advance online publication. DOI: 10.3390/su17010098

Tigges, M., Mestwerdt, S., Tschirner, S., & Mauer, R. (2024). Who Gets the Money? A Qualitative Analysis of Fintech Lending and Credit Scoring Through the Adoption of AI and Alternative Data. *Technological Forecasting and Social Change*, *205*, 123491. DOI: 10.1016/j.techfore.2024.123491

Turel, O., & Serenko, A. (2012). The benefits and dangers of enjoyment with social networking websites. *European Journal of Information Systems*, *21*(5), 512–528. DOI: 10.1057/ejis.2012.1

Ullah, S., Nobanee, H., & Iftikhar, H. (2023). Global financial integration, governance-by-technology, and green growth. *International Review of Financial Analysis*, *90*, 102838. Advance online publication. DOI: 10.1016/j.irfa.2023.102838

United Nations Conference on Trade and Development. (2024). Credit rating agencies, developing countries and bias: Policy review (UNCTAD/GDS/2024/3). https://unctad.org/publication/credit-rating-agencies-developing-countries-and-bias

Vafaeimehr, A., Ansari, S., & Rahmani, M. (2023). Confirmation bias in investment decisions: A behavioural finance review. *Journal of Behavioural Finance Studies*, *8*(2), 45–62.

van Deursen, A. J. A. M., Bolle, C. L., Hegner, S. M., & Kommers, P. A. M. (2015). Modeling habitual and addictive smartphone behavior. *Computers in Human Behavior*, *45*, 411–420. DOI: 10.1016/j.chb.2014.12.039

Vanden Abeele, M. M. P. (2021). Digital wellbeing as a dynamic construct. *Communication Theory*, *31*(4), 932–955. DOI: 10.1093/ct/qtaa024

Veeramani, K., & Jaganathan, S. (2020). Land registration: Use-case of e-Governance using blockchain technology. *KSII Transactions on Internet and Information Systems*, *14*(9). Advance online publication. DOI: 10.3837/tiis.2020.09.007

Veerankutty, F., Ramayah, T., & Ali, N. A. (2018). Information technology governance on audit technology performance among Malaysian public sector auditors. *Social Sciences (Basel, Switzerland)*, *7*(8), 124. Advance online publication. DOI: 10.3390/socsci7080124

Voigt, P., & von dem Bussche, A. (2017). *The EU General Data Protection Regulation (GDPR): A practical guide*. Springer. DOI: 10.1007/978-3-319-57959-7

von Schomberg, R. (2025). On Technological and Innovation Sovereignty: A Response to Carl Mitcham's Call for a Political Theory of Technology. *NanoEthics*, *19*(1), 2. Advance online publication. DOI: 10.1007/s11569-025-00469-w

Wang, K., Liu, X., Chadwick, D. R., Yan, C., Reay, M., Ge, T., Ding, F., Wang, J., Qi, R., Xiao, M., Jiang, R., Chen, Y., Ma, J., Lloyd, C., Evershed, R. P., Luo, Y., Zhu, Y., Zhang, F., & Jones, D. L. (2025). The agricultural plastic paradox: Feeding more, harming more? *Environment International*, *198*, 109416. Advance online publication. DOI: 10.1016/j.envint.2025.109416 PMID: 40215920

Wang, S., Asif, M., Shahzad, M. F., & Ashfaq, M. (2024). Data Privacy and Cybersecurity Challenges in the Digital Transformation of the Banking Sector. *Computers & Security*, *147*, 104051. DOI: 10.1016/j.cose.2024.104051

Weil, M. M., & Rosen, L. D. (1997). *Technostress: Coping with technology @work @home @play*. John Wiley & Sons.

Weinert, C., Maier, C., Laumer, S., & Weitzel, T. (2020). How does technostress influence the coping of information system users? Conceptualizing a model of technostress coping. *Management Information Systems Quarterly*, *44*(3), 1199–1228.

Wilkin, C. L., Couchman, P. K., Sohal, A., & Zutshi, A. (2016). Exploring differences between smaller and larger organisations' corporate governance of information technology. *International Journal of Accounting Information Systems*, *22*, 6–25. Advance online publication. DOI: 10.1016/j.accinf.2016.07.002

World Bank. (2020). *Consumer risks in fintech: New manifestations of consumer risks and emerging regulatory approaches*. World Bank Publications.

Wu, W., Huang, T., & Gong, K. (2020). Ethical Principles and Governance Technology Development of AI in China. In *Engineering* (Vol. 6, Number 3). DOI: 10.1016/j.eng.2019.12.015

Wu, Y., & Li, G. (2024). Technology governance and governance technology: From the perspective of regulatory research on blockchain digital assets. *Bulletin of Chinese Academy of Sciences*, *39*(8). Advance online publication. DOI: 10.16418/j.issn.1000-3045.20240323001

Yar, M. A., Hamdan, M., Anshari, M., Fitriyani, N. L., & Syafrudin, M. (2024). Governing with intelligence: The impact of artificial intelligence on policy development. *Information (Basel)*, *15*(9), 556. DOI: 10.3390/info15090556

Yin, R. K. (2018). *Case study research and applications: Design and methods* (6th ed.). Sage Publications., https://opac.atmaluhur.ac.id/uploaded_files/temporary/DigitalCollection/YTE3NDlmYTY0ZjE2MDA5ODE4NGI1Y2FhMjdkMjRmYWNkMDA2MTVhOQ==.pdf

Yuslaini, N., Widya Setiabudi Sumadinata, R., Fedryansyah, M., Abdillah, A., Prianto, A. L., & Febriyanti, D. (2023). Sustainable investment strategies in the palm oil industry in Indonesia. *Journal of Infrastructure. Policy and Development*, *7*(3), 2288. Advance online publication. DOI: 10.24294/jipd.v7i3.2288

Yusuf, H., Fitri, A., & Razzaq, A. (2026). Using artificial intelligence for human-AI collaboration in knowledge management systems to improve organizational efficiency and learning. In *Driving Organizational Transformation Through Human-Robotic Collaboration* (pp. 35–48). IGI Global Scientific Publishing.

Yu, X., & Zhao, L. (2023). Textual disclosure complexity and analysts' weighting of information. *Journal of Contemporary Accounting & Economics*, *100395*. Advance online publication. DOI: 10.1016/j.jcae.2023.100395

Zhang, M., & Zhang, C. (2025). The Political Economy of the Fintech Regulation in China and Its Implications. *Computer Law & Security Review*, *56*, 106089. DOI: 10.1016/j.clsr.2024.106089

Zuboff, S. (2019). *The age of surveillance capitalism: The fight for a human future at the new frontier of power*. PublicAffairs.

Zwitter, A. (2024). Cybernetic governance: Implications of technology convergence on governance convergence. *Ethics and Information Technology*, *26*(2), 24. Advance online publication. DOI: 10.1007/s10676-024-09763-9

Zwitter, A., & Hazenberg, J. (2020). Decentralised Network Governance: Blockchain Technology and the Future of Regulation. *Frontiers in Blockchain*, *3*, 12. Advance online publication. DOI: 10.3389/fbloc.2020.00012

About the Contributors

Muhammad Anshari is an Associate Professor of Business Information Systems at the Universiti Brunei Darussalam School of Business and Economics (UBDSBE). After completing his PhD at the Faculty of Business, Economics and Policy Studies, Universiti Brunei Darussalam, he served as a Research Fellow at National Taiwan University, following an earlier research fellowship at King Saud University, Saudi Arabia. He has completed eight research grant projects and three industry research consultancies. Since 2022, Dr. Anshari has been listed among Stanford University's Top 2% World Scientists in the fields of ICT and Business and Management. He received two Outstanding Paper Awards at the Emerald Literati Awards 2023, and his work has been cited in three U.S. patents. In 2024, he was awarded the Research Excellence Award for Senior Academic Career (Social Sciences) at Universiti Brunei Darussalam. His research primarily contributes to the United Nations Sustainable Development Goal 9 (Industry, Innovation, and Infrastructure), with interests spanning Business Information Systems, Knowledge Management Systems, Digital Business, Digital Humanities, Digital Governance, and Digital Health.

Mohammad Nabil Almunawar is currently a professor at the School of Business and Economics, Universiti of Brunei Darussalam (UBDSBE), Brunei Darussalam. Hwe was the former dean of UBDSBE. He received his bachelor's degree in 1983 from Bogor Agricultural University, Indonesia, master's degree (MSc) from the Department of Computer Science, University of Western Ontario, London, Canada in 1991, and Ph.D in Computer Science/Information Systems from the University of New South Wales in 1998. Dr. Almunawar has published more than 250 papers in refereed journals, books, book chapters, encyclopedias, and international conference proceedings. He has more than 30 years of teaching experience in the area of information systems. His overall research interests include applications of IT in management, e-business/commerce, digital marketplace/

platform, digital business ecosystem, health informatics, information security, and cloud computing. Currently, he focuses his research on digital transformation, digital marketplace, digital platform, and digital business ecosystem.

Hazri Kifle is the Vice-Chancellor of Universiti Brunei Darussalam (UBD), and is recognized for his leadership in higher education, public sector innovation, and digital transformation. His vision aligns UBD with Brunei's Vision 2035, emphasizing sustainability, global partnerships, and preparing graduates for future industries. He has contributed significantly to e-Government development, focusing on ICT's role in governance and service delivery, and has published research on teacher professionalism, youth leadership, and innovation in education. Beyond academia, he actively promotes regional cooperation and has delivered keynote addresses on AI literacy, maritime governance, and strategic trust. His expertise spans public sector innovation, digital transformation, higher education leadership, and youth development, making him a pivotal figure in shaping Brunei's academic and policy landscape while positioning UBD as a hub for sustainability and innovation.

K. Balaji is an Assistant Professor in Business and Management, Christ University, Bangalore. He did Ph.D. from KLU Business School, KL University,Vijayawada. He is having 12 years of teaching experience. He has to his credit 23 Research Articles published in reputed National and International Journals. He has participated and presented more than 12 papers in both National and International Seminars/Conferences and also attended more than 50 workshops/ FDPS organized by various reputed organizations. He has also participated in more than 50 seminars / webinars organized by various reputed organizations. He has also attended in 6 Short Term Training programs.He has successfully conducted 3 webinars, one 5 day FDP and one International Conference on Reimaging marketing in New Normal. He is a ratified as Assistant Professor by both JNTUH, JNTU Anantapur and Sri Venkateswara University,Tirupati. His specialized areas include, Accounting and Financial management, Marketing Management, Retailing Management, Consumer Behavior studies, Entrepreneurship and Business Laws.

Annisa Fitri Anshari is a young researcher and student at the University of Melbourne. Her academic work and research interests are situated at the intersection of psychology, education, and public health. Professionally, she has demonstrated a commitment to academic support and community engagement, having served as an Academic Peer Mentor at RMIT University Melbourne Australia, where she provided guidance in various psychology disciplines, and as a teacher for the Indonesian Community of Victoria.

Nasir Ahmad Ganaie works at the Department of Humanities and Social Sciences, Indian Institute of Technology Guwahati, where his academic and research engagements are closely aligned with the institute's interdisciplinary and policy-oriented vision. His work primarily focuses on counter-insurgency and de-radicalisation strategies, youth empowerment and peacebuilding in conflict-affected regions. At IIT Guwahati, he contributes to advanced research and teaching that bridges the humanities and social sciences with contemporary security, governance and development challenges. Dr. Nasir brings to IIT Guwahati a strong academic background and a robust research profile. He holds a PhD in Political Science from the University of Hyderabad and completed his Postdoc at the Department of Political Science, University of Kashmir. Dr. Nasir has published in reputed Q1 journals indexed in Web of Science and Scopus, demonstrating sustained engagement with high-quality international publications. He has also authored several book chapters published by leading academic publishers, including Routledge (Taylor & Francis), SAGE and also holds 23 approved patents.

Nur Hidayah is a professor in the Department of Guidance and Counseling at Universitas Negeri Malang, Indonesia. Her research focuses on counseling education, digital counseling innovation, and the integration of technology in psychological services. She has published widely in the areas of counseling theory, educational psychology, and AI-supported counseling practices.

Mujaddid Afkar Izzuddin is a Geophysics student at the Faculty of Mathematics and Natural Sciences, Universitas Indonesia. His academic focus includes geophysical data analysis, subsurface structure interpretation, and earth modelling, alongside broader interests in the intersections between science, technology, energy, education, and social development. To strengthen this interdisciplinary perspective, he has taken courses in the philosophy of economics and the philosophy of technology, deepening his understanding of how technological innovation, economic systems, and social values shape contemporary societies. His professional experience includes internships at the Directorate General of New, Renewable Energy and Energy Conservation (EBTKE), Ministry of Energy and Mineral Resources of the Republic of Indonesia, and the Institute of Policy Studies, Universiti Brunei Darussalam, where he engaged with issues related to energy transition, public policy, and regional development. Beyond his academic and professional engagements, Mujaddid is actively involved in science writing and interdisciplinary research that bridges geoscience, energy studies, and sustainable development. His works include Geophysical Interpretation of Gravity and Magnetic Data Revealing Ancient Magma Intrusion, 3D Modelling Using Gravity Methods for Identifying Geothermal System, and Why Geothermal Energy Remains Underutilized and How to Unlock Its Potential.

Nasrudin is a lecturer in the Department of Communication at Universitas Islam Kalimantan Muhammad Arsyad Al-Banjari, Banjarmasin. He specializes in communication studies and is involved in teaching and research. Email: nasruddin3100@gmail.com

Nofriansyah Nofriansyah earned a Bachelor's degree in Economics Education from Universitas Sriwijaya in 2017 and a Master's degree in Economics Education from Universitas Negeri Padang in 2019. Currently, the author is pursuing a doctoral degree in economic education at Universitas Pendidikan Indonesia (UPI) with an LPDP scholarship in 2024 until now. His areas of expertise include education (evaluation, learning models, instructional media, and learning strategies) and economics, microeconomics, macroeconomics, and management).

Bagas Noval Ramadhani, a student at Universitas Islam Negeri Jurai Siwo Lampung with a deep passion for sharia accounting. I am highly interested in learning about Islamic financial principles, ethical accounting practices, and Sharia-based business systems. I enjoy exploring how sharia accounting promotes fairness, transparency, and sustainability in the economy. As a motivated learner, I aim to apply my knowledge to support the growth of Sharia-compliant financial institutions and businesses.

Yansen Alberth Reba is a lecturer in the Department of Guidance and Counseling at Universitas Cenderawasih, Indonesia. His academic interests include counseling psychology, educational psychology, digital counseling innovation, and the integration of artificial intelligence in guidance and counseling services. He has published several books and scholarly works in the areas of counseling, educational philosophy, and educational psychology. His current research focuses on the ethical implications of artificial intelligence in counseling services, critical digital literacy among students, and the development of technology-assisted counseling practices in higher education.

Taufikur Rohman, a bachelor's degree graduate and the top student at STIS Alwafa Bogor. I am currently pursuing a Master's degree at UIN Sunan Kalijaga Yogyakarta. My academic interests focus on the development of Islamic economics and finance, with particular emphasis on social justice, sustainability, and institutional governance. I am actively engaged in research and academic writing as a contribution to the advancement of knowledge and the promotion of Islamic economic practices that are adaptive to contemporary challenges.

Wahyu Wibowo is a graduate student in the Master's Program in Shariah Economics at UIN Sunan Kalijaga Yogyakarta. His academic interests include the Halal industry, Islamic philanthropy, and economic literacy. He received four DIKTI-funded PKM grants (2012–2014), three of which focused on community service—ranging from Jarimatika training to literary-mathematical education for orphans, one of which was selected as a national finalist. He also initiated an entrepreneurship project titled IBU SASTIKA (Innovative Mathematical Literature Book) that combines educational innovation with creative content.

Hamza Yusuf is a young researcher currently based in Melbourne, Australia. He is studying at RMIT University, focusing primarily on data science and software engineering. His studies involve programming, data analysis, software development, and computational problem-solving. Through his academic work, Hamza is building a strong foundation in using technology to understand data, develop software solutions, and support informed decision-making. He has also been involved in research activities and has submitted several research projects, including conference papers, book chapters, and journal papers, demonstrating his growing engagement with academic research.

Index

A

B

C

D

R

S

T

U

V

www.ingramcontent.com/pod-product-compliance
Lightning Source LLC
LaVergne TN
LVHW081523300926
849161LV00006B/1280